W9-DCW-686

# we have your daughter

## THE UNSOLVED MURDER OF JONBENÉT RAMSEY TWENTY YEARS LATER

PAULA WOODWARD

PROSPECTA PRESS
WESTPORT AND NEW YORK

Published by Prospecta Press, an imprint of Easton Studio Press
P.O. Box 3131
Westport, CT 06880
(203) 571-0781
www.prospectapress.com

Cover and interior designed by Barbara Aronica-Buck

First Edition
Manufactured in the United States of America

Hardcover ISBN: 978-1-63226-077-2
eBook ISBN: 978-1-63226-078-9

*When your child is murdered, the anger, pain and grief are compounded by the crushing realization that another person intentionally took the life of someone so precious, so innocent.*

*To see your child's name on a headstone is impossible.*

—Parents of Murdered Children, Inc.
Two mothers on their daughters' murders

*There's no tragedy like the death of a child. Things never get back to the way they were.*

—Dwight D. Eisenhower
Supreme Commander, Allied Forces, World War II
US President, January 1953 to January 1961

*Reason is not automatic. Those who deny it cannot be conquered by it.*

—Ayn Rand
Novelist, philosopher, playwright, screenwriter

*Logic is the technique by which we add conviction to truth.*

—Jean de la Bruyère
17th Century Philosopher and Moralist

Steve:
Thank you for your incredible support of this book and me
and your values which have always encouraged me.

I love you. I miss you.

# CONTENTS

we have your daughter

# INTRODUCTION

ON DECEMBER 26, 1996, the brutally beaten body of six-year-old JonBenét Ramsey was found by her father in a rarely used storage room in the basement of the Ramsey home in Boulder, Colorado. The little girl had been strangled and her skull fractured either late on Christmas Day or sometime the morning after. Evidence showed she'd struggled helplessly with her tiny fingers to free the rope that was pulled tight around her neck.

The case was initially classified as a kidnapping because of a ransom note that had been left in the home. I began reporting on the story on December 27, 1996, the day after JonBenét's body was found. The murder of the "child beauty pageant queen" became worldwide news and, in the midst of their excruciating grief, John and Patsy Ramsey, parents of JonBenét, became the prime suspects.

Twenty years later, memories have evolved and fewer details are remembered, but one strong and inviolate premise remains: every discovery that members of law enforcement, the media and the public have made through the years about a possible killer in this case has only strengthened their beliefs in their own theories. The perception, whether misguided, that either an intruder or a member of the Ramsey family murdered JonBenét has been solidified in many minds. And that is what this book examines.

The JonBenét Ramsey case is still one of this country's most famous unsolved mysteries. In 2012, the Boulder Police Chief declared it a "cold case." The Boulder County District Attorney, Stanley Garnett, however, wrote at that time that "no homicide is ever 'closed' while I am DA, meaning we will investigate them until we solve them and, as an office, have made solving all unsolved homicides a top priority." He described the Ramsey case as "inactive."

Four years prior, JonBenét Ramsey's parents and her brother, Burke, had been exonerated through DNA evidence by then Boulder District Attorney Mary Lacy, who stated, "we do not consider your immediate family to be under any suspicion in the commission of this crime." However, through the years others in positions of power stated publicly that John and Patsy Ramsey remained "under the umbrella of suspicion," a stigma they were forced to carry beginning in 1997, when then Boulder District Attorney Alex Hunter and then commander of the Ramsey investigation Mark Beckner, who would later become chief of the Boulder Police Department, labeled them in this way.

There is no statute of limitations on murder.

This is the first investigative examination and book on the Ramsey case that has involved the cooperation of people with varied points of view, including police investigators who worked the case, district attorneys who were part of the investigation, John and Patsy Ramsey and members of their family, and the Ramsey's defense attorneys. I have remained in contact with these people, and others who've operated on the fringe of the investigation, since I began reporting on this case.

The involvement of three Colorado governors in the case has been considered and those individuals interviewed as well. More than 10,000 pages of confidential case notes, unpublished police reports and prosecution documents, defense documents and accumulated evidence never before made public have been studied and nearly one hundred people interviewed.

The new evidence unearthed through this research includes information from a rare, never-before-published, 3,000-page JonBenét Ramsey Murder Book Index. Organized and prepared by the Boulder District Attorney's Office, this index is a summary of the many Boulder Police Department Ramsey case reports that also includes evidence, public input and documentation from the numerous Ramsey Murder Case Files. The JonBenét Ramsey Murder Book Index has been verified as authentic by three people who worked on the case.

Accessed along with the Murder Book Index was information from an additional and confidential 1,000-page file of all Boulder Police Department officers involved in the Ramsey case. This file describes the officers' participation by dates and police report numbers and includes references to some in law enforcement outside the department who aided in the investigation. Also accessed as part of the research for this book was information from a 182-page confidential Boulder Police Department Master Witness List. This information came from the BPD for use by the Boulder District Attorney's Office and is labeled "JonBenét Ramsey 1st Degree Murder Case—Report DA 96-21871." This last file is, in essence, one of the prosecuting attorney's trial preparation outlines. It includes the name of each witness to be called at trial, the name of the person who interviewed that witness and a short synopsis of expected testimony information.

Also included in this book are written reports from the first police officers and detectives who arrived on the scene, critically important documents that have never been published. These documents answer questions related to this case that have been asked for years such as "Why didn't the police find the child's body when they arrived at 6 a.m. that day?" and "Why did it take seven long hours for JonBenét to be found, and why was it her father who found her and not police officers?"

Information from an evaluation of Boulder Department of Social Services confidential interviews with JonBenét's brother, Burke, shortly after the murder has also been reviewed, as has private information provided by JonBenét's teachers. New information is disclosed as well about what JonBenét actually ate before she was killed, and why this matters. In short, many urban myths related to this case that have been considered as fact for so many years are finally here exposed for what they are—myths.

This book also includes content from a confidential 60-page journal written by John Ramsey over a period of eleven months beginning in January 1997, shortly after his daughter was murdered. Portions of the journal are being made public now in order to provide a rare look at a family under siege following a murder of one of their own.

The acting defense attorneys at the time of the murder never voiced their personal perspectives on the Ramsey case, but they have now in this book. There is also new information that helps explain why, from the fall of 1997 to present day, the three principal Ramsey family attorneys, Pat

Burke, Hal Haddon and Bryan Morgan, represented John and Patsy Ramsey at no cost.

JonBenét's brother, Burke, also talks publicly for the first time in this book. Rare conversations with JonBenét's half-sister and half-brother, Melinda and John Andrew Ramsey, are included as well. Patsy's primary cancer doctor has also gone on the record in an exclusive interview to discuss his patient, including her disease and treatment.

Only three people have known that, until Patsy Ramsey's death in 2006 from ovarian cancer, she and I would occasionally talk in what she called "do you have a few moments" conversations.

Patsy made it clear that she wanted to relay candid bits and pieces of family information, conversations among them and thoughts about her children, her cancer, the police and the killer whenever she could. Her rules: everything she said was off the record, at least for the time being.

Whatever people thought about Patsy Ramsey, she was a woman who bore the scars of tremendous suffering. Accused by many—including the powerful and the merely shrill—of the most heinous crime a mother could commit, she stood straight, facing into the gale. At some level, my response to her remained simply human to human. I would listen to her off the record, in private conversations, as long as she did not admit to criminal acts.

Patsy said I could reveal all the information she shared with me only if and when she decided it was OK, or upon her death. After that, she said, it would be my decision on when to release it. I could ask her whatever I wanted, and she would choose whether to answer. She answered all my questions.

I took notes of these conversations, and then we went over them in detail after we were finished to make sure they were accurate.

Now is the time to release what is a deeply personal perspective on Patsy Ramsey via conversations in which her husband did not participate, though he did know about them. Approximately eighty-five percent of the quotes from Patsy noted in this book are from those sessions.

"Someday it may help John just to hear my thoughts after I'm gone," she told me. That was part of my last conversation with her. She was in

Denver in late 2005, meeting with members of her defense team for what was, in her mind, her goodbye to them. We spoke by phone.

"Someday," she added, "this may build enough publicity so the right person who is dedicated to the truth can really help find the killer, if he hasn't been found." In reality, of course, that may never happen.

Also included in this book are examples of the misinformation that was continuously and deliberately provided by the Boulder Police Department and the Boulder District Attorney's Office in attempts to influence reporters and public perceptions of the Ramsey case. These are included so erroneous assumptions based on such misinformation can be debunked once and for all.

It's important to note that several law enforcement officers and others involved in the Ramsey case who cooperated on this book asked that their names not be used for fear of losing current jobs. Still others were apprehensive about openly criticizing their colleagues who are still in law enforcement despite such colleagues' apparent lack of regard for administrative rules and criminal evidence procedures. Now, twenty years later, this case still has that much power.

The people who requested that their names not be used are well known to me and were intimately involved in some phase of the Ramsey murder investigation. They have also met my editor's tough requirements for allowing anonymity in rare but necessary cases.

Accepted law enforcement protocol is discussed throughout this book in order to clearly present instances in which such protocol was not followed during the Ramsey case investigation. Several law enforcement research manuals and books that provided such information are noted as utilized resources. Concluding statements in reports from the six handwriting experts consulted on both sides of the case, some of which have never been published, are included as well.

There are also instances in which a person quoted is described as a family friend or a female friend, etc., rather than identified by name, even if such names are noted in previously unreleased police reports or in information from key witnesses. This is done for members of the public who are not in law enforcement for the sake of their privacy after so many years. It is also done for the sake of simplicity in telling this story.

Additional research for this book utilized resources from the Vanderbilt University Television News Archive in Nashville, Tennessee; NewsLibrary.com; LexisNexis; the Norlin Library at the University of Colorado in Boulder; and the Auraria Library in Denver (which supports the Metropolitan State University of Denver, the University of Colorado in Denver and the Community College of Denver). Researchers from the Denver Public Library were also consulted.

While researching this book, I wasn't prepared for my personal reaction to seeing and studying JonBenét's personal belongings. As a journalist, I have found it necessary to prepare emotionally for stories and trials involving child deaths, child abuse or other disturbing events. Such stories inevitably have a harsh impact, one a reporter has to consciously work to guard against. When I first set out to cover this story, I knew I could not let it take a part of me with it.

As I brought this thinking into my more recent coverage of JonBenét's case, I realized in looking at her drawings, writings, photographs and autopsy photos that I hadn't allowed myself in the late 1990s to view her as an innocent child who was tortured and murdered. Rather, I had held her at a distance as the child beauty contestant—the one-dimensional JonBenét of the tabloids and sensational TV shows. That was my loss.

This is one reason there are so many previously unpublished photographs, drawings and writings of hers included in this book. My hope is that such documentation of the life ended through murder in December 1996 may give others the same richer, more fully formed understanding of the little girl named JonBenét Ramsey that I now have. Some crime scene photos and diagrams are used as well in order to contribute to a more complete understanding of the facts of this case and enhance the reader's ability to analyze them.

Through the window of all the materials that have been collected and researched for this book, which include additional defense papers, communications between prosecutors and Ramsey attorneys, personal tape-recorded interviews, DNA findings, letters and other documentation related to the case, a new transparency is revealed. The entire collection of the researched material is used for listed reference as needed under the umbrella name "WHYD Investigative Archive." "WHYD" is an acronym for the title of this book, *We Have Your Daughter*, which is from words used in the ransom note.

The bits and pieces of information related to this case, some factual and some not, that have been disseminated by so many with no proof should no longer stand as correct. What is publicly known is both accurate and false. Now, with newly disclosed documentation, evidence and contributions from the people involved in this tragic story, the case of the murder of JonBenét Ramsey can be portrayed as never before. And you, the reader, can make your own decisions related to it.

# PROLOGUE

"I WANT TO KILL THE KILLER."

He said it with fists clenched, his face taut with anger and the smoldering frustration of many years unfulfilled by resolution.

John Ramsey and I were sitting on a restaurant balcony next to a short waterway, the Pine River Channel connecting Lake Charlevoix and Lake Michigan in Charlevoix, Michigan, a quaint summer resort where John and his family had spent their summers for many years. It was June 2009, and town residents had held art and bake sales to raise money to buy and plant petunias along the boulevards. The town was draped with hanging flower baskets full of bright pink, purple, red, white and yellow blossoms.

We were seated near the drawbridge that allowed mostly pleasure boats to pass under Bridge Street, the main street of Charlevoix. It was early evening, quiet and calm. The people in the boats smiled and waved as they passed by. In the fading sunlight, the glint of the blue water rebounded in mirrored reflections.

I was stunned. There had been nothing about the serene setting or peaceful moment to suggest that the man across the table from me was contemplating revenge.

In the time I had known John Ramsey, the stoic, long-suffering father and central figure in an infamous murder investigation, I had never heard him say anything like this. He stared at me for several seconds, and there was silence between us. Then he gradually released his fists and said, "For years I had such rage that I told my friends just let me alone in a room with the monster that killed my daughter. We won't need a trial. I will tear him to shreds and it will take time because I want him to suffer, just as my daughter suffered. I will have no remorse."

The lines in John Ramsey's face slowly faded as he reflected on this statement. "But," he added, "I found I could not live with that kind of anger. My soul was rotting inside. Forgiveness came painfully slow, but I had to go in that direction. I couldn't spend each hour in every day still hating him."

"Then why did you just say you wanted to kill him?" I asked. "Where did that come from?" There was a long pause as John Ramsey appeared to think about this contradiction.

"Forgiveness is constant work," he said finally, "and as I just showed you, I'm not perfect. I'm not sure why it happened right now."

We had been talking about Charlevoix, with John offering descriptions and anecdotes in his gentle voice, when the conversation took its stark turn.

John knew I was in Charlevoix to talk with him about this book, a definitive account of the investigation into JonBenét's killing covering what had been discovered in the years since the murder, including new evidence . . . and new revelations related to the politics of the murder investigation. I wanted to know if he would cooperate. The case had dominated tabloid life and the public imagination for more than a decade by that point. No one seemed truly able to let it go.

In 2000, both John and Patsy Ramsey co-authored a book about their daughter being killed. But their defense attorneys heavily edited *The Death of Innocence,* because they feared one of the parents would be arrested for the murder and the book would be used against them.

John also wrote a faith-based book published in 2012, *The Other Side of Suffering: The Father of JonBenét Ramsey Tells the Story of His Journey from Grief to Grace.* It is about his struggles with his faith and the acceptance and mingling of his religious beliefs with regard to the multiple tragic deaths his family has endured.

He did not speak freely in either of those books about the facts of JonBenét's murder case.

But the barricade that has held his emotions and candor back has at long last been breached with this book. *We Have Your Daughter* offers a very personal look at the Ramsey family and their story of what happened related to the investigation of JonBenét's murder as reflected in interviews, documents, photographs and videos. It also includes observations from many other people who were involved in the case from the beginning.

"I have always said the crushing blow was the loss of our child," John Ramsey told me. "The police accusations and media lynching were just noise level stuff at the time. We were devastated and hurt so much that we couldn't be hurt anymore by the actions that followed. Now, I view the police as incompetent bullies, made very dangerous because of their power, bias and inability to analyze or discern objectively."

His disillusionment with the police and clearing his family's name are why John Ramsey agreed to cooperate with me in writing *We Have Your Daughter*.

"I want you to tell the story of what happened from your perspective as an investigative reporter who covered this from the beginning," he told me that June day in Charlevoix. "I will answer any questions. Just please get accurate information to the public. It matters very much what happened here. Investigate the circumstances. Do it for justice. If you affirm that either Patsy or I was involved, then go ahead and write it. Maybe some of what you learn will help find the killer."

"I have complete editorial control and will report what I find," I reminded him.

"Yes," he said. "I will sign a document saying you have complete editorial control. I will not look at the book before it's published unless you need me to do so."

The warning bells for the drawbridge clanged. Once on the hour and once on the half-hour, the bells rang out, the cars on Bridge Street stopped, the gates on the drawbridge glided smoothly upward, and the boats on Pine River Channel flowed through from one lake to the other. Some boaters blew their air horns in a signal to the bridge operator to please wait for them to get through. It was a cacophony of sound that gradually faded into background as I waited for John to speak once again.

He drew in a long breath and seemed to gather himself as he straightened in his chair. "I no longer view the lynch-mob behavior of the media and the police incompetence and vengeance as just background noise," he said. “They were fundamentally and deeply wrong in what they did. They affected our entire system of justice and our lives. They need to be held accountable, too. Can you tell people about that?”

“I’ll try,” I said. “Will you tell me how you survived?”

The question stopped him. He put his fingertips to his temples and rubbed them in a half-circle. His face looked pained. Here was the man alone, the survivor of a great storm that in many ways still washed down upon him.

“Without Patsy by your side,” I continued, “can you look into the chasm at all that has been lost? To understand? To explain? To try to help find your daughter’s killer?”

“I’ll try,” he said.

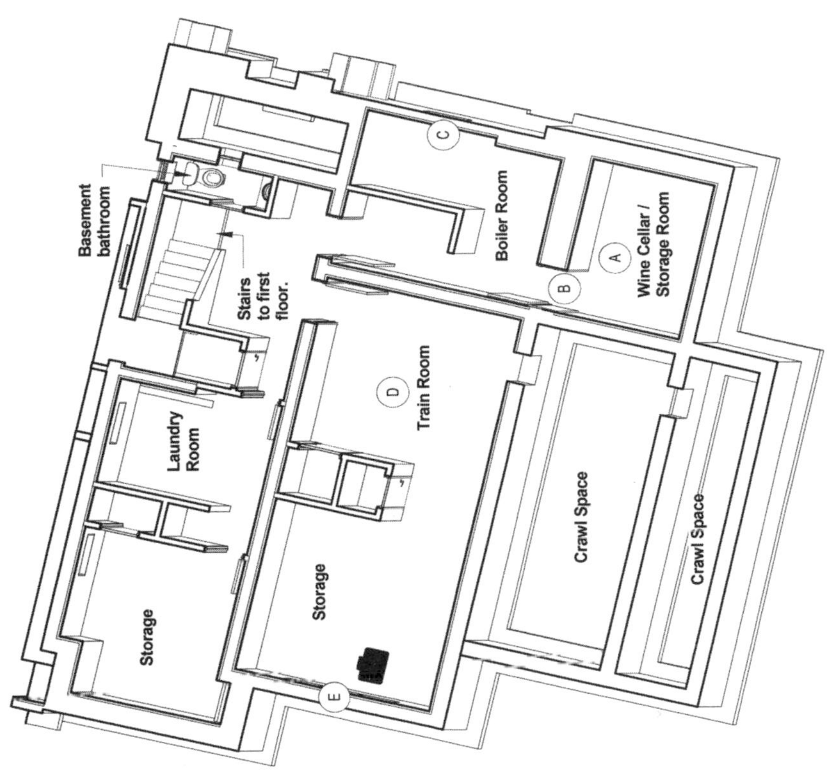


## Ramsey Basement

A JonBenét's body.
B Wine cellar door opens outward.
C Exposed ventilation duct.
D Train room.
E Broken window and suitcase.

N

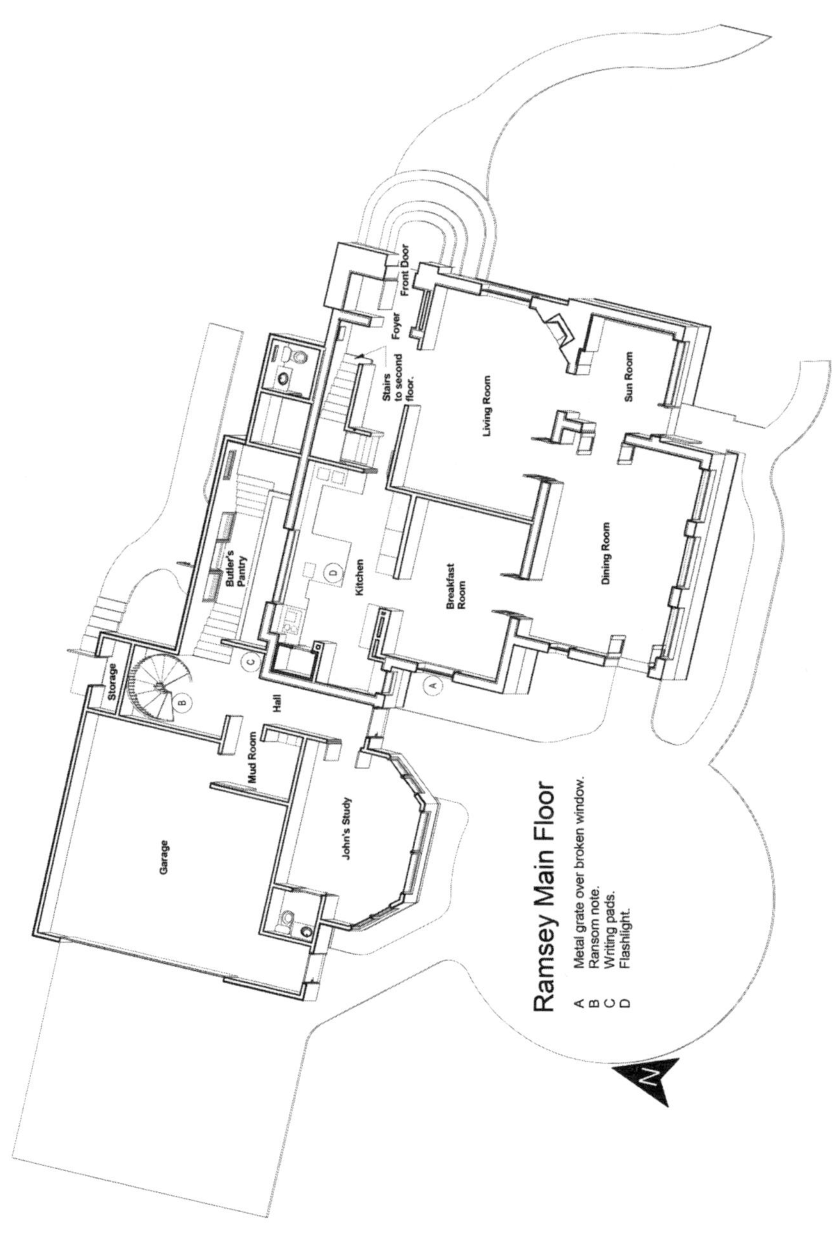
Ramsey Main Floor
A Metal grate over broken window.
B Ransom note.
C Writing pads.
D Flashlight.
Front Door
Foyer
Stairs to second floor.
Living Room
Sun Room
Dining Room
Breakfast Room
Kitchen
Butler's Pantry
Hall
Storage
Mud Room
John's Study
Garage
N

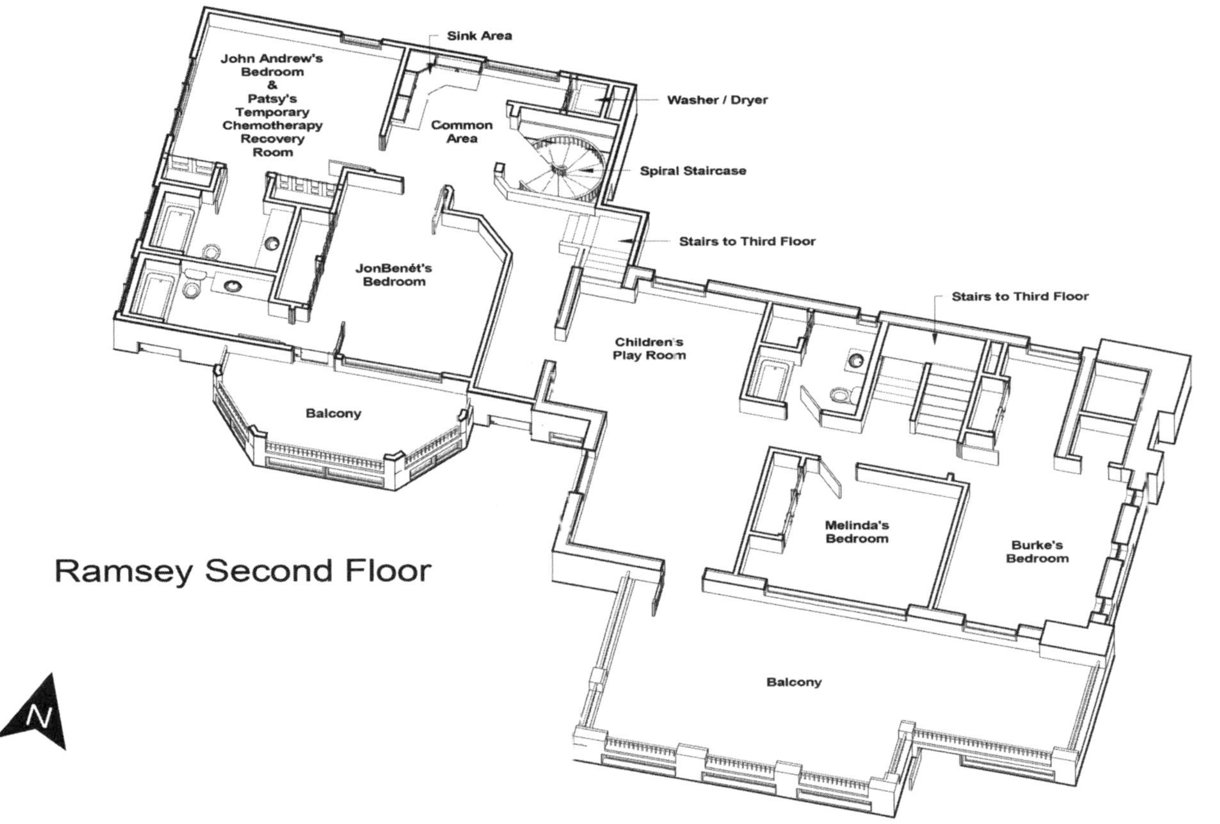


Ramsey Second Floor

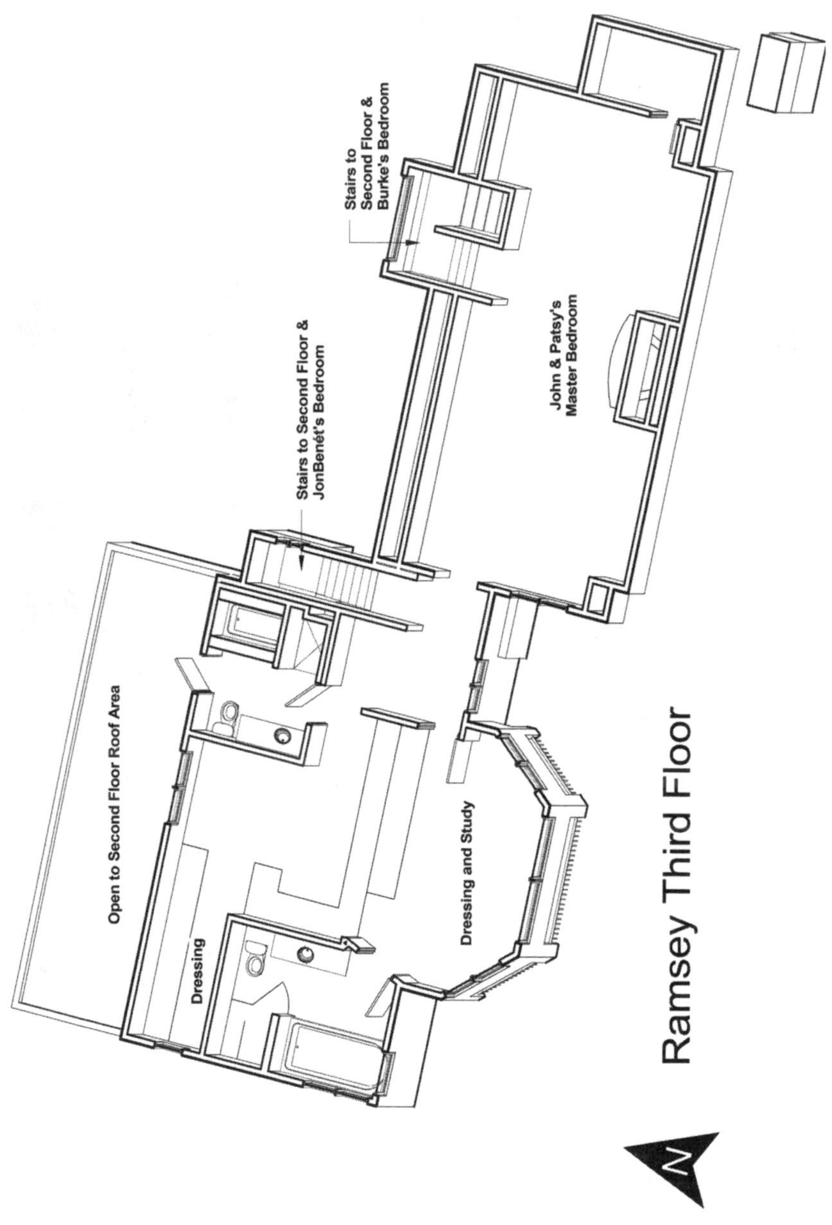


3-D Floor Plans used by permission of the architect, Nolan Carl, 10-Nine Design Group, Las Vegas, Nevada.

# CHAPTER 1
# THE FAMILY

Christmas decorations and police crime scene tape, December 27, 1996. Outside of Ramsey home.

THE SOUND WAS JOYFUL, constant, often high-pitched and boisterous. The various scout troops—Brownies, Cub Scouts, Girl Scouts and Boy Scouts—voiced their excitement as they marched along the route of the ninth annual Boulder Parade of Lights with the gleaming fire trucks, school bands, brightly lit floats and, of course, Santa Claus. That year, 1996, the Boulder parade fell on December 6. It was a chilly night filled with colored lights and sparkles and with steaming exhausts from the floats and fire trucks and the visible breaths of those out in the cold.

Four pretty girls, three younger ones and a teenager, were riding on the top of the back seat of a red convertible. They wore crowns, warm holiday coats, woolen gloves and their best smiles. They were representing AmeriKids, a non-profit youth development group in Denver. All of the girls, including six-year-old JonBenét Ramsey, were excited, shivering a little from the cold.

JonBenét in Boulder Christmas Parade, December 6, 1996. © John Ramsey.

JonBenét's grandparents, Patsy's mom and dad, walked next to the car and carefully watched JonBenét, just as adults from other families watched out for their children while the floats, cars and bands slowly started and stopped and started again in the typical dance of a local parade.

Christmas was still the Ramseys' favorite season. They loved the festivities.

Being in the annual Boulder parade was a tradition in their family. JonBenét's brother, Burke, who was nine, and his Scout troop had also walked or ridden on floats in prior parades, handing out candy to the crowd along each route, as they were doing this year. While she'd waited for the parade to start, JonBenét had called to her brother, "Burke! Burke! Please save some for me." He'd stopped and teased her as he gave her a piece.

Christmas was the best of times for the Ramsey family, but 1996 would be the last year that statement would hold true for them.

Patsy had started decorating early that year. With the number of trees and decorations in her home, her housekeeper and others had also been very involved. After two years, the extensive renovations on the Ramseys' 1927 three-story red brick and stucco house were finally finished, and Patsy was no longer ill from a frightening bout with ovarian cancer that had threatened her life since 1993. The family had much to celebrate.

Burke's Christmas tree in his bedroom.

For their part, JonBenét and Burke "sort of" helped their mom with some of the five or six Christmas trees in the house. They picked out the decorations they wanted to hang on the tree in each of their bedrooms. While

(Left) Sitting Room Christmas tree, main floor. (Right) JonBenét and Burke helping to decorate, December 1996. © John Ramsey.

JonBenét invariably selected red, pink and blue bulbs and angels, Burke chose trains or planes for his tree. Another tree in an adjacent sitting room had a big golden angel on top of it.

Santa Clauses of all kinds could be found in various corners in the Ramsey home. And there was garland on the spiral staircase that went from the main floor near the kitchen in the back of the home up to the second floor near JonBenét's bedroom.

(Left) Garland decorating spiral staircase. (Right) Spiral staircase.

Burke's room was also on the second floor, but at the opposite end of the house. Patsy and John's bedroom stretched the length of the third floor. It was a converted attic space that now held their bedroom as well as closets and bathrooms. Staircases went down each end of their room to the second floor, past their children's rooms and then on to the main floor.

The priorities in the Ramseys' lives had changed since mid-1993, when Patsy was given a "no-chance" prognosis after she was diagnosed with ovarian cancer. She'd entered an experimental treatment program whose exclusive inclusion allowed only Stage IV ovarian cancer patients. The treatments worked for her; she'd survived and was cancer free. Because of this, the Ramsey family lived less for the future and concentrated more on every day. And to Patsy, who never forgot her cancer could come back at any time, that included making Christmas as magical as she could. "I overdid the decorations. I know I did," she later said, smiling. "But it was part of living in the moment."

As the *Daily Camera,* the local Boulder newspaper reported on December 21st, "a gathering was held by Access Graphics . . . with about

Ramsey Family with Santa Claus, December 1996 Ramsey Christmas Party. © John Ramsey.

three hundred employees where John Ramsey thanked everyone for the company reaching the one billion dollar mark." (BPD Report #1-74.)[1]

On December 23, the Ramseys had a Christmas party for some friends and their children. Santa Claus was there played by a man Patsy had hired before.

The next day—Christmas Eve—JonBenét and Burke each went to play with friends while their mom and dad finished up some last-minute shopping for presents. JonBenét told the little girl she was visiting about a Secret Santa Claus who had promised he would visit her after Christmas. She also told this information to the little girl's mother, and another mother also learned of this. Neither mother gave a lot of thought about JonBenét's genuine delight in the promised "Secret Santa visit" until after JonBenét was killed. (BPD Reports #1-1167, #1-1149, #1-1874.)

And no one, except the person who killed JonBenét, if that person is still alive, or any accomplice he or she might have had, knows whether that promised visit had anything to do with her death.

That Christmas week, JonBenét drew a picture for her parents of baby Jesus in the manger with her brother and her standing next to the manger. It was one of her Christmas presents to them. On Christmas Eve night, the Ramseys went to church, then out to dinner at a friend's restaurant. After that, they drove up to see the big star that had been installed on a hill above Boulder for the holidays. Then they returned home. "We set out food for Santa," Patsy recalled. "John read *The Night Before Christmas* . . . and Burke, JonBenét and I would try to remember the next line in the story while he waited to tell us. We were happy."

"We spent some time shaking packages under the tree," Patsy continued, "guessing what was inside and admiring how pretty some of the bows and wrapping on the gifts were. The big challenge of the night," she added, laughing at the memory, "was getting them both to bed and asleep because as we all know Santa Claus can't come and leave his presents unless the children are asleep."

"Patsy and I sat down briefly just to enjoy the evening after the kids were asleep," John later reflected, "and to marvel at the blessings and happiness of our lives and just what plain fun this was." And then the

Drawing of JonBenét, Burke and Baby Jesus. Christmas present from JonBenét to her parents. © John Ramsey.

Actual book read by John to the family on Christmas Eve.

Ramsey family went to bed for what they knew was going to be an early Christmas morning.

"The kids ran into the bedroom at 6:30 that morning," John remembered. "They were thrilled. I made them stay in our room until I went downstairs and turned on the Christmas tree lights. I brought in Patsy's bicycle from the garage. Burke's and JonBenét's new bikes were already in front of the tree."

Santa Claus had brought a look-alike doll for JonBenét and a Nintendo video game system for Burke. There were lots of toys and gifts.

"We just smiled and laughed," John continued. "JonBenét gave me a jelly bean dispenser, which she was very excited about as she knew I loved jelly beans."

Patsy talked about that holiday, saying it "was fun, happy, the way we wanted it to be, especially for our children."

The rest of the day was full of JonBenét and Burke playing with other kids in the neighborhood, showing off their new toys and trying them out wherever they could, indoors or out. Patsy began packing for their trip to Michigan scheduled for the next day. They were planning to meet with John's two children from his first marriage to celebrate Christmas in Charlevoix, Michigan, where the Ramseys had a vacation home. At one point on that Christmas day, John went to Jefferson County Airport, which was about ten miles from the Ramsey home. He wanted to check out the private plane scheduled to transport them the next day and stow some luggage in it. Having their own plane, and the wealth that fact implied, would contribute to turning members of the public and law enforcement against the Ramseys in the months ahead.

At one point in the late afternoon, Patsy heard her daughter's voice call her from her bedroom. "Mom," JonBenét said, "this is what I want to wear." The little girl was referring to the clothes for an evening get-together with family friends and their children. When Patsy arrived in her daughter's bedroom, she noted that the new outfit JonBenét held up had different colors than the traditional red the two had planned to wear that night.

JonBenét's bedroom had pale pink walls and darker pink bedspreads

JonBenét jumping with excitement because Santa Claus has left a bicycle for her. © John Ramsey.

Burke and JonBenét opening Christmas presents. © John Ramsey.

on two twin beds. On one bed, a doll with blonde bangs, an elaborate white bonnet and a matching long, flowing white dress was propped up in a seated position against the headboard. A Santa Claus bear lay on a pillow at the feet of the doll. The bed skirts of the two beds matched the curtains on the bedroom's three windows. A regular one-panel glass door led to a covered balcony outside the second-floor bedroom. It opened inward. A blue, white and pink-striped dresser stood between the two twin beds, and a tall beige dresser was next to JonBenét's bed. The room's closet doors were painted with a mural of blue, pink and green hats hanging off a colorfully painted hat pole.

In one corner of the room sat a small Christmas tree decorated with red, pink and blue bulbs . . . and an angel.

Child beauty contest trophies were displayed on shelves along one wall in the common area outside her bedroom.

JonBenét was a beautiful little girl with blonde hair and a sweet and

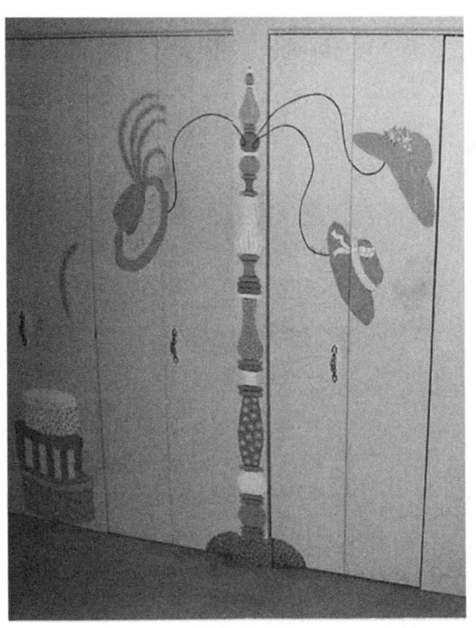

(Left) JonBenét's painted closet doors. (Right) Christmas tree in her bedroom.

Pageant trophies in the common area outside her bedroom.

fun smile. According to her parents, she was a type A extrovert who liked to be busy and involved in a number of activities. She had a personality that was "on" all the time, they said. Her dad added that JonBenét was "effervescent." She was also stubborn.

"Johnnie-Bee," Patsy encouraged, using the nickname she often called her daughter, "let's wear the same colors like we planned."

"No, Mom," JonBenét insisted, "this is what I want to wear." The six-year-old liked to pick out her own clothes, and Patsy could rarely predict which outfit her daughter would finally select.

Sometimes parents know when to give up and give in, and this was one of those times, Patsy decided. JonBenét ended up wearing what she wanted: a white top instead of the red one her mom had chosen.

When everyone was dressed and ready to go, Patsy helped the children put on their warm winter coats and finally the family left home that Christmas evening for another festive holiday event.

At the party, JonBenét nearly fell asleep on the floor while playing a game with her dad, her girlfriend, and her friend's father. By the time the Ramseys left the party and dropped a few presents off to other friends that evening, JonBenét had fallen asleep from the many thrills of the day.

Back at home around 9 p.m., John Ramsey carried JonBenét upstairs and placed her on her bed, where Patsy removed JonBenét's shoes, left the white top on her daughter and replaced the bottom part of JonBenét's outfit with a pair of long underwear. She then covered her daughter with her bedspread and kissed her on the forehead. "I took a moment just to smile and absorb this exhausted little girl sleeping before me and [having] what must have been happy dreams," Patsy said. "Then I went to bed."

John helped Burke with a new toy for a few minutes until they both went to bed as well.

John Ramsey's Journal about Christmas Day 1996:

*JB begged me with her sweet little smile to help her ride her new bike around the block again before we went to dinner. I told her we were late and we would do it another time. I helped her ride it around the patio. I will always remember her face . . . saying, "Daddy, please help me ride my bike around the block, just once more." Why didn't I do it?*

## CHAPTER 2

# THE DAY AFTER CHRISTMAS—MORNING

(Above and following pages) Exteriors of Ramsey home reflecting its size.

## THURSDAY, DECEMBER 26, 1996*

CHRISTMAS NIGHT, 1996, and into the early morning after was below freezing in Boulder. Even the neighborhood holiday lights seemed frozen, twinkling in the muted distance. The moon was just past full and, when it occasionally emerged from an overcast sky, made patches of snow on the ground turn silver. To the south and west, the university town's landmark jagged rock formations called the Flatirons faded in and out of the gliding shadows. The house at 755 15th Street stood in apparent peace and silence, undisturbed by the ice-laced currents from the heights of the Rockies that had turned a 54-degree day into a frigid night. A passerby would have noticed a few lights on in the Ramsey home on the main and second floors and in JonBenét's bathroom, all part of a normal routine for the family.

**A chronology of this morning's events is listed at the end of this chapter.*

From the east-facing front of the house, the size of the Ramsey family home was deceiving. Only when you looked at it from the south did you realize how high and far back the home stretched and how large it really was, which was more than 7,000 square feet.

## THEIR STORY

At about 5:45 in the pre-dawn darkness, a horrible piercing scream tore through the house.

"JOHNNNNN!!!!!!!!"

Patsy's urgent cry hit John with an impact that caused him to flinch in alarm. His heart pounded and adrenalin rushed as he ran down the stairs from the third floor toward Patsy's terror-filled voice.

When John reached his wife in the hall outside the open door to their daughter's bedroom on the second floor of their home, Patsy's face appeared stricken, her eyes wildly unfocused. She was looking at everything and at nothing. There was a ransom note, she told him, sobbing, for their daughter, JonBenét. "She's gone!"

Fear and dread engulfed John and Patsy Ramsey as each felt a rising sense of panic in their chests and throats. It was suddenly hard to breathe.

John stared at his daughter's empty bed. Her bed covers were pulled halfway back, and there was a crease in her bottom sheet. JonBenét's dresser was undisturbed, its lamp and array of little-girl knick-knacks just as they should be.

The second twin bed in the room was still neatly made with a doll sitting at its head. A smaller Santa Claus bear lay on a pillow at the feet of the doll, just as it had the night before, and a few of JonBenét's clothes had been placed on that bed.

But John didn't notice them. He was struggling to make sense of what he was looking at. Just hours before, he had carried his sleeping daughter to her bedroom and placed her safely in her bed. He'd left the bedroom while Patsy changed JonBenét's clothing. He then played with

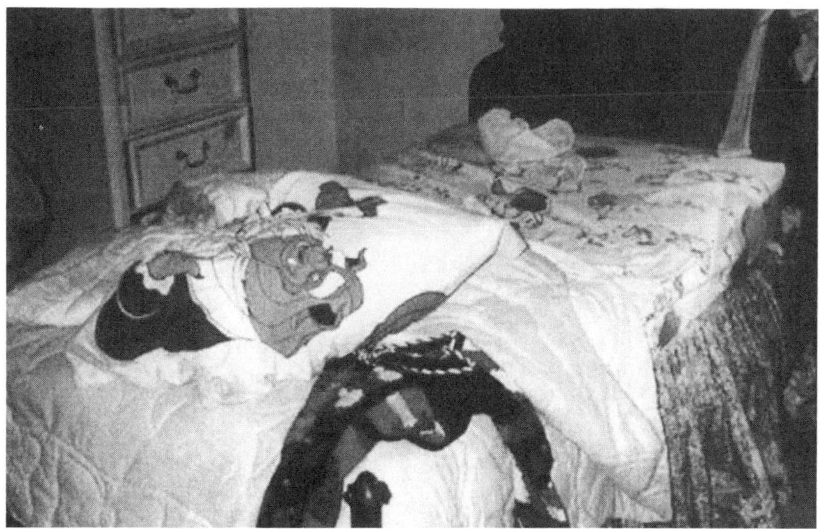

JonBenét's bed as it was found that morning. Courtesy Boulder Police and Boulder County District Attorney.

Second twin bed in JonBenét's bedroom. Courtesy Boulder Police and Boulder County District Attorney.

his son and his new toys, took a melatonin pill to help him sleep, and gone to bed.

What about nine-year-old Burke? Confusion muddied clarity that awful morning. Both parents raced to their son's room, which was also on the second floor, on the opposite end of the hallway from JonBenét's bedroom.

Please, God, let him be here.

He was. Burke was in his bed, curled beneath a blue bedspread. His bedroom was decorated with wallpaper featuring model airplanes.

Burke would later say in an interview that he pretended to be asleep that morning when his parents checked on him, because hearing his parents so upset had scared him.

Though John and Patsy tried to take deep breaths and think clearly, Patsy was quickly growing more hysterical and began physically shaking, her muted sobs coming in gasps. The fright kept building, tightening both their chests, and the next few moments became a panicked blur. They ran to the bottom of the back spiral staircase with its green garland decorations, where a note lay on a lower step.

The note was handwritten. In the two and a half pages of bizarrely worded threats, there was a demand for ransom.

Burke's bed and bedroom.

Bottom three stairs of spiral staircase.

Mr. Ramsey,

Listen carefully!

His voice rising, John told Patsy to call the police. It was 5:52 that morning. Every second was fueled by desperation.

You will withdraw $118,000.00 from your account. $100,000 will be in $100 bills and the remaining $18,000 in $20 bills.

"Hurry, hurry, hurry," she begged the 911 operator.

John spread the ransom note on the floor of the kitchen as he tried to absorb what was in it, but most of the words didn't make sense. One message got through:

we have your daughter

His mind was racing. He wondered how someone had gotten into the house, and who could have possibly done this. He also started thinking about how to get the ransom money.

Why hadn't he heard anything? How could this have happened right in his own home?

John and Patsy looked into each other's faces, silently sharing a horrible fear. In the middle of the night, someone had entered their home, left a ransom note and taken their daughter. They were too dazed to speak. How was it possible? Wouldn't they have heard her cry out? Wouldn't they have heard something? Wouldn't they?

John quickly rushed through the house, haphazardly checking for anything—something—while Patsy finished placing the 911 call and proceeded to call family and friends to come help them.

One of Patsy's best friends received a phone call from Patsy, who was screaming into the phone, "Get over here as fast as you can. Something terrible has happened!" (BPD Report #5-402.)[1]

John's Journal:

*We were out of our minds. I looked under JB's bed. If I could keep my wits about me I could get her back. She is smart and strong—she knows her Dad will get her back.*

A uniformed Boulder police officer arrived in a marked police car within eight minutes of Patsy placing her 911 emergency call. John and Patsy Ramsey had a traditional belief in the police. When you needed help, you called them, and they knew what to do. They were comforted by the officer's arrival. John showed Officer Rick French the ransom note and tried to explain as clearly as he could what was happening. He told the officer their daughter had been kidnapped. She was only six years old. Officer French listened, took notes and asked John, "Do you think she could have run away?" John said, "No. She's only six years old. She wouldn't run away."

Officer French took a brief look in various areas of the home but reported finding nothing suspicious. Within two minutes, a family friend had arrived, pulling into the alley driveway and then running to the east-side front of the house. Another officer also arrived.

In the moment, the unknown—as cruel as it was—would turn out to be better than the terrible certainty that was coming.

Soon Burke was roused from his bed and dressed so he could be hustled away from the growing turmoil inside his house and go to a friend's house to play. Both John and Patsy walked with their son down the path in front of their home, accompanied by one of the police officers, to a friend's waiting car. Bundled in his winter jacket, Burke carried an armful of toys he had received for Christmas just the day before. He was crying. His parents hugged him tightly, trying to convey all the reassurance they could muster.

"JonBenét has been taken but we're going to get her back," John told his son. He also told Burke that it would be better if he went to a friend's home for now, that his mom and dad were there for him and this would all soon be resolved.

After Burke left, the morning wore endlessly on, and Patsy felt her mind slowly closing down. "I was unable to hold onto the fact that my daughter was gone." All around her, she saw blurred images of kind-faced people, their mouths moving with distant and faint sounds as she sat collapsed on the floor in the Christmas wonderland she had created. The beautiful tree with its shimmering ornaments stood in one corner, yesterday's symbol of joy not only irrelevant but a brutal reminder of how quickly things had turned. Her agony could not be suppressed.

She vomited into a bowl between her legs.

People continued to arrive. Detectives. Friends. Victim Advocates whom the police had called. Patsy tried to answer everyone's questions, but to those around her she seemed frozen in slow motion at times and then broke down in out-of-control crying just short moments later. For Patsy, one thought—a stubborn focus—provided a lifeline connection to JonBenét. She felt that as long as she held that thought and let nothing else in, then her daughter was still with her. She had to communicate with JonBenét by concentrating only on her, and she was determined to hold onto that connection. It was a fragile and desperate attempt subject to the sharp realities of the intrusions all around her. Patsy Ramsey was willing her daughter to be there, to hear her. In her anguish, she was trying to hold the world away.

Patsy couldn't have known this at the time, but in the minds of some of the people moving around her that morning, the roots of suspicion, even of judgment, were already taking hold.

John was in another room. He, too, was answering questions, trying to offer what help he could. Unlike Patsy, he was allowing his mind to contemplate the terrible realities at hand. John was consumed with thoughts of the kidnappers, of the freezing temperatures and darkness of the night that had just passed, of the fear he had for JonBenét. What was she thinking? Was she crying for her mom and dad?

Were they hurting her?

Was she alive?

He offered the police anything they wanted. What can I do? What do you need? Ask me anything. Anything. Just tell me what you need.

John's Journal:

*We would get JB back & I couldn't wait to hold her in my arms. The FBI had been called we were told but would take a couple of hours to get here. I wanted to block roads, put police at the airport are we doing enough? We gave the detectives more leads.*

*We are worried the kidnapper hasn't called.—Where is the FBI?—We're told they're reachable by telephone for advice. I'm thinking who can I call to get all resources on this? I'm getting desperate now.*

He tried to focus on the one goal of getting his daughter back. Unspoken, his thoughts tumbled as he wavered between thinking about "when" they'd get JonBenét back versus "if" they'd get her back.

His more optimistic thoughts led to planning how he and Patsy would take JonBenét and Burke away when this was over.

But that was just a wishful daydream that faded as despair seized him. There might not be a happy reunion. There might not be a trip away for JonBenét and Burke to overcome this trauma. Whatever had happened to his daughter, life would never again be "normal." His thoughts tumbled over themselves all morning.

At one point very early on December 26, there were at least five police officers and two detectives in the Ramsey home. In fact, at varying times throughout the morning, there were a total of eighteen family members, friends and law enforcement personnel on the premises, most freely wandering the home, contaminating the crime scene and whatever evidence might have been there.

John continued his search, which was erratic. He looked in a closet, behind a chair and under a bed, picking up a magazine and even looking in their walk-in refrigerator. In fact, the refrigerator was the first place he looked. And while telling himself to "focus," he was incapable of an organized and logical search. He was trying to find his daughter, but he didn't know what else he should be looking for. He was traumatized. By the time John got to the basement, he simply wandered through some rooms, which were messy from the Christmas season preparations, not seeing or knowing what might be out of place until he got to the train room, the room where Burke had set up a model train on a table.

It was there that John Ramsey saw something that terrified him: an open broken window with a suitcase underneath it and a scrape mark on the wall near it.

The suitcase would later be moved from its horizontal position along the wall to a vertical angle, as shown, by a family friend.

That suitcase shouldn't be there, John thought. The window shouldn't be open. And what is that scrape on the wall?

He immediately returned upstairs and told an officer what he'd seen. He explained that the window had been broken the summer before, when

(Left) Suitcase, which was originally horizontal next to the wall when John said he found it. Courtesy Boulder Police and Boulder County District Attorney. (Right) Detail of possible shoe scrape on wall. Courtesy Boulder Police and Boulder County District Attorney.

he'd been locked out of his home. He'd gotten into the house by breaking that window. But the suitcase was normally kept under the basement stairs with the other luggage. And the window shouldn't have been open. He knew something was very wrong. A Boulder police report added more information: "(sometime before 1000 hours) [10:00 a.m.] John Ramsey went down into the basement to the train room and he found the train room window open so he closed it." (BPD Report #5-2473.)

The second officer on the scene that morning wrote in his report that he "examined the outside of the residence . . . initial inspection of the west basement window grate." (Sergeant Paul Reichenbach—Date of Report 1-26-1996.)

The "west basement window grate" was located above the broken basement window.

The Boulder sergeant also wrote in his report that he "observed actions of occupants of house."

When the winter sunrise allowed, John grabbed his binoculars and went to one of the highest points in the home on the third floor. He scanned the neighborhood to see if he could spot anything unusual. Perhaps there would be a car, a van, a person, something that struck him as suspicious and might help police.[2]

He also checked his mail, hoping it might contain a clue. The mail was delivered through a mail slot near the front door that dropped the mail inside the house. Even that well-intended act would be misconstrued, as John Ramsey would later be criticized in a leak to the media for taking time during the crisis to sort through his mail.

At a time when it would seem of critical importance that the family and police should be working in careful concert, the investigation was already teetering on the edge of disaster, like a snow-packed mountain in which unstable particles of snow are shifting beneath the surface, about to cause that first gigantic surface crack, the signal of the beginning of an unimpeded avalanche.

Commander-Sergeant Bob Whitson, the on-call supervisor that morning, didn't arrive at the Ramsey home until more than three hours after Patsy's frantic 911 call. Before his arrival, he had gone through a deliberate process of notifying necessary personnel, contacting and setting up a meeting with the FBI, and searching for a recently created kidnapping protocol document that hadn't yet been distributed to Boulder police officers. Only a few detectives had the document, and they were on vacation over the Christmas holidays.

Even though his arrival was delayed, Whitson knew he needed to observe the scene firsthand and talk with the Ramseys. When he arrived, they were in different rooms of the house.

The sergeant went first to John. To Whitson, John appeared to be a distraught parent who was forcing himself to respond calmly. John was able to answer questions, and Whitson thought he was earnestly trying to contribute.[3]

JonBenét's bedroom was the supervisor's next stop. Whitson walked upstairs to the second floor with the two detectives who'd been on the scene since earlier in the morning. Upon arriving outside the door to JonBenét's bedroom, Whitson looked in the room for any signs of crime such as blood or broken items, something that wasn't as it should be. He didn't find anything. He also had no idea how many people had already traipsed through the little girl's bedroom. According to his report, he ordered the detectives to block the door with yellow crime scene tape and stressed that no one should go in the room except police. He made a point of telling John that no one but investigators should go into his daughter's bedroom.

Then, Whitson asked one of the two detectives present, Fred Patterson, to obtain handwriting samples from John and Patsy Ramsey. From a desk located just outside the kitchen in an area near the back staircase, John produced two tablets the family used to write notes to each other. On one tablet that contained samples of John's own handwriting, John also wrote more at the top for additional comparison. The other tablet contained samples of Patsy's handwriting.

In his initial police report, Detective Patterson said he "gave the pads to Sgt. Whitson for later comparison with the ransom note. Sgt. Whitson maintained custody of the pads." Whitson would take them directly to

BOULDER POLICE DEPARTMENT

SUPPLEMENTAL REPORT

CASE: P96-21871

DATE: DECEMBER 27, 1996

REF: HOMICIDE INVESTIGATION
JONBENET RAMSEY

BY: ROBERT WHITSON

On Thursday, December 26, 1996, at about 6:05 a.m., I received a page to call the Watch 3 Supervisor, Paul Reichenbach. Sgt. Reichenbach advised me that he had responded to a reported kidnapping involving a six year old girl from 755 15th in Boulder. He was requesting detective assistance.

I telephoned Detectives Linda Arndt and Fred Patterson and asked them to respond to 755 15th.

While driving into Boulder, I telephoned Detectives Arndt and Patterson and they advised me they were almost at 755 15th. Therefore, I responded to the Police Department to make several telephone calls. Those included to following:

Portion of Commander-Sergeant Whitson's police report.

the Boulder Police Department. The ransom note had already been taken to BPD headquarters.

Unknown to other on-scene law enforcement personnel, the second of the two detectives, Linda Arndt, kept a sample of John's handwriting and didn't submit it to Whitson, who at that point was the custodian for the handwriting collection. This action was contrary to the way a trained investigator or lab processor would collect a significant forensic sample. Accepted forensic protocol dictates the investigator or processor "selects a team of trained personnel to perform scene processing, collects the evidence at the scene, bags and labels it and then transports it to the lab where scene evidence is being collected."[4] Although there was nothing wrong with someone not specifically designated to collect such evidence doing so at the scene, the manner of the collection was less than scientific and could easily have raised chain-of-custody questions at a later trial, especially when the other officers didn't know Arndt had kept a sample of John Ramsey's handwriting.

Sgt. Reichenbach, the second officer on the scene, reported his findings to Whitson. "I was told there was [sic] no signs of forced entry" (Commander-Sergeant Robert Whitson—Date of Report 1-27-1997).

Even though Reichenbach had examined the "west basement window grate," Whitson did not mention that he had been told this information, or the fact that John Ramsey had reported that he'd found a known broken basement window left open with a suitcase underneath it and a scrape along the wall near it, when he wrote in his report:

> Detective Patterson advised me that telephone traps and traces had been placed on the Ramseys' telephone and a tape recorder was attached in case the suspect called. I was advised that Officer Barry Weiss had already photographed the house and didn't find any signs of an obvious crime scene where there had been a struggle. (Commander-Sergeant Robert Whitson—Date of Report 1-27-1997.)

Examining the case years later in a three-day Boulder Police Department review, several invited and experienced homicide detectives from throughout the state of Colorado would voice concerns that officers on the scene failed to report to Whitson the other signs in the basement: the suitcase out of place, the broken window and the scrape mark on the wall. "The scene briefing is the only opportunity for the next in command to obtain initial aspects of the crime scene prior to subsequent investigation."[5]

Information about the handwriting samples collection and the police photographs of the Ramsey home was contained in Detective Linda Arndt's report dated January 8, 1997: "Ofc. Weiss was photographing the interior and exterior of the residence. Ofc. Barklow was attempting to obtain latent fingerprints. Areas checked included: possible points of entry and exit to the residence; as well as the spiral staircase leading from outside JonBenét's bedroom to the first floor; and the door leading into JonBenét's bedroom."

There was limited documentation of evidence gathered during those first critical hours. Forensic officers only documented parts of the scene when the whole house, inside and out, had been important. The two forensic officers should have looked everywhere and documented everything, especially since at that early stage no one could have known what might be useful evidence. "Conducting a scene walk-through provides the investigator(s) in charge with an overview of the entire scene."[6]

After directing the collection of the handwriting samples, Whitson then approached Patsy. She was sitting with two friends in a small sunroom. Whitson's conversation with Patsy was brief, lasting less than a minute. Whitson introduced himself, telling Patsy he had contacted the FBI and everyone was trying to help her and John get their daughter back. Whitson would later state, "She was extremely upset and mumbling 'my baby.'"

While the difference in behavior between the husband and wife was dramatic, Whitson later said, "I didn't think it was unusual." He added that, in his twenty-two years of police experience, "I saw people respond all sorts of ways to stress and grief."

Whitson got little information from Patsy, but one of his detectives reiterated that both John and Patsy had been interviewed and the process was ongoing. The interviews had not been recorded because the two detectives had only one tape recorder between them, and they'd decided to hook that to the telephone in case the kidnapper made his promised ransom call.

Whitson left with one of the two detectives for a 10 a.m. meeting he had scheduled with the FBI. He told the remaining patrol officers they should also leave.

After leaving the home, Whitson wrote in his report: "Det. Patterson and I checked the area near the Ramseys' home for any suspicious looking people or vehicles and did not see anyone unusual. I responded to the Police Department and met with several Detectives and representatives from the FBI. During this meeting, [Boulder] Det. Jeff Kithcart came into the room and I handed him the two note pads which I was given as samples of Mr. and Mrs. Ramsey's handwriting." (Commander-Sergeant

Robert Whitson—Date of Report 12-27-1996.)

The promised phone call from the kidnapper was supposed to occur "between 8 and 10 a.m.," yet all police personnel except one detective had left the Ramsey home before 10 a.m.

By then, hell and its resultant misery were ready to open their doors for all to see.

## CHRONOLOGY

## DECEMBER 26, 1996—THURSDAY

According to standard police protocol, only law enforcement (detectives and lab personnel) should have been in the Ramsey home the morning of December 26, 1996, because the entire home was part of a presumed kidnapping, and therefore a crime scene. Yet there had been eighteen people in and out of the house that morning: eight police officers, two Victim Advocates, three Ramsey family members and five family friends.

An accurate and signed police entry/exit logbook from the crime scene was not kept. Logbooks represent another way of gathering evidence. They are signed by each officer, who is also supposed to note their times of entering and exiting the scene. In the Ramsey logbook, there are occasionally several times listed for what should have been one sign-in and sign-out for each of the officers.[7] Here are the best records available from the JonBenét Ramsey Murder Book Index:

**5:52 a.m.—Patsy calls 911.**

**6:00 a.m.—First officer, Rick French, arrives at the Ramsey home.**

**6:01 a.m.—Friend of the family arrives at the Ramsey home. The records never mention his wife's arrival, but she appears a short while later.**

**6:02 a.m.—Second officer, Sergeant Paul Reichenbach, arrives at the home.**

**6:10 a.m. and 6:20 a.m.—More friends arrive after being called by Patsy. Two arrival times are listed for them in police records.**

**6:10 a.m. and 6:16 a.m.—Third officer, Karl Veitch, arrives at the scene. Two arrival times are listed in police records.**

**6:30 a.m.—First Victim Advocate arrives.**

**6:30 a.m. and 7:00 a.m.—Second Victim Advocate arrives. Two arrival times noted.**

**6:40 a.m. and 6:56 a.m.—Fourth officer, Barry Weiss, arrives. Two arrival times noted.**

**7:00 a.m. and 7:10 a.m.—Fifth officer, Sue Barklow, arrives. Two arrival times noted.**

**7:00 a.m.—JonBenét's brother, Burke, is roused from his bed by his father and a friend and taken to a family friend's home.**

**7:13 a.m.—The Ramseys' minister arrives.**

**8:10 a.m. and 8:11 a.m. and 8:30 a.m.—Two detectives, Fred Patterson and Linda Arndt, arrive. It is two hours and 18 minutes, two hours and 19 minutes or two hours and 38 minutes after the 911 call. By protocol, the detectives are in charge of the scene.**

**9:15 a.m.—Commander-Sergeant Bob Whitson arrives.**

**9:45 a.m.—Whitson and one of the detectives leave.**

**10:00 a.m.—All officers except Detective Arndt leave the home. Nine civilians remain. JonBenét is still missing.**

The wife of one of the Ramseys' friends was never listed in the entry/exit log. The friend had been the first civilian to arrive, reportedly at 6:01 a.m. There is no indication in the log that his wife arrived, but she was in the Ramsey home early that morning.[8] Several witness statements were taken from her about being in the home, and she and others have verified that she was there.

# CHAPTER 3
# FINDING JONBENÉT

Burke and JonBenét at Atlanta 1996 Summer Olympics. © John Ramsey.

## CHRONOLOGY

# DECEMBER 26, 1996—THURSDAY

1:00 p.m.—Detective Arndt suggests John Ramsey and his friend search the home to see if anything is out of order.

1:06 p.m.—(Approximate time) John finds his daughter's body in an old basement storage room.

1:30 p.m.—(Approximate time) John's children from his first marriage (son, John Andrew, and daughter, Melinda, as well as Melinda's boyfriend) arrive in Boulder after flying to Denver International Airport from Minneapolis.

1:30 p.m. to 2:00 p.m.—(Approximate time) The Ramseys leave their home and go to a friend's home to stay. The police have interviewed them and don't ask to continue to interview them. Nor do they take the family to the police department for interviews, forensic physical examinations and DNA testing.

Early evening and that night—John's brother, Jeff, family friends and Patsy's sisters arrive at the airport in Denver from Atlanta.

TO LOOK AT THE GOOFY SMILE on the handmade turtle, which sports a painted and shaped paper plate for its shell, is to see what she saw.

Turtle with paper plate shell made by JonBenét. © John Ramsey.

Her art teacher wrote that she "draws happy, sunny pictures. She is talented and a care-giver to other students."

Her music teacher said JonBenét "loves to dance and sing. She always makes sure that each student has his/her turn."

Her homeroom teacher wrote on JonBenét's report card after her first few months in Kindergarten: "JonBenét is a pleasure to have in class. She is a confident, positive student who works hard on all assignments. JonBenét's mature behavior makes her a positive role model for other students."

EVALUATION OF PROGRESS

- \+ = Things I do well.
- ✓ = Things I'm working on.
- x = Things I will learn to do.
- · = Needs to improve.

| ATTENDANCE | TRIMESTER 1 | 2 | 3 |
|---|---|---|---|
| Days present | 55.5 | | |
| Days absent | 4.5 | | |

TEACHER COMMENTS:
1st semester JonBenét is a pleasure to have in class. She is a confident, positive student who works hard on all assignments. JonBenét's mature behavior makes her a positive role model for other students.

(Left) Self-portrait made by JonBenét. © John Ramsey. (Right) Homeroom teacher's comment about JonBenét.

## THURSDAY, DECEMBER 26, 1996

Although John, Patsy and their friends had been allowed to wander throughout the home during the morning, after nearly all the police officers left before 10 a.m., all civilians on site were instructed by the remaining detective to stay in a back section on the main floor. This is where the detective, John and Patsy, their friends and the two Victim Advocates waited for the ransom call. The phone rang several times that morning. Some were return calls from acquaintances John had called while trying to arrange the $118,000 ransom money for when the call came from the kidnapper. Others were from friends, unaware of the devastating circumstances inside the home, who were calling to wish the Ramseys happy holidays. With each call, John experienced brief seconds of relief and then despair. He answered with a simple hello, trying to keep his voice calm. With each call, he thought, "Maybe this is the kidnapper. Maybe he'll let me hear my daughter's voice."

One call that morning was unlike the others. With this call, there was a split-second pause on the line, and then the caller hung up. In 1996, the family didn't have caller ID, and the call was not long enough to complete a trace of it through the phone company.

"I thought it was the kidnapper," John said later. The caller had waited just long enough to hear his voice. Why did the caller hang up? Who was it?

There was nothing he could do.

It was a long, slow morning of suffering. The small group of people waited and prayed while their hearts were slowly torn apart . . . As Patsy negotiated with God, at one point she was overheard by a police officer saying, "If only it was me, I would trade places with . . . I would trade places . . . oh please, God, let her be safe oh please, let her be safe." (BPD Report #5-2627.)

JonBenét Ramsey was born August 6, 1990.

*Patsy and John Ramsey*

*joyfully announce*

*the birth of their daughter*

*JonBenét Patricia*

*August 6, 1990*

*1:36 a.m.*

*6 pounds, 9 ounces*

(Above) JonBenét's birth announcement. © John Ramsey. (Below) Patsy holding newly born JonBenét on her lap. © John Ramsey.

She was named after her father, whose full name is John Bennett Ramsey. Her mother used the soft, French J when she called her by name. Her father used the hard J.

As a baby, JonBenét didn't cry much. When she did, her mother knew she either needed a diaper change or it was time for bed. Otherwise, JonBenét smiled a lot and was delighted to sit and watch what was going on around her, always searching for a new sight. As she got a little older, her mom once said, she loved airplanes. When she heard one, she would point and wave toward the sky and say "pane."

Her half-sister, Melinda, remembers how much JonBenét liked to play outside and be with other children. "Kids!" JonBenét would yell out, pointing and turning all different ways in her stroller. "Kids!"

Patsy kept her children busy. When asked what she did for a living, Patsy said she "invested in futures." Most assumed that meant she worked in the stock market, but Patsy was talking about her children. She was a mother.

JonBenét and Burke took piano lessons.

At various times, JonBenét took violin lessons and acting lessons, participated in a children's choir and attended gymnastics, singing and dancing classes.

Both children skied, ice skated and were enrolled in rock climbing and Bible study classes.

Patsy and John wanted them to be well rounded and to participate in family activities that included sports as well as educational and artistic endeavors. Burke had his father's genes. He was quiet and became easily involved in activities by himself.

JonBenét had Patsy's personality times ten; she was gregarious and outgoing, and she liked people. She talked in her own language from an early age and then just talked a lot. She was "exuberant," Patsy would say, adding that yes, "JonBenét went through the two-year-old phase." She was very strong-willed and verbal, according to both parents.

Once, when the family was skiing in Aspen, John thought JonBenét was skiing at too fast a speed and could lose control. He remembers them being at the top of an advanced run on a clear day of vivid blue skies and sunlight and snow. The grandeur of the Colorado Rockies was all around them, and here was his little girl, racing her way down the mountain. He skied down and tackled her.

"Man, she was mad," he remembered, smiling. They had both face-planted in the snow. JonBenét looked around, startled, trying to figure out what had happened. Then, sputtering with indignation, she demanded, "Dad, did you do that? I was just getting going!"

"JonBenét, you were going too fast. You could have gotten hurt."

"No. Only if I couldn't stop. I could stop."

"Well," her dad answered, "I'd like you to slow down a bit."

They helped each other up and brushed themselves off, and then off they went, skiing again. JonBenét took off just as quickly but, this time, her dad was very close behind.

On her first report card in kindergarten, JonBenét got thirty-nine plusses and needed work on recognizing the differences between a penny, nickel and dime and between a letter, word and sentence. She also needed

**High Peaks Elementary**
**Core Knowledge School**

**KINDERGARTEN REPORT CARD**

3740 Martin Drive
Boulder, CO 80303
303 494-1069

Student JonBenet Ramsey Grade K

Teacher __ School Year 1996–97

Assignment Next Year ____

| WORK HABITS | 1 | 2 | 3 |
|---|---|---|---|
| Listens to directions | + | | |
| Follows directions | + | | |
| Works independently | + | | |
| Completes work | + | | |
| Works in a careful manner | + | | |
| Works well in groups | + | | |
| Shows positive attitude toward given tasks | + | | |
| Uses time constructively | + | | |

| SOCIAL HABITS | 1 | 2 | 3 |
|---|---|---|---|
| Plays well with others | + | | |
| Is thoughtful and courteous | + | | |
| Listens when others are speaking | + | | |
| Accepts responsibility for own actions | + | | |
| Practices self-discipline | + | | |
| Respects authority & property | + | | |
| Is developing self-confidence | + | | |
| Tries to do what is expected | + | | |

| READING | 1 | 2 | 3 |
|---|---|---|---|
| Shows interest in books | + | | |
| Exhibits reading-like behavior (imitates reading, memorizes stories, reads pictures) | + | | |
| Understands left to right sequences | + | | |
| Reads color words | ✓ | | |
| Knows address, phone#, and birth date | + | | |
| Can identify and supply rhyming words. | + | | |

| WRITING | 1 | 2 | 3 |
|---|---|---|---|
| Demonstrates fine motor readiness | + | | |
| Participates in writing activities | + | | |
| Is willing to use temporary spelling | + | | |
| Knows difference between letter, word, & sentence | ✓ | | |
| Beginning sounds | + | | |
| Uses beginning & ending sounds | + | | |
| Transitional (almost readable) | + | | |

| ORAL LANGUAGE | 1 | 2 | 3 |
|---|---|---|---|
| Listens without interrupting | + | | |
| Expresses ideas clearly | + | | |
| Contributes to class discussions | + | | |

| NUMBER READINESS | 1 | 2 | 3 |
|---|---|---|---|
| Recognizes and draws basic shapes | + | | |
| Identifies top, bottom, middle, inside, outside | + | | |
| Can compare numbers (as many as, less than, more than) | + | | |
| Can count to 100 | + | | |
| Can write numbers to 13 | ✓ | | |
| Recognizes shape or color patterns | + | | |
| Recognizes number patterns | X | | |
| Recognizes penny, nickel, dime | ✓ | | |

| SCIENCE/SOCIAL STUDIES | 1 | 2 | 3 |
|---|---|---|---|
| Participates in group activities | + | | |
| Shows curiosity and interest in topics studied | + | | |
| Observes for varied purposes | + | | |
| Recognizes likenesses and differences | + | | |

JonBenét's kindergarten report card.

to work on writing out her numbers past thirteen and reading color words. The only "x" she got was for a failure to recognize number patterns.

JonBenét had a certain vitality and was always active and busy. During a parental interview for kindergarten, Patsy wrote in some paperwork that "activities [JonBenét] liked were artwork, coloring, ceramics, reading, monkey bars, rollerblading and bicycling." Patsy also wrote that JonBenét would rather "play with others than play alone," got along "great" with her brother, and loved "scary stories." She felt JonBenét did "well in printing, reading, art, computer, writing and letters." With regard to discipline, Patsy wrote JonBenét was "very sensitive" and that "it was important not to pull her from a group, but to reach compromises."

In one Boulder Police Department report related to another caregiver for Burke and JonBenét, a long-time babysitter said, "JonBenét and Burke were the most loving brother and sister I've ever seen" (BPD Report #5-3610). Another report, however, related to a former nanny, stated that the nanny had "bad-mouthed the Ramseys a lot." (BPD Report #5-1343.) It was reported by police that the same nanny "who babysat while Patsy was ill" had hit Burke: "Burke said she had hit him and he did not like her. She had been mean." (BPD Report #5-3044.) That babysitter resigned or was let go as the children's nanny soon after the incident involving Burke.

When they weren't in school, JonBenét and her brother were often outside playing with friends. JonBenét was an all-day person, which meant she'd wake up cheerful and ready for the day ahead. During the school year, she'd get up, get dressed and go to school. She and her brother carpooled to a local public school. She had a few after-school activities, and then she was home for dinner, family time and bed.

Once, on a jungle gym with her mother standing by, JonBenét missed a rung, fell and landed flat on her back. Her parents had stressed laughter through playtime accidents. As Patsy ran up to her stunned, unmoving child, JonBenét suddenly burst into laughter and told her mom, "I'm not hurt, Mom. I'm going to get back on, and this time I won't fall." Patsy recalled, "I was always amazed by the confidence and maturity of statements like that from both Burke and JonBenét. I'm not so sure I would have climbed back on those monkey bars."

In a previously unreleased police report, Detective Linda Arndt, the only law enforcement person in the Ramsey home after 10 a.m. on Thursday, December 26, 1996, wrote about what she did that morning. According to this report (Detective Linda Arndt—Date of Report 1-8-1997), Arndt talked with Patsy about when she found JonBenét missing, who had keys to the home, their vacation plans and if Patsy had any ideas related to who might have kidnapped her daughter. Patsy told the detective about her housekeeper, the housekeeper's family and how the housekeeper had recently asked to borrow $2,000. Arndt also wrote that Patsy's mother, by phone from Atlanta, had said she wanted Detective Arndt to know the housekeeper had told her "many times" that JonBenét was such a beautiful girl and asked if she (JonBenét's grandmother) wasn't afraid someone was going to kidnap her granddaughter.

Arndt also interviewed John about his wife's recent recovery from cancer. They talked about any suspicious people around the house but, according to Detective Arndt's report, John said there hadn't been any, as far as he knew.

Detective Arndt also discussed the wording in the ransom note[1] with John, the amount of the ransom, the strange signature on the note—"S.B.T.C"—and "things to say when the author(s) of the suspected ransom note called." She also asked him about any employee of his company, Access Graphics, "who might be responsible for the disappearance of JonBenét." "John did tell me that there was one employee he was forced to 'let go' approx. 5 months ago," Detective Arndt wrote, adding that she and John then considered the employee in more detail.

As Patsy lay on a couch, she talked with Arndt about the ransom note. "Patsy explained to me that [the housekeeper] did not use the words 'hence' or 'attaché case.' Patsy did not know why someone would ask for the amount of $118,000. Patsy said that amount had no significance to her. Patsy asked me why the author of the note had not asked for a larger sum of money, or at least a round sum of money. Patsy said the author of the note referred to John as being a Southerner. Patsy told me that anyone who knows John Ramsey knows he's not from the South."

"John Ramsey's friends made the following observations about the note: The author of the note directed the note to John Ramsey; the amount of $118,000 was an odd amount; the author of the note appeared to be somewhat educated, since the words 'hence' and 'attaché case' were used; the sentence 'don't try to grow a brain John' seemed to be a slap in the face to John Ramsey; the closure 'Victory! S.B.T.C' did not make sense; and the reference to John Ramsey being a southerner [sic] indicated to the friends the person did not really know John Ramsey because John was originally from Michigan."

A family friend who at one point that morning left the home to arrange to have the ransom amount of $118,000 immediately available from John's bank also spoke with Detective Arndt. "[Friend of John] told me that $118,000 is a relatively insignificant amount compared to John Ramsey's wealth. He told me that the persons who demanded the ransom could easily have asked for $10,000,000 and . . . obtained that amount."

Arndt also noted in her report, "No one in the house made any obvious comment to me that it was after 1000 hours [10:00 a.m.] and the suspected kidnappers had not called." In the ransom note, the kidnapper said he/she would call between 8 a.m. and 10 a.m., so Arndt was questioning why John and Patsy hadn't noted the time, even though the officers who'd left at 9:45 a.m. and 10 a.m. had failed to stay with Detective Arndt for that crucial ransom call.

By nearly noon, after six frustrating hours with no word, the home was suffocating from inaction.

Detective Arndt paged her supervisor, Sergeant Larry Mason, at noon and at 12:30 p.m. She reported that he did not respond to her pages. She noted in her report: "Patsy Ramsey had been repeatedly asking me for an update. John Ramsey seemed to isolate himself from others."

Arndt suggested that John and his friend search the home "to keep John Ramsey's mind occupied." The two men then went to the basement.

In the basement, they both went directly to the room with the suitcase and the broken window and then investigated further, each moving in a different direction. John went past the basement stairs and down the basement hall to the door of a storage room that was located next to the one he'd just been in. The door was straight down the hall from the staircase and was accessed through an open boiler room door. The door to the storage room was about five feet into the boiler room and in direct line of sight of the staircase.

The old door had no handle. It was painted bright white, and a black metal plate covered the space where a handle would otherwise have been located. The door led to a room that had been used to dump and store coal from the main floor when the home was originally built in 1927. The Ramsey family used the room as a space to store Christmas decorations and presents as well as window screens and other construction paraphernalia. At the top of the door, a makeshift block of wood was held in place by a screw. A latch that hung straight down from the block of wood

Wine cellar door/storage room door with latch (highlighted) at top to keep it closed. The door opened outward only.

kept the door closed when it was secured.

John undid the latch and pulled the door open. Inside, the darkness of the bare storage room was solid and still.

He turned on the light. Milliseconds of reality blasted toward him.

It was an ugly room that was mostly square, with a short left-side wall that led to a corner and then a longer straight wall around that corner. The room was all concrete from the walls up to the ceiling and down to the moldy floor. The open door allowed light from the hallway to help illuminate the dimly lit, rarely used space.

Just around the corner, JonBenét was sprawled on the dirty floor, arms above her head, a blanket from her bed casually, or tightly (there is differing opinion on this), covering part of her body. Her favorite pink Barbie nightgown was on the floor next to her. (BPD Report #2-8.)

Where JonBenét's body was found in the basement.

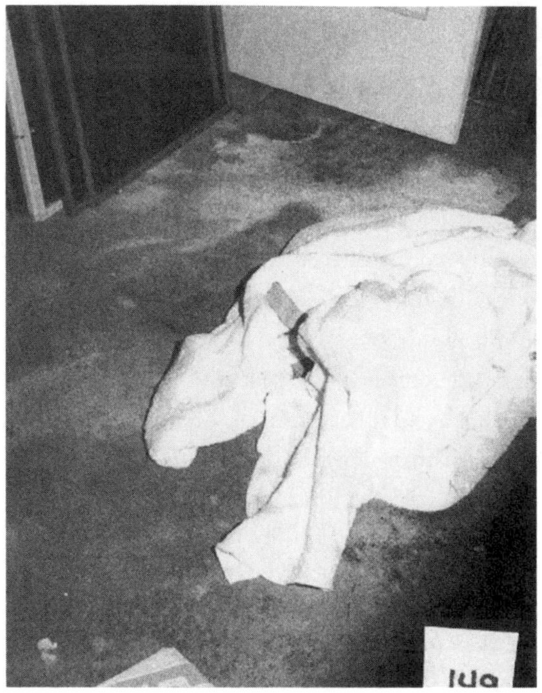

Duct tape binding JonBenét's mouth and blanket that was partially covering her. John had removed the duct tape from her mouth when he found her. The friend right behind him picked the duct tape up and then dropped it. Courtesy Boulder Police and Boulder County District Attorney.

John's Journal:

*I see instantly what I know is JonBenét. A white blanket from her bed and her face is turned to the left, black tape on her mouth. Her arms are above her head tied together with a shoestring type cord. I notice a red spot beneath her skin at her esophagus. A rush runs over me, thank God I have found her. I fall down over her saying come on baby, talk to Daddy. I rip the tape from her mouth. Her delicate eyelids are closed and her skin is cool to the touch. Come on honey. Oh God, no, talk to me, talk to me. I start to untie her arms as they are bound tightly. I've got to do something. I'm totally out of my mind now. I pick up JonBenét and start to rush upstairs. All I can do is scream. My screams are those panic kind of scream you have during nightmares just before your body shakes awake with a start.*

There was a brief second of relief . . . his heart beating against his chest . . . as John pulled the duct tape off JonBenét's mouth and frantically tried to untie her hands. And then there was the scream. A deep primal scream, a father's anguish welling from the depths, a tortured cry that reached those on the floor above, foretelling news of a child's death. John kept screaming, his body shaking. "I realized she wasn't alive and picked her up and carried her upstairs," he later said. The coroner would determine the cause of death had been either strangulation or a blow to the head. The force of the blow that JonBenét endured caused a crack eight-and-a-half-inches in length that ran along the interior of her skull, including a portion of her skull that was caved in. But none of that damage to her skull was visible on the outside of her head.

As he ran from the basement to the main floor carrying his daughter with her arms frozen above her head in rigor mortis, John Ramsey thought for at least a fleeting moment that maybe it wasn't too late. His denial was so strong that he held onto the hope that the stiff, cold little girl who was his daughter somehow was alive and could be saved. He laid her on the floor of the main floor hallway and Detective Arndt desperately tried to find JonBenét's pulse. But this was not a day for such mercies. The detective told him, "She's dead." Any chance was gone, and the helplessness John Ramsey felt at that moment was crushing. At that point, the detective moved JonBenét's body into the living room next to the Christmas tree.

Years later, Patsy would remember the scream from the basement. "It was kind of this hoarse, deep scream. I was in the den with a couple of our friends. They held me back and wouldn't let me go. Eternity passed and John came in. I knew from his face. I can't describe how he looked, but it was in his face and his walk and his eyes. He told me she was dead. I thought I ran into the room where she was, but friends tell me they had to support me to even walk into the living room to see my baby girl." One of those friends would later tell police that she "thought it was strange that Patsy did not move" when the body was found. (BPD Report #1-1194.)

Soon, however, Patsy Ramsey did make it to where JonBenét's body lay on the living room floor. John had covered his daughter with a blanket. Patsy lay down and held the body of her little girl. "My mind snapped," she later remembered. "I couldn't cope, understand or reason."

According to Detective Arndt, "Patsy was crying and moaning while she was with JonBenét. Patsy raised herself onto her knees, lifted her arms straight into the air, and prayed. Patsy said 'Jesus! You raised Lazarus from the dead, raise my baby from the dead!'"

The Christmas tree and sparkling decorations as well as figurines of the Three Wise Men in the beautifully decorated living room stood as mute witnesses over the murdered child who lay, a rope still embedded in her neck, on the floor in front of them.

Tree with three wise men figurines in front of it. It was where JonBenét's body was laid by the only detective in the home. Courtesy Boulder Police and Boulder County District Attorney.

The Ramseys' friends joined hands as the family minister, who had arrived earlier that day, began Last Rites. They then recited "The Lord's Prayer" while gathered on the floor around JonBenét's body.

When Commander-Sergeant Bob Whitson returned to the Boulder Police Department at 10 a.m. that day for his meeting with the FBI, he turned John and Patsy's handwriting samples over to the department's forgery detective, who was already in possession of the ransom note. The meeting with the FBI, which also included Boulder Police Chief Tom Koby and Sergeant Larry Mason (supervisor of the other detectives that day), lasted nearly three hours. And then, quite suddenly, the meeting was interrupted.

Whitson remembers that the forgery detective who had been examining the ransom note and the handwriting samples burst into the conference room with the tablet with Patsy's handwriting on it. But it was something else on the tablet that brought the meeting to a stunned halt. In the middle of the tablet, where there should have been empty pages, the detective had found the words "Dear Mr. & /" in that same odd block-letter handwriting of the ransom note. Patsy's tablet, which contained samples of her handwriting, had also been used by someone for practice writing the beginning words of the ransom note. Seven pages had been ripped from the middle of Patsy's tablet as well. The ransom note had been written on the eighth, ninth and tenth pages of the tablet; what was left of those pages in the tablet had tears that matched up with tears at the top of the ransom note pages.

"And that was when it coalesced," Whitson said. "The meeting came to a conclusive halt. It was the first indication law enforcement people in the room had that the Ramseys might have been involved in their own daughter's disappearance."

The anomalies of the day continued to mount. "I tried to call the Ramsey home line to tell the detective about the new ransom note development, and it was busy," said Whitson. The phone line was busy because, at that exact moment, the only detective in the home was calling 911 to report a body had been found by John Ramsey in the basement of the home.

In a later police report, on-the-scene Detective Linda Arndt said she used a cell phone to call in the dead-body discovery, which wouldn't account for a busy home phone line at the exact same time. The discrepancy about the busy phone signal in the home was never resolved.

The death of JonBenét Ramsey was quickly conveyed to those meeting with the FBI at Boulder Police Department headquarters. Whitson would later describe the scene that he and other officers rushed back into at the Ramsey home as surreal.[2] "Patsy was standing and holding JonBenét and rocking back and forth with a banshee-like wail. I was focused on her so everyone else was a blurred surround."

Downstairs, the friend who had helped John Ramsey search the basement at the request of Detective Arndt was stationed in front of the closed basement door. Arndt had asked him to stand guard there and allow no one to enter. Involving a civilian once again in the crime scene was another mistake by the detective. "Controlling the movement of persons at the crime scene and limiting the number of persons who enter the crime scene is essential to maintaining scene integrity, safeguarding evidence and minimizing contamination."[3]

At the suggestion of the Ramsey family's minister, Patsy finally set JonBenét's body on the floor. John and a family friend literally carried and half-dragged Patsy, who had collapsed, out of the room. Later Patsy Ramsey would state, "Nothing. Nothing. I could do nothing on my own." She also recalled that in her mind she was screaming, "No! No! No!"

When John's son and daughter, John Andrew and Melinda, along with Melinda's boyfriend, arrived via a flight from Atlanta at the Minneapolis airport, where they'd planned to meet John, Patsy, Burke and JonBenét after their flight from Boulder, a flight attendant told them to call their father in Boulder. They suspected something was wrong and quickly found a pay phone at the airport. John Andrew called and his dad answered the phone. Melinda would later recall that the color drained completely from John Andrew's face as his father spoke to him. "JonBenét's been kidnapped," John Andrew said.

"I fell to the ground when John Andrew told me that," Melinda said. "He was still on the phone. I knew it was bad. We scrambled and were able to fly stand-by to Denver. My boyfriend was with us. We got a cab in Denver."

By the time the three arrived in Boulder, JonBenét's body had been found. "When we got to the house in Boulder," Melinda said, "I remember seeing police setting up yellow tape around the yard. Dad and Patsy were outside with friends, and Dad was crying. Patsy looked awful. Dad said, 'JonBenét is with Beth.' That's my sister who was killed in a car crash. My mind played tricks on me. I was already in shock. My first reaction was that JonBenét had not died. It was that Beth was taking care of JonBenét while she was still kidnapped."

Melinda continued, "We all almost immediately got into cars and went to a family friend's home. When we got there, Patsy couldn't even sit up, so I went to comfort her." Melinda told Patsy, "We're going to get her back. It's going to be OK." And Patsy told Melinda, "No, Melinda, you don't understand. Your dad found her in the basement. She's dead."

"I remember thinking this would kill them," Melinda said. "After my older sister, Beth, was killed in a car wreck, it was just so awful. I didn't think they could take another loss like this. I thought they'll be dead in a year from sheer grief. Patsy already seemed dead inside. Her whole body was pale and gray. She just wasn't there. Dad was sobbing continuously. His way of dealing was to pace and cry."

Melinda, her brother and her boyfriend had started the day in the best of holiday spirits, looking forward to being with the rest of the family. While they tried to absorb the enormity of what had happened, lives had already toppled and collapsed.

John's Journal:

*John Andrew and Melinda both started to cry. Oh why do my children have to bear such burdens so early in their life.*

John's brother, Jeff, other friends and Patsy's sisters arrived that night from Atlanta. Jeff would later say he was unable to acknowledge that JonBenét was dead until he saw his brother's face and helpless sobbing.

Jeff dwelled on memories of his niece and focused on comforting his brother and his wife. He recalled JonBenét's boundless enthusiasm, and he remembered them playing in the leaves in his brother's yard in Boulder two years before. "One more time, Uncle Jeff," JonBenét had called to her uncle. It had been one of those golden Colorado fall days with a brilliant blue sky and temperatures still warm enough to play outside, but the air vibrated the skin with the promise of a cool night ahead. The temperature in Boulder at 5,400 feet descends with the sun. The September days were growing noticeably shorter, the sun slanting in at different angles, its western light this time of the day diffused by gold. The game they were playing involved JonBenét hiding in a pile of leaves. It was up to her Uncle Jeff to "find" her. She would then jump and yell, "Boo!" and he would pretend to be surprised. Then the game would start over again with JonBenét hiding in a new pile. After the seventh or eighth time, Uncle Jeff said maybe they should quit and go inside. But JonBenét, with that endless supply of energy most kids have when they're having fun, wanted to keep going. "Again?" she'd ask her uncle.

Susan Stine, whose family the Ramseys lived with for four months after the murder, found out what had happened on December 26 when she and her family arrived home from a movie that day. The phone rang and another friend said, "Did you hear what happened to the Ramseys? JonBenét was murdered!"

"Everything was so crazy," Susan reflected. "At the time, it's something you would never have thought possible. Not someone going into a house and murdering a child. We were all dazed for weeks, just operating on automatic pilot."

Terror, fear and depravity had slipped quietly into the home of a seemingly content family of four in the town of Boulder, Colorado. And it was all magnified by the bizarre evidence of the case with its many interpretations.

# CHAPTER 4
# RANSOM NOTE

Five movies examined for ransom note phrasing. © Tommy Collier.

## CHRONOLOGY

**Lines from all these movies, which were in circulation before the Ramsey ransom note was found, were compared to it. Police reports said John and Patsy Ramsey didn't go out to see movies (BPD Report #5-431.):**

**1971—*Dirty Harry* released**
**1986—*Ruthless People* released**
**1994—*Speed* released**
**1995—*Nick of Time* released**
**1996 (November)—*Ransom* released**

THE RANSOM NOTE was the first solid evidence discovered at the scene. To see and read the words of the person who killed JonBenét Ramsey, or had knowledge of her murder, is still eerie even after all these years.

While there is no profanity in the ransom note, the odd and perverse personality of the writer seeps through its words. The note conjures images designed to strike pure terror in the heart of a parent of a kidnapped child via words such as "beheaded." Parts of the note seem disjointed, while others seem strangely concise. There are hints of terrorism and fragments of text from movie scripts. The first paragraph includes spelling and punctuation errors and perhaps a minor shaky handwriting disguise, but in the remaining text there are no errors, and the block-style writing evens out. Although the note seems to indicate some knowledge of the family, it chillingly alludes to the Ramseys' daughter but never once mentions her by name. According to forensic psychiatrists, such a strategy helps a killer to disassociate from the victim as a person. But it could also mean the killer didn't know her name or how to spell it.

The killer or accomplice who wrote the ransom note used a black Sharpie, a felt-tip pen, that was in the Ramsey home. "United States Secret Service document Examiner Larry Stewart found the pen marked CBI exhibit 292 had the same type of ink as was on the ransom note." (BPD Report #3-199.)

The note is approximately 372 words in length, depending on how you count abbreviations, and two-and-a-half-pages long. It was left on the back spiral staircase between the first and second floors of the Ramsey home, on one of the lower steps, where Patsy found it. She later said those were the stairs she always used to come downstairs. The pen with the same ink as the ink used to write the note was found with pens in the first-floor kitchen area near the back staircase. It may be one of the longest, if not the longest, ransom notes in recent history, according to researchers.

A close family friend in the home with the Ramseys that morning stated, "Whoever wrote the note has a very superficial knowledge about John Ramsey. They probably got the stuff from reading bibliographies [sic] in the press about Patsy because she's from the South" (BPD Report #5-52). Another close friend in the home with the family that morning said the note contained some "fakey stuff" and seemed "so personal." (BPD Report #5-413.)

When the Ramsey home was part of a holiday tour of homes in Boulder in 1994, flyers about the Ramseys were made available to visitors. According to the Boulder Police Department, there was a "copy of the flyer found in the basement near where JonBenét's body was found. This flyer provides information regarding the background on the family and could contain information observed in the ransom note." (BPD Report #19-1.)

With regard to the ransom note, one of the detectives familiar with the investigation later remarked, "Imagine what type of person would be able to write those words while in essence lying in wait for the Ramseys to come home that Christmas night, knowing at least in part what was going to happen. What kind of sheer, coldblooded ruthlessness would it take by the parents to write these ransom words after torturing, sexually assaulting and killing their little girl?" He added, "Or what about the person who might have written the note days earlier, knowing what was planned for the child?"

Mr. Ramsey,

Listen carefully! We are a
group of individuals that represent
a small foreign faction. We ~~do~~
respect your bussiness but not the
country that it serves. At this
time we have your daughter in our
posession. She is safe and un harmed
and if you want her to see 1997,
you must follow our instructions to
the letter.

You will withdraw $118,000.00
from your account. $100,000 will be
in $100 bills and the remaining
$18,000 in $20 bills. Make sure
that you bring an adequate size
attache to the bank. When you
get home you will put the money
in a brown paper bag. I will
call you between 8 and 10 am
tomorrow to instruct you on delivery.
The delivery will be exhausting so
I advise you to be rested. If
we monitor you getting the money
early, we might call you early to
arrange an earlier delivery of the

money and hence a earlier
~~delivery~~ pick-up of your daughter.
Any deviation of my instructions
will result in the immediate
execution of your daughter. You
will also be denied her remains
for proper burial. The two
gentlemen watching over your daughter
do not particularly like you so I
advise you not to provoke them.
Speaking to anyone about your
situation, such as Police, F.B.I., etc.,
will result in your daughter being
beheaded. If we catch you talking
to a stray dog, she dies. If you
alert bank authorities, she dies.
If the money is in any way
marked or tampered with, she
dies. You will be scanned for
electronic devices and if any are
found, she dies. You can try to
deceive us but be warned that
we are familiar with Law enforcement
countermeasures and tactics. You
stand a 99% chance of killing
your daughter if you try to out
smart us. Follow our instructions

and you stand a 100% chance
of getting her back. You and
your family are under constant
scrutiny as well as the authorities.
Don't try to grow a brain
John. You are not the only
fat cat around so don't think
that killing will be difficult.
Don't underestimate us John.
Use that good southern common
sense of yours. It is up to
you now John!

Victory!

S.B.T.C

The language in the note generated tremendous speculation. One theory suggested that parts of the ransom note might have used lines from movies involving kidnappings. Boulder County Sheriff Homicide Detective Steve Ainsworth, on loan to the Boulder District Attorney's Office for the investigation, remembered hearing quotes similar to those in the ransom note in a *Dirty Harry* movie. Detective Ainsworth talked with other investigators to see if they might remember other movies that might have similar language.

Ainsworth and retired Colorado Springs Homicide Detective Lou Smit compared the words in *Dirty Harry* and several other movies involving ransoms. Smit was hired by the Boulder District Attorney with approval from the Boulder Police Department to work the homicide case and provide a different perspective since he did not live in the Boulder area.

Ainsworth and Smit reasoned that, if the author had used quotes from movies demanding ransoms, then he would have had to spend time watching those movies and gathering the quotes. They concluded it was possible the killer brought the quotes to the Ramsey home and wrote the ransom note before kidnapping and killing JonBenét, or took Patsy's tablet outside of the home and wrote the ransom note earlier before bringing it back into the home.

The first *Dirty Harry* movie is about the search for the Zodiac Killer, a real-life serial killer who operated in the San Francisco area during the late 1960s. He murdered at least five people and claimed to have killed many more. The Zodiac Killer has never been apprehended.

The *Dirty Harry* movie featured a dramatic and suspenseful beginning, much like the Ramsey murder did, as well as a sinister and macabre story line:

The bells toll mournfully as the movie camera zooms in on a list of San Francisco police officers who have been killed in the line of duty. It pans up to a San Francisco Police Department badge. Then it moves down the list of killed officers, whose names have been memorialized in stone. The badge is visible once more before dissolving into the scope of a sniper's rifle being sighted from the top of a high-rise building. The music intensifies; the sniper locks his rifle crosshairs on a young woman swimming in a rooftop pool a few streets away. As the weapon fires, the riflescope follows the woman as she's hit and sinks into the water of the pool. It's the opening and classic scene from *Dirty Harry,* the first in a series of movies produced about a detective, Harry Callahan, played by actor Clint Eastwood.

The serial killer in the *Dirty Harry* movie threatens the mayor of San Francisco for ransom in exchange for not killing more people. The comparisons:

**Ramsey Ransom Note**

Mr. Ramsey,
Listen carefully!

*Dirty Harry*

"Now listen to me carefully. Listen very carefully." (The killer says this while beating Callahan.)

"Now listen." (The killer says this to the mayor of San Francisco.)

**Ramsey Ransom Note**

If we catch you talking to a stray dog, she dies.

*Dirty Harry*

"If you talk to anyone, I don't care if it's a Pekingese pissing against a lamppost, the girl dies." (The killer says this to Callahan in a call related to the ransom drop.)

**Ramsey Ransom Note**

The delivery will be exhausting so I advise you to be rested.

*Dirty Harry*

"It sounds like you had a good rest. You'll need it." (The killer says this to Callahan.)

The person who wrote the ransom note to John Ramsey about JonBenét warned him four times what to do to get his daughter back, or "she dies." The killer in the movie *Dirty Harry* warns what to do three times or "the girl dies."

Another movie, *Speed,* involves a bus filled with passengers that's been rigged with a bomb. The man requesting money says the bus will explode if it slows to less than 50 miles an hour.

*Speed* features actors Keanu Reeves, who plays a Los Angeles police officer named Jack Traven, and Sandra Bullock, who plays a passenger on the bus who becomes its driver after the actual driver is accidentally shot. The ransom demand is $3.7 million dollars for the killer to remotely disarm the bomb.

**Ramsey Ransom Note**

Don't try to grow a brain John.

*Speed*

"Do not attempt to grow a brain." (The killer says this to Traven.)

A third movie compared to the ransom note, *Nick of Time,* stars actor Johnny Depp, who plays a protective father named Gene Watson. Watson's daughter is kidnapped and, to get her back, Watson is supposed to kill the governor of California. He is told he is being constantly watched and supervised by one of the kidnappers.

**Ramsey Ransom Note**

Speaking to anyone about your situation, such as Police, F.B.I., etc., will result in your daughter being beheaded.

*Nick of Time*

"You talk to a cop; you even look at a cop too long and your daughter's dead . . . I'll kill her myself. Cut the head off right in front of you." (The killer says this to Watson.)

**Ramsey Ransom Note**

You and your family are under constant scrutiny as well as the authorities.

*Nick of Time*

"Don't forget. I'll be watching you." (The killer says this to Watson.)

**Ramsey Ransom Note**

Listen carefully!

*Nick of Time*

"I need you to listen to me carefully. Three lives depend on it . . . Very carefully." (Watson says this to the governor of California.)

The fourth movie compared to the Ramsey ransom note, *Ruthless People*, stars Danny DeVito, who plays millionaire Sam Stone, and Bette Midler, who plays Stone's despised wife. Stone wants to get rid of his wife, but she's kidnapped before he can. The kidnapper calls Stone using a disguised voice.

**Ramsey Ransom Note**

Listen carefully!

*Ruthless People*

"Listen very carefully!" (The kidnapper says this to Stone.)

**Ramsey Ransom Note**

You and your family are under constant scrutiny as well as the authorities.

*Ruthless People*

"You will be watched at all phases of execution." (The kidnapper says this to Stone.)

The movie *Ransom* starring actors Mel Gibson and Rene Russo was showing throughout the country, including in Boulder, at the time of JonBenét's murder. It involves the kidnapping of the son of a very wealthy and influential high-profile businessman named Tom Mullen. The first few minutes of the film show Mullen and his son playing hide-and-seek during a party at their home.

After the kidnappers take Mullen's son, they e-mail Mullen a video of the child with silver duct tape over his eyes. (JonBenét had black duct tape placed over her mouth.) One of the kidnappers calls Mullen using a mechanically disguised voice and gives him detailed instructions on how to get his son back. He details the terms, including denominations of the money and the type of briefcase to use, and warns Mullen not to involve the police or the FBI. The kidnapper also says Mullen's family is being watched and gives conditions that, if violated, will result in the child being killed.

None of the movies police compared with the note was found in the Ramsey home. All videos in the Ramsey home had been made for children to watch. Boulder police checked numerous video stores to see if John and Patsy had rented any movies with kidnapping themes. They hadn't, as far as investigators were able to determine. The couple also told police they didn't go out to watch movies (BPD Report #5-431).

Four of the five movies noted use words such as "listen," "listen up," "now listen to me carefully," "now listen," and "listen very carefully," all of which are echoed in the JonBenét ransom note:

Listen carefully!

There is other unusual wording in the demand note, which ends with:

Victory!
S.B.T.C

Although there have been many theories about what "S.B.T.C" stands for, no one has found the answer yet. When Boulder Police Department investigators searched for a connection to S.B.T.C, they found phrases that matched but appeared to lead nowhere: Southern Bell Telephone Company (BPD Report #1-813), a family in Florida with those initials on their license plate (BPD Report #1-618), Santa Barbara Tennis Club (BPD Report #26-189) and Saved by the Cross (BPD Report #26-148). There were other matched comparisons, but no leads.

Experts say $118,000 is a peculiar amount of money to request for a ransom amount. Other actual ransom notes in kidnappings typically request amounts in evenly rounded numbers, according to research.

The amount in the Ramsey ransom note is also close to the amount John Ramsey received from a deferred compensation bonus from his employer that year. But it wasn't exact. John's bonus was slightly more than $118,000—it was $118,117.50.

"How many people would know what my bonus was?" John Ramsey later asked. "If I or my wife were writing that note, why would we choose a ransom amount that would cause the police to ask us questions about it because it was close to my bonus amount?"

John kept his pay stubs in his unlocked desk at home, where a stranger could have found them. Almost immediately after investigators working for the Ramseys told two Boulder Police Department detectives about the bonus and the pay stubs, this information—including payment amounts—was leaked to the media, and another brick was cemented in the wall of public opinion against the Ramseys.

What wasn't reported publicly were ties that linked the ransom request amount of $118,000 with two former employees of Access Graphics, where John Ramsey was CEO.

The BPD report states that one employee told police that it was an "'odd coincidence that $118,000 happens to be the amount of the difference between what we W-2'd [this deleted pronoun from the report referred to the person fired] as a result of what we felt we gave up in the settlement and the promissory note, the unpaid note, the promissory note. And it's such an obtuse connection, but since you asked, $118,000.' (Pertaining to a settlement: re: [the ex-employee] who stole money from Access Graphics)" (BPD Report #5-3295).

The controller of Access Graphics at the time stated about the same former employee that the person had been "involved in a fraud for approximately that amount" (BPD Report #5-795).

And a second employee stated: "It is either the bonus or also a number close to the claim that [ex-employee] made against the company." (BPD Report #5-3488.)

One recurring rumor about the case stated that a book found in the Ramsey home was connected to the ransom note. The Ramseys said they didn't have the book in question, but rumors and publicity still swirled that they did and used ideas from it in the murder of their daughter. *Mindhunter: Inside the FBI's Elite Serial Crime Unit*, was written by retired FBI profiler John Douglas and published in August 1996. Douglas's book details how profilers working from crime scene evidence try to predict the behavior, motivation and patterns of serial killers. The book also discusses the limitations of profiling and how a profile is apt to fit a lot of people and can't substitute for hard evidence.

Douglas was hired by the Ramsey attorneys. He thought the killer was an intruder who specifically hated John Ramsey. With the permission of the Ramsey attorneys, Douglas conferred with the FBI, the Colorado Bureau of Investigations and the Boulder Police Department. Another former FBI profiler, Greg McCrary, who worked for the prosecution, felt the Ramseys were involved in the death of their daughter and countered Douglas's conclusions. Both men were criticized publicly, which was typical of the case. And anyone who publicly declared support for one side or the other automatically qualified as a source for gossip shows, tabloids and sometimes traditional media outlets.

The rumor mill asserted the Douglas book also contained the "Listen carefully" phrase found in the ransom note. Although there is no information in the WHYD Investigative Archive that indicates the Douglas book was found in the Ramsey home and introduced as evidence, mounting rumors about it further damaged the public's view of John and Patsy Ramsey.

Another rumor about the ransom note concerned the phrase "Use that good southern [sic] common sense of yours."

Information was circulated that this was an "insider" phrase that John and Patsy used. It was rumored that this was a family joke because John was not a Southerner, and Patsy teased him about this fact. John was born in Nebraska and raised for the most part in Michigan. He lived in Atlanta for twenty years before moving to Boulder in 1991. Family friends Mike Bynum and Susan Stine, as well as Patsy and John, have said the couple never talked or joked about whether or not John was a Southerner. It wasn't an issue.

Also questioned: the use of the slang term "fat cat" in the ransom note: "You are not the only fat cat around, so don't think that killing will be difficult."

The term "fat cat" was first used in the 1920s to refer to a wealthy political donor, but it has evolved to mean any wealthy person. It is not a flattering phrase, and it was not commonly used in 1996. However, it would eventually appear to come back in vogue. In 2011, the term was used during a broadcast of *NBC Nightly News with Brian Williams* to refer to Wall Street and Congress.

The ransom note has proven to be an enigmatic element of the Ramsey murder investigation. It raises many questions, including whether it was written before or after the murder, and continues to stimulate speculation about JonBenét's torturous death.

# CHAPTER 5
# JOHN AND PATSY

John and Patsy in Michigan. © John Ramsey.

## CHRONOLOGY

**November 1980—Patsy and John are married in Atlanta. It's his second marriage.**
**January 1987—Burke is born.**
**August 1990—JonBenét is born.**
**February 1991—The Ramsey family moves to Boulder.**
**January 1992—John's oldest daughter from his first marriage, Beth, is killed in a car accident. She was Burke's and JonBenét's half-sister. John had three children from his first marriage.**
**July 1993—Patsy is diagnosed with Stage IV ovarian cancer.**
**December 1996—JonBenét is murdered.**

IN 1979, WHEN HE WAS THIRTY-SIX YEARS OLD, John Ramsey borrowed money from his father for an engagement ring for Patsy. He then asked Patsy's dad for permission to marry his daughter and, when her father said yes, rehearsed "in great detail" when and how he would ask. He chose the white clapboard Old Vinings Inn in Atlanta. The restaurant had been a general store and post office before becoming a popular restaurant. It boasted charm and Southern-style food.

Most people who only know Atlanta from traveling through Hartsfield-Jackson Atlanta International Airport would be amazed by the large city's beauty in the spring. Atlanta is filled with blossoms of every scent and color from azaleas, dogwoods, wisteria, red bud and all manner of fruit trees as well as jonquils and iris in full bloom.

"There is nothing prettier than the South in the springtime," John has said. The gorgeous landscape matched perfectly his plans for the romantic proposal. John wore a suit and a tie he'd bought especially for that night, and after dinner he and Patsy went out to a pretty little gazebo surrounded by the glory of spring. John was "very nervous." But he mustered his courage and asked, "Will you marry me?"

Patsy's answer: "I'm honored, but I need to think about it and talk with my mother first."

John, ever the gentleman, told her "of course," but this certainly wasn't the answer he'd wanted to hear. He found himself thinking immediately, "The heck with that. She's just trying to find a nice way to say 'no.'"

Patsy remembered being "delighted, excited and of course I wanted to say 'yes' right then." But Patsy was an old-fashioned girl. "I really did want to talk with my mom and give her the respect that John had given my dad by asking him first. He'd asked my dad. I'd talk with my mom! And, my mom and I were really close."

Three days later, she said "yes." John remembered later only that they were in Atlanta and that Patsy agreed to marry him.

John was divorced when he met Patsy. He'd met his first wife, Lucinda, at Michigan State University, where they both went to college. When John graduated, he and Lucinda got married. He went to Naval Officer Candidate School, and they spent two years in the Philippines, where John was a naval officer, and one year at the Naval Air Station in Atlanta. They then returned to Michigan, where John earned a master's degree in Business Administration before he and Lucinda moved back to Atlanta.

After eleven years and three children, "it just didn't work out. We grew apart," John said. The divorce was a "real failure for me. I should have worked harder on the marriage."

Lucinda staunchly supported John throughout the investigation of JonBenét's murder, saying, "John would never murder his child, nor would he support anyone he thought did."

John had been single for two years when he first saw Patsy. Enough time had passed since his divorce that he always "kind of had [his] eyes open." He was walking to the parking lot of his apartment, and she was walking toward him. He absorbed a lot in the simple hello they exchanged as they walked past each other.

"She was attractive. Even in that glance and the way she walked, she struck me as really grounded. She wasn't a phony, and she wasn't trying to be sweet, just matter of fact. It was a weird sensation. She seemed like a strong woman. Someone who knew where she was going. She wasn't flirty."

Patsy would later state she didn't remember the encounter, which may have contributed to why John had found her so interesting. But she had noticed him before and thought he was "good-looking with a nice smile."

In his mid-thirties, John was a good-looking man in excellent physical shape who ran for exercise. He was quiet and had a quick laugh, dry wit and wry sense of humor. He was well rounded and versed on numerous subjects. In college, he had been his fraternity's president. He tended to be a little serious and concentrated on getting his work done. He had a very sharp mind. When he met Patsy, he hadn't yet had the business success he wanted.

Patsy was pretty and very smart. She'd been Miss West Virginia in the Miss America Pageant and graduated magna cum laude from West Virginia University's P.I. Reed School of Journalism.

Patsy also had a Southern graciousness that led her to make people around her comfortable. She had a good sense of humor, and laughter

Patsy's college photo.

was always part of her day. Patsy loved being with others. Her friends said she was a great pal, a great mom, very loyal and supportive, a full-time friend who could be very funny.

After college, Patsy worked as a secretary at an advertising agency in Atlanta, though she found her job frustrating because she wanted to learn to handle client accounts. In the late 1970s, however, such work was still considered a man's job. Patsy reasoned that working as a secretary in an advertising firm might eventually "open an opportunity" for her.

A week after their first encounter, John and Patsy were formally introduced when a business partner and friend of John's happened to invite them both to dinner. When he found out Patsy was just out of college and only twenty-two-years old, John didn't consider her as someone he would date. He did notice, though, that "she was real lively, energetic, fun" as well as "more mature" than he expected. By the end of the evening, he was kind of "intrigued" by her and "invited her to a party the next week." Although at first Patsy found John to be "enjoyable and good company," she didn't think much more about him until he called and asked her out. They connected very quickly, and before long she fell in love with him because he was a "truly wonderful person, and he had honesty, character, a gentle nature, and humor, and besides, he was really attractive." Patsy added, "I liked that he was smart, and we were ultimately great partners in marriage, as parents and in business."

They dated for nearly two years before they married in November 1980. John was thirty-seven-years old. Patsy was twenty-four. She loved and adored his three children from his prior marriage, and John's children loved and adored her, too, thinking of her as a "favorite aunt."

That was another reason why John loved Patsy. That and, as he has said, she was "classy."

The Ramsey wedding took place at the Peachtree Presbyterian Church in Atlanta, in the heart of the city's leafy northwest neighborhoods. Physically, the church's building recalls the movie *Gone with the Wind* with its massive white columns in front of a pristine white entrance, its red brick walls and towering steeple. Generations of Atlanta families have attended Peachtree, lending it an Old South resonance. The main

Patsy, Melinda, John Andrew, Beth and John Ramsey shortly after their wedding. © John Ramsey.

Peachtree Presbyterian Church, Atlanta, Georgia.

sanctuary is soaring, filled with light and welcoming. While its side windows are clear, at the head of the sanctuary is a magnificent stained glass window that portrays the Ascension of Jesus. Huge organ pipes line the sides of the minister's podium. "If they ever played that organ to its full potential," John has said, smiling, "you probably wouldn't be able to stay in the church because it would be so loud." He has called the church a place of "comfort." "It was a big area and we hadn't invited many people."

The Ramseys kept their wedding simple because they didn't have much money. Patsy wore a beautiful white full-length wedding gown with an elegant train. The gown had a high neck and long sleeves that tapered near her wrists. She wore a white hat with a veil and carried red, white and yellow flowers. John wore a black tux with a red rose in his lapel. He had a full beard and mustache then. Happiness radiates from the couple's wedding photographs.[1]

John remembers looking out at the huge main area of worship, waiting for Patsy to appear and "really sweating." His son, four-year-old John Andrew, was the ring bearer. With his white-blonde hair and sporting a bow tie, John Andrew whistled as he walked down the long aisle. Everybody

Mr. and Mrs. Donald R. Paugh
request the honour of your presence
at the marriage of their daughter
Patricia Ann
to
Mr. John Bennett Ramsey
on Saturday, the fifteenth of November
nineteen hundred and eighty
at seven-thirty in the evening
Peachtree Presbyterian Church
Atlanta, Georgia

John and Patsy's wedding announcement and invitation. © John Ramsey.

laughed. It was a happy occasion. John's two daughters, the flower girls, wore green dresses that matched the bridesmaids' dresses. Patsy remembers standing in her white gown and looking down the aisle. "I was so happy, and there was so much potential in our lives together already with three wonderful children. The steps going forward were just part of the joy."

Their reception, which was also simple, was held at a small hotel and featured a quartet the couple had hired to play dance music. They stayed the first night in John's home, and then left for their honeymoon in Acapulco, Mexico. John wished they could have taken his children, too.

On their honeymoon, the newlyweds quickly got to know how the other handled adversity when they became ill from food poisoning. John and Patsy were sick for two days before they were healthy enough to fly home.

At the time of their marriage, Patsy was extremely devout, while John went to church on an irregular basis and considered himself a "casual Christian." Eventually Patsy influenced John's interest in religion, and they both developed the faith they would rely on so much in the future.

The couple's first home together was the Atlanta house John had bought before he and Patsy married. It was a basic, small, three-bedroom ranch built in the 1950s. John particularly liked the knotty pine paneling in the living room. He worked as a manufacturer's representative of computer-related products. It was the early 1980s, before computers had become an accepted part of everyday life, but John had confidence in the products he sold and felt computers represented the future.

In 1982, John and Patsy bought a larger home in the suburbs of Atlanta so John could save money by working in a home office after he'd finished the basement. They made the mortgage affordable by borrowing money from Patsy's parents. Burke and JonBenét hadn't been born yet, but the couple had frequent visits from John's three children, Beth, John Andrew and Melinda. John and Patsy lived in that home for the next nine years. They created many good memories there, and even today John will say, "Wish I still had that house." They sold it to move to Boulder in 1991. Their plan was to stay in Boulder for a time and eventually return to Atlanta, which they considered home.

John always felt he was lucky he entered the computer business so early. He and Patsy began their life together by stretching their paychecks to make ends meet. But John understood the computer business and invented a software product that enabled him to be in business for himself. "Patsy was my secret weapon," he has said. "She and I would go out to dinner together with business associates. They were captivated by her and her knowledge of the business. She was instrumental in helping us get contracts and products that we needed to move forward. She was smart."

John's company merged with two other computer distribution companies to reduce costs and increase visibility. The consolidated company was headquartered in Boulder and called Access Graphics. Lockheed Corporation was a twenty-five percent owner. When Lockheed merged with Martin Marietta in 1995, Lockheed Martin was born, a global powerhouse with divisions in aeronautics and electronics as well as information, global and space systems. Eventually, Lockheed Martin bought all the remaining shares of Access Graphics, and John became president and CEO and no longer owned any interest in the company. He was now a Lockheed employee.

In January 1992, John's oldest daughter from his first marriage, twenty-two-year-old Beth, was killed with her boyfriend in a car accident near Chicago in bad weather. John learned of his daughter's death when his brother, Jeff, called to tell him.

"I was screaming," John would later recall. "I don't know if I stayed on the phone or threw it down. I just don't remember. I stormed around my office, yelling 'There is no God. There is no God.' I remember screaming that out."

John was given a ride home. Patsy hadn't heard yet, but she knew as soon as John arrived home that something was wrong because he was so upset. When Patsy asked what was wrong, John said, "Beth was killed," prompting Patsy to cry out and fall to her knees.

"It was just so unexpected," Patsy later recalled. "I looked at John's face, and he was crying. It took me a while to understand it had really happened, and then it was endless."

Beth was John's oldest daughter, his first-born child, and the two had a special relationship. Beth was the first of his children whom John heard say "Da-da" and watched as she learned to walk. Beth was very sensitive and compassionate. She'd worried about her dad after her parents' divorce, called him often and always wanted to know his plans for the holidays in order to make sure he wasn't alone. "We could talk about anything," John has said.

One twenty-degree day in Atlanta before he and Patsy moved to Boulder, John asked who wanted to go to the lake and look at boats with him. His children looked at him "like I was nuts," John later recalled. Then he added, "But Beth raised her hand and said 'I'll go.' She always liked to go with me. So we ended up shivering in the wind, looking at boats, and had a great time."

Beth was very mature, but very delicate. "After the divorce, I can remember her crying and saying, 'Oh, Daddy' when I dropped them off after a visit, which always broke my heart." Her mannerisms touched her father's soul; he knew that she loved him through it all. "Beth was wildly excited when we told her Patsy was pregnant with Burke," John said. "Beth didn't think of it as competition. It was genuine excitement. Beth saw them all as one big family that was now getting an addition as opposed to two separate families." Beth once described herself to her dad as "a very loyal friend." "And, you, Dad," she said, "are one of my best friends."

"Beth," said her dad, "was wonderful and innocent."

Beth's death shaped the way John would handle tragedies like Patsy's cancer and JonBenét's supposed kidnapping. "With Beth, there was no chance. She was dead. With Patsy's cancer and what we thought was JonBenét's kidnapping, we had a chance, because there was life."

Patsy remembered John sobbing alone in the nights after Beth was killed. Sometimes he would just break down. They both learned the best way to deal with Beth's death was to take care of the living, the rest of their children and each other. John said there was still a terrible emptiness that took a long time to begin to heal. "It never heals completely. You still have a scar in your heart that will never go away."

Beth, John and Patsy. © John Ramsey.

According to Patsy, "We just kept going and tried to stay positive and looked toward every new day being a better one. But life and living just aren't the same when your child dies. The despondency is very difficult to overcome. There is always the void, and you work very hard to regain faith."

Up until Beth's death, John's life had been happy, for the most part. "But happiness is circumstantial," he said. "Happy is a four-year-old getting a chocolate chip cookie. Happy is the bill on your car being much lower than you expect when you're low on money. The challenge became learning how to establish a deeper emotion of joy when you have such a deep scar from your child's death."

He began to study certain people to see how they coped with their life burdens. And he thought, "Beth's death was my burden, and dealing with that grief was my challenge. I needed to learn to find the more steady joy again in honor of her." He found it, in his other children, in a sunrise while on a run, in being married to Patsy, in the sound of his children's laughter. The concept of joy wobbled within him for a very long time, but eventually it steadied. Then he built on it with memories of Beth to help him. He lived for every day and trusted less in the future.

John also felt no foreboding about the life that lay before him. He held Beth in his heart. He moved forward, step by step, until his sense of loss gave way to renewed optimism, that would too soon be crushed.

## CHAPTER 6

# PATSY'S CANCER

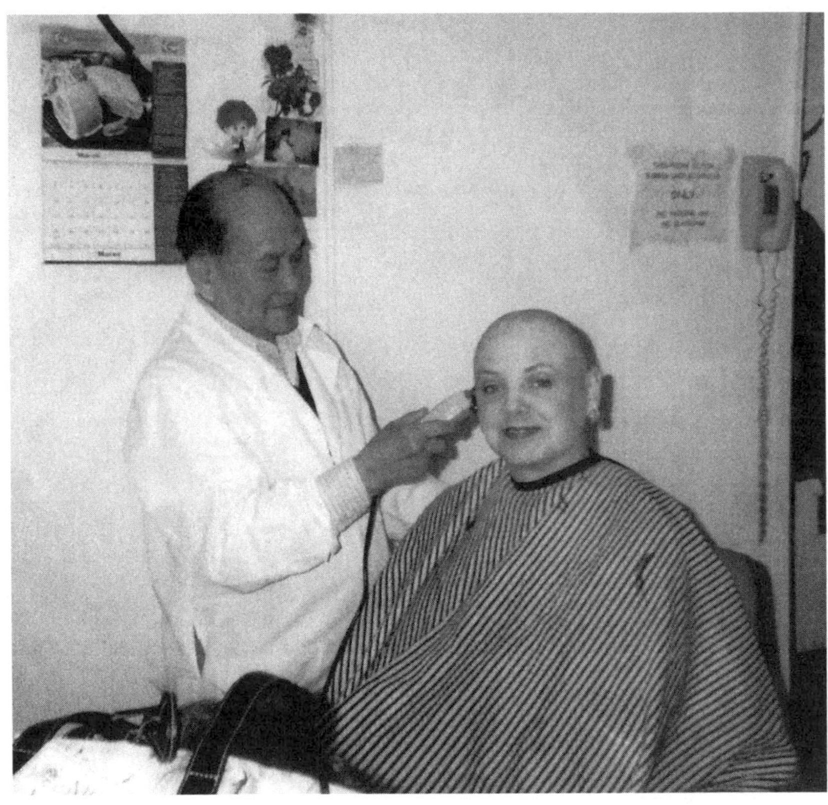

Patsy's hair being shaved at the beginning of her chemotherapy treatment at the National Institutes of Health in Maryland, July 1993. Chemotherapy would cause her to lose all of her hair. © John Ramsey.

## CHRONOLOGY

**July 1993—Patsy is diagnosed with Stage III ovarian cancer in Atlanta.**

**July 1993—Patsy is diagnosed with Stage IV ovarian cancer at the National Institutes of Health in Bethesda, Maryland. There is no Stage V.**

**July 1993—Patsy begins a series of experimental, last-chance chemo treatments in Bethesda, Maryland. The treatments are scheduled every three weeks.**

**January 1994—Patsy is found "clear" of cancer. She will undergo two more chemo treatments and then have six-month checkups until 2002 when her cancer returns.**

WHEN A DOCTOR TELLS YOU that you are going to die, it swallows all else in your life. Some accept the facts. Others collapse and give in. Still others decide to fight with everything they've got. And not one of us knows which person we'll be until we've been given that sentence.

Elisabeth Kubler-Ross in *On Death and Dying* lists five stages of grief or emotional behavior that people experience when told they are going to die, and their typical order. The stages of denial, anger, bargaining, depression and acceptance apply both to those who are going to die and those who are losing or have lost a loved one. These emotions matched Patsy's reactions to her own grief about the prognosis she was given in July 1993.

The National Cancer Institute has identified more than 200 kinds of cancer. Patsy was diagnosed with ovarian cancer. When she found out after surgery in Atlanta that she had Stage III ovarian cancer that was most likely terminal, she went into denial. She collapsed. "I tried to sleep it away. I didn't think about my chances of living," she said. Denial, anger and bargaining merged quickly. "Why did we lose Beth and then, why was I going to die? We always tried to live with wisdom and kindness and as Christians. Why would God give me two wonderful children and then take me away from them?"

When Patsy was diagnosed with cancer, John remembered his helplessness when he learned Beth had been killed. So he decided to take control and fight as hard as he could to save his wife. He launched a computer search for the latest treatments and experiments related to ovarian cancer. Access Graphics employees volunteered to help. They found what they thought would be Patsy's best chance: an experimental ovarian cancer treatment program offered by the National Institutes of Health (NIH) at the National Cancer Institute (NCI) in Bethesda, Maryland.

John and Patsy flew immediately to Washington, D.C., with her medical history and a recommendation from a family friend who was a doctor. In Washington, they entered a seemingly endless maze of bureaucracy. The National Cancer Institute is on the campus of the National Institutes of Health. The NIH campus is enormous and has 27 research centers. Approximately 18,000 employees work on the main campus along with 6,000 scientists, enough people to populate a good-sized town.

Upon arriving at the NCI, Patsy and John experienced the extensive security measures that had been put in place after the first World Trade Center bombing in February 1993, when six people were killed and at least 1,000 injured after a truck bomb blew up in underground parking. Just to get into an NCI parking lot, the Ramseys had to go through two security checks that required them to show identification and step out of their car while everything was searched, including their vehicle's underbelly via poles with mirrors attached to them.

The NCI building that Patsy and John had been directed to was a brick high-rise that was at once intimidating in size and encouraging as it represented the nation's best cancer facility . . . and Patsy's best shot for treatment.

Inside, the NCI building had a massive lobby with a high ceiling and was buzzing with activity. The lobby was filled with people waiting at elevators, doctors in different-colored lab coats and patients and visitors either coming or going. There were lecture halls. There was a large cafeteria in the basement as well as a hair salon, barbershop, history museum and transportation center. It was an enormous place. It was overwhelming. "You just didn't walk in the front door and find a reception desk," John said.

Patsy realized what she was in for when they first entered the building. "I lost what little identity I had and became a person with cancer," she would later say. As she and John made their way through the facility to find where she needed to be, the people who stood out to her were the ones just like her. People with cancer. "They were in various stages, in wheelchairs, in wheeled beds with turbans around their heads. It was their eyes I noticed. Some had so much pain and misery in them. But I kept looking and I found others who were in a different place with strength and a will to live in their eyes. That helped."

Patsy was "afraid, yet . . . desperate to get started." "I felt like every minute wasted was in favor of the cancer. I needed to do something to fight." She and John went to the floor designated for ovarian cancer patients and found there were 75 people ahead of them at the information/reception area. Most of their time that day was spent sitting in line, hoping they would get to the front to see who could help them. There were other people hurting in the line, too. "We never got to the head of the line that day and left pretty defeated," John later remembered.

The next day, John tried a different strategy, stopping nurses and approaching clerks on the floor where ovarian cancer specialists were located, asking who could help, whom they could even see, who might point them in the right direction. It worked. They found the offices of the right group of doctors where the "experimental protocol" was taking place. Patsy was appraised. The results were devastating. According to her medical records, the doctors told her that her ovarian cancer was actually Stage IV, and she was eligible for experimental treatment.

Stage IV is the last stage of ovarian cancer. There is no Stage V. The cancer had spread to her lymph nodes. The doctors at NCI also found an additional tumor behind her pubic bone. "We only take the ones who really have no chance, except for this experimental program," Patsy later recalled one doctor telling them. "You qualify because you're dying. We don't know if the treatment will work. It will be painful. You will be very sick, and you still may die. The doses we are using for the chemotherapy are double what are usually used."

Patsy wept. John fought his own tears. As scared as he was, however, he also heard the words "she's been accepted into the experimental protocol." Whatever dwindling chance his beloved wife had, she at least would have this last desperate bid to live.

Patsy later said this "was the kick-start" she needed. "All I heard was the treatment might work. I would work [as] hard as one of their lab mice. I decided I was being given a chance, and my goal was to fight with every good cell in my body. That's when my whole attitude changed. This treatment was the base I would build on regardless of how tough it was. But I would also utilize groups of people to pray together for me, meditation, positive thought and my love for my family to fight." She had her head shaved before starting chemotherapy, because it would fall out from the treatment.

It took Patsy a while to fully embrace that attitude and, even then, it ebbed and flowed. "I cried, was exhausted and was almost paralyzed by the fear of the chemotherapy and dying." Patsy began the first treatment within a week of her first appointment with the doctors at the NCI in July 1993. There would be eight treatments, with each given every three weeks, and three toxins would be used at the same time to try to kill the cancer.

The treatments were absolutely brutal by anyone's definition. Patsy's whole body was ravaged from being pumped full of poison to try to kill the cancer cells, and the chemo would cause collateral damage on her good, or normal, cells. Her doctors gambled that enough of her normal cells would survive, and she would live. It was a delicate balancing act. A port was implanted in her chest for direct access to her veins for the duration of the treatment. The port provided access for chemotherapy administration, IVs and blood transfusions. The blood transfusions would refortify the cells that had been destroyed and help keep Patsy alive. Each session of chemotherapy lasted thirty-six to forty-eight hours.

For each session, Patsy was admitted to the NCI hospital, where dedicated people took care of her. The people, she would say, "who try to make the impossible better."

Her room at NCI was white with pale tan walls. There were two beds in her room and a pull-curtain between the beds for privacy. The atmosphere was as soothing as it could be. There were paintings on the walls. Some were standard hospital prints. Others were pictures and paintings donated by those who had been at NCI as patients in the past or by patients' families. Patsy would later say that the presence of these donated paintings emphasized to her that "someone else understood, too." Her room was a sterile environment with no plants or flowers allowed, yet it gave her comfort and a sense of belonging. For the short while she was there for each treatment, this was her room and her bed. "I welcomed it and dreaded it," she said, reflecting on the paradox; the treatment that might give her life could also kill her. The room was imbued with confidence and pessimism. She felt more responsibility than she probably should have about whether she lived or died. "I sometimes felt I should be awake to fight it instead of sleeping when sleep was the recovery I needed," she noted.

Patsy's treatment involved being tested on Monday and beginning continuous chemotherapy on Tuesday morning. She would finish by Thursday afternoon. Then, before the impact of the chemotherapy set in, even though she felt sick, she usually flew back to Boulder on Saturday for her three weeks off from chemotherapy. Her goals came in increments. Prior to each trip home, the goal was to get an airplane seat with no one sitting next to her so she could lie down during the flight.

"The person who kept me alive was Dr. Pat Moran," she would say. Moran is an oncologist in Boulder. John had researched the best oncologists in Boulder and the metro Denver area, and Dr. Moran was one of those at the top of the list. He was experienced, calm and helpful, and he and Patsy got along well. Each time she returned to Boulder from Bethesda, Patsy would almost immediately check into Boulder Community Hospital for a week to recover and ensure that she didn't get an infection from her weakened condition. At home after these Boulder hospital visits, Patsy would stay in a bedroom, only five steps away from the bathroom because of her constant nausea.

"This wasn't a normal treatment," said Dr. Moran. "Patsy was on an experimental protocol. That meant the Washington D.C. doctors were trying out new medications, and combinations of them, to see which combination might work for her."

Dr. Moran added that Patsy was "a tough lady." "There were a number of times she needed to be hospitalized because of a fever or a low white cell count," he said. "It's very risky when that happens. People can clearly die in that situation. Her chemotherapy was very fatiguing. She had received a death sentence. The cure rates were quite low. The expectation was that the vast majority of people in this experiment would die. Averages [were] measured in one to three years."

But, Dr. Moran continued, "Patsy . . . was extremely determined. This was something that she was going to fix. She was exhausted, had significant nausea, hair loss. She developed anorexia because she didn't want to eat. It was easier not to, because eating made her nauseous.

"I thought she was very intelligent, had a good handle on her disease and what it meant and the potential implications. She really had it together. Cancer can be a real devastating experience. It causes some to lose their moorings. Patsy seemed very grounded. She would tell me, 'This is what I'm going to do. I'm going to fly to DC and get my treatments, and then I'll fly back and you'll help keep me alive here in Boulder.'"

Dr. Moran projected confidence. He was a young doctor, a specialist in cancer and diseases of the blood. Patsy felt he was always very pleasant and professional, and he was "dedicated" to helping her live through the chemotherapy from NCI. He was quiet and reassuring. He wore glasses, and Patsy noticed when he was especially concerned about her condition, he would adjust his glasses with one hand and then tell her what she needed to know.

Dr. Moran knows about the illnesses afflicting patients, but he also seems to have a natural grasp of the person within the illness. He is always inspired by how deep some of his patients dig to find the resources to fight. "Everyone has their own way," he says. "But ultimately, people want to live. They rely on friends, family and children. How people survive is a combination of their own inner strength. The medical profession tries to help where it can. A lot is self-driven. Patsy definitely had that drive to live.

"What struck me about Patsy was, despite how wiped out she was from the treatments . . . [s]he was barely able to take care of herself . . .

yet, she maintained a pretty good sense of humor. She could smile. She could crack a joke. In spite of how very, very sick she was, she'd get as well as she could during the three weeks between treatments. And then she'd go back for more."

"Patsy's battles with cancer give insight into her personality and faith," her attorney Pat Burke has said. "To understand what she went through helps [one] get to know her and brings into question, in my mind, why one would think someone this determined to live because of her family and the differences she could make with them would be a suspect in her daughter's horrible murder."

Patsy's family, especially her parents, understood that Patsy's cancer and frequent absences for treatment would affect her children. They just didn't know how. JonBenét, who was three years old when her mother's treatments began, was lonely when her mother was away. Neither Burke nor JonBenét could understand why their mom wasn't with them at home. At one point, JonBenét went to Atlanta and spent five weeks with Patsy's family, but for the most part the two children stayed in Boulder. John tried not to travel so he could spend more time with them. "JonBenét," he said, "needed reassurance and asked for her mommy a lot. At times, she would cry, this little girl, just inconsolable, because she needed her mom with her."

Patsy once recalled "Johnnie-Bee" playing quietly in her mother's bedroom at home while she (Patsy) lay in bed recovering from her latest round of chemotherapy. "It was another thing we could do together when I was too weak to do much else," Patsy explained. "She would talk and play with her toys, and I would just listen. At times, she would do a sort-of somersault and it was just being together. I loved it, and so did she."

JonBenét and Burke would wear protective masks, and so would their mother. The rare play times in their mother's bedroom were allowed as long as Patsy didn't have a fever. Patsy couldn't have physical contact with them, so her children weren't allowed their familiar hugs. Patsy's most vivid memory of that time is of her two children walking down the long hospital hall in Boulder, holding hands, being there for each other.

That's when she knew she had to live, for them, but she didn't know if she would.

In Bethesda, Patsy usually had a roommate who was in the same delicate balance between life and death. They would become close during their short time together. Even if they were too weak to talk, too nauseous to hold their heads up, they shared the same fight and desperation to live. They tried not to give the cancer any more power than it already had, and fought their fears together. Desperation would visit in many forms. "There were times I lost faith. There were times when I was so sick I questioned living," said Patsy, whose life was based on living through Christianity. At times, she felt as though she had lost her soul.

With one roommate, Patsy would practice a meditation that prompted her to concentrate on killing one cancer cell in her body at a time. "It would take a lifetime, which we didn't know if we had, but it was something to try and keep our minds off the after-effects of the chemotherapy."

One of her cancer friends was Vicki. Of all Patsy's roommates, Vicki was most often scheduled for chemotherapy at the same time as Patsy. They were always at their worst while becoming friends. They got their chemo together and then fell into a "nightmare of sickness." Patsy was "kind, caring and giving," Vicki once said. "She fought as hard as the rest of us, and she tried very hard not to become too involved in the 'why me?' that we all went through." Vicki felt the treatment protocol was agonizing. Yet she also believed there was a reason she met Patsy during the treatment. Patsy encouraged Vicki to be baptized and was with her in Bethesda in the hospital chapel when she was. Vicki died in 1997.

In December 1993, after eight treatments, Patsy was ready for surgery to determine her new prognosis. Although Patsy had already undergone several encouraging CAT scans, her doctors needed to operate in order to determine whether any cancer cells remained. Her CAT scans were clear, but for a thorough exam, surgeons cut a twelve-inch opening from her breastbone to her pubic bone. They then rinsed out her pelvic area and checked it and other organs for microscopic traces of cancer. Patsy would vividly remember waking up from the four-hour surgery to an excruciating rush of pain. And then there was the thirteen-day wait while all her tests were analyzed and she recovered from the brutal surgery. After those thirteen days, one of her nurse friends walked into her room and sat down beside her. "Her eyes sparkled," Patsy later said, "and then she said, 'I'm not supposed to tell you, but I can't wait. It's gone. The cancer is gone.'" The pain seemed to lessen with that news. "There was serenity in hearing that," Patsy said. "A release of the fear. Hope became a friend again."

Her doctors decided to give Patsy two more chemotherapy treatments "just to make sure." Her total treatments with the experimental protocol that began in July 1993 lasted nine months.

She always lived knowing it could come back. "I felt every second I was alive was a blessing because at the edge of it all, even though I'd beaten it this time, it could still win. And I was so afraid it would," Patsy said. "I'll never know that I would have changed much of how I lived my life if I hadn't gotten cancer, but I do know that because I did, all that mattered was family, my beliefs and friends. I pray daily for all those who have it because now I know what they endure."

Looking back at the cancer, the treatments and the brutal suffering, Patsy knew she'd become a different person. "I learned after a while not to be affected by the little stuff in life. The details mattered, but not to the extent that I would worry or get upset about them. My perception of life and living changed, and my attitude about what really mattered was reinforced."

In 2002, Patsy called one of her dear friends. Linda Boss and Patsy had an advertising business together in Charlevoix. Linda remembers Patsy saying, "Are you sitting down?" Patsy was sobbing. Linda said, "What's wrong?"

Patsy answered, "It's back." Her reprieve had lasted eight years. "The cancer," she said. "It won't give up."

# CHAPTER 7
# POLICE MISTAKES

Two Boulder police detectives at the Ramsey home searching the crime scene outside. December 28, 1996.

A SIX-YEAR-OLD HAD BEEN SAVAGELY MURDERED, and the Boulder Police Department was in charge of finding her killer. Yet the department had no homicide unit. Boulder Police Chief Mark Beckner talked about that in 2001, when he testified in a deposition in a civil case called *Wolf vs. Ramsey*. Under questioning, Beckner said, "In our department, we don't have a specific homicide unit. Our detectives handle a variety of cases. They aren't specialists in homicide, per se." The attorney questioning Chief Beckner asked, "Has that been true the entire time that you've been involved with the Boulder Police Department from 1978 until the present time?" Beckner answered "Yes."

So Boulder Police had no homicide department when JonBenét was killed. Then Boulder Police Chief Tom Koby had never worked on a homicide case as a homicide investigator. The commander of the investigation, John Eller, had never worked on a homicide. One of Eller's friends, Detective Steve Thomas, who was available and brought in from the BPD Narcotics unit, had no homicide experience. The city of Boulder had reported no homicides in 1996 until the Ramsey murder. Very few of the investigators ultimately assigned to the Ramsey investigation had homicide experience, and what they had was limited. Very few of them had children, an experience that could have aided them in dealing with the parents.

"The type of power that was inevitable in this case can corrupt, or provide wisdom and compassion," said one district attorney. "It can allow for greatness or magnify incompetence. One never knows what kind of person will turn up until the shake-out on who has it emerges." Commander Eller had an extremely high-profile type of power that demanded immediate answers. Chief Koby allowed Eller free run of the investigation, according to those who worked it. The investigative approach was much like that used in drug investigations like those Narcotics Detective Steve Thomas had experienced. In a narcotics investigation, a suspect is targeted and a case is built as evidence is gathered to prove the suspect's guilt.[1]

Homicide investigations are different from narcotics investigations.

Homicide detectives follow the evidence. "Death investigation requires strict adherence to guidelines . . . In the case of homicide, investigators must carefully collect evidence to help identify suspects."[2] The crime is identified, the evidence gathered and analyzed and only then is a potential suspect identified. But within the first few hours of JonBenét's murder, some investigators on the case voiced their opinions to other case officers and a few members of the media that the Ramseys had been involved in their daughter's death. And then they set out to prove it.

## THURSDAY, DECEMBER 26, 1996

When Commander-Sergeant Bob Whitson's pager went off shortly after six the morning after Christmas, it woke him from sleep. Whitson, a narcotics sergeant with the Boulder Police Department, was also the on-call supervisor for that day.

The page had been sent from Sergeant Paul Reichenbach, who was on night shift. When Whitson returned the call, he was told there had been a reported kidnapping of a six-year-old girl complete with a ransom note. Whitson was surprised by the nature of the crime. During his twenty-two years with the Boulder Police Department, he had answered no calls for reported kidnappings. Kidnappings in Boulder were always related to custody disputes. And there were never any ransom notes.

Reichenbach read portions of the ransom note over the phone to Whitson. He also told him the police, the victim's father and the father's friends had all searched parts of the home, but the little girl had not been found there. Whitson asked that patrol cars in front of the house be moved out of sight, since the ransom note threatened to hurt the missing child if the police were called.

During this phone call, Whitson asked a lot of questions about the Ramsey family. He'd never heard of them. Reichenbach told Whitson the family was composed of a father, mother, a nine-year-old son and the missing six-year-old daughter. He said the family appeared to be wealthy based on the appearance of their home. He also told Whitson there was a recent newspaper article in the home about the extraordinary success of the company where John Ramsey worked.

There was an alarm in the home, but it hadn't been set.

Police had searched the records and learned the Ramseys had no criminal history. But there was some glamour attached to the family. Patsy was a former Miss West Virginia in the Miss America Pageant, and her daughter had performed in child beauty pageants. From what Reichenbach communicated, Whitson envisioned the Ramseys as an "All-American family."

Commander-Sergeant Whitson lived in Loveland, a town twenty-five miles north and east of Boulder. After he finished his call with Sergeant Reichenbach, he showered, dressed and started the forty-five-minute drive to the Boulder Police Department.

It was cold and dark. Sunrise wasn't until 7:20 that morning, and the sky would remain cloudy.

Before he left his house, Whitson called two detectives to report to the Ramsey home. As he was driving in, he heard the two detectives use the police radio to contact Sergeant Reichenbach. They asked to meet the night-shift sergeant a few blocks away before they responded. Whitson thought then it was a mistake for them to use their police radios. A kidnapper could have easily been monitoring police radio calls. In 1996, personal cell phones were not in wide use.

While driving, Whitson remembered the just-released movie *Ransom* and thought someone might be copying the movie. He thought about the child who had been kidnapped and how they would get her back. If someone was copying *Ransom,* Whitson thought, "The Boulder Police Department did not have the experience or the equipment to handle the case."

He was thankful that since the kidnapping of aviator Charles Lindbergh's baby in 1932, new laws had been passed that resulted in all kidnappings of children nationwide being handled by the FBI. He called them the moment he arrived at BPD headquarters.

But there were jurisdictional questions that had to be satisfied. The person he spoke to at the FBI told Whitson an agent would page him back. At this point, Whitson called the Boulder commander in charge of the detectives. The commander couldn't come in because his family was sick, but he told Whitson to rely on the department's new kidnapping policy. Whitson called the city's press information officer. He put out an emergency page to all command staff and detectives about the apparent kidnapping and then tried to locate a copy of the new policy, which was being developed for all law enforcement officials in the county.

The police detective who had a copy of the policy was on vacation, as were about half of the other detectives who might have had it. It was the day after Christmas, and a lot of people were off. Whitson couldn't find the policy. He called a Boulder County Sheriff's lieutenant he thought might have it. The lieutenant was off-duty that day. He told Whitson where to find it in his office, which was a few miles from the Boulder Police Department.

Whitson drove frantically to the Boulder Sheriff's Department, and then it took him at least twenty more minutes to find the paper he was looking for. He knew he was using up valuable time. He stopped by the Boulder District Attorney's Office, which was, at the time, in the same building as the Sheriff's Department, to advise two district attorneys about what was happening. While at the DA's office, he got a page from an agent with the FBI Emergency Response Unit in Denver. They set up a meeting for ten that morning at the Boulder Police Department.

Whitson arrived at the Ramsey home, conducted a brief investigation and left at 9:45 a.m. with Detective Patterson, one of the two on-scene detectives. Patterson needed to provide information, answer questions and be debriefed by the FBI at the Boulder Police Department Command Center. Whitson released the other officers from the home, except Detective Linda Arndt. In retrospect, he would later say, that was a mistake.

Whitson was forthright in admitting other mistakes to me, including not clearing the home of all non-official personnel when he first arrived. He would also admit that he told police officers they could leave when he should have instructed them to stay and support Detective Arndt. He realized later that he should have "ensured for himself the home had been searched and photographed, even though he was told it had been." The detectives and the night-shift supervisor should have asked the same questions about a house search, he said. The much-sought-after kidnapping protocol that he finally found at the Boulder Sheriff's Department was never studied or used that morning.

Then Boulder District Attorney Alex Hunter's most trusted professional confidant, then First District Attorney Bill Wise, is still angry about the investigation even to this day:

> It was the most screwed-up investigation. It was just terrible. They shouldn't have had marked police cars and officers out in front. They left the one detective up there at the house. Her very sophisticated equipment to track and tape any kind of call that might be from a kidnapper was a small recorder and a little suction cup that you lick and you stick on a telephone. It was just silly that they left her there with that house full of people and her trying to figure out how to put the people to work and keep them out of her hair. And then, of course, they find the body. Is there any way in its initial stages that the investigation could have been botched more badly? Not that I know of.

The Boulder Police Department's behavior was a "mess" according to then Adams County District Attorney Bob Grant. It was "chaos."

According to Wise and Grant, the mistakes made by BPD officials from the very beginning of the Ramsey murder investigation have marred and shaped it to this day.

Marked police cars were parked in front of the Ramsey home, and uniformed officers responded when the ransom note author had warned John Ramsey not to contact police.

When the first police officer arrived, he should have had Patsy and Burke removed from the home and taken to the police department for interviews and physical forensic examinations. John Ramsey should have been left behind for interviews and to answer the kidnapper's promised phone call referenced in the ransom note.

The home was a crime scene. Only law enforcement officers

involved in the investigation should have been inside and the only ones to search the premises. Family friends and Victim Advocates should not have been allowed in the home at all. That is underscored by the fact that, according to numerous Boulder Police Department reports (#5-447, #5-461, #5-397, #5-873, #5-445, #5-447, #5-451, #1-363, #5-4134, #5-4128, #5-448, #5-239, #5-240), the following took place beginning at approximately 6:20 a.m.:

> Within approximately 10 to 15 minutes of his arrival, [John and Patsy's friend] searched the basement of the Ramsey residence. He noticed the lights were on [in the main basement area], saw the broken window in the train room and suitcase and looked for broken glass and found a small piece of glass. The latch on the window was in the unlocked position and his impression was that the window was closed.

The friend moved the suitcase under the window, which would cause confusion for investigators. He also "looked in the storage room but could not see anything and went back upstairs."

The reports also state that the friend "did not turn on lights in the wine cellar" during his search, which may have been why he didn't see JonBenét's body. (For some reason, the storage room where JonBenét's body was eventually discovered was at times referred to as a "wine cellar" in police reports, although no wine was stored in it.) The light switch in the storage room was right next to the door, not on an adjacent wall. According to scene officers, it was "difficult" to find in the dark. (BPD Reports #5-447, #5-461, #5-397, #5-873, #5-445, #5-447, #5-451, #1-363, #5-4134, #5-4128, #5-448, #5-239, #5-240.)

This friend and others shouldn't have been in the home or searching it, even though they were trying to help, yet police didn't prevent them. When he went back upstairs from the basement, that friend "told an officer about the suitcase and broken window."

"After JonBenét's body was found in the wine cellar later that day by her father, the same friend picked up and dropped the duct tape that

Light switch in wine cellar/storage room.

her father had torn off her mouth," further affecting the crime scene. (BPD Report #5-887.)

When the forensic investigators arrived, everyone should have left the home, including the detectives. The forensics investigators need to get what information they can from an uncontaminated crime scene. "It is essential to maintain a proper chain of custody for evidence."[3]

All major crime scenes have an official police entry-exit log. Every person going in and out of the scene logs entry and exit times, then initials each. The log at the Ramsey home was poorly kept based on its conflicting and duplicate arrival times for certain people and discrepancies related to how many people were in the home as documented in the JonBenét Ramsey Murder Book Index.

Police officials should have made a thorough top-to-bottom search of the home immediately upon arrival that included a complete inspection of every door, window, cabinet, closet and drawer. This is a basic premise of a police investigation, yet none of the law enforcement officers on the scene took the responsibility for ensuring that this was done. The fact that police had failed to search the basement storage room and it was the father of the victim who discovered his own daughter's body changed the whole course of the investigation.

According to the National Institute of Justice,[4] the following mistakes occurred:

- No one was in charge that morning. In order of arrival, first the patrol officer, the sergeant, and then the detectives should have taken over, removing all non-essential people in the home and maintaining an accurate entry-exit log.

- The first two on-call detectives should have gone to the home immediately. Instead, they arrived anywhere from two hours and ten minutes to two hours and thirty minutes after they were first called, having stopped by BPD headquarters first.

- The detectives were not properly equipped. Together, they had one tape recorder between them, so they were unable to record their interviews with the Ramseys.

- If a kidnapping had occurred, as was first assumed, yellow crime scene tape should have been used for the entire home, not just for JonBenét's bedroom, and the entire home should have been photographed and inspected for fingerprints.

- The one detective who was left by herself in the home after 10 a.m. should have had other law enforcement support. There was still the question as to whether the kidnapper would call, and more interviews with John and Patsy were necessary.

- John should never have been allowed to search the home unless a police officer was with him. As the parents of the victim, the Ramseys had a proprietary interest in the scene and could have changed it. Although there was nothing at that time to suggest that they were suspects, there was nothing to support that they were not.

Also, since no law enforcement officer was with John when he found his daughter's body, his reaction could not be noted.

Error compounded error. Later, experienced officers within the BPD who were not on the scene that day would react with shame and disbelief about such humiliating and ongoing mistakes. Detective Lou Smit, hired by the Boulder District Attorney's Office during the investigation, later shared his concerns: "The lone detective should not have moved JonBenét's body from the main floor hallway to the living room after John brought his daughter's body upstairs from the basement, as this served to further contaminate the crime scene."

- The Ramsey family should have been taken to the police station immediately after JonBenét's body was found for videotaped interviews, collection of clothing, physical forensic examinations of their bodies and immediate tests for drugs and alcohol. The examinations of their bodies were critical to determine whether any of them had injuries that could have been caused when JonBenét fought back against her attacker.

According to correspondence between the Boulder Police Department and a Ramsey defense investigator, clothing John and Patsy were wearing on the evening of December 25, 1996 wasn't requested by investigators until *one year later* in December 1997. On March 3, 1998, "Detective Trujillo of the Boulder Police Department met with [a Ramsey private investigator] during which time Det. Trujillo collected clothing purported to belong to the Ramsey's [sic]." (BPD Report #1-1429.) A letter from the investigation commander on the case at that time supports the request for clothing one year after the murder.

However, another police report indicates some pieces of clothing belonging to Patsy and John were turned over to the police on January 28, 1997, approximately four weeks after their daughter's murder: John—two black shirts; Patsy—black pants and a red and black sweater. (BPD Report #1-1430.) There is no indication if one or both of these reports

IS January 28, 1998

Commander Mark Beckner
Boulder Police Department
1805 33rd Street
Boulder, Colorado 80301

**HAND-DELIVERY**

**RE: Ramsey Investigation**

Dear Commander Beckner:

In December of 1997, you requested that representatives of John and Patsy Ramsey provide to the Boulder Police Department the clothes that they were wearing as depicted in the attached photograph. This request was made to John Ramsey's attorney, Bryan Morgan, who in turn contacted me.

I have collected from the Ramseys the following items of clothing:

1) Black shirt from John Ramsey.
2) Black shirt from John Ramsey.
3) Black pants from Patsy Ramsey.
4) Red and black checked sweater from Patsy Ramsey.

Ms. Ramsey is still attempting to locate a red shirt which might match the shirt that is depicted in this photograph. Mr. Ramsey cannot be sure which black shirt he was wearing; thus we are providing two shirts which resemble the one in the photograph.

Response letter to BPD about getting clothing Patsy and John wore the day JonBenét's body was found.

may be correct or if there is a mistake related to the date discrepancy.

The parents should have also been interrogated thoroughly and separately after JonBenét's body was found. The Ramseys have said they would have continued to talk with police if they'd been asked. They have repeatedly said they didn't know what to do after their daughter's body was found but leave their home and go to a friend's home. No one from law enforcement insisted or suggested that they go to the Boulder Police Department. At that time, they had no defense attorneys.

One BPD investigator has said that Commander Eller wanted to turn the home back over to the family that afternoon but the investigator on the case said no, explaining that he would need two to three weeks of unrestricted access to the home.

When FBI agents arrived at the Boulder Police Department at approximately 10 a.m. on the day of JonBenét's reported kidnapping, they were unaware so many mistakes had already been made related to the investigation. Police Chief Tom Koby wanted their help, and one of the first questions he asked the special agent in charge of the FBI Emergency Response Team was, "When are you going to take over the investigation?" While this would not happen immediately, this transition would occur within a few hours. FBI Supervisory Special Agent Ron Walker needed to gather facts, determine that the case was a kidnapping and "get the massive movement of other FBI resources underway." He and his agents had responded to the Boulder Police Department, instead of the home, because the department's headquarters was the site of the incident command post. During the next three hours of fact gathering and getting FBI resources into place, the agency would transition into taking control of the case.

"I made calls to FBI headquarters in Denver, to the FBI Special Operations Group and the Swat Team," Walker has stated. "The ransom money package needed to be put together. An airplane was put on standby to track devices with the ransom money. The technical agents who would manage the telephones for a possible ransom call were on their way. The focus was a kidnapping investigation and it took valuable, but necessary, time to get people in place. A Boulder Police sergeant and I were headed out the door to go to the Ramsey home in response to requests for help from the detective on the scene. That's when we got the call the child's body was found."

The murder meant the case jurisdiction went immediately to the Boulder Police Department. Even so, FBI agents went to the scene to offer initial law enforcement assistance. One agent has said he was "stunned" by the number of people in the home when he arrived and the "completely compromised crime scene."

Within a few days of the murder, Boulder Police Chief Koby appeared to change his mind about help and rejected outside assistance. When the chief of the Denver Police Department called to offer his own experienced homicide detectives' help, according to him, Chief Koby's response was, "What for?"

They would all soon learn they were dealing with a murder that would mesmerize the nation and play out in the media for years.

# CHAPTER 8

# FIRST ON-SCENE POLICE OFFICER'S REPORT

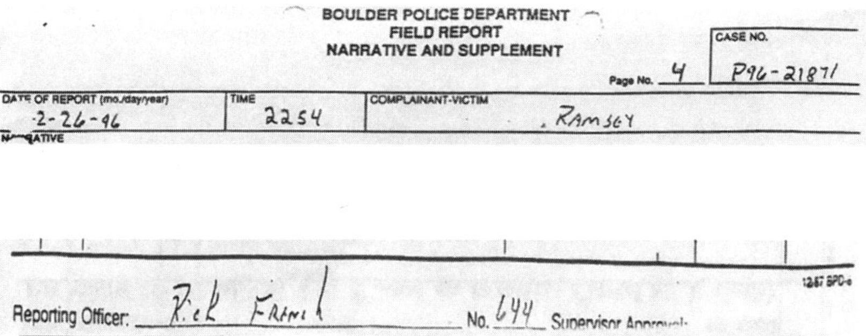

BOULDER POLICE DEPARTMENT
FIELD REPORT
NARRATIVE AND SUPPLEMENT

Page No. 4

CASE NO. P96-21871

| DATE OF REPORT (mo./day/year) | TIME | COMPLAINANT-VICTIM |
| --- | --- | --- |
| 12-26-96 | 2254 | RAMSEY |

NARRATIVE

Reporting Officer: Rick French No. 644 Supervisor Approval:

1287 BPD-6

Signature of Boulder Officer Rick French on his police report detailing the events of December 26, 1996. French was the first officer on the scene.

## CHRONOLOGY

## DECEMBER 26, 1996—THURSDAY

**6:00 a.m.—The first Boulder Police Department official to arrive on the scene, Officer Rick French, arrives.**
**6:02 a.m.—The second BPD official to arrive on the scene, Sergeant Paul Reichenbach, arrives.**
**1:00 p.m.—Officer French begins writing his report about the Ramseys.**
**1:06 p.m.—Approximate time JonBenét's body found. Officer French returns to the Ramsey home after the discovery of JonBenét's body is reported.**
**10:54 p.m.—Officer French resumes writing his report.**

## DECEMBER 27, 1996—FRIDAY

**The second officer on the scene, Sergeant Paul Reichenbach, files an amended report. His first report from the Ramsey home was one paragraph long.**

FOR YEARS, MEMBERS OF THE MEDIA, the public and law enforcement agencies have asked why the first two on-scene officers failed to find JonBenét's body. They arrived only two minutes apart.

The answers were in first responder Officer French's police report and also in a statement made to Officer French by the second officer to arrive. Despite a case littered with police leaks, this information was not leaked and was known by only a few officers and attorneys.

"In the basement I attempted to open the door leading to the area where JonBenét was ultimately found, but it was secured by a wooden latch above the door. The door opened inward and I was looking for access out of the house. Since the door could not have been used for that purpose, and it was latched closed, I did not open it." (Officer Rick French—Date of Report 12-26-1996 Time written: 2317—11:17 p.m.)

French wrote this part of his report slightly more than ten hours after JonBenét's body was discovered. Here's why these statements he wrote about the door are incorrect and misleading:

- The door opened outward only, not inward.
- French could not have known if there was an exit out of the room unless he opened the door and looked into the room to find out where it led. "I did not open it," he wrote.

Officer French gave even more contradictory and incorrect information about that critically important basement door in a formal debriefing two weeks later on January 10, 1997. According to the JonBenét Ramsey Murder Book Index, at this time he told the two senior officers who reported:

"Officer French finds the wine cellar locked." (BPD Report #5-3853.) (Date of Formal Interview: 1-10-97.)

"Officer French thinks the wine cellar door is nailed shut." (BPD Report #5-3854.) (Date of Formal Interview: 1-10-97.)

These erroneous statements created questions related to the accuracy of perceptions noted in other parts of French's report, including:

"She [Patsy] found JonBenét's room empty and then discovered the note as she walked down the stairs." (Officer Rick French—Date of Report 12-26-1996 Time written: 1300—1 p.m.)

In the later formal debriefing/interview, Officer French clarified and disagreed with his own report, according to police reports by senior BPD officers:

"Officer French does not know whether Patsy said that she went in to get her daughter ready or whether she came downstairs first." (BPD Report #5-3834.) (Date of Formal Interview: 1-10-97.)

Lone on-scene Detective Arndt also contradicted the information about Patsy's actions described in Officer French's report:

"Patsy had gotten up on the morning of Dec. 26 1996 and had gone down the stairs from her bedroom to the kitchen . . . At the bottom of this spiral staircase Patsy discovered a 3 page handwritten note. . . After Patsy looked at the note and read it she ran to JonBenét's bedroom. JonBenét was missing" (Detective Linda Arndt—Date of Report 1-8-1997).

Another discrepancy from Officer French's report again referred to Patsy. After she found her daughter's room empty, French wrote:

"She immediately called the police." (Officer Rick French—Date of Report 12-26-1996.)

The Ramseys have said Patsy did not immediately call police when she found the ransom note and her daughter missing. She first called out for John. Together they checked their daughter's room and then went to check on their son, Burke. According to John, he was then on the floor in the kitchen with the ransom note spread out before him while Patsy placed the 911 call.

Another question about perception from Officer French's report:

"Mrs. Ramsey told me that she had gone into JonBenét's room at about 0545 hours [5:45 a.m.] to wake her in preparation for a short trip the family was to take later that day." (Officer Rick French—Date of Report 12-26-1996 Time Written: 1300—1 p.m.)

Here's why this information was incorrect:

"The Ramseys were planning to travel from Jefferson County Airport near Boulder to Minneapolis to pick up their other children and then fly on to Traverse City, Michigan. From there, they were to drive more than an hour to their vacation home in nearby Charlevoix, Michigan. The total trip would have taken approximately seven hours and covered about 1,000 miles." (Source: JonBenét Ramsey Murder Book Index.)

Regardless of whether Patsy described the pending trip in this way or the way Officer French did, the Ramseys weren't preparing for a "short" trip. It's a small detail, but that lack of extended information about the trip should have been used as an avenue for more questioning by the officer, in case the trip had any bearing on JonBenét's disappearance.

A defense attorney has said it was another reason why defense attorneys would eventually question French's entire report.

French wrote this next part of his report nine and a half hours after JonBenét's body was found:

"[T]hey arrived home at 2200 [10:00 p.m.] hours. Mr. Ramsey said he read to both kids for a short time and then they were in bed by 2230 [10:30 p.m.] hours." (Officer Rick French—Date of Report 12-26-1996 Time written: 2254—10:54 p.m.)

The report is countered by other police reports regarding what the Ramseys said:

"(2100 to 2115 hours) [9:00-9:15 p.m.] The Ramsey's [sic] returned home. JonBenét had fallen fast asleep. John carried her inside, took her upstairs, put her on her bed and then Patsy came in to her bedroom behind him. John went down to get Burke ready for bed who was working on a little toy and John worked on that toy with him for 10 or 15 minutes then he took him to bed, got his pajamas on and then John Ramsey went upstairs and got ready for bed." (BPD Report #5-2449.)

"(2130 to 2200 hours) [9:30-10:00 p.m.] Patsy Ramsey went upstairs to bed." (BPD Report #5-2364.)

"(2130 to 2140 hours) [9:30-9:40 p.m.] John Ramsey was in bed and all the lights were out." (BPD Report #5-2449.)

There were questions about what JonBenét was wearing when she went to the Christmas party and afterwards when she went to bed. She was found dead in a white top with a silver star. Officer French wrote:

"Ms. Ramsey said that JonBenét had been dressed in white long underwear and a red turtleneck." (Officer Rick French—Date of Report 12-26-1996 Time written: 2254—10:54 p.m.)

This statement would be contradicted by:

- Detective Lou Smit, who reported that fibers from the white top were found on JonBenét's bed sheet.

- Patsy, who has explained that while the two were going to dress alike in red tops that evening, JonBenét opted to wear a white top instead before they left for the dinner party, and Patsy did not change JonBenét out of that white top when she put her daughter to bed.

When John Ramsey spoke with the Boulder Police Department in a June 1998 interrogation, he described how his daughter had been dressed in this way: "She had on a little top with a silver star on it and a black-color pair of pants. I don't remember if she had color—she probably did. I don't remember what color it was." (John Ramsey Interrogation—June 23, 1998.) (Present for the interrogation: investigators for the prosecution Lou Smit and Mike Kane, John's attorney Bryan Morgan and a private investigator for the Ramsey attorneys, David Williams.)

The white top JonBenét was wearing when her body was found had a white silver star on it. The red top didn't. Smit and Kane would ask no more questions about a red top, indicating, said a Ramsey attorney, "the red top wasn't an issue."

Detective Arndt's initial report supported Officer French, however:

"JonBenét had last been seen wearing a red turtleneck and white long underwear." (Detective Linda Arndt—Date of Report 1-8-1997.)

Arndt didn't list a source of information for this statement in her report.

Former Adams County District Attorney Bob Grant would later question when Officer French wrote the above information in his report. Then he'd ask whether the discovery of JonBenét's body affected what French wrote so many hours later at 10:54 p.m., 11:17 p.m. and 11:44 p.m. about activities in the Ramsey home. Those times are listed on French's own report, which is available in the Documents Section of this book.

His report was written in one continuous flow of words with no delineations for time changes.

As for why the second officer on the scene and first-responding supervisor, Sergeant Paul Reichenbach, didn't open the basement storage room door where JonBenét's body was eventually found: "Sgt. Reichenbach told Ofc. French that he had seen the wine cellar door, but he didn't go in it." (Source: JonBenét Ramsey Murder Book Index.)

Reichenbach's first report does not reflect why he didn't go in the storage room/"wine cellar" door. He filed an amended report the next day, December 27, which is not available. His first report contained information "concerning the initial inspection of the house and basement and outside. Also contact with John Ramsey." (Sergeant Paul Reichenbach—date of report unclear from available documentation.)

The first twenty-four to forty-eight hours of a death investigation are vital.

It is during this short period that investigators must interview witnesses, gather a wide array of information and sort out facts. They must rely on people's memories and get their statements quickly. They normally write new reports on a daily basis from their notes, so each day's work can be recalled later, clearly and concisely. Other detectives assigned to a case also need access to all written reports. The detective in charge of a case oversees the investigation and ensures that developing detective reports are filed on a daily basis in what some law enforcement officials call the Murder Book. Such oversight did not happen with regard to the murder of JonBenét Ramsey. Lou Smit, brought in by the Boulder District Attorney and approved by Boulder Police, has criticized the lack of organized control and oversight at the Boulder Police Department during the Ramsey investigation for even the most elementary and ordinary process of writing reports. Smit's main job was to organize and coordinate the Boulder Police Department reports on the case.

Formal interviews of some BPD officers were conducted by high-ranking officers to verify, clarify and, in some cases, question what was in each individual officer's report. Formal interviews of officers are not the norm in a homicide investigation. They're used as a form of damage control when too many questions exist about what someone has reported. According to a report sponsored by the U.S. Department of Justice, such interviews should involve a "'devil's advocate'" who "should review investigative conclusions to ensure they were made and documented with transparency and integrity to combat any occurrence of investigative bias."[1]

Despite such attempts to control and learn more from the errors made that first day of the Ramsey murder investigation, high-ranking Boulder Police Department officials compounded problems by scheduling formal interviews an astonishing number of days later. Officer Rick French's formal interview took place more than two weeks (fifteen days) after JonBenét's body was found, and Sergeant Paul Reichenbach's formal interview occurred more than a month (thirty-six days) after. Memories and details become vague over such long periods of time, and this was a death investigation. By allowing such lengthy delays, BPD officials failed to fulfill one of their basic responsibilities. As stated in a guide to investigating deaths from the National Institute of Justice, "Local death investigators must do their best to find answers for families who have lost loved ones."[2]

During the formal interview of Officer French on January 10, 1997, senior officials sought to learn whether French had actually checked the doors in the Ramsey home on the morning of December 26, 1996. In addition to a quote from Officer French which states "John Ramsey said all the doors were locked," the report related to this interview includes the following statements:

- "Det. Patterson had asked Ofc. French if there was any sign of break in and (French) told him no because he asked Mr. Ramsey if everything was locked and he [Ramsey] said yes; is anything broken; he said no; and (French) noted that but he does not know that for sure."

Experts insist that police officers must check such information themselves.

- "It is not clear if Officer French determined that JonBenét's patio door was locked."

All possible points of entry in a home must be thoroughly checked to determine whether an intruder was involved in a kidnapping case, say experts. That's a key and elementary area of investigation.

During the formal interview of Sergeant Reichenbach on January 31, 1997, senior officials sought to learn more about any locked or unlocked doors at the Ramsey residence. The report related to this interview includes the following statements:

- "Sgt. Reichenbach did not check the doors to see if they were locked."

- "Sgt. Reichenbach could not recall observing the butler kitchen door when he was at the house."

That last statement is important, because both the first family friend to arrive at the Ramsey home the morning of December 26, 1996, and a neighbor had noticed that this particular door was partially open at 6 a.m. and 8 a.m., respectively. While case notes from December 27, 1996, as well as February 1 and February 24, 1997, state that BPD officers discussed their concerns about the open butler kitchen door on those dates, such statements as well as supporting documentation should have been provided in initial reports and observations from the first day of the investigation, December 26, 1996. The butler kitchen door in the Ramsey home was located on the north side of the house and led to a small utility room that shared a wall with the kitchen. At each end of the butler kitchen, a few steps led up into the main kitchen.

After subsequent and more thorough investigations of the home, BPD police report excerpts state that multiple doors and windows in the Ramsey residence were found to be unlocked and some were open, providing more than eight areas of possible entry. (Source: JonBenét Ramsey Murder Book Index.)

The Boulder District Attorney's Office became involved in the Ramsey murder investigation the afternoon of December 26, 1996, when the body of JonBenét was discovered. However, Boulder DA Alex Hunter was on vacation in Hawaii, and First Assistant DA Bill Wise decided not to call him while he was away. The gravity of the case was just not registering.

A Boulder Police Department officer was left to guard JonBenét's body while the DA's Office acquired a search warrant. Even though the family said the police could have access to the home, the DA's Office wanted the legal protection of a search warrant. While one was obtained, no one re-entered the home for several hours. It was the right thing to do when so much hadn't been done correctly. "With a search warrant," said one attorney consulted for this book, "you're golden."

After the paperwork was in order at 8:00 that Thursday night, the coroner signaled that the body could be removed from the home.

By then, a few local reporters had arrived on the scene to videotape and photograph the careful removal. JonBenét's small, broken body, contained inside two coroner body bags layered one inside the other, lay on a gurney that was wheeled outside the front door of her family's home to the coroner's wagon that cold, frozen night. There was a hush as the reporters realized what they were witnessing. Stillness enveloped them and seemed to expand throughout the neighborhood. You could almost feel it as it traveled. The only sounds were the crunching from the wheels of the loaded gurney when it hit a few patches of crusted snow and then the slam of the rear door on the coroner's station wagon as they prepared to drive JonBenét Ramsey's body away.

# CHAPTER 9

# LONE ON-SCENE DETECTIVE'S FIRST REPORT

**Detective Supplemental Report: P96-21871**
**First degree murder**
**Det. Linda Arndt**
**Date of Report: January 8, 1997**

On Dec. 26, 1996 at approx. 0635 hours I received a phone call at my home phone number from Det. Sgt. Robert Whitson. Sgt. Whitson informed me that officers were on the scene of a reported kidnapping. The reported kidnapping had occurred at 755 15th St. located in Boulder, Boulder County, Colorado. JonBenet Ramsey, a 6 year old female, was reported to have been kidnapped from her home. JonBenet's mother had found a ransom letter inside the home at approx. 0550 hours this morning. JonBenet had last been seen inside her home at approx. 2200 hours on Dec. 25, 1996. There was no apparent forced entry to the residence. Other family members who were inside the home from the night of Dec. 25 through the morning of Dec. 26 had not been harmed. These family members included JonBenet's mother, father, and brother.

In the note left by the reported kidnappers, the author of the note stated the reported kidnappers would phone the Ramseys between 0800 hours and 1000 hours. Sgt. Whitson requested that I respond to the Ramsey address on 15th St. Sgt. Whitson was going to make attempts to have US West Communications place a trace on all incoming calls placed to the Ramsey home.

Portion of Boulder Detective Linda Arndt's police report about events of December 26, 1996.

## CHRONOLOGY

## JANUARY 8, 1997

**Detective Arndt's police report is dated thirteen days after JonBenét's body was found. The significance of this is that the three largest police departments in Colorado—Denver, Colorado Springs and Aurora—dictate violent crime reports must be turned in within twenty-four to forty-eight hours of the investigator's observations.**

**"Each department or agency has a method which they use for written documentation of the crime scene. There [sic] investigator/technician should follow his/her departments assigned procedures for written documentation. The importance of sharing information can never be over-looked."[1]**

**The Boulder Police Department referred me to its Policies and Procedures online report which was under the name of its new police chief who took office in July of 2014. Under the Written Reports Section, reports must be turned in at the "end of the work day" unless supervisory approval is needed. So BPD's policy as of 2014 would be the twenty-four- to forty-eight-hour rule.**

"WHERE'S HER REPORT? What's she going to say?"

That was overheard in Boulder, where a group of cops had gathered with media close by. They were describing the thirteen days it was taking for the lone Boulder police detective who had been in the Ramsey home when JonBenét's body was found to turn in her report. Once it was in the system, that report actually reiterated some continuing errors and created new ones. Bob Grant, then Adams County District Attorney has said he wouldn't have factored in the information from this report because it had taken so long for the detective to file it, but he would have included reports from each day as long they were turned in the day the observations were made.

Adams County District Attorney Bob Grant was one of four metro-Denver district attorneys who would later assist the Boulder DA in the Ramsey investigation. Grant and the other DAs were asked to help by then Governor Roy Romer in 1998. Grant said he was alarmed when looking at evidence in the case because of "recall" reports that were filed and considered part of the chain of evidence by the Boulder Police Department.

"I was disturbed during the Boulder Police Department presentation of the case when I determined to reject the 'recall' reports provided by the police department," Grant said. "These were reports written after the fact by officers, sometimes a month later. I didn't consider 'recall' reports as valid. An officer should be writing reports the day of his/her investigation."

Detective Arndt's report was regarded by District Attorney Grant to be a "recall" report. Yet her report was still considered by the Boulder Police Department to be a viable part of the case file. This meant that, if there was a trial, her report and testimony would be part of it. It would give future defense attorneys information that could be considered to raise reasonable doubt because of the time it had taken for the report to be filed and because of the questions the report raised.

Arndt began her report by writing about the phone call she'd received asking her to respond to the Ramsey home. After receiving the call, she wrote, she went to the Boulder Police Department and met with the officer who had collected the original ransom note from the scene.

According to homicide detectives, Arndt's first priority should have been to report to the scene, but she and Detective Fred Patterson did not follow this protocol. At the police department, Arndt asked for copies of the note and got a tape recorder. After leaving the police department, she and Detective Patterson met with Sergeant Paul Reichenbach, the overnight watch supervisor, behind a small shopping center. The two detectives then proceeded to the Ramsey home.

Portions of Detective Arndt's January 8, 1997 report contain errors, some of which are noted below. (Sixteen pages from Arndt's report are contained in the Documents section of this book.)

Errors or misperceptions in the report include:

- Regarding the ransom note: "No police or law enforcement were to be notified, otherwise JonBenét would be 'decapitated.'"

The word in the actual ransom note was "beheaded." The wording needed to be exact since the report would become part of the record of the case.

- "Det. Patterson and I sealed the entrance to JonBenét's room at approx. 1030 hours [10:30 a.m.]."

The sealing of JonBenét's bedroom at this time would not have been possible if Detective Patterson had left with Commander-Sergeant Whitson for a 10 a.m. meeting with the FBI at the Boulder Police Department. Furthermore, Whitson's report stated that he was present with Detective Arndt and Detective Patterson when JonBenét's bedroom was sealed with crime scene tape at approximately 9:30 a.m. And finally, Patterson left with Whitson at 9:45 a.m., so the sealing of the room had to have happened before 9:45 a.m.

- "At approx. 1035 hours [10:35 a.m.] all BPD officers, detectives, and victim advocates cleared the Ramsey residence. The only persons remaining in the residence were: John Ramsey, Patsy Ramsey, [five family friends] and myself."

According to various other police reports, the home was cleared of all law enforcement personnel by 10 a.m., not 10:35 a.m. Arndt also failed to mention the continued presence of the Victim Advocates, who remained in the home at varying times that morning.

- "At an unknown time between approx. 1040 hours [10:40 a.m.] and 1200 hours [12:00 p.m.] John Ramsey left the house and picked up the family's mail. I was not present when John left. I did witness John Ramsey opening his mail in the kitchen."

No one saw John leave his home that morning except when he walked his son to a friend's car accompanied by Patsy and a police officer. He didn't leave the house to get the mail; it was delivered through a mail slot next to the front door. He'd hoped there might be a clue in the mail.

The Ramsey family's minister said that he "never, during the time that he was in the house, saw John Ramsey leave the first floor of the house." John has said he felt he needed to be "glued" to the home in case he got a ransom call. At the time he went to the third floor with binoculars to search the neighborhood, the pastor had not arrived yet.

- "John's adult children from another marriage, John Andrew and Melinda, had taken the family's private plane from Atlanta and had flown to Minneapolis, MN. John Ramsey, Patsy, JonBenét and Burke were going to fly to Minneapolis, MN and meet with John Andrew and Melinda."

That information was wrong. John Andrew, Melinda and Melinda's boyfriend had flown commercially from Atlanta to Minneapolis in order to meet the rest of the family there on the morning of December 26. John, Patsy, Burke, JonBenét and a private pilot had planned to fly in the Ramseys' private twin-engine plane from Jefferson County Airport near Boulder to Minneapolis to pick up the older children in Minnesota and then go on to Michigan so the family could enjoy a late Christmas celebration there.

- "After officers had been dispatched to this call, all further communication was done by telephone rather than radio traffic."

That contradicts Commander-Sergeant Bob Whitson's statement that he heard Det. Arndt and her partner over the police radio just before they reported to the scene after the 911 call. Whitson has recalled thinking at the time it was a bad idea for the detectives to be talking by radio when a kidnapper could be monitoring them.

- "The first officer on the scene was Ofc. Rick French. Ofc. French had told Sgt. Reichenbach that something didn't seem right."

There are no available police reports or excerpt records from either Officer French or Sergeant Reichenbach, the second officer on the scene, that support this statement. If Arndt herself did not hear Officer French say this, then this statement is considered "hearsay." Arndt did not add any information or perspective to this statement in her report. Furthermore, according to available records, neither Officer French nor Sergeant Reichenbach reported this statement in their own reports or in later debriefings.

- "John told me that he personally checked all of the doors and all of the windows in the home this morning. All of the doors and windows were locked."

Again, basic yet critical information related to whether the doors and windows in the Ramsey home were locked or unlocked was not gathered by initial responders. This statement parrots what Officer French's report said and reveals that Arndt also failed in those critical first few hours to check any, much less all, of the possible points of entry into the house.

- "John told me no interior lights were on when he went to bed. I asked John which exterior lights were on when he went to bed . . . John told me that he didn't know if any exterior lights were on."

This statement contradicts what the Ramseys stated as recorded in the JonBenét Ramsey Murder Book Index: "John and Patsy Ramsey went to bed and left some of the first floor lights on as well as one more lights [sic] on the landing on the second floor and JonBenét's bathroom light was also left on." (BPD Report #90-10, Source.)[2]

Furthermore, a neighbor "who lives immediately south of the Ramsey's [sic] residence, got up to use the restroom and saw that the light in the southeast corner of the house, which had been left on every night for the past five years, was out." (BPD Report #1-1196.)

Another neighbor, who lived just north of the Ramsey home, told police investigators that at midnight between December 25 and 26, he "looked out his kitchen window at the Ramsey residence and observed the upper kitchen lights were on and dimmed low." He added that "this was the first time that he had seen these particular lights illuminated in the five years that he'd lived next door to the Ramseys. He said these lights are located in the ceiling above the kitchen window." (BPD Report #1-99.)

- "John told me that Patsy and Burke immediately went to bed. John had read a book to JonBenét, tucked her into bed, then John went to bed."

This contradicts what Patsy and John told police in their interrogations. They said Patsy put the sleeping JonBenét to bed and John stayed up and worked with Burke on a new toy for a little while before putting his son to bed and then turning in himself.

Also in this report, Detective Arndt described what happened after she suggested to John and his friend that they search the house, even though this suggestion went against most violent-crime investigation protocols. Only the police should have searched the home or been involved in crime collection.

- "I suggested to [John's friend] that he and John Ramsey check the house 'from top to bottom' excluding JonBenét's bedroom. I suggested to [friend] that John Ramsey check to see if anything belonging to JonBenét had been taken or left behind."

- "After I had spoken to John he immediately went to the basement door." . . . "The time was approximately 1300 hours [1:00 p.m.]." Again, John was accompanied by his friend, but Arndt did not accompany the two men.

- Within five minutes, Arndt stated, she heard "some type of shout or scream before I saw [John's friend]. I saw [John's friend] grab the phone in the den, dial 2 to 3 numbers, then hang up the phone. [John's friend] then ran back towards the basement door. Yelled for someone to call for an ambulance."

- Arndt described what happened next in this way: "I was standing in the hallway, facing the door to the basement, when I saw John Ramsey coming up the final three or four stairs. John was carrying a young girl in his arms. The young girl had long blonde hair. John Ramsey was carrying the young girl in front of him, using both of his arms to hold her around her waist area. The young girl's head was above John Ramsey's head while he was carrying her. From a distance of approx. 3 feet, as John was walking up the stairs, I was able to make the following observations to this young girl: both of her arms were raised above her head and were motionless; her lips appeared blue; her body appeared to have rigor mortis; there was a white string attached to her right wrist; there was a bright red mark, approx. the size of a quarter, at the front of her neck; the lower portion of her neck and the right side of her face appeared to have livor rigor mortis. I told John to place the young girl's body on the rug just inside the front doorway. John did as he was instructed. The young girl was JonBenét. JonBenét appeared to have been dead for a period of time. I touched JonBenét's neck in an attempt to locate any sign that she was alive. JonBenét's skin was cool to the touch. There was dried mucus from one of JonBenét's nostrils. My face was within inches of JonBenét's face. I detected an odor of decay. John Ramsey asked me if JonBenét was alive. I don't remember the specific words John Ramsey used. I told John Ramsey that his daughter was dead. John Ramsey moaned. I told John Ramsey to go back to the den, where the other persons in the house were congregated."

Ramsey doesn't remember why he carried his daughter upright instead of horizontally; possibly, he's said, it was instinct because her body was stiff from rigor mortis and wouldn't have fit through the storage room door or the basement door to the main floor.

- ". . . After John Ramsey left I picked up JonBenét and carried her into the living room. I laid JonBenét on the rug located inside the living room . . . Shortly after I had moved JonBenét into the living room I heard a loud guttural moan and wail coming from the den area of the house. The noise sounded as though it was made by a woman. John Ramsey came into the living room area approx. 1 to 2 minutes after I had sent him back to the den. As John entered the room he asked me if he could cover up JonBenét. John grabbed a throw blanket that was lying on a chair located immediately inside the living room. John placed this blanket over JonBenét's body before I had a chance to speak. I adjusted the blanket on JonBenét's body so that her clothing was covered from her neck down. I also covered the neck area of JonBenét. I had covered the wound on JonBenét's neck with her long sleeved shirt before John Ramsey arrived in the living room. I told John Ramsey he could say good-bye to his daughter, but he could not move her body, touch her hands, or lower the blanket. John knelt on the floor next to JonBenét. John repeatedly referred to JonBenét as 'my little angel'. John stroked JonBenét's hair with one of his hands. John Ramsey laid down next to JonBenét, placed an arm around her body and made sounds as though he was crying. I did not notice any tears. John Ramsey then rolled away from JonBenét's body and went into a kneeling position . . . John Ramsey then knelt by JonBenét's body, hugged her, and called her his little angel."

- Detective Arndt also noted that John looked toward the den where Patsy was and then added her observations of Patsy making her way into the living room: "I saw Patsy Ramsey. It seemed as though Patsy was unable to walk without the assistance of some-

> one on each side of her, holding her up . . . When Patsy saw JonBenét's body she immediately went to her and laid on top of her."

These acts described are among the most serious that occurred that day. It was wrong that police allowed an unsupervised search of a crime scene by non-police personnel, and major complications occurred due to John and his friend cross-contaminating the fragile evidence from the body of JonBenét. John did this when he tried to untie his daughter's hands, ripped the tape off her mouth and carried her upstairs. His friend picked up the duct tape that John had ripped from JonBenét's mouth and then dropped the piece of duct tape on the blanket in the basement. Experts say the situation was further compromised when Detective Arndt moved JonBenét's body, allowed John to place a blanket over it, adjusted JonBenét's shirt and the blanket to cover the neck wound and allowed Patsy Ramsey to lie on and then hold the body of her daughter in her arms.

According to the US Department of Justice, the following actions are among those that should have been, and were not, taken by Detective Arndt:

- "Upon arrival at the scene, and prior to moving the body or evidence, the investigator should: A. Remove all nonessential personnel from the scene."[3]

- "The investigator shall ensure that all property and evidence is collected, inventoried, safeguarded and released as required by law."[4]

By January 8, 1997, the date of Detective Arndt's written report, a media maelstrom had begun swirling around the Boulder Police Department's mishandling of the case and the Ramseys' possible involvement in the death of their daughter. Whether such public pressure may have influenced Detective Arndt when she wrote her report thirteen days after the child's body was found and whether she remembered information clearly at that point is not known. She gave only one interview to the media, and the information in her police report was not discussed.

Boulder Police Chief Tom Koby removed Detective Arndt from the Ramsey murder case in May 1997. Arndt told another detective at that time that she would not talk about anything related to the investigation and could not recall anything about it other than what was in her police reports.

Detective Arndt sued the City of Boulder in February 1998, alleging that defamatory and damaging statements had been published repeatedly about her. She asked for $150,000. The case would be dismissed in 2001. She testified in that case that she hadn't talked with the media because Chief Koby had imposed a gag order.

In 1999, Arndt gave her first public interview. She told Elizabeth Vargas of ABC's *Good Morning America* about the moment she saw John walking up the stairs with JonBenét:

"I saw black with thousands of lights and everything that I had noted that morning that stuck out instantly made sense. JonBenét was clearly dead and had been dead for a while.

"I leaned down to her face and John leaned down opposite me and his face was just inches from mine. We had a nonverbal exchange that I will never forget and he asked if she was dead and I said, 'Yes, she's dead,' and I told him to go back to the room and to dial 911.

"As we looked at each other . . . I remember—I wore a shoulder holster—tucking my gun right next to me and consciously counting out the 18 bullets."

Vargas asked Arndt why she counted her bullets.

"'Cause I didn't know if we'd all be alive when people showed up. I knew what happened. I knew what happened to her."

"Do you think your fear was well founded?" Vargas asked.

"You bet I do," Arndt said. "There was no doubt in my mind."

Nowhere in the obtained portion of Detective Arndt's police report written by her for the day of the initial investigation did she state such information.

# CHAPTER 10

# JONBENÉT'S AUTOPSY

JonBenét on her way to school. Her dog, Jacques, is also in the photo. © John Ramsey.

## CHRONOLOGY

**December 25 or 26, 1996—JonBenét Ramsey is murdered either Christmas night or early the next morning.**[1]

**December 26, 1996—Thursday**

**1:06 p.m.—JonBenét's body is found.**

**December 27, 1996—Friday**

**8:15 a.m.—JonBenét's autopsy begins.**

**2:15 p.m.—JonBenét's autopsy ends.**

**7–9 p.m.—A pediatric expert is called in by the coroner for a second opinion on whether there was a recent sexual assault on JonBenét Ramsey's body.**

WHEN SHE LAUGHED, her laughter was full of delight and happiness and sounded like little bells tinkling in a breeze according to her family. The sound reverberated throughout her whole body. Her laughter would cause anyone with her, adult or child, to join in. Those who loved her say JonBenét found complete joy in her world.

## FRIDAY, DECEMBER 27, 1996

Her body had been stored overnight in a refrigerated room kept just above freezing. It remained in the original body bags and on the same gurney. The day before, a coroner's assistant had sealed and numbered the body bags to preserve the chain of custody and ensure the bags wouldn't be opened before the autopsy. Just minutes now before the autopsy was to begin, the gurney was wheeled into the room.

It was time.

Her autopsy began at 8:15 a.m. on the day after her body had been found. It was performed at Boulder Community Hospital, the same hospital where her mother had struggled to live three years before while recovering each month following out-of-state chemotherapy sessions for Stage IV ovarian cancer.

The Boulder County Coroner, Dr. John Meyer, had been in his position for over nine years, since 1987. He was a board-certified forensic pathologist. Forensic pathologists are trained to look for and determine the cause and manner of death in sudden, unexpected and violent deaths. The autopsy is the primary tool in a pathologist's investigation.

Dr. Meyer was well regarded by other forensic pathologists. He was elected to four terms as coroner in Boulder County until he was term-limited out of office in 2002.

The autopsy room at Boulder Community Hospital had one stainless steel table. The room was brightly lit, like a surgical theater, and had a rust-colored floor. Several cabinets lined the white walls. Today, the room was crowded with people.

This was the autopsy of a murdered child who had died under mysterious circumstances in a town that hadn't had a single murder that year. Her body was the most valuable evidence left behind by her killer. Seven people attended the autopsy: two attorneys from the Boulder District Attorney's Office, two detectives from the Boulder Police Department, Boulder County Coroner Dr. John Meyer and two medical assistants. All wore bluish-green caps and gloves. Dr. Meyer and one of his assistants were fully dressed in surgical gowns, caps, gloves and footwear to prevent contamination. The coroner's verbal observations during the autopsy would be recorded while the law enforcement officers in attendance used cameras to document every step of the process.

Any murmur of conversation had fallen away when the body bags containing JonBenét's tiny remains were wheeled into the room. The understanding of what had happened, the murder of a lovely little girl in her own home, surely hit all those in attendance hard. "Brutal" was one way some familiar with the case saw it. "Sadistic," others thought. The awful reality made for a solemn, sober moment.

The body bags were removed from the gurney and placed with a soft thump on the cold stainless steel autopsy table. The evidence cameras from the detectives and attorneys began to click, flash and whir.

Dr. Meyer cut the seal. The zipper on the first bag grated as it was unzipped, provoking a feeling of dread. The witnesses braced themselves as the second bag was opened and JonBenét's body was slowly exposed. And they winced almost as one with the horrific realization, again, of why they were there.

Dr. Meyer began speaking into his tape recorder while he examined the outside of her body. JonBenét was still dressed in a long-sleeved white knit collarless shirt with an embroidered silver star decorated with silver

NAME: RAMSEY, JONBENET

DOB: 08/06/90

AGE: 6Y

SEX: F

PATH MD: MEYER

TYPE: COR

AUTOPSY NO: 96A-155

DEATH D/T: 12/26/96 @1323

AUTOPSY D/T: 12/27/96 @ 0815

ID NO; 137712

COR/MEDREC# 1714-96-A

FINAL DIAGNOSIS:

I. Ligature strangulation

- A. Circumferential ligature with associated ligature furrow of neck
- B. Abrasions and petechial hemorrhages, neck
- C. Petechial hemorrhages, conjunctival surfaces of eyes and skin of face

II. Craniocerebral injuries

- A. Scalp contusion
- B. Linear, comminuted fracture of right side of skull
- C. Linear pattern of contusions of right cerebral hemisphere
- D. Subarachnoid and subdural hemorrhage

Portion of JonBenét's autopsy report.

sequins. She wore white long underwear with an elastic band containing a red and blue stripe. Her panties were white with printed rose buds. The elastic band proclaimed it "Wednesday." Wednesday had been Christmas Day, two days earlier. A small red-ink heart had been drawn into the palm of her left hand. It was never determined who drew the heart, although her mother sometimes drew one on her daughter's hand. Perhaps, her parents later suggested, JonBenét had drawn this one.

JonBenét's body was lifted by the shoulders and ankles as the body bag was slid out from underneath her. According to the autopsy report, there was a "rust colored abrasion" on her cheek near her right ear that was clotted with blood. There was also a similar mark on her back. "On the left lateral aspect of the lower back, approximately sixteen and one-quarter inches . . . are two dried rust colored to slightly purple abrasions."

One end of a piece of white rope was wrapped loosely around her right wrist.

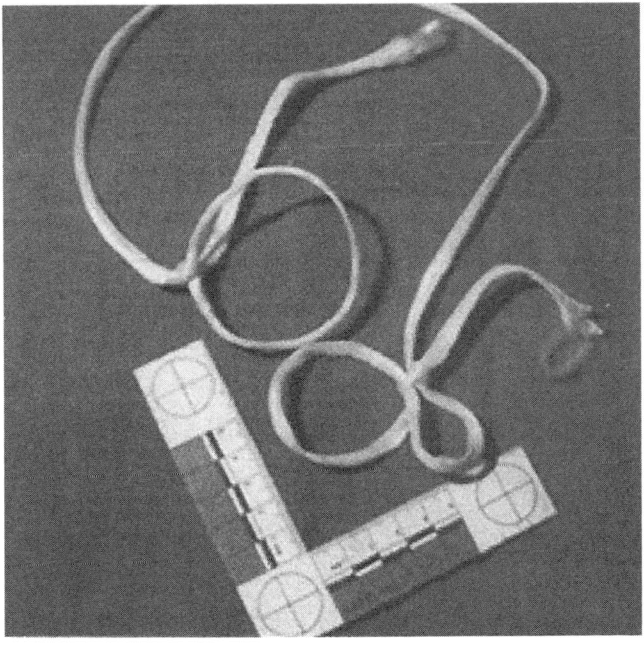

Wrist binding found tied on JonBenét. Courtesy Boulder Police and Boulder County District Attorney.

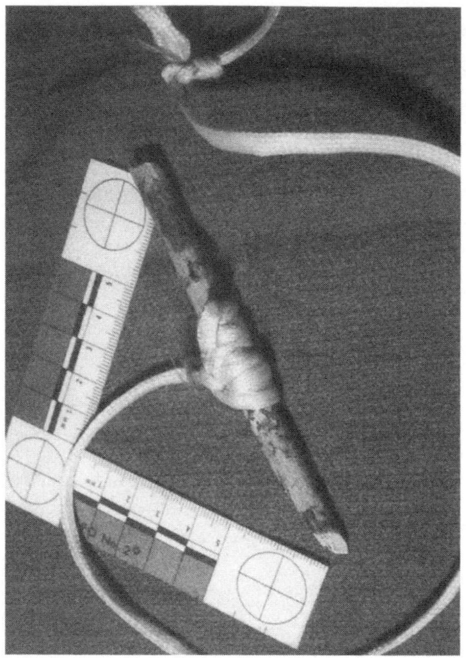

Garrote found embedded around JonBenét's neck. It was used for strangulation. Courtesy Boulder Police and Boulder County District Attorney.

Her killer had turned another piece of rope into a weapon by using slip knots to create a noose and squeezing the noose closed around her neck. It remained embedded there indicating the force of the strangulation. Dangling from the end of the noose was a wooden handle. Another deep ligature furrow, or rope mark, encircled her entire neck, the coroner observed. The two areas of furrow marks meant the rope may have been squeezed very tightly at least two times around her neck, or the rope and something else had been used to encircle the neck to cause the two marks. The handle on the end of the rope was used to control the amount of pressure on the noose around her neck—a garrote, it's called. The rope could be tightened until unconsciousness and then loosened on her neck by her attacker at will to bring her back to life. Garrotes are often made of wire and thrown over someone's head from the back and then tightened through pressure against the front of the neck according to a military officer. This garrote was made from rope. Those who saw it said it was an unusual device that had been carefully crafted. The wooden handle was part of a broken paintbrush from Patsy's painting supplies, which were kept in the basement. Patsy was an amateur painter. She painted mostly landscapes and flowers. She also painted pictures of roosters and gave them to friends.

During the external exam, the coroner found very small petechial hemorrhages on the inside of both upper eyelids. "There are possible petechial hemorrhages on the right lower eyelids, but rigor mortis on this side of the face makes definite identification difficult," the coroner's report would later read. While these hemorrhages can be attributed to more than twenty possible causes, they also can be a sign of a death by asphyxiation.[2] The coroner would list asphyxia by strangulation associated with craniocerebral trauma as the two possible causes of JonBenét Ramsey's death.

Once the coroner cut the cord from JonBenét's neck, he discovered a necklace, "a gold chain with a single charm in the form of a cross." JonBenét is pictured wearing this necklace in the Christmas Day photograph on the cover of this book.

Dr. Meyer also noted scratches on JonBenét's neck that appeared to have been caused by fingernails. Investigators would suggest the little girl had struggled against the tightened noose around her neck. The Ramseys would later say knowing their daughter had struggled to fight her killer as she was being strangled caused them nights and days of agony.

The coroner also clipped JonBenét's fingernails to look for DNA under them that might belong to her killer. Later tests would find the same foreign DNA in three places: under fingernails from each hand and mixed with blood in her panties.

After thoroughly examining the outside of JonBenét's body, the coroner began the internal examination while the cameras documenting the evidence continued making their now-familiar sounds.

After opening her scalp area, the coroner discovered a horizontal fracture in her skull that was eight and a half inches long. A small portion of her skull measuring one and three-quarters by one-half of an inch was hit so hard that the blow broke off part of her skull bone along the fracture line. There had been extensive bleeding, but her scalp had not been broken, so the hemorrhage had remained contained within her skull. While there was no external evidence of bruising or swelling of the head, the hemorrhage indicated to Dr. Meyer that the head injury had occurred when JonBenét was still alive.

Police never identified the weapon that likely caused the head fracture, but speculated that it had been a smooth object with no protrusions such as a baseball bat, a flashlight or a board because it had crushed her skull but not broken the skin of her scalp. A baseball bat found just outside the Ramsey home did not belong to the family but could not be traced.

A flashlight similar to one carried by police officers was found on the kitchen counter of the Ramsey home but also could not be traced.

Dr. Meyer found evidence that JonBenét was sexually assaulted, perhaps with an object like the paintbrush handle. Wood fibers found in her vaginal area were later traced to Patsy's paintbrush handle. A small amount

Baseball bat found outside the Ramsey home. Courtesy Boulder Police and Boulder County District Attorney

of blood in JonBenét's vaginal area indicated she was alive during the assault.

Four possibilities raised by the autopsy report of JonBenét Ramsey would be debated at length among members of law enforcement, the media and the public:

ONE: Whether a stun gun had been used to incapacitate and control JonBenét. In the autopsy report, the coroner noted two abrasions on her lower left back. These, along with similar abrasions on her right cheek, were spaced the exact same measurements apart.

The abrasions became a major controversy when, several months after the murder, Detective Lou Smit, who'd been hired onto the case by the Boulder District Attorney's Office, theorized that the marks had been caused by a stun gun.

Smit also took autopsy photographs to a forensic pathologist in the greater Denver metropolitan area and asked him to examine them. Dr. Michael Dobersen, a coroner/medical examiner for Arapahoe County, a southern suburb of Denver, is a soft-spoken man who is described by others as thoughtful and meticulous and is highly regarded by his peers.

In the summer of 1994, Dobersen had conducted several stun gun tests on anesthetized pigs to determine the kind and size of markings stun guns would make. He chose pigs because their skin composition is most similar to humans.

Because of his research and testing, Dobersen had been called as an expert witness in multiple cases thought to have involved stun guns. One involved the murder of multi-millionaire Robert Theodore Ammon, an investor killed in 2001 in Suffolk County, New York. At the time, Ammon was involved in a divorce from his second wife. Prosecutors stated the killer used a stun gun to incapacitate Ammon while beating him to death. Dr. Dobersen testified in that trial that a stun gun had been used twice on Ammon's neck and perhaps twice on his back. Ammon's second wife's new husband was eventually convicted in 2004 of the murder.

With regard to the Ramsey murder, Dr. Dobersen said it was very probable that the abrasion marks found on JonBenét had been caused by a stun gun.

After his office had "looked at the possibility extensively," Boulder Coroner Dr. John Meyer said, "I would not rule out one or the other with regard to a stun gun being used."

The stun gun theory was controversial because it contributed to the "intruder" theory in the Ramsey murder case since a stun gun would only need to be used if it was necessary to control a victim. Presumably the Ramseys would not have needed to use a stun gun to control their own child. The parents said they'd never owned or used a stun gun. And no stun gun that might have been used by JonBenét's killer was ever recovered.

Definitive information on a stun gun being used on the little girl could have been determined if her body had been exhumed and her skin examined for burn marks from a stun gun. By the time the stun gun theory came to light several months after the murder, however, Dr. Dobersen stated that it was too late to do this since JonBenét's skin would have deteriorated too much for an accurate determination to be made.

According to a police report, an officer from the Colorado Bureau of Investigation supported the possibility that a stun gun had been used on the child. "Sue Ketchum of the CBI [Colorado Bureau of Investigation] is shown the photos of the marks and she indicated that they could very well be made from a stun gun." (BPD Report #26-58.)

Other possible weapons that might have caused the abrasions included protrusions from the bottom of JonBenét's brother's toy train track, which was kept in the basement not far from where JonBenét's body was found. According to an investigator in the Boulder District Attorney's Office in charge of the Ramsey murder case in the mid-2000s, the protrusions reportedly matched the abrasions exactly. The district attorney at the time, Mary Lacy and other attorneys from her office listened to the investigator's presentation, but she said, "we discounted the information."

TWO: Whether JonBenét was sexually abused before her murder. The autopsy found "chronic inflammation" in JonBenét's vaginal wall. At least two detectives on the Ramsey police investigation speculated in media leaks that this condition had been caused by ongoing sexual abuse. Two highly reputable metro-Denver coroners, Dr. John Meyer (who performed the autopsy) and Dr. Michael Dobersen (noted above), both stated that the inflammation could have had several other causes, including improper wiping after going to the bathroom. JonBenét's pediatrician said she was not sexually abused. And physicians from the Kempe Center, a child abuse prevention organization in Denver, stated publicly after studying the evidence that JonBenét had not been subjected to long-term sexual abuse.

However, considerable speculation continued on this front, especially when the public learned of JonBenét's many contacts with family doctors including her pediatrician, Dr. Francesco Beuf of Boulder, and questioned whether this signaled a history of trouble at home. JonBenét and her mother had made more than thirty such contacts via either visits or phone calls with Dr. Beuf and with doctors in Michigan near the Ramseys' summer home over a three-year period from March 1993 to December 1996. (BPD Report #14-1.) After JonBenét's murder, information related to this number of contacts with these doctors was leaked to media, despite medical records indicating most of the calls and visits had been for coughs, fever, colds and flu-like symptoms.

JonBenét's medical records show her mother either called or had her daughter visit a doctor several times due to chronic sinus problems and allergic rhinitis as well as irritation and inflammation of portions of the nose. There were also four references in the medical records to accidental injuries: "cheek hit by golf club," "fell on nose," "fell and bumped forehead on stairs," and "fell and bent nail back." Five references in the medical file were about JonBenét's vaginal area. One was about a phone report from her mother related to a possible bladder infection, another was about how to treat chicken pox in her vaginal area, another (which was filed under vaginal in medical notes) was about diarrhea. Medical records also show JonBenét received two well-child checks by her pediatrician that included examinations of her vaginal area, and both results were "clear."

**Francesco G. Beuf, M.D., FAAP**
2880 Folsom, Suite 100
Boulder, CO 80304
(303) 442-2913
Caring for Infants, Children, and Teenagers

January 18, 1997

My office treated JonBenet Ramsey from March, 1993, through December, 1996. Throughout this period, there has been absolutely no evidence of abuse of any kind.

Francesco Beuf, M.D.

Dr. Francisco Beuf, JonBenét's pediatrician, and his letter to Boulder police stating no prior sexual abuse.

In a statement to Boulder police, Dr. Beuf wrote: "My office treated JonBenét Ramsey from March 1993 until her death. Throughout this period, there has been absolutely no evidence of abuse of any kind." (Dr. Francisco Beuf, January 18, 1997.)

Dr. Beuf told two Boulder Police Department detectives the same information in an interview the first week of January 1997. He gave similar information to KUSA TV, when I interviewed him on videotape for broadcast in February 1997:

WOODWARD: When you talked with the police, did they ask you about sexual abuse of JonBenét?
BEUF: Yes, of course they did.

WOODWARD: What did you tell them?

BEUF: I told them absolutely, categorically, no. There was absolutely no evidence, either physical or historical.

WOODWARD: And that's from seeing her thirty times in three years?[3]

BEUF: About that—

WOODWARD: What else did they ask you?

BEUF: Well, they asked me mainly the same questions you've been asking.

WOODWARD: Relationships with her parents?

BEUF: Relationships with her parents and what sort of child she was. If there was any indication of depression or of sadness.

WOODWARD: And your answers?

BEUF: Only that it was appropriate that she was sick and wasn't feeling too well. The mother was off getting treated for her cancer. She was sad at that.

WOODWARD: Was she an ordinary kid?

BEUF: I think she was extraordinary in the amount of charm she had and the sweetness, I guess, was the quality I appreciated the most. How she was doing things with her friends here, going to Michigan with her parents. Just the fun things in life, and beauty pageants just didn't seem to be at the top of the heap by any means.

WOODWARD: Tell me what she said to you.

BEUF: To be honest with you, I can't remember. I just remember it made me feel good to see that much happiness and niceness in one spot.

Dr. Beuf would have been required by Colorado law to report any signs of sexual abuse to authorities. In May 1963, a Colorado statute was passed regarding mandatory reporting by physicians about physical injuries of children. The statute was amended to include expanded reporting powers and, by 1969, included mandatory reporting required by a variety of people for suspected physical and sexual abuse of children.

Patsy Ramsey talked with me about her daughter's frequent visits to the pediatrician: "I was an overprotective mother when it came to my children's medical needs," she said in early 2000. "It's because I had cancer and the fears that go with it, so every symptom with them became something that I needed to have checked out and verified in order to be sure they were okay."

Patsy also said her cancer doctors told her she needed to keep her children as healthy as possible to protect her own immune system, which had grown weak from her struggles with ovarian cancer.

THREE: Whether JonBenét had wet her bed. The autopsy stated: "The long underwear was stained with urine." Detective Lou Smit said while fibers from JonBenét's night clothing had been found on her bed sheets—indicating that those particular sheets hadn't been changed during the night—no urine was found on them. Other sheets were found in the dryer next to JonBenét's room, and the Ramseys' housekeeper said she "believed she last changed JonBenét's sheets that Monday before Christmas." (BPD Report # 1-461.) That would have left the options of Monday, Tuesday or Wednesday for the sheets to be changed.

The Ramseys, their attorneys, and some law enforcement officials have stated that JonBenét probably urinated from the brute force of being stun-gunned, strangled or struck in the head, or upon her death. At least one Boulder police narcotics detective, Steve Thomas, however, became convinced very early in the investigation that Patsy had hit her daughter in a rage after JonBenét wet her own bed, then staged the elaborate cover-up with or without John.

Patsy said JonBenét had regressed in her potty training and using the bottle when Patsy was away for her first long period of cancer treatments, but JonBenét had only been three years old when her mother's treatments began. With regard to anyone in the Boulder Police Department coming to the conclusion that she had killed her daughter because of bedwetting, Patsy would later say, "They just really didn't get it. JonBenét's bedwetting wasn't a big deal to me, but it was to her. I felt badly for her because she would get embarrassed, so I always made sure not to make an issue of it for her sake. The bedwetting was because of my cancer and being gone so much for treatments." More recently, John said, "Bedwetting really wasn't an issue. It just wasn't."

The fact is that by December 1996, JonBenét was no longer a chronic bed wetter, according to her mother and her father, though Patsy kept a plastic sheet over JonBenét's mattress and kept overnight diapers handy. A housekeeper in Charlevoix, Michigan, where the family had their summer home, said in a police interview that JonBenét only had "occasional accidents." Still, some officers used the occasional bedwetting problem to advance their theory that JonBenét was deeply troubled and sexually abused.

According to a website article on Children's Hospital Colorado, "Doctors don't know for sure what causes bedwetting or why it stops. But it is often a natural part of development, and kids usually grow out of it. Most of the time, bedwetting is not a sign of any deeper medical or emotional issues."[4]

FOUR: Whether material in JonBenét's stomach indicated a timeline of when she was killed and who killed her. According to the coroner's observation written into his autopsy report, JonBenét's stomach contained "fragmented pieces of yellow to light green-tan vegetable or fruit material which may represent fragments of pineapple." Actual laboratory testing had not been completed at the time the coroner's report was written.

This statement, however, was enough to add to the speculation that Patsy Ramsey was guilty of murdering her daughter. The morning of JonBenét's disappearance, a bowl that included chunks of pineapple was photographed by Boulder Police Department investigators on the kitchen table in the Ramsey home. Later tests would reveal both Burke's and Patsy's fingerprints on the outside of the bowl.

For more than ten months following the murder, it was assumed and accepted by law enforcement officers and members of the public that, prior to her murder, JonBenét had eaten pineapple that came from inside the home from the bowl in the kitchen. This theory was first floated to the media as a leak, and it became a huge topic of discussion and publicity when the presence of pineapple fragments in JonBenét's stomach was assumed to be confirmed from the published autopsy report observation.

Bowl of pineapple on kitchen table in Ramsey home. Courtesy Boulder Police and Boulder County District Attorney

Somehow public opinion tied these "facts" to the belief that Patsy and John Ramsey had killed their daughter.

The exact material in JonBenét's stomach and intestines was first discussed with experts at the University of Colorado on October 15, 1997 (BPD Report # 1-1156), more than ten months after JonBenét was killed. Their reports about the contents of her stomach/proximal area were given to the Boulder Police Department more than a year later in January of 1998, (BPD Report #1-1349) one year after JonBenét's death. And that's when the mystery deepened and the misconception about what JonBenét actually ate was discovered.

According to previously unreleased BPD reports, laboratory testing revealed that JonBenét also ate cherries and grapes as well as pineapple. Remnants of cherries were found in the stomach/proximal area of her small intestine. "Another item besides pineapple was cherries." (BPD Report #1-1348.) In that same report: "Another item besides pineapple was grapes." (BPD Report #1-1348.) Another report expands on the grapes, saying "grapes including skin and pulp." (BPD Report #1-349.) The food described resembles what is included in most cans of fruit cocktail.

The new information wasn't released publicly, and the pineapple-only myth with its handy bowl of fruit on the kitchen table of the Ramsey home continued to be circulated. Why does this matter?

- The Boulder Police Department and the Boulder District Attorney's Office had been operating on an assumption for a year. Who knows where the correct information could have led?

- Among the reasons for checking food content in the body as soon as possible are the possible suggestions related to a timeline of death or perhaps poisoning that it could provide.

Related to establishing a timeline of death, consulted experts disagreed about when JonBenét could have eaten the fruit and how long it would have taken to digest. Her parents said JonBenét was already asleep in the car when they arrived home the evening before she died, and they took her in the house and put her to bed without her waking up. The friends who hosted the dinner party the Ramseys had attended that evening said JonBenét ate no fruit at their home. So, when and where did JonBenét eat it?

Some forensic experts state that digestion time can vary highly from 30 minutes to a few hours to several hours. If JonBenét had eaten some of the food in the afternoon of Christmas Day, which she might well have done without her parents being aware, the longer transit time for digestion would support John and Patsy's statement that they put their daughter right to bed after arriving home that night. But if forensic experts who contend there is a much shorter digestion period are correct, then it would seem JonBenét's parents were lying about her being asleep when she arrived home.

Other theories suggested by those familiar with the case state that JonBenét could have been fed later that night by her "Secret Santa" (a person she told a friend's mother was going to make a secret visit to her after Christmas) or forced to swallow the fruit by a stranger.

According to Dr. Michael Dobersen, the forensic coroner from Arapahoe County south of Denver, assumptions should be avoided and only the facts from an autopsy and summarized police reports considered. "She ate part of the fruit about an hour before she was assaulted and killed," he has stated. "There are no existing facts on who gave it to her. The assault on her would have stopped her stomach digestion. The digestion also would have stopped when she died."

JonBenét's autopsy took six hours. It was finished in the early afternoon, when her body was prepared for shipment to Atlanta for her funeral.

Early that evening, Coroner Meyer stated that he had sought an outside, second opinion on the nature of his vaginal findings. Dr. Andrew Sirotnak, then an assistant professor of pediatrics at Children's Hospital, who also worked at Denver's Kempe Center, consulted with Meyer at the morgue. (BPD Report #7-15 Source.) He agreed with Dr. Meyer that there had been a recent genital injury.

Since the coroner formally released JonBenét's body to her family in late December 1996, he has rarely spoken publicly about his personal perspective on her autopsy.

"There are so many aspects of it," Dr. Meyer said. "The things I look at now that bother me the most are [that] this was a tragic death of a beautiful little girl, and my concern is that we'll never know what happened. That's the bottom line. My biggest concern is that we won't find out who killed her."

The autopsy provided another insight into the killer. Law enforcement officials had learned from it that they were dealing with a person who was either enraged, brutal and cruel or ruthlessly detached and heartless. How else could they explain this murder of a child, especially with the overbearing and torturous violence involved?

"If it doesn't strike you personally in some way, then it's time to get out of the business," Dr. Meyer said. "That having been said, you can't let that interfere. You do what your job requires and focus on that exclusively. That's your responsibility to the deceased. Philosophical thoughts are for another time."

The Boulder Coroner's Report concluded, "Cause of death of this six-year-old female is asphyxia by strangulation associated with craniocerebral trauma." Dr. Meyer did not indicate in what order the injuries happened, and another forensic coroner consulted said it would be difficult to determine injury order in this case.[5]

JonBenét Ramsey was sexually abused, strangled, suffered a horrific blow to the head . . . and fought back.

CHAPTER 11

# THE DAYS AFTER—DECEMBER 26 TO 31, 1996

(Above) JonBenét's casket. (Below) JonBenét's body being carried in a casket out of the church in Atlanta. December 31, 1996.

## CHRONOLOGY

Thursday, December 26, 1996—After JonBenét's body is found, the Ramseys go to a friend's home to stay. Boulder Police Department officers accompany them to observe, write reports and protect.

Friday, December 27, 1996—The Ramseys stay with their friends. BPD officers are still with them day and night, observing and writing reports.

John asks a BPD sergeant to come to the friend's home to interview him.

Saturday, December 28, 1996—John, Patsy, Burke, John Andrew and Melinda give DNA samples and are interviewed and monitored by police, who take notes at the Boulder Sheriff's Department. John, Patsy and Burke give handwriting samples at the home where they are staying.

Attorney Mike Bynum says there will be no more interviews without an attorney for the Ramseys present.

The commander of the investigation, John Eller, attempts to stop the release of JonBenét's body to her family unless the Ramseys come to the Boulder Police Department to be interviewed. He has no legal authority to do this and is rebuked by the coroner and the Boulder District Attorney's Office.

Sunday, December 29, 1996—A memorial service for JonBenét is held in Boulder. The Ramsey family then flies to Atlanta for her funeral. It is Patsy Ramsey's fortieth birthday.

Monday, December 30, 1996—Visitation is held for JonBenét in Atlanta.

A Boulder police spokeswoman erroneously says Patsy Ramsey has not had her DNA taken. The information is published in the media.

Tuesday, December 31, 1996—JonBenét's funeral is held in Atlanta.

John's friend causes a disturbance in Atlanta at a private residence. (BPD Report #5-4583.)

THE RAMSEYS WOULD NEVER GO HOME AGAIN.

They had spent hundreds of hours making their home a happy retreat. It was a pretty place filled with family photographs, colorful wallpaper, paintings and relaxed furniture. Patsy later would say, "Yet there was so much tragedy. John's daughter Beth was killed in a car accident when we lived there, I was diagnosed with cancer and then JonBenét was killed inside. The house seemed to have turned against us, and we wouldn't ever go back." She shivered as she said this.

Within an hour of JonBenét's body being discovered, Patsy and John Ramsey were told by police that they had to leave their home because it had become a crime scene. They left a house, though, a place that was no longer their home. Instead, it was now a series of still and lifeless rooms, stripped empty of the people who had made them a comfort. They retreated to the home of close friends who had been with them, caring and supporting them, all morning. The police went with the family for both protection and to gather more information. Soon their son, Burke, joined them, as well as John Andrew, Melinda and her boyfriend.

One Boulder Police Department officer who remained with the Ramseys observed John and Patsy the night of December 26 and into the morning of December 27. He wrote in his police reports observations about Patsy and John's behaviors that provided a professional insider's look of their states of mind. The officer also talked with the Ramseys' friends about them. The information from his report shows how closely the family was being monitored and reveals their emotional conditions; information that hasn't been released until now. Information leaked after the first week following JonBenét's death showed a stark difference between what was noted in the confidential police reports and what was published and broadcast by the media and online. Publicly, the couple was variously described as "cold," "seemingly uncaring," and "not acting right." John was even described as "ice man" by Boulder District Attorney Alex Hunter months after JonBenét's murder.

But in unreleased police reports, details regarding John and Patsy's behaviors seemed to contradict what was publicly disclosed about them that first night after their daughter's murder:

12:05 a.m. 12-27-96: "Both John and Patsy get Valium." (BPD Report # 1-112, Source.)
12:20 a.m. 12-27-96: "John and Patsy Ramsey fall asleep on the living room floor." (BPD Report #1-112, Source.)
01:50 a.m. 12-27-96: "Patsy gets up and asks if someone is with her son, Burke. She also asks for more pills and says 'I just want to stay asleep.' She also asks if all the doors and windows are locked. She is drowsy and drugged." (BPD Report #1-112, Source.)

The police reports continue:

02:00 a.m. 12-27-96: "Patsy gets up to go to the bathroom. She is drowsy and dazed. Sobs every once in a while. At times needs to be supported." (BPD Report #1-112, Source.)
02:35 a.m. 12-27-96: "Patsy Ramsey goes back to bed." (BPD Report #1-112, Source.)
02:40 a.m. 12-27-96: "John Ramsey gets up and asks for two pills and walks around crying." (BPD Report #1-112, Source.)
02:45 a.m. 12-27-96: "John Ramsey goes back to bed." (BPD Report #1-113, Source.)
02:50 a.m. 12-27-96: "John Ramsey is back up crying and sobbing at times." (BPD Report #1-113, Source.)
03:50 a.m. 12-27-96: The police officer's report ends when he is relieved by another officer. (BPD Report #1-85.)

Another police report written from an interview with a family friend said: "Per [Patsy's friend] . . . Patsy looked dead herself . . . was up every 30 minutes throughout the night. John was pacing when I got there . . . was pacing and crying throughout the night . . . Patsy would ask . . . me to check on Burke every 10 minutes." (BPD Report #1-1881.)

John's Journal:

*We spend the next 24 hours in a numbed, body-shocked daze. I sleep a little bit on the floor, totally in agony.*

## FRIDAY, DECEMBER 27, 1996

On that Friday morning, John began trying to find a child counselor for Burke. The Ramseys had taken nothing from their home when they left, so friends organized to get some basic clothing for them and began preparing for a memorial in Boulder and a funeral service in Atlanta.

That afternoon, the police knocked on a few doors in the Ramseys' neighborhood to find possible witnesses. According to an attorney in the DA's Office and Detective Lou Smit, however, the Boulder Police Department never completed a thorough canvass of the neighborhood. Ever.

Some of the police reports from a brief canvass that was done would list an address and then, "Nothing of significance reported." Smit responded to this finding by saying, "A short while into a homicide investigation and snap judgments were being made about what was and was not important. Everything was important at that point in the investigation."

The Stine family, friends of the Ramseys, went to visit the couple where they were staying on Friday, December 27. "Patsy looked like she had aged a thousand years. She was so distraught," Susan Stine said. "We said what little we could say and hugged her and John and then just did what little we could to help. We'd brought our son with us to be with Burke. We thought it was important that Burke have a friend with him to distract him from the grieving adults."

John's business attorney and friend also saw them the day after the murder was discovered. Mike Bynum viewed the developments in the immediate days that followed as the lawyer he was. In spite of consistent rumors floated in the media that the Ramseys were not cooperating, Bynum knew both Patsy and John had been interviewed or observed every day since that first morning and would be until they left Sunday afternoon for JonBenét's funeral in Atlanta.

"After that first day, I could tell they were being targeted by police," said Bynum. "That was why it was so important to get attorneys for them immediately."

The lead police commander on the case began insisting the Ramseys come to the Boulder Police Department to be interviewed. John replied, "Come and interview us as much as you want where we are staying, but Patsy can physically barely get out of bed." That's when the legal side of Bynum kicked in fully. "These were people who literally couldn't tie their shoelaces," he said. "The trauma of seeing their dead daughter's body strangled with a rope embedded in her neck when they had never seen a victim of a violent crime left them incapable of making decisions. The Ramseys didn't hire an attorney. I did. I asked John if he would trust me to make a decision for him that I felt was critically important. He didn't ask me what it was and just said 'go ahead.' Neither one of them knew my decision was to hire attorneys to represent them."

Friday afternoon, a family friend "put Patsy Ramsey to bed and Patsy made some comments that concerned the friend such as 'can't you just fix this' and 'why did they kill my baby' as well as other comments [the friend] was not ready to share." (BPD Report #1-1186.)

On that same Friday, John got a call from a close friend at Access Graphics, the company where he was CEO. The man voiced concerns similar to those Bynum was thinking and told John, "I need to convey a message to you. It's from someone in the DA's Office on the inside of the investigation. I can't tell you who it is, but the person said I'm supposed to get this message to John Ramsey." The message was a warning. "You need to get the best defense attorney you can. They think you killed your daughter, and they're out to get you." John, who was still paralyzed with grief, was simply incapable of acting on any information. He told no one about the call, and its message didn't penetrate until weeks later.

The last time John Ramsey had seen his daughter was after she'd been tortured and killed. He couldn't get that image out of his mind. Nothing else mattered.

Bynum thought the BPD insisting the family go to the police department for more interviews and the commander in charge of the case, John Eller, refusing to go to the home where the Ramseys were staying to interview them was "counter-productive and unreasonable." He called the person he thought was one of the best defense attorneys in Colorado, Hal Haddon of Haddon, Morgan and Foreman in Denver. Haddon remembers the phone call from Mike Bynum. Bynum told him, "The most terrible thing has happened. This little girl was kidnapped and murdered. These are family friends of mine, and even though they are cooperating, the police are trying to frame them."

Haddon listened. "I didn't know Mike Bynum or the Ramseys," he said, "but from what Mike told me, it sounded like it was an awful tragedy and the police had targeted the parents. These are the kinds of cases we do. We represent people who are involved in serious criminal investigations."

Haddon called his partner, Bryan Morgan, who lived in Boulder. Morgan had seen the news of the murder on a local television station on Thursday night, December 26, but few details had been revealed at that time other than the fact that a child had been murdered.

That Friday morning, the *Rocky Mountain News*[1] had reported that Boulder Police Department Commander John Eller had said, "The family has been more than cooperative." In the same article about the kidnapping and murder, however, an attorney from the Boulder District Attorney's Office was quoted as saying, "It's not adding up."

On the phone, Haddon and Morgan agreed to take on this case.

## SATURDAY, DECEMBER 28, 1996

Two days after her murder, JonBenét was once again held for ransom. The commander of the Ramsey investigation, John Eller, threatened to hold the child's body indefinitely unless her parents agreed to an immediate and lengthy interrogation at the Boulder Police Department that Saturday morning. "It exacerbated the feelings in an already terribly flawed investigation," said Ramsey attorney Mike Bynum. "Not only was this threat extremely inappropriate, it was unconstitutional unless there was probable cause to continue the hold on the body."

John and Patsy weren't told about Eller's exact threat of trying to keep their daughter's body from them.

John's Journal:

*Patsy is in extremely bad shape, unable to walk . . . Chuck [Dr. Francisco Beuf] tells Mike [Bynum] that in his professional opinion we are in no shape to be taken out of the house to the police station for lengthy interviews. Mike relays that medical opinion to the Detectives, who continue to insist that we must come to the Police station to give them the help they need to solve this crime.*

According to Colorado law, the custody of the body of JonBenét Ramsey belonged to the Boulder County Coroner, who had released it to the family for burial. Attorneys from the Boulder District Attorney's Office told Eller to back off because he had no legal standing on the custody of the child's body. Eller did drop his demands, but the damage lingered. In the continuing days, as the Ramsey attorneys were hired and became active in the case, they told me they were incensed by what they perceived as Eller's unprofessionalism and hostility.

"Think if it was your child and someone threatened to keep your child's body from burial even though you legally had already been given the right to it. How could anyone even think of something that cruel?" asked Bynum.

John's Journal:

*We are confused. We want to help any way we can. We agree to go to the Sheriff's Dpt. to give DNA samples and handwriting because that will take only 15 minutes each, the police tell us. We trust them when they tell us going to the Sheriff's Dpt. is the only way they can do this. We find out later they could have taken DNA from us at the house. We agreed because we were trying to help. But the interviews would be hours. Can't they ask questions for interviews where we're staying?*

The Ramseys spent that desolate Saturday morning with Patsy in bed, Burke closely and constantly watched and John finding out that Bynum had hired attorneys for the family.

"John had great difficulty in understanding why I hired attorneys for them," said Bynum. "He was a law and order supporter. He trusted the police would do what was right and just. I explained to him there's a way that allowed you to cooperate and allowed you to protect your family and help the police. And that's what we're doing by hiring attorneys."

John remembers Bynum telling him he had hired two attorneys to represent him and Patsy.

John's reaction was, "Why do we need attorneys?" and "Why do we need two attorneys?" He said later he was unable to comprehend the seriousness of the forces gathering against him. In his mind, he and his family were innocent, and he was certain the police would feel the same way.

When attorney Bryan Morgan initially spoke with John in that first week following JonBenét's murder, he told him why he and his wife would need separate attorneys. Under the Colorado Rules of Professional Conduct, Rule 1.7, the same attorney could not represent Patsy and John under the circumstances of the case, which included the fact that they were both suspects.

The two attorneys would meet with John and Patsy personally and individually upon the Ramseys' return from JonBenét's funeral in Atlanta. To escape the pressures of the case, Morgan and John drove east of Boulder to a hiking trail, where they would walk for an hour and just talk. It was a private session held out in the open country for the two of them to get to know each other. Morgan says he remembers John as initially very emotional; they didn't talk about JonBenét or the murder investigation during this first meeting. John recalls immediately finding Morgan to be very thoughtful, compassionate, intelligent and sincerely interested in him.

"I felt very good about him," John remembers. "Morgan was a warm man and extremely professional. This was not a meeting to decide whether to hire him. Mike Bynum had already hired him. It was a very relaxed environment and talk."

Patsy met defense attorney, Pat Burke, a highly skilled trial lawyer, in Boulder. He had talked with Patsy by telephone when she was in Atlanta, and met with her at the family friend's home where the Ramseys were staying.

Pat Burke remembers their meeting well. "She was curled up in a ball on a couch. She was incredibly sad. I thought she was sincere and smart and continued to think that throughout our relationship. We met for three hours. She was completely distraught. She cried repeatedly. Still, there were moments when she became composed enough to talk about her family and their lives."

Patsy would later say her new attorney made her feel "very secure and protected." "I respected him and admired his approach to me and about JonBenét and the case. I felt comfortable with his guidance."

Prior to these meetings on the Saturday afternoon before the Ramseys attended a Sunday memorial service in Boulder and then left for Atlanta for their daughter's funeral, they had to leave the bleak solitude of their friends' home for DNA testing at the Boulder Sheriff's Department. They did this with the understanding that the process would take no more than 15 minutes for each of them. The family didn't understand they would also be observed and briefly interviewed by Boulder Police Department detectives at the Boulder Sheriff's Department. They also didn't realize they could have given DNA samples from the home where they were staying. Patsy and John Ramsey were each accompanied that afternoon by a legal representative whose presence Mike Bynum had arranged. Bynum also told the Boulder DA's Office there would be no further interviews of the Ramseys without an attorney present.

While detailed and confidential records of the Ramseys' DNA exchanges from that afternoon would be kept, the same standard of confidentiality wouldn't hold when information about those DNA collections—and what the Ramseys said while at the Boulder Sheriff's Department—was leaked publicly.

The Boulder Sheriff's Department was in the same building as the Boulder County Courthouse and the Boulder District Attorney's Office. The Boulder Police Department was in a separate building five miles away. Detectives had scheduled brief times for each family member at the Boulder County Sheriff's Department Records Section, a sparse room with a sink and long table at which fingerprinting was normally completed.

John Andrew Ramsey, JonBenét's half-brother, was the first to give DNA samples. He was also photographed. His testing began at 3:12 p.m. (Source: WHYD Investigative Archive.)

According to police reports, at approximately 3:50 p.m., JonBenét's half-sister, Melinda Ramsey, began giving blood and hair samples and fingerprints. She, too, was photographed. Melinda was described as being "friendly/cooperative/talkative" while "samples were obtained." "Some basic personal information was obtained" as well. Times were listed in the report for when actual samples were taken:

> 3:50 p.m. blood draw
> 3:55 p.m. hair samples
> 4:00 p.m. fingerprints
> (Boulder Detective Steve Thomas, 12-28-1996.)

Burke Ramsey gave his DNA at the same time as Melinda, at 3:50 p.m., according to excerpts from police records in the WHYD Investigative Archive. His photograph was also taken.

At approximately 4:09 p.m., Detective Thomas noted that John began giving blood and hair samples and fingerprints. "A photo was taken and some basic personal information was obtained . . . John Bennett Ramsey was cooperative and reserved and samples were obtained." John was accompanied by a private investigator who conducted work for the Haddon, Morgan and Foreman law firm.

4:09 p.m. blood draw
4:16 p.m. hair samples
4:24 p.m. fingerprints
(Boulder Detective Steve Thomas, 12-28-1996.)

At approximately 4:37 p.m., the same two detectives met with a heavily medicated Patsy Ramsey.

"Patricia Ramsey was cooperative in our requests, but was crying/sobbing, withdrawn and non-speaking, and unsteady on her feet. Samples were obtained without incident. A photo was taken and some basic personal information was obtained." Blood and hair samples and fingerprints were taken.

"During this processing, Patricia Ramsey sobbed/cried and during fingerprinting asked Detective Gosage 'Will this help find who killed my baby?' and made the statement 'I did not murder my baby.'" (BPD Report #1-143.)

Those statements were later leaked to the news media by "sources," and would be used against Patsy Ramsey in the months to come. A representative from Haddon, Morgan and Foreman accompanied Patsy.

4:37 p.m. blood draw
4:42 p.m. hair samples
4:50 p.m. fingerprints
(Boulder Detective Steve Thomas, 12-28-1996.)

At 6:00 p.m. that Saturday, according to the WHYD Investigative Archive, Melinda Ramsey arrived at the Child Advocacy Center for an interview. She was interviewed by detectives for more than two hours from 6:10 p.m. until 8:25 p.m. and gave handwriting samples.

At 6:55 p.m., according to the WHYD Investigative Archive, two Boulder Police Department detectives interviewed John Andrew. He, too, was interviewed for two hours from 6:55 p.m. to 8:52 p.m. and gave handwriting samples.

About the same time, 6:40 p.m., at the home where they were staying, John, Patsy and Burke Ramsey gave more handwriting samples. They were observed and supervised at this time by Detective Linda Arndt. The samples of all the immediate family members were collected and received at the BPD Property Bureau later that Saturday night.

That same Saturday, Patsy's sister, Pam, went to the Ramsey home to collect clothing and personal items for the family. Pam said the police officer on duty at the front door told her she could go in and get what she wanted. She insisted he accompany her and make a list of what she took. The WHYD Investigative Archive, however, states from a police report that the officer only allowed Pam to stand in the doorway of each room and tell the officer what she wanted to bring back. The officer would then take the item and catalog it before giving it to Pam. The police report and Pam's accounting of what happened are different.

While in the home, Pam felt she had missed something in JonBenét's bedroom and returned there.

John's Journal:

*Pam returned to the room and was drawn to a small medal that JonBenét had won at the last little pageant that she had done . . . When Pam told me of this and handed me the medal with the comment, I felt like JonBenét wanted me to get this to you, I was overwhelmed with emotion. JonBenét had many medals and trophies, but I had always told her that the most important thing was talent, not beauty. So she began working very hard on talent. The last pageant was in early December and I had planned to go there for her talent performance, but the program was running ahead of schedule and I arrived after her performance and after she had been awarded her medal. She lit up like a Christmas tree when I arrived and as soon as I sat down beside her she took the medal from around her neck and placed it around mine. During the days after JonBenét's death, I had thought that I must find this medal as it was something very special to me. Having Pam now tell me that she was strangely drawn back to JonBenét's room to retrieve what seemed was an insignificant medal among all of her much larger awards, and to deliver it to me, felt like a direct message from JonBenét. No one knew about that medal except JonBenét and me. No one knew its significance to me. JonBenét had spoken to me and let me know that she was alright and with God. I was so thankful for that gift and to this day that medal never leaves my neck and it was placed by JonBenét. Whenever I hit bottom, I touch the medal and it reminds me that JonBenét is with God and will be there to escort me home when my tasks are completed here.*

Boulder District Attorney Alex Hunter called in that Saturday from vacation to his First Assistant DA, Bill Wise, and asked to be informed of the developments of the day. That night, Wise called Hunter back about the Ramsey DNA samples, fingerprints, photographs, interviews and handwriting samples. Hunter remembers being angry about Commander Eller's demand to use the child's body to force her family to talk at the Boulder Police Department. It didn't make sense to him that Eller would even consider doing that when Wise had told him the family was willing to be interviewed at the home where they were staying. Wise continued to keep District Attorney Hunter informed of further developments in the case in the days ahead.

While the Ramsey family plodded through the necessary responsibilities in the investigation of the murder of their daughter, the Boulder Police Department was striving to manage the investigation while dealing with public relations realities.

Over the weekend, Police Commander John Eller defended BPD officers' actions when they first responded to a call about a possible kidnapping that Thursday morning, saying in a *Rocky Mountain News* article that responding officers did not immediately search the Ramseys' home because they "had no reason to believe the child would be in the house at the time."[2]

One experienced police officer in the department not involved in the case later stated that he shuddered at Eller's public comments. Concerns existed about the closeness of the relationship between Commander Eller and BPD Chief Koby, and between Eller and BPD Detective Steve Thomas. Some wondered whether Eller had the experience to handle the case and whether the three Boulder Police Department officers already lacked objectivity about the investigation.

Only two days after JonBenét's body was found, the story of her murder had spread nationally. Outside Colorado on that Saturday, the story was covered in newspapers in Los Angeles, Houston, Miami, Alabama, St. Petersburg, San Jose, New York, Philadelphia, Kansas City and Trenton, New Jersey.[3] There is no accurate accounting available on what television newscasts and radio broadcasts mentioned the murder.

## SUNDAY, DECEMBER 29, 1996

It was Patsy's fortieth birthday, but that wasn't even an afterthought.

"That didn't matter," Patsy would later say. "What mattered was our daughter. How could we ever accept that she was gone?"

The service at St. John's Episcopal Church in Boulder was private. John spoke and wore JonBenét's medal around his neck. After the service, the family flew to Atlanta for the funeral and burial.

In Boulder, turmoil and now hostility continued inside the investigation with relentless scrutiny and finger-pointing in the media about the botched investigation.

In Denver and beyond, confusion reigned from an article published in the *Rocky Mountain News* (January 1, 1997) that contained this information:

"John Ramsey pilots plane to Atlanta for daughter's funeral."

*Rocky Mountain News* reporter Charlie Brennan reported the story in the days after the Ramsey family's trip to Atlanta. Reporters seeking off-the-record reactions to the headline found people who had read the article and thought John Ramsey was a cold, uncaring father focused enough to be able to fly a jet to Atlanta.

This statement, however, was wrong.

John Ramsey didn't fly the plane. He says he was too shocked to even consider piloting a plane. Two pilots working for Lockheed flew it. The company had loaned the Ramseys the corporate jet and pilots for their trip to Atlanta for their daughter's funeral.

In an interview years later, Brennan admitted that he'd made a mistake.

"No reporter ever likes making a mistake, and I regret that it was made . . . It was based on a source, and yet that's one, not two, whose information had been highly reliable in the past, and I had every reason to have faith that the information was accurate in this case, and that's regrettable."

John's Journal:

*We learned that the media frenzy had already begun with the false report that I had piloted my personal jet, I don't have one, back to Atlanta and then accusations in the local Denver hate radio shows that John Andrew, my son, was a suspect even though he was in Atlanta with his mother and sister for Christmas.* (BPD Report #1-752 stated a radio talk show host said that John Andrew had murdered JonBenét.)

## MONDAY, DECEMBER 30, 1996

The last time John and Patsy saw their daughter privately was during a visitation at the funeral home in Atlanta. It was the fourth day after her body had been found. Hundreds of family and friends attended. After the others had left, Patsy, John, Burke, Patsy's parents and two sisters, JonBenét's half-brother and half-sister (John Andrew and Melinda) and John's brother, Jeff, as well as a few other relatives gathered around JonBenét's coffin.

One at a time, they said goodbye. Some of them left a personal remembrance to be put into her casket. Nearly all of them leaned over and whispered special words. And each of them told JonBenét, "I love you."

"She was so small and so was her coffin. I couldn't understand what was happening," John would later recall.

## TUESDAY, DECEMBER 31, 1996

It was now five days after JonBenét's body had been discovered, and this day was the day of her funeral. The same church in which her family had witnessed so much happiness, including her parents' wedding and her own christening, was now reserved for JonBenét's funeral. Her casket, covered with pink roses, sat in front of the mourners at the front of the church. The melody and words of the song "Jesus Loves Me" were accentuated by the sobs of the mourners as they sang before the coffin that held JonBenét's body.

Family in church standing before JonBenét's casket.

# CHAPTER 12

# INTERVIEWS, FORMAL INTERVIEWS AND INTERROGATIONS AND WHY THEY MATTER

VOLUME 1 OF 4
PAGES 1 - 246
JUNE 23RD, 1998
FOR JOHN RAMSEY'S INTERVIEW
THE FOLLOWING WERE PRESENT

**LOU SMIT**
**MIKE KANE**
**BRYAN MORGAN**
**DAVID WILLIAMS**

**Page 0003**

**LOU SMIT: Do you remember how JonBenet was dressed?**

**JOHN RAMSEY: She had on a little top with a silver star on it and a black pair of pants. I don't remember if she had color -- she probably did. I don't remember what color it was.**

LOU SMIT: How about Patsy? How was she dressed?

JOHN RAMSEY: You know I don't remember other than I've looked at pictures of their party and that's my memory. But I couldn't have told you without looking at the pictures.

LOU SMIT: And what did the pictures show?

**Page 0107**

JOHN RAMSEY: I think in the pictures she had like a red Christmas sweater on.

LOU SMIT: These pictures that you have of the party, are these pictures that the police got or were these extra pictures?

JOHN RAMSEY: No, I think they are the ones that the police got. I think they were taken at the White's. I don't think we took any pictures.

LOU SMIT: Okay. Did anybody take any pictures that you know that were at the party?

JOHN RAMSEY: No. Not that I remember.

LOU SMIT: Okay. So you drive to the Walkers, that's the first one. And you were driving, do you remember what the road or weather conditions were like that night?

JOHN RAMSEY: I believe there was no weather because I would've have been concerned because I knew we were flying out the next morning. So I know I wasn't aware of any weather. It wasn't snowing. It was dry. I don't think the drive was bad.

Labeled as an interview when it was an interrogation. The two words were used interchangeably by Boulder Police and the Boulder County District Attorney.

THE RUMORS, SPECULATION AND OPINIONS from those who knew and didn't know what had happened emerged like lightning strikes in a fierce Rocky Mountain storm. So much was developing suddenly, from so many different directions, and with it misinformation deliberately leaked to the media.

## MONDAY, DECEMBER 30, 1996:

According to their own records, police had interviewed Patsy and John multiple times since the murder. Yet that Monday, four days after JonBenét's body had been found, the *Rocky Mountain News* and the *Daily Camera* published inaccurate stories based on false information provided by a Boulder Police Department spokeswoman.

> . . . Police, however, have not interviewed JonBenét's parents, John and Patricia Ramsey. They're still grief-stricken. They're not in any condition to be interviewed, Police Department Spokeswoman Leslie Aaholm said.
>
> *(Rocky Mountain News,* December 30, 1996.)

> They have been in no condition to be interviewed up to this point, she [Boulder Police Department Spokeswoman Leslie Aaholm] said.
>
> *(Daily Camera,* December 30, 1996.)

It was the beginning of a pattern through which most media outlets accepted the word of Boulder Police Department officials without verifying information with the Ramseys or their attorneys. Verifying and double-checking information at that time in the investigation was a difficult thing to do, several reporters who covered the case said. John Ramsey's attorney, Bryan Morgan, "wasn't talking because it was an active investigation," according to one reporter. The Ramseys were also surrounded and protected by their friends. Patsy later recalled, "We hadn't even thought about talking publicly. We were just trying to survive each minute."

With regard to the Ramseys' interactions with the Boulder Police Department, it is important to differentiate between what exactly a police interview involves and how it differs from a formal interview or an interrogation conducted by police. All of these terms—interview, formal interview and interrogation—were used frequently with regard to the Ramsey murder investigation, further contributing to the confusion surrounding the case.

"An interview is a non-accusatory question and answer session with a suspect, victims or witness. The goal of an interview is to gather information."[1] The Ramseys were interviewed several times in the first few days of the investigation by Boulder Police Department investigators.

An "interview" is also a way to gather any information, including behavior, that can be analyzed during and after the interview. According to widely used police protocol, the BPD did "interview" the Ramseys, multiple times, during the first few days of the investigation.

"A formal interview means the investigator's demeanor is non-accusatory and non-judgmental, the interview is conducted in a controlled environment, and the primary interview questions are prepared ahead of time."[2] The "formal interview" reference was used by the Boulder Police Chief in his first news conference in January 1997, when he stated that the family had not been "formally interviewed." But the word used by BPD Spokeswoman Leslie Aaholm on December 30 had been "interviewed." There was a lot of disagreement going on within the Boulder Police Department related to this investigation and how they wanted to present it, but deliberate leaking to the media seemed the winner.

"The purpose of an interrogation is to elicit the truth from a person whom the investigator believes has lied during an interview."[3] The Ramseys were separately "interrogated" by Boulder Police Department officials multiple times beginning in April 1997.

If reporters had been able to check police records, they would have found the following:

- Thursday, December 26, Morning: The officers and two detectives on the scene interviewed Patsy and John periodically and observed them constantly while they were in the Ramsey home. Their interviews were not tape-recorded that morning, because the only tape recorder the detectives had was attached to the home phone in anticipation of the expected ransom call. Officer French, Sergeant Reichenbach, Detective Patterson, Detective Arndt and Commander-Sergeant Whitson all confirmed in their police reports that they spoke with and observed the Ramseys while in the home that day.

- Thursday, December 26, Mid-Morning: Detective Patterson also interviewed Burke Ramsey, the Ramseys' nine-year-old son, at a friend's home, where he had been taken. Burke's words were recorded. Most major police departments have a child expert on stand-by in case a child needs to be interviewed. The Boulder Police Department, however, did not. Whether such an interview is conducted by a child expert or not, the child usually needs to be interviewed as soon as possible because of memory issues. Burke's interview that day was conducted by BPD Detective Fred Patterson without his parents' permission. Yet Detective Patterson's interview and written report listed someone unrelated to the Ramsey family as Burke's grandmother, which was not true. It is not known if Detective Patterson had specifically directed this person to pretend she was Burke's grandmother when she was not or why this was done.

Parental permission is usually obtained in order to help build trust and rapport with the family. It would have caused a problem for the Boulder Police Department, however, if Patsy and John had said no, as was their right, because it would have affected BPD's information gathering.

As part of that interview, Detective Patterson asked Burke about discipline in his family. The boy's response was recorded in another officer's report:

"John and Patsy Ramsey disciplined each of their children by talking to them . . . Burke said there had been no family arguments prior to, nor on, December 25." (Detective Linda Arndt—Date of Report 1-8-1997.)

- Thursday, December 26, Early Afternoon: After JonBenét's body was found, the Boulder Police Department continued to observe and write reports on the family. The hours immediately following the discovery of JonBenét's body represented the most critical time for the police to gather further information, interview, or interrogate, since the Ramseys hadn't yet "lawyered-up" and were willing to talk. John recalls, "At that point, we didn't know what else to do but leave our home and go stay with our friends. We were given no direction by police other than that our home was a crime scene and no one could go back inside."

- Thursday, December 26, Afternoon and Overnight and Friday, December 27 All Day: The observations of the family's behavior had never stopped. Police guarded the Ramseys and wrote reports on their behavior and comments. They also spoke with friends of the Ramseys while observing the family.

- Friday, December 27, Afternoon: John asked if BPD Supervisor Larry Mason would come and talk with him. Sergeant Mason and Detective Arndt arrived and interviewed John. Patsy, according to her doctor, was too medicated to participate. The two officers remained on site for approximately forty minutes. Other Boulder Police Department officers stationed in shifts at the home continued observing the family and writing reports.

- Saturday, December 28, All Day: Officers stationed in the home observed the family members and wrote reports. That afternoon, two detectives interviewed and got basic information from John,

Patsy, John Andrew, Melinda and Burke as they collected DNA from them at the Boulder Sheriff's Department. Everything that a member of the Ramsey family said and did was written in police reports and recorded. Each session lasted about fifteen minutes. The Ramseys agreed to extensive interviews at their friends' home, but their doctor felt Patsy was too ill to go to the Boulder Police Department for a sustained interview/interrogation. Boulder Police Commander Eller refused to interview the Ramseys at the home where they were staying. This was another move with which many experts disagreed. "Interview them anywhere you have a chance to," Detective Lou Smit has said. "Get as much information as soon as you can."

- Saturday, December 28, Early Evening: Melinda and John Andrew were interviewed for approximately two hours each that Saturday after DNA testing at the Boulder Sheriff's Department, and their interviews were recorded.

- Saturday, December 28, Early Evening: Detective Arndt conducted short interviews with and took handwriting samples from John, Patsy and Burke at the home where they were staying with friends.

- Sunday, December 29, Morning: Police remained with the Ramseys constantly until the family left for Atlanta following a memorial service. During this time, officers continued to observe behavior, gather information and write reports related to the Ramseys without the family's attorneys present.

Despite the many times the Ramseys were indeed interviewed by the Boulder Police Department in the first days of the investigation, on Monday, December 30, BPD Spokeswoman Leslie Aaholm stated for the media: "Police have not interviewed JonBenét's parents, John and Patricia Ramsey." This was simply not true.

Chief Koby talked about BPD "interviews" of the Ramseys on January 10, 1997, during his first recorded meeting about the case, which was held with selected members of the media.

"Police have not formally interviewed JonBenét's parents," he said, "but did talk with them immediately after the crime."

A "formal interview" is a one-on-one single interview in a police-controlled environment, which can easily evolve into an "interrogation" when the police are or become suspicious of the individual being questioned. By the time Boulder Police Department officers decided it was time to sit down separately with the Ramseys under controlled circumstances, the Ramsey attorneys had come on board and at that point said "not yet."

Based on standard criteria with regard to interviews as well as formal interviews and interrogations of someone the police suspect has committed a crime, the following list notes accurate and inaccurate information that was released to the public by the Boulder Police Department during the Ramsey murder investigation.

- During the first two weeks after the murder of JonBenét and continuing for several months, the Boulder Police Department stated that "Police have not interviewed the Ramseys." This was false.

- Sixteen days after JonBenét's body was found, when Boulder Police Chief Tom Koby stated in a news conference that "Police have not formally interviewed JonBenét's parents," this was in fact true. The BPD had failed to conduct necessary formal interviews or interrogations of the Ramsey family early that Thursday afternoon on December 26. Instead, the police told the family to leave their home because it was now a crime scene.

- April 30, 1997: The Boulder Police Department announced that "formal interviews" had been scheduled with the Ramseys. This was false. What had been scheduled were "interrogations." Well before this date, Patsy and John Ramsey had been considered suspects in their daughter's murder. On April 18, 1997, Boulder District Attorney Alex Hunter had announced that the Ramseys were "the focus of the investigation." Indeed, investigators had been focused on Patsy and John Ramsey as suspects from the very first day of the investigation. The Ramseys did submit to interrogations by Boulder Police detectives on April 30, 1997.

- On June 23, 1998, approximately 18 months after their daughter was murdered, Patsy and John Ramsey were subjected to what turned into three days of interrogations by the Boulder District Attorney's Office. There seems to be no argument that these were indeed "interrogations."

Why does the terminology matter? Because it's accurate. The parents weren't being interviewed, they were being interrogated. They were suspects and had been since their daughter's body was found.

When the Ramsey defense attorneys first met with John and Patsy about reasonable cooperation with the police, they encountered naiveté from the couple. Both declared in those first few days that they were ready to talk with the police, get involved full-time and do what was asked of them. The Ramseys said that included whatever the police wanted them to do. They didn't know why this might cause them serious problems down the line. "We were innocent," each of them said. John added that the police were welcome to talk with them all they wanted, although he and Patsy had begun to wonder why Boulder Police Department officials hadn't done more of what they'd said they needed to do after JonBenét was found.

The Ramseys' attorneys, however, wouldn't cooperate with what they considered was intimidation and suspicion on the part of BPD detectives. The Saturday after JonBenét's body was found, John's business attorney, Mike Bynum, told the Boulder DA's Office, "No more questioning without an attorney present." Soon after that, John and Patsy finally became convinced that Boulder Police Department officials suspected that one of them had killed their daughter, and were considering no other suspects.

John's Journal:

*This is lost time in finding the real killer.*

The Ramsey homicide was a worldwide breaking news story. Reporters and their editors and the owners of the media outlets that employed them all understood this was a story of immense public interest because it involved everything from beauty, wealth, and child pageant video tapes to a ransom note and a mysterious murder. This story also had the potential of generating considerable amounts of inaccurate information. There was fierce competition among reporters and their media outlets to be first to provide the public with new information about the Ramsey case, and this often led reporters to ignore their responsibility to also be right. In many cases, reporters failed to ensure the accuracy of the information they were reporting due to the immense pressure they faced to be first.

The Ramseys would realize the intense and full-blown interest in their daughter's murder at her memorial service in Boulder and at her funeral in Atlanta.

"There were numerous photographers and cameramen at the church," John would recall, "and later they had to be forced to leave the cemetery grounds, relenting to camp out off the property, but within camera view of the burial site. I walked through our friends and family at the cemetery, unable to realize the enormity that JonBenét was gone. Mixed in was the fact that every move I made I felt was being recorded. Instead of mourning our daughter fully, quietly and completely, we were trying to bury our daughter and they were trying to make money off her death."

"It was a vague haze," Patsy later said. "I was on medication so I could function. I remember the cemetery and the blur of color and noise coming from the media outside the cemetery grounds."

And while Patsy and John Ramsey attended their daughter's funeral that Tuesday, December 31, a Boulder Police spokeswoman put out more false information to the media. BPD Public Information Officer Leslie Aaholm told the *Rocky Mountain News* that blood, hair and handwriting samples had been collected from John and from JonBenét's siblings, "but not from her mother."

> "I assume it's because she is still extremely grief-stricken and not in any condition to be interviewed," Aaholm said.
>
> (*Rocky Mountain News,* December 31, 1996.)

On Wednesday, January 1, the *Daily Camera* in Boulder repeated this inaccurate information about Patsy that had been provided by the Boulder Police Department.

> Police collected blood, hair and handwriting samples from John Ramsey and his children. No samples were collected from Patsy Ramsey.
>
> (*Daily Camera,* January 1, 1997.)

Aaholm did not correctly report that the entire family, including Patsy, had given DNA, handwriting samples and short interviews on Saturday, December 28. On January 2, Boulder Police finally issued a news release saying they "concurred" that Patsy had given blood, hair and handwriting samples the Saturday before. But that was two days after the first of two erroneous newspaper articles had been published based on the false information that an official spokesperson for the police department had provided. In the age of the Internet, those false stories weren't going to end up at the bottom of anyone's bird cage. They had already been reprinted and discussed and they also became topics on cable and radio talk shows. In two short days, they had become facts in the minds of readers, viewers and listeners, and why shouldn't they? The information had come from an official source with the Boulder Police Department.

When recently contacted about these errors and where she had gotten this particular information regarding Patsy Ramsey, Aaholm said, "I don't remember. It was too long ago." She then added, "I am not interested in participating."

Public opinion, which included the opinions of outside law enforcement officers who would later become involved in the Ramsey murder investigation, was being cemented against the Ramseys. Even though John and Patsy had cooperated with authorities, the false messages that the Boulder Police Department continued to present to the public countered this fact and were instead perceived, and eventually believed, to be true.

Also around January 1, 1997, reports in the media attributed to "unnamed sources" began. Most mainstream news organizations require off-the-record information to be confirmed by two or more sources, usually one from each side of an issue. These widely accepted rules were rarely followed in the Ramsey case. The following statement, which was only partially true, provides just one example of how leaks from one side of the story were used to portray the Ramseys poorly: "Authorities also found evidence that the killer may have sexually assaulted the little girl, the source said." (*Rocky Mountain News*, January 1, 1997.)

Blogs and radio talk shows went into a frenzy at the reporting of this news. The first prevailing opinion: John Ramsey had killed his daughter because he had been molesting her.

"Sources" continued to bet that both John and Patsy Ramsey were either involved or knew who was.

The Ramsey murder story had gone national on major evening newscasts within the first week after JonBenét's death. From the start, speculation ran rampant: "Experts say the 'ransom demand is too low and too specific.'" (*NBC Nightly News,* December 31, 1996.)

One newspaper headline called for restraint:

DON'T RUSH TO JUDGEMENT, EXPERTS WARN
(*Daily Camera,* January 1, 1997)

But it was too late.

## CHAPTER 13

# THE FIRST MEDIA INTERVIEW—CNN

Patsy Ramsey with her husband John (not shown) in their first public media interview on January 1, 1996. Courtesy CNN.

## CHRONOLOGY

**Wednesday, January 1, 1997—Ramseys give first public interview to CNN.**

## WEDNESDAY, JANUARY 1, 1997

"WE HAD NO IDEA WE WERE SUSPECTS," John said about the first media interview he and Patsy gave, which was with CNN. "We knew they would have to look at us first because we were immediate family. We didn't know about the threatened refusal to return our daughter's body because our attorneys hadn't told us. They dealt with it because they thought we couldn't handle it then, and they were right. We weren't reading about the case. We knew something about the publicity, but we were concentrating on burying our daughter and the devastation that comes with that. When we did the interview, we were in shock. We really didn't know what we were doing."

Patsy agreed. "We didn't know how the case had already been shaped against us. Our reaction was to help as much as we could. That's what we thought we were doing with the CNN interview. It was hard for us to understand that the police, who were supposed to support us as innocent people, were actually working to arrest us."

The decision to talk with Cable News Network (CNN) wasn't really a decision, both said years later. They just "kind of moved in the direction we were pointed." According to CNN reporter Brian Cabell, who interviewed the Ramseys, the president of CNN had contacted a Ramsey family friend in order to encourage John and Patsy to communicate with the public to help find their daughter's killer and correct misperceptions. At this point, John and Patsy were still operating on the assumption that that's what they were doing, and should do.

Their attorneys, however, had told them not to talk with the media and didn't know about the January 1 interview until it was airing nationally that night on CNN.

Patsy, who was on heavy anti-anxiety medication and tranquilizers at the time of the interview, did not come off well on camera with her halting and disorganized speech. Her eyes didn't seem focused. Her voice ranged from calm to almost hysterical. She did not appear sympathetic, according to some viewers, which created a conundrum due to her normally poised appearance and the fact that she had a beauty pageant background. Others who had watched and were asked their opinions after the interview aired said they wondered if perhaps she was guilty.

According to an expert in photojournalism who has studied people under stress in interviews, there is another perspective that should be considered.

"I always thought Patsy had built a wall, albeit psychologically and unconsciously, when she appeared on camera," said Sonny Hutchison, a partner in High Noon Entertainment, a national television production company. "Every time she faced the glare of cameras, lights and microphones, it was a reminder of her daughter's death and that she had not prevented it. With that weighing on her, how could she possibly let down her guard, raise her eyes and face the world as the person she was?"

The CNN interview didn't quell the initial interest in the Ramseys. It exacerbated it. Television and radio talk show hosts sounded off about the couple's behavior and their answers to questions. Photos and videos of JonBenét in beauty pageants, many of which had been slowed down and had seductive music added, rolled over and over across television screens and dominated newspaper and magazine covers. The glamour, the money, the strange and cruel killing, the ransom note, the inside views being expressed . . . all of this contributed to an explosion of voyeuristic interest and, along with it, satellite and cable television access.

From the media perspective, the Ramsey murder was viewed as a "great story" that was especially helpful for the numerous news shows required to fill a 24-7 news cycles. The mid-1990s—1994, 1995 and 1996—were just the start of the pressure of the 24-7 news week. Human interest stories were always needed. First, there was Susan Smith, who strapped her two children in car seats and drove her car into a lake to drown them. She initially reported them kidnapped and was found guilty in July 1995. In October 1995, football great O.J. Simpson was acquitted in a criminal trial of the brutal murders of his ex-wife and a friend. Those stories had kept the 24-7 cycle going, and now the media managers, reporters and producers were hungry for more. The Ramsey case stepped right up and provided exactly what was needed. It was a story "with legs" in the media vernacular; one that had the ability to keep going and going and going, creating its own momentum.

CNN had done something unusual with the Ramsey interview, especially since it was of such high interest. They'd edited it. Normally, an interview of this magnitude would be broadcast unedited so viewers could watch, hear and dissect every nuance and expression of the people being interviewed.

CNN's Brian Cabell has since said the story was edited because the first ten minutes involved just "getting to know them." "It was edited because we didn't want to use 45 minutes for a sometimes rambling interview," he explained. Cabell covered the story in Atlanta and said, "I knew the story was a pretty big deal."

John felt the editing by CNN had changed the accuracy and total impact of their interview.

John's Journal:

*Media people criticized our interview. She was too emotional.—He wasn't emotional enough. Interestingly, CNN had cut out the part where I wavered with tears and emotion. We stated during the interview that now that we had properly laid JonBenét to rest, we wanted to return to Boulder to help with the investigation. The police had already leaked the false information that we had refused to be interviewed. That wasn't true, but was to be the first of many lies told by the police department in unofficial leaks to the press.*

During the interview, Patsy made the statement:

> There is a killer on the loose. I don't know who it is. I don't know if it's a he or a she. But if I were a resident of Boulder, I would tell my friends to keep your babies close to you.
>
> (*CNN*, January 1, 1997)

Over the next few days, reactions from Boulder officials were swift, dismissive and accusatory:

Boulder Police Chief Tom Koby:

> That's not rocket science . . . There is a person who is responsible for a homicide and who has not been apprehended.
>
> (*Daily Camera*, January 2, 1997)

Boulder Mayor Leslie Durgin, held a nationally televised press conference related to the Ramsey case on Friday, January 3:

> It's not like there is someone walking around the streets of Boulder prepared to strangle young children.
>
> (*Daily Camera,* January 3, 1997)

> There was no forced entry into the house. The person who did it apparently knew the house. That does not imply to me a random act.
>
> (*Rocky Mountain News,* January 3, 1997)

> People in Boulder have no reason to fear there is someone wandering the streets of Boulder looking for someone to attack. Boulder is safe, she said. Boulder is a safe community and will continue to be.
>
> (*Rocky Mountain News,* January 4, 1997)

Similar messages from Boulder officials were also communicated to the public by the media in headlines and statements such as these:

> NO NEED TO WORRY ABOUT KILLER ON THE LOOSE, COPS AND MAYOR SAY
>
> (*Rocky Mountain News*, January 3, 1997)

> No reason for alarm for residents of Boulder.
>
> (*CBS*, January 3, 1997)

> No killer lurking in the streets . . . No signs of forced entry, according to Boulder Police.
>
> (*CNN*, January 4, 1997)

John's Journal:

*It was the start of what was going to develop into a media fabrication of who we were that was fed by police leaks and foolish statements by Boulder's pinheaded mayor, Leslie Durgin.*

The JonBenét Ramsey Murder Book Index provides stark examples that show the mayor and Boulder Police Department were wrong or not being honest about there being no forced entry or access into the Ramsey home on Christmas Day and night, 1996. There are at least 100 windows in the home. More than half opened to the outside. The locks on them were mostly twist-type locks which, according to police, can easily be opened.

One door on the third floor of the Ramsey home opened to the outside. Two doors on the second floor opened to the outside. Six doors on the main floor opened to the outside, plus one more door opened into the garage. The total: ten doors opened to the outside in the Ramsey home, if you included the door from the home into the garage. More than eight areas of possible entry were discovered, including the solarium door, the broken basement window with the suitcase under it and the northeast basement bathroom window.

Window lock.

From the JonBenét Ramsey Murder Book Index:

"Solarium door (facing south): fresh pry mark damage near the dead bolt appeared to be two or three separate and distinct areas of attack. The 'missing wood chips' were not located in the vicinity of the door." (BPD Report #1-59.)

"Living room: three-paned window; a wreath covered the middle pane, which was unlocked but closed. An extension cord ran between the window and its frame and led to the outside." (BPD Report #1-59.)

"Formal dining room: the middle panes of the eastern- and western-most windows were both closed but unlocked. Statue and flower arrangements were in front of these windows, which prevented the windows from being opened." (BPD Report #1-59.)

"French door along the west wall: no signs of forced entry to the door, which was ajar." (BPD Report # 1-59.)

"South rear residence door northwest of the grate: the exterior screen door appeared to have damage in the area of the handle lock consistent with the door being forced open with the lock engaged. It looked like the force supplied to the lock mechanism came from the inside out. No pry marks on the exterior." (BPD Report #1-59.) The pry marks on this door had been pointed out to Patsy Ramsey the summer before, according to a family friend, but there is no indication in the archive as to whether there were both recent and older pry marks.

"Butler kitchen entrance: non-opening windows are located on either side of the door. No forced entry observed at this location." There was no forced entry, but an excerpt from interviews with two witnesses state the door was open. When John's friend arrived at the Ramsey home at 6:01 a.m., he "found the butler kitchen door standing open about one foot while it was still dark outside and before the evidence team or Det. Arndt arrived." (BPD Report #1-1490, BPD Report # 1-1315.) The time noted was 6 a.m., so it was one of the first things the friend noticed. At 8 a.m., a neighbor whose home was just to the north of the Ramsey home "got up and observed a basement door leading into a kitchen area was standing wide open." (BPD Report 1-100, Source.) In another report, the same neighbor "said that this door was approximately 1/3 of the way open when he saw it." Since there was no basement door on the north side of the house (or any other side of the house) that opened to the outside, it is understood that this was the same butler kitchen door the family friend noticed was partially open at 6 a.m. . . . and told police about. (Source: JonBenét Ramsey Murder Book Index.)

"Northeast basement bath: two areas on the bottom frame were clear of dust. The impressions were consistent with the application of fingers to the area. The associated area inside the residence showed smudge marks on both walls above and just south of the toilet. A piece of garland similar to that found in the wine cellar [storage area where the child's body was found] was found stuck to the wall in the east impression." (BPD #1-59.) The garland had decorated the spiral staircase from the first floor to the second.

"Metal grate: below the broken basement window directly under the grate were observed leaves and other exterior debris." (BPD Report #1-61.)

The information about the open doors and possible forced entries was never publicly released in its entirety. What was written in the first police reports and leaked to the media and published repeatedly was "No forced entry," which was not accurate. Even today, some reporters familiar with the case say they weren't aware there was any evidence of forced entry into the home.

I interviewed former Boulder Mayor Leslie Durgin in June 2010 about her misstatements about "no forced entry" at the Ramsey home.

"The comments were innocent," Durgin said. "I was not being fed information from Police Chief Koby about the case."

"We had an agreement that he would not give me information that the full city council did not have," Durgin told me in a later interview. "The comments were to calm the fears and try to quell some of the media hysteria in the community. There was a slight drumbeat that there was a killer in Boulder stalking young children, and I wanted to send the message there wasn't."

Yet in a 1999 documentary, which aired on various cable and network television stations in the U.S. and in Britain, Durgin said she regularly consulted with Chief Koby, and specifically cleared her statement there was not a killer on the loose with him.

From *The Case of JonBenét—The Ramseys vs. the Media*, (1999 Documentary):

> Mayor Leslie Durgin: It was done in large part to allay the fears of the children in our community and to let people know that the information that I had at the time was that we did not have some crazed person wandering the streets of University Hill.
>
> Interviewer: And who did you clear it with?
>
> Mayor Leslie Durgin: The police chief.

But how could she have known that there wasn't a killer in Boulder stalking young children?

## SATURDAY, JANUARY 4, 1997

District Attorney Alex Hunter returned from his Hawaiian vacation and "couldn't understand the atmosphere in Boulder and the media attention." He told a few confidants that maybe he should have come back to Boulder earlier.

Meanwhile, more stories were published or broadcast that involved information acquired from quoted "sources."

> CLUES: NOTE WRITTEN IN HOUSE: PAPER MATCHES PAD IN RAMSEY HOME
>
> (*The Denver Post,* January 4, 1997)

This information was only partially correct and was detrimental to the Ramseys. Only the killer knew whether the note had been written in the home or not. And yet the story also ran in the *Daily Camera* and the *Rocky Mountain News* and on *NBC Nightly News.* The consistency of the leaks that contributed to public suspicions of the Ramseys continued.

> Boulder, Colorado police say there are new and disturbing clues.
>
> (*CBS Evening News,* January 4, 1997)

The Ramsey story was reported for sixteen consecutive days on all of the four then-dominant national evening newscasts: ABC, CBS, CNN, and NBC.[1] National, international and local newscasts continued to report on the story for years after.

## JANUARY 5, 1997

Ten days after JonBenét's body was found, the *Daily Camera* in Boulder summed up the status of the case based on a few details that had been publicly released and on a lot of leaked information from unnamed sources. The story provided significant insights into how some detectives on the case were thinking:

> Sources say the investigation is tightly focused on the home, and that key events associated with the murder appear to have taken place in the home.
>
> Police and city of Boulder spokespeople repeatedly have told residents of the city there is no cause to worry that a killer is on the street.
>
> The ransom note appears to have been handwritten inside the house, on paper taken from a pad in the house, casting doubts on whether it was a premeditated crime. Writing in the first portion of the note has been described as "shaky," then improving.
>
> Questions linger about the methods of the alleged kidnappers: Why kill the girl before giving the Ramseys an opportunity to meet ransom demands? Why not remove the girl from the house? Why request the relatively paltry sum of $118,000? Boulder police sent five detectives to Roswell, Ga., to interview friends and family members of the Ramseys.
>
> Police were not casting a "wide net for suspects."

The Ramsey attorneys, stating that they couldn't handle the onslaught of requests from the media for information, hired a media consultant. The media consultant was quickly labeled a "paid spokesman," "publicity relations manager" and a "spin doctor" in the ensuing weeks of reporting. This was an untenable situation, according to a well-known defense attorney in Denver, in which the media used the Ramsey lawyers' response to its own demands to further condemn the family.

# CHAPTER 14
# MANIPULATING THE MEDIA

Q. Let me ask you about that. How many cases have you been involved in where you were analyzing the demeanor and conduct of parents who had a child found murdered in their home; what was your experience in that type of a case?

A. None.

Q. Do you have any experience, formal training, in how psychologically or otherwise one expects a parent to grieve when a child has been murdered?

A. No.

Deposition with testimony of former Boulder Detective Steve Thomas.

IN JANUARY 2007, Special Counsel to the Los Angeles County District Attorney Devallis Rutledge wrote an article for *Police* magazine entitled "The Lawful Use of Deception: Sometimes you have to resort to trickery to get confessions from suspects." In that article, Rutledge said, "It might be nice if law enforcement officers never had to lie to a criminal suspect in order to solve a crime . . . Unfortunately, the reality is otherwise."

Rutledge then noted that the US Supreme Court has repeatedly supported the use of deception in criminal investigative work and quoted the following statements from two Supreme Court rulings: "'Criminal activity is such that stealth and strategy are necessary weapons in the arsenal of the police officer.' (*Sorrells v. U.S.*)."

"'Nor will the mere fact of deceit defeat a prosecution, for there are circumstances when the use of deceit is the only practicable law enforcement technique available.' (*U.S. v. Russell*)."

In other cases noted in the article, the Supreme Court has ruled that it is acceptable for police to falsely tell a suspect he has been implicated by his accomplice in a crime; use an informant to set up a drug sale between an undercover agent and a suspect; and tell a suspect his fingerprints have been found at a crime scene. As Rutledge stated, "The general rule is that deception can be used as long as it is not likely to induce an innocent person to commit a crime or to confess to a crime that he or she did not commit."

While such use of deception in police work may be considered by many to be necessary, during the Ramsey murder investigation, the Boulder Police Department used deception in a different way.

A former FBI profiler consulted by the Boulder Police Department developed the idea, and the blueprint of attack was simple and insidious. The first step was to turn media attention away from what had been called "the bungled investigation." The second step was to convict the Ramseys in the press. The plan was to put pressure on John and Patsy by leaking information, accurate or not, to the media, which was desperate to feed the voracious public appetite for details about the brutally murdered child beauty queen.

The practice of leaking information to favored reporters is a shopworn method law enforcement uses for one of two possible reasons: to get correct information out or to put a certain slant on a story. Reporters work hard to develop trust with a source or two within law enforcement so they, too, can get the inside story, and they sometimes maintain a relationship with a source for years. But reporters have a responsibility to double-source, or talk with sources from opposing sides of an issue, in order to verify that the information they present to the public is accurate. During the investigation of the murder of JonBenét Ramsey, that was hardly ever done.

Hundreds of journalists were pursuing the story. Every leaked morsel of information—and many of those tidbits were either blatantly wrong or maliciously misleading—spread across the media universe with unparalleled speed.

Just as the Boulder Police Department completely blew the early stages of the investigation of the Ramsey murder, the mainstream media, for the most part, was far from experiencing its finest hour. JonBenét's sordid death sold print copies and air time in the same way that the upcoming death of Princess Diana, in August 1997, would. After Diana's tragic accident, John Ramsey wrote about her death in his journal:

John's Journal:

> *We are shocked and saddened along with the rest of the world to learn of Princess Diana's death over the weekend . . . I think we have particular empathy because we have been pursued for months by the tabloids stalking us.*

Three Boulder law enforcement officers on the Ramsey case later confirmed the "deliberate and misleading leaking strategy." They were there when the strategy was being developed, but they won't allow their names to be used for fear of repercussions. The name of the FBI agent who is alleged to have developed the active "manipulation" protocol put into effect in late December 1996 is also not being used in this book. In a phone conversation, he denied to me that he had developed the strategy, saying, "I would never leak on an active case."

More details about the early plan to manipulate the media in relation to JonBenét's murder were revealed in a transcript from a civil lawsuit against the Ramseys in September 2001. That defamation lawsuit, *Wolf v. Ramsey*, was filed by a man who thought the Ramseys had defamed him because they had called him a potential suspect in their book.

During the deposition phase of the lawsuit, former Boulder Detective Steve Thomas testified while under oath. He had worked on the Ramsey murder case before resigning from the Boulder Police Department in August 1998.[1] Ramsey civil attorney Lin Wood questioned Thomas in the deposition about the BPD strategy of using the media:

WOOD: Was there any plan or strategy on the part of [the] Boulder Police Department or any other law enforcement agencies to try to put pressure on the Ramseys through the public?

THOMAS: I think so.

WOOD: And isn't it true that [retired Colorado Springs and El Paso County, Colorado Homicide Detective] Lou Smit's approach to build a bridge with the Ramseys really was in conflict with the Boulder Police Department's strategy of putting public pressure on them?

THOMAS: Yes.

WOOD: And the FBI was involved . . .

THOMAS: . . . I believe there were discussions with the FBI, yes, about how to exert some public pressure on people who are not cooperating, yes.

WOOD: Part of that was to try to portray [the Ramseys] clearly to the public as being uncooperative and therefore appearing to be possibly involved in the death of their daughter, right?

THOMAS: I think it was two different things. I don't think they were necessarily trying to further paint them as uncooperative. I think they were using the media to get them back in to help us with the case.

WOOD: Were they also thinking that they might use the media to apply pressure so that there might be a possibility that one of the parents might confess involvement in the crime? Was that ever discussed?

THOMAS: That may have been—that may have been some motivations.

WOOD: Do you believe from your recollections that that was discussed?

THOMAS: I wouldn't disagree with it. I don't have any concise, clear recollection of a conversation like that.

The judge reviewing the depositions in the *Wolf v. Ramsey* lawsuit, Federal Judge Julie Carnes, supported the evidence of a stated plan to manipulate the media when she dismissed the case before trial and issued a written 93-page summary statement. As part of the March 2003 statement, Judge Carnes wrote:

> Pursuant to the FBI's suggestions that the Boulder Police publicly name defendants as subjects and apply intense media pressure to them so that they would confess to the crime, the police released many statements that implied defendants were guilty and were no longer cooperating with police.

Here is a sampling of what was published or broadcast during the week after JonBenét's murder, all of which supports Judge Carnes's written statement:

**Friday, Dec. 27, 1996**—Assistant Boulder District Attorney Bill Wise is quoted by the *Rocky Mountain News* as saying, "It's not adding up." Wise should have elaborated on this comment. What wasn't adding up? The reporter who wrote this article also should have asked the question, and included the answer.

**Monday, Dec. 30, 1996**—False statements related to the Ramseys not having been interviewed early in the investigation by the Boulder Police Department: "Police, however, have not interviewed JonBenét's parents, John and Patricia Ramsey. 'They're still very grief-stricken. They're not in any condition to be interviewed,' Police Department spokeswoman Leslie Aaholm said."

(*Rocky Mountain News*)

"Police . . . have not interviewed the girl's parents, . . . " Aaholm said. "'They have been in no condition to be interviewed up to this point.'"

(*Daily Camera*)

**Tuesday, Dec. 31, 1996 and Wednesday, January 1, 1997**—False statements published in three separate articles in the *Daily Camera* related to whether DNA samples had been collected from Patsy Ramsey by the BPD:

"Police would not comment on when the Ramseys will return to Boulder or when, or if, they plan to take samples from Patsy Ramsey."

"No samples were collected from Patsy Ramsey."

"Police have taken blood and hair samples from all family members except JonBenét's mother, Patsy Ramsey, who police said was too distraught to give the samples."

**Tuesday, Dec. 31, 1996**—"Experts say 'ransom demand too low and too specific.'"—Statement aired on *NBC Nightly News* that was accompanied by no statistics to back up this claim.

**Wednesday, Jan. 1, 1997**—"John Ramsey is a pilot, and the family traveled to Georgia in his plane." False statement published in the *Rocky Mountain News* that led the public to believe John Ramsey had flown his family in his plane to Georgia for his daughter's funeral. The family traveled to Georgia for JonBenét's funeral on a Lockheed plane flown by Lockheed pilots.

In response to the January 1, 1997, Ramsey CNN interview, during which Patsy said, "There's a killer on the loose," the following reactions were published and broadcast by the media:

**Friday, Jan. 3, 1997**—Boulder Mayor Leslie Durgin told the *Daily Camera*: "It's not like there is someone walking around the streets of Boulder prepared to strangle young children." What evidence had been collected relative to the Ramsey case that would have allowed anyone in a position of authority to make this statement?

**Friday, Jan. 3, 1997**—According to a *Rocky Mountain News* headline, Boulder "cops and mayor" have stated there is "no need to worry about killer on loose." How could they have been certain of this? Why did they continue saying this? What evidence had been collected to support such a statement?

**Friday, Jan. 3, 1997**—CNN reported in a story about the Ramsey murder the false statement by Boulder Mayor Leslie Durgin that "there were 'no visible signs of forced entry in the house' where JonBenét was found dead."

**Saturday, Jan. 4, 1997**—*The Denver Post* reported with apparent certainty that the Ramsey ransom note had been "written in house," even though no proof to support this claim had been collected. In fact, the location in which the ransom note was written—a key element related to whether there was premeditation involved in the murder—has never been determined.

According to those inside the investigation, the Boulder Police Department quickly began to operate under the presumption that if they put enough pressure on the Ramseys, Patsy and John would break and turn against each other. The media—and then the public—fell quickly into line, creating an uproar around the case.

One law enforcement person who worked on the case said, in looking back, "Little consideration was given by those in charge as to whether or not the Ramseys were innocent or the inevitability of the family being tainted for the rest of their lives by a barrage of erroneous information published by the media. In the minds of many readers, viewers, outside law enforcement and even reporters, the Ramseys were involved in the death of their daughter; it was that simple."

When a case has reached the courts, leaks to the media can be stopped through a court-issued decree called a gag order. A gag order applies court-ordered penalties to all officers of the court and witnesses in order to prohibit them from talking to the media and help ensure a defendant gets a fair trial. Gag orders are used in notorious cases.

Boulder District Attorney Alex Hunter couldn't have gotten a gag order through a trial judge for the Ramsey murder case because there hadn't been any arrests that might have led to a criminal trial.

Contributing to the turmoil and perceived lack of accountability related to the Ramsey murder case was the type of government in effect in Boulder at the time, a council-manager (also known as a "weak-mayor") form of government. Floyd Ciruli of Ciruli Associates, a political consultant in Denver, says, "The weak-mayor form of government, which is typically the council manager form of government, was developed at the turn of the early 1900s as part of a reform movement and part of increased municipal control of government. It was an answer to the strong-mayor form of government when sometimes the strong mayor system became corrupt.

"The downside to weak-mayor government is that the power is extremely diffuse. Whether you are a constituent or a member of the media, it is often difficult to make any one individual accountable. There is no one location or . . . individual in complete control. The city manager has control of employees and hires the police chief. The council, which is elected, hires the city manager and therefore has control of the city manager, but can't order the city manager what to do. The mayor is mostly ceremonial and selected by the city council. If anyone in the government doesn't want to cooperate, it is impossible to make them."

That diffused accountability within the ranks of the Boulder city government led most reporters to rely on unnamed sourcing in order to gather information related to the Ramsey murder case.

The following statement from a confidential defense memo underscored the attitude of the Boulder Police Department related to the Ramsey murder case: "[I]f you don't hate the Ramsey's [sic] a lot, then you are not a good team player."[2] Supporting the Ramseys in any way was considered a very poor career move within the Boulder Police Department at that time, according to Lou Smit, a retired detective who'd worked on the Ramsey case and eventually changed his initial opinion that the Ramseys were guilty. After analyzing the related police reports on a daily basis, Smit has said, he came to the conclusion that the Ramseys were innocent.

Less than a week after JonBenét's death, the Boulder commander of the investigation, John Eller, contacted a business in Colorado Springs that put cases together for computer courtroom presentations. One of the owners of the business, Ollie Grey, a law enforcement officer with homicide experience, said he met with Eller and with a district attorney and police personnel at that time. Eller told the business owners he wanted to hire the company to help put together a case for court. Their suspects, Eller told Grey, were "the Ramseys."

Grey told Eller, "Let's look at the evidence." But according to Grey it became clear after several meetings that the Boulder Police Department had no physical evidence to support their theory that the Ramseys were guilty in the murder of their daughter. He added that there wasn't anything his company could have utilized to move forward in preparing a trial presentation related to the case.

Meanwhile, leaks from various sources continued to make headlines:

> **Wednesday, Jan. 8, 1997**—"2nd Note Found in Ramsey Residence"—Misleading headline run in *The Denver Post* with a story that, quoting sources, said the second note "could be a draft of the ransom note . . ." The article was accurate in that it referred to the partially finished greeting for the ransom note, "Dear Mr. & /," that had been written on Patsy's notepad and found in the home on Thursday, December 26—the day JonBenét's body was also found. What was wrong with the article was it assumed the note had been written in the home, and no one but the killer knows where the note was written. It could have been written at an earlier time somewhere else. The leak cast suspicion on the Ramseys and was reported in the *Rocky Mountain News* and the *Daily Camera* and on *CBS Evening News.*

"It's a mystery to me how it got so sideways," Patsy's attorney, Pat Burke, has said. "I think the media does have so much control over what happens in daily life in America . . . I think it influenced the wretched behavior of the Boulder Police Department. I think it was sad. And I'm very upset that Patsy went to her grave with people still thinking she had something to do with the death of her daughter."

Susan Stine, with whom the Ramseys lived during the first months after JonBenét's murder, since then has discussed the animosity displayed toward the Ramsey family by certain Boulder Police Department officials. In the spring of 1997, Stine and her neighbors called the BPD to complain about members of the media harassing their children at a neighborhood school bus stop. While several Boulder patrol officers helped in this situation, they told Stine that they were risking their jobs to do it. Two officers told Stine that they had been ordered not to help the Ramseys and their friends, and that this order had come "from the top," i.e., from the Boulder police chief and the Boulder city attorney. Neither official has responded to requests for information about that order.

Bryan Morgan, John Ramsey's attorney and a Boulder resident, is still appalled by the behavior of the Boulder Police Department during the Ramsey investigation. "With all the indicators, the hard evidence that pointed outside," Morgan has said, "they tried to railroad these people. When people in a position of power act like that, all of our liberties are at risk. They were frighteningly and terrifyingly unprofessional."

While speculation circled related to the murder of six-year-old JonBenét Ramsey, an awful reality had shifted into full motion. On Wednesday, January 8, in a quiet area of Boulder County, nine-year-old Burke Ramsey, JonBenét's brother, underwent a mandatory Colorado Department of Social Services Boulder Child Protection Team interview.[3] Boulder detectives, Social Services staff, attorneys for the prosecution, and Pat Burke (Patsy's lawyer) watched the interview from behind a one-way mirror. Patsy had brought her son to the department's Child and Family Advocacy Center, but was not allowed to watch the interview, which is not unusual. The location for the interview had been chosen by Boulder Police Department Commander John Eller. Child psychologist, Dr. Suzanne Bernhard from Boulder, was chosen by the Boulder County Department of Social Services/Human Services. She interviewed Burke.

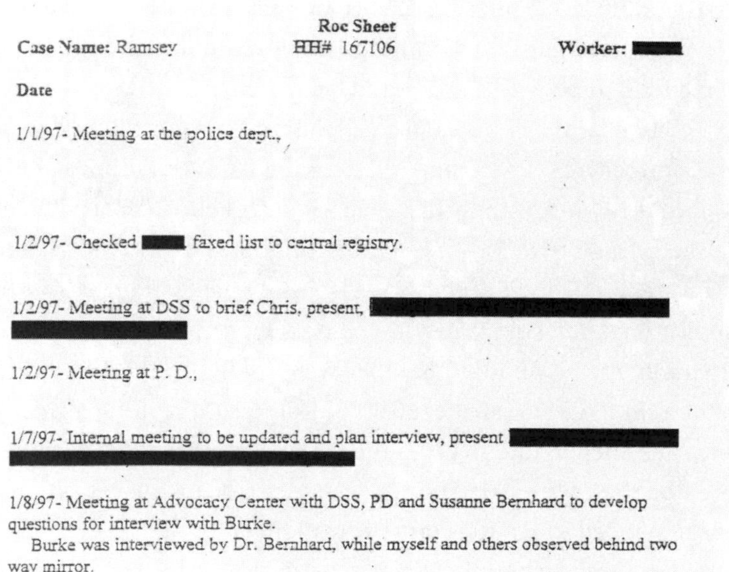

**Roc Sheet**

**Case Name:** Ramsey HH# 167106 **Worker:** [redacted]

**Date**

1/1/97- Meeting at the police dept.,

1/2/97- Checked [redacted] faxed list to central registry.

1/2/97- Meeting at DSS to brief Chris, present, [redacted]

1/2/97- Meeting at P. D.,

1/7/97- Internal meeting to be updated and plan interview, present [redacted]

1/8/97- Meeting at Advocacy Center with DSS, PD and Susanne Bernhard to develop questions for interview with Burke.

Burke was interviewed by Dr. Bernhard, while myself and others observed behind two way mirror.

Notes regarding planning for Burke Ramsey's interview by Boulder Social Services.

Following quotes are from portions of Dr. Suzanne Bernhard's Interview—Boulder Department of Social Services "Evaluation of the Child" report on Burke Ramsey—January 8, 1997:

> The parents refused to allow DSS [Department of Social Services] and the police to interview Burke. They agreed that Burke could be interviewed as long as a psychologist conducted it.
>
> Although Burke is just shy of his tenth birthday, he appears younger than his years. Initially he was rather reserved and then later "warmed up'" during the interview. He was articulate and bright. His answers to questions were rather brief, as he did not elaborate. It was clear that the parents did not discuss with him how JonBenét died. Burke stated that "she was probably stabbed with a knife." At one point in the interview, Burke described a nightmare he has had since his sister's death. Burke said he had a dream that he and his mother were tied up and a big axe was above them, swinging back and forth above them, getting closer and closer, "like it was going to cut us in half."

Dr. Bernhard talked with Burke Ramsey about his relationships in the family:

"When asked, Burke said he didn't think he received any more or less attention than JonBenét."

"He wants to be a pilot like his dad. His dad works long hours and his mom takes care of him."

"Reportedly both JonBenét and Burke were bedwetters, but during the interview Burke denied that he had a problem with wetting the bed."

"Burke also denied any sexual touch between him and his family members."

From the psychologist: "I reviewed both JonBenét and Burke's medical records. Their pediatrician is Dr. Beuf. The medical records did not indicate any history of abuse of either child."

The interview with Burke elicited a strong opinion about any possible involvement the brother may have had in his sister's death and was included in the Human Services "Evaluation of the Child" report: "From the interview it is clear that Burke was not a witness to JonBenét's death. He does not appear fearful at home. However, he seems somewhat disconnected and isolated in his family. According to Dr. Bernhard, it seems as though Burke has not begun to grieve his sister's death."

Two weeks after JonBenét's death, in his first public question-and-answer session with the media in which he met with five selected reporters, Boulder Police Department Chief Tom Koby defended his department's investigation of the Ramsey murder case with some startling statements. His department had come under scrutiny for the way the investigation was being handled. The *Rocky Mountain News* published a related article on January 10, 1997 that featured the following headline and direct quotes from Koby:

> I've been in communication with police personnel around the country and most legal experts will tell you we've done it just right.
>
> There is nothing that's been done either by us or the Ramsey family that is out of order.

The article also stated that, according to Koby, BPD "detectives do not consider the Ramseys' decision to hire attorneys incriminating," and "to insinuate the girl's parents are guilty . . . 'is totally unfair.'"

That comment by Koby contradicted what his commander on the case, and some of his detectives, were telling reporters "off the record" about the Ramseys hiring attorneys.

Boulder District Attorney Alex Hunter had watched the Koby news conference on television. He and Koby were good friends, but the police chief's "we've done it just right" statement unsettled Hunter. There were also several editorials published in local newspapers that disagreed with the "we've done it just right" statement. Hunter had been fortunate in his several terms in office to have good media relations and few controversial cases in his county. He had been hopeful that Koby's news conference would help him out as well. But by the end of the news conference, he did not think it had gone well at all.

"The police were still keeping quiet officially and denying the obvious," he would later state. "I decided I needed to attempt to talk more to the reporters and keep up good relations."

Within weeks, Hunter was meeting with mainstream reporters, tabloid reporters, even the editor of the *Globe* tabloid.

"I was very careful not to tell the media specifics on the case," Hunter said. "I needed to try to handle the media better and get to know them on a personal basis so I knew who I could trust and who I didn't. That's one of the reasons I did it." He also enjoyed the celebrity, according to someone in his office who spoke on the condition of anonymity.

Ramsey attorney Hal Haddon has said, "Alex's biggest mistakes on the case were he tried to be all things to all people. He could have taken control of it early on by putting this grand jury on and that would have had the effect of controlling the police, controlling the rumors that became endemic in the case. Which would have put him in charge. But it ended up that nobody was in charge. The police envisioned they were in charge. The prosecutors thought they were in charge. They worked at cross purposes."

By state statute in Colorado, the chief law enforcement officer in a judicial district is the district attorney. This meant Hunter should have been in charge of the Ramsey murder case. His leadership in the case was so lacking, however, that he was criticized publicly in multiple media editorials for "not taking charge."

Hunter was Boulder County's District Attorney for seven terms for a total of twenty-eight years. He looked like the ideal grandfather, was charming in a politician's way and his "Aw, shucks" persona worked in Boulder. It did not, however, work in national news conferences with their unrelenting focus. Hunter could be temperamental, but those in his office at the time have suggested he might have behaved that way for show. He fretted over the Ramsey media coverage and how it portrayed his office and the Boulder Police Department, yet wasn't sure what he should do to correct it other than to visit more with reporters in order to promote "good will." During all his years in office, Hunter was considered a hands-off district attorney who let others in the office handle day-to-day operations while he dealt with politics.

"He rarely came to the office," said one of his colleagues, "until the Ramsey case. Then he was here nearly every day. At his very core, during those many years in office, he was a politician."

Within a few weeks of Koby's news conference, Hunter found out that the Ramsey case commander and his detectives were not sharing forensic results from the Colorado Bureau of Investigation, including the DNA report from JonBenét's body, with his office. Hunter went from being temperamental to furious. The Colorado Bureau of Investigation, which was analyzing the reports, agreed to copy Hunter's office on the reports they had analyzed for the BPD, but having to resolve such difficulties between two agencies that should have been working together took more time away from the investigation. The situation also underscored the difficulties that existed between the Boulder District Attorney's Office and the Boulder Police Department.

Although most police agencies share investigative material with their county's district attorney's office, according to homicide experts, they are not obligated to do so until a case is offered for criminal filing or another criminal proceeding. Sharing information, experts say, however, is the best practice.

By this stage in the Ramsey murder investigation, the manipulators had become the manipulated. The Boulder Police Department and the Boulder District Attorney's office were actively using and trying to control each other, while both were manipulating the media. Also by this point, the Ramsey attorneys had become aware they needed to get involved and fight back using the media.

# JONBENÉT

JonBenét and Burke on his birthday. © John Ramsey

JonBenét on bicycle. © John Ramsey.

JonBenét taking piano lessons. © John Ramsey.

© John Ramsey.

© John Ramsey.

Family on Fourth of July in Michigan. © John Ramsey.

Last photo John Ramsey took of his daughter. It's on Christmas Day after the family had finished opening Christmas presents. JonBenét and her mom were relaxing together. This is approximately fourteen hours before she was killed. © John Ramsey.

## CHAPTER 15

# CHILD BEAUTY PAGEANTS

The contrast between JonBenét, the pageant contestant and JonBenét, the little girl throwing rocks into the lake. © John Ramsey

CHILD BEAUTY PAGEANT PHOTOS AND VIDEO became the criminal record the Ramseys didn't have.

Initial shock at the murder of a child was quickly overridden with broadcasts of the pageants of the dead girl. According to then-Adams County District Attorney Bob Grant, who was asked in 1997 by Colorado Governor Roy Romer to become involved in the Ramsey murder investigation, "Those tapes caught fire and people rose to that publicity bait like hungry jackals. Those in the case and on the periphery. Anyone who was seeking a moment of media spotlight or wanted to be a hero. It was a call of 'all aboard' and there was a scramble to see who could be the most important. The investigation was competing with that."

Five days after JonBenét's body was discovered, her child pageant videos and still photographs were shown nationally by NBC and CBS on their evening newscasts. Two days later and a week after her body had been found, the videos and photos were broadcast again on January 2 by NBC and CBS. ABC began using JonBenét's child pageant videos on January 3 and CNN on January 5. From then on, all four national newscasts used the pageant videos and photos of JonBenét in some format nearly continuously for weeks. Local television stations throughout the country got the JonBenét pageant videos and photos from their national affiliates. Photographers who had originally recorded the videos and shot the photos sold them to the media. The Ramsey family did not own any of these rights, nor provide any of the videos or photos.

"Pageants were put on trial," Betsi Grabe, PhD, a professor of Mass Communications at Indiana University-Bloomington, who studies the effects of news images on public opinion, has said. "If pageants were evil, then who is putting these children into them? The parents. That made them bad parents. The Ramseys were made into 'look what they made their child do.' Then you can make the next step in their guilt. It's a very slippery slope, especially when the video of JonBenét is playing over and over and over on television."

The underlying apprehension and, in some cases, rage that others possessed regarding John—and especially Patsy—Ramsey were soon on full display. In private conversations and very public radio talk shows, the public demanded to know why a parent would subject their child to the demands of the beauty pageant circuit. "Isn't there enough pressure in children's lives already?" people asked. "What kind of lesson does a child learn when they earn success based on how they look?"

The answers did not give a caring portrait of the Ramseys as parents. According to NewsLibrary.com, more than 125 negative articles were written and published throughout the country on child beauty pageants in January and February 1997. At least twice that number referred to JonBenét Ramsey as the "murdered child beauty queen." The *Kansas City Star* ran an editorial on January 19, 1997, about John and Patsy entitled "Pillars of a community? These parents are creeps."

According to Hilary Levey Friedman, PhD, a Harvard sociologist who has studied child beauty pageants as well as JonBenét Ramsey's involvement in pageants, "This combination of wealth, attractiveness, the mystery of the murder and then the child beauty pageant angle made [the Ramsey murder investigation] a national and international story. The child pageants weren't something that people were very aware of until JonBenét's murder. Their reactions to what they saw on television were that the child pageants were extreme and crazy."

Patsy had represented West Virginia in the Miss America Pageant, entering the pageant when she was in college and winning an award on the national level for dramatic interpretation. She had been in pageants growing up, and her mother had been a big part of this experience with her. "It was fun and we got very close to each other," Patsy would later say.

JonBenét was first exposed to pageants in 1993 when Patsy was invited to host a Miss West Virginia Pageant and brought her family with her. Patsy also performed a song at the event. It was after this pageant that JonBenét told Patsy she wanted to dress up and dance and perform "like you do, Mom."

Jeff Ramsey, John's brother, remembers a family talk during which Patsy asked others about whether JonBenét should be allowed to be in pageants at so young an age. Patsy had started in pageants when she was older than her daughter, who was three at the time. Patsy was reluctant about it, Jeff said, but they all agreed it would be fine for JonBenét to enroll in singing and dancing lessons. What started as singing and dancing lessons soon evolved into pageants.

"Once she made up her mind to do something, she was very committed," Patsy later explained. "I can assure you if Johnnie-Bee didn't want to do something, she simply wouldn't. The pageants were another bonding experience for us." At home, JonBenét and her girlfriends would play a game of presenting each other to an imaginary audience and pretending to walk across a stage. JonBenét would also do other activities with these same friends, like playing dolls or going sledding.

In the book she and John wrote, Patsy said, "In two years, JonBenét participated in nine pageants. Only two of these were national pageants, an earlier Royale Miss and the Sunburst." JonBenét primarily competed locally in Colorado and Georgia.[1]

In June 1995, a few months short of her fifth birthday, JonBenét was voted "Little Miss Charlevoix" in a contest that welcomed girls of all ages. Her competition had been two other girls her age. JonBenét rode in parades that same summer as "Little Miss Charlevoix." In October 1995, when she was five years old, she won "Little Miss Colorado," which resulted in her riding in the Boulder Christmas Parade that year. In the first months of 1996, JonBenét competed in a contest at a local Colorado mall, but didn't place.

According to available records, JonBenét's participation in pageants increased in 1996. In April, she was in the Colorado All-Stars Kids State Pageant, which awarded all participants a prize. JonBenét won for Cover Girl.

In July 1996, JonBenét was in the Gingerbread Productions of America and won a division title as "Mini Supreme Little Miss." Also that summer, she won an award in the national America's Royale Tiny Miss competition and competed in the Sunburst Beauty Contest in Atlanta. She then competed at the national level in the same contest in Atlanta. JonBenét was in a beauty pageant in early November in Denver, and in

Georgia's Dream Star Pageant over the Thanksgiving break.

The many trophies that had been on display outside JonBenét's bedroom at the time of her death suggest she had won or placed in several pageants. On December 22, 1996, JonBenét also participated in a performance with other children in the Denver metropolitan area as part of AmeriKids, a local non-profit focused on children.

"A couple of times Patsy didn't want to go to a pageant," John would later say, "but JonBenét was so excited they decided that yes, they would." Patsy said in private conversations that child beauty pageants were mostly a Southern activity. "The girls who competed and were serious about it usually did so every weekend," she added.

John and Patsy Ramsey were deeply affected by how the media portrayed their daughter after she was murdered. As John put it: "A huge amount of the public knew her and formed opinions of her after she was killed because the only pictures and video they saw were those sold by the photographers who had videotaped them at the pageants so they owned the rights to them. We had no say in what was published. We were stunned that we had no rights to the video or the still pictures we hadn't taken ourselves, but it was something that never occurred to us until then."

"It was a part of her life that became her identity because it was what the media focused on—the murdered child beauty queen," said Patsy. "Can you imagine what it was like to have her killed and then her image and who she was reshaped and taken from us, too? In reality, she was our darling girl, and a normal everyday busy child who happened to be in pageants and a lot of other activities because we all enjoyed them."

According to Dr. Friedman, there is "a range of child beauty pageants." She puts them into four types with the following descriptions:

Natural beauty pageants: "No makeup is allowed. These pageants are not as prevalent as they once were."

Hobby Glitz beauty pageants: "They're local. The children have their hair made up and use makeup. JonBenét participated in these pageants."

National beauty pageants: "JonBenét participated in these pageants.

Qualification is necessary. Hair is professionally made up and makeup is used."

High-Glitz pageants: "These are the ones you see on television with the current focus on the 2012 television show *Toddlers and Tiaras.* They wear makeup, including false eyelashes, hair falls, and fake embellishments. There is more award money in these pageants, and it is definitely part of the pageant circuit. Some parents have pageant businesses they've developed on their own. This supports the pageant habit." Dr. Friedman added, "Based on what I have seen and read, JonBenét did not do High-Glitz pageants."

"Child pageants are predominantly [held] in the South," Dr. Friedman said. "JonBenét's murder had a huge impact in the decline of them. But in 2000 they came back and increased in popularity, because parents wanted their children to be involved in them."

In January 1997, three weeks after JonBenét's murder, *Newsweek* magazine published an article with a sentence that launched the dyed-blonde-hair myth about JonBenét and her pageants:

"Patsy Ramsey regularly had her kindergartner's hair lightened at a beauty salon."

No attribution or beauty salon name was given, and none was needed for this to be instantly accepted as a true fact. The story that JonBenét's hair was chemically altered to blonde for beauty pageants spread and is still considered accurate. And yet that wasn't true, according to Patsy, her father, her sister Pam,

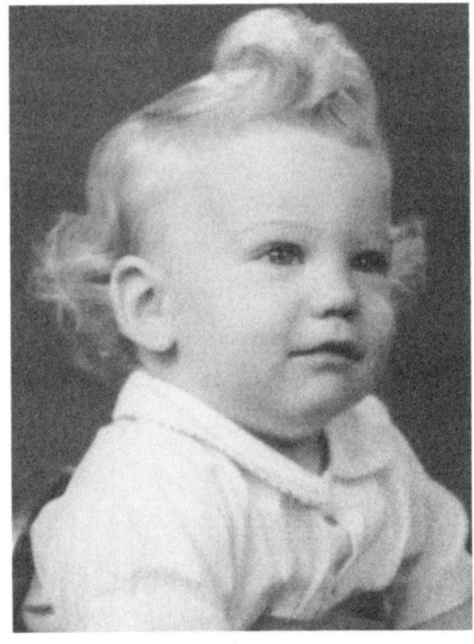

John Ramsey with white-blonde hair as a baby. © John Ramsey.

John Ramsey holds his son John Andrew. John Andrew has the same white-blonde hair as his father and his half sister, JonBenét. © John Ramsey.

and JonBenét's half-sister, Melinda. The blonde hair color came naturally from the Ramsey side of the family. John and his son, John Andrew, both had curly white-blonde hair until they reached eight or nine years of age.

While JonBenét had naturally light brown hair, it often turned blonde from the summer sun and darkened just a little in the winter. According to Patsy, she sometimes had her daughter's hair professionally rinsed and conditioned in order to get rid of the greenish tinge it acquired from chlorine when JonBenét spent a lot of time swimming in pools. Patsy also told John and a friend at one time that she had JonBenét's hair "touched up and conditioned" because it had been bleached white from the sun.

Both John as well as Patsy's sister Pam, have said that Patsy never colored JonBenét's hair, nor had it colored. According to Melinda, JonBenét's half-sister, "That is just something they wouldn't do because she was a child." John added, "It's just not something we would do."

Yet, according to the JonBenét Ramsey Murder Book Index, one of Patsy's best friends told police that, during the Christmas party at the Ramsey home on December 23, 1996, "[She] also noticed that JonBenét's hair was died [sic] blonde" or "appeared really bleached out." (BPD

Reports #1-229, #5-4724.) This was the only allegation obtained by police from someone who knew the Ramsey family that JonBenét's hair may have been dyed blonde at any time.

"JonBenét and I could practice dance routines together and design costumes," Patsy explained. "I didn't think of it as anything negative because it was part of what I had experienced as I grew up in the South and it seemed positive and fun. The picture the public got was from the beauty pageant videos that were aired continuously. It seemed she was a child whose life was 100 percent beauty pageants because the only pictures and video available were of the pageants. But that was really a small part of her life and who she was."

Susan Stine shared school carpooling duties with the Ramseys. Burke, JonBenét and the Stine's son went to High Peaks Elementary School, part of the Boulder Valley School District. "There was no dress code," Stine said, "so JonBenét would mostly wear sweatpants, play pants, t-shirts, turtlenecks and sweatshirts. The school was very casual, and so was she. She never wore make-up to school." Dresses were for the rare school pictures or end-of-the-school-year events.

Another friend of the Ramsey family said that "many of the parents, after the murder, had commented that JonBenét just looked like a regular kid at school." She "would often wear just jeans to school." This friend explained that many parents of students at the school had not known JonBenét was involved in child beauty pageants before seeing the Ramseys' daughter in the child pageant video aired on the news.

Patsy's attorney, Pat Burke, offered this insight regarding the effect of JonBenét being in child beauty pageants and its relationship to public doubts about Patsy: "Show me one thing, honestly and objectively, that you would ever criticize about her. The honest response is that some people criticize her because she put her daughter in beauty pageants. Yet that was what Patsy was raised doing. That was the culture of her upbringing in West Virginia. To her growing up, it was a good experience that improved her self-confidence and brought her closer to her mother. The worst thing people would be able to say about Patsy was that they didn't like it that she put her daughter in beauty pageants."

In addition to the pageants, JonBenét liked skiing, skating, rock climbing, piano lessons, and just being and interacting with friends and family, according to both of her parents.

She liked to be part of whatever was going on. On one Thanksgiving, when the whole family was going to her Uncle Jeff's home, each family was going to bring a side dish. JonBenét insisted she bring her own food to share. She brought white bread rolled up with jelly inside, which she made herself with a bit of help from her mom. She called them "jelly roll-ups" and watched carefully to make sure everyone at the dinner had one. Patsy smiled remembering how she was JonBenét's assistant that day. "I loved all my children dearly, and I sure was happy having that little girl telling me how to help her make jelly roll-ups."

"She was always going full speed and laughing and smiling," JonBenét's dad has said.

Her Uncle Jeff said JonBenét was a loving, sweet, normal little girl who just wanted to do all the things other little girls did. "I cannot remember her in any pageant clothes or dresses. She was just a typical little girl in jeans and a t-shirt, dressed up in a little-girl dress only for a special occasion like Thanksgiving or Christmas."

Uncle Jeff is one of John's best friends. Because Jeff lived in Atlanta and John and his family lived in Boulder, their families didn't see each other as much as they would have liked. But his memories of his niece are of a little girl who adored her big brother and loved playing with him and his friends, her little friends, and any adult who would agree to play her "kids" games like hide-in-the-leaves or hide-and-seek.

JonBenét was "very smart and talented, wise beyond her years," her dad remembers. "She had unusual insight. If I came home from a particularly rough day at work looking serious, she would notice and tell me, 'I don't think that's a good face to wear, Dad. I think you should smile.'

"She was very aware of people around her," John added. "She loved the colors of flowers, the fragrance of them and was always surprised when some of them that were so pretty had thorns on them."

Family friend and business attorney Mike Bynum didn't know Burke and JonBenét well, but he once spent several days in Charlevoix, Michigan, where the family had a summer home.

"I went sailing with them on Lake Charlevoix where, even though they were six and nine, both kids had jobs on the boat. Both were treated with respect and showed respect back to their parents." Sailing was another family activity that was important to both John and Patsy.

When John and Mike had to leave Charlevoix on business, Bynum says JonBenét was upset that her dad was going. The two stood for a few minutes in the entryway of their home in Charlevoix. "He got down on one knee and gave her a big hug and then talked with her about why he needed to go and when he would be back," Bynum said. "He was on her level and talking with her face-to-face. I was impressed with the interaction between the two of them." Bynum remembers the picture of them, down on the floor, talking it out.

When police interviewed JonBenét's teachers after her murder, her homeroom teacher said: "JonBenét was a most unusual gifted student who was very humble and compassionate. Other children loved JonBenét and she was a very sweet girl." That teacher said she was only vaguely aware that her student may have been in some sort of pageants. JonBenét's music teacher said JonBenét was a "very humble little girl and very poised and very non-assuming. Not boisterous or egotistical. Very caring and compassionate. No signs of abuse." And JonBenét's art teacher described her as a "very mature" student who "seemed to be very normal." (BPD Reports #5-3145, #5-3150, #5-3437, #5-3355, #5-3146, #5-3375.)

JonBenét's teachers were equally enthusiastic about Patsy Ramsey. "Patsy was a volunteer that was a teacher's dream," said JonBenét's homeroom teacher.

In a basement in a home in a Southern town, there is a room with JonBenét's drawings as well as some photographs and clothing neatly stacked together. There are costumes from her pageants. The room gives off a wisp of loss that grows as one continues to look at the items this little girl left behind. On one piece of paper are words she printed: "Mom," "Dad" (with a sailboat after her dad's name), "Cat," "Dog,"

"Boy," "Bat," "Burke," and then "JonBenét" in her own cursive style. There's a smiling face after her brother's name and a hat after hers. The words give a sense of promise.

There is also a cut-out Christmas tree on a paper sack. The decorations on the tree are bright shiny dots of red, green, lavender, gold, silver and blue. Glue has soaked through and whitened parts of the tree, and then there's her name at the bottom, something she was just learning to write at the time. One can picture her head bent over her drawing, brow furrowed in concentration, working proudly on this Christmas creation of hers.

Or there's the construction-paper US Mail truck; the whimsical drawing with several suns; the finger painting in bright yellows, blues, greens and pink; the ever-present smiling sun in other drawings shining down on cheerful flowers. There's what might be a self-portrait of a blonde girl with blue eyes, a pink dress and a big smile, created seven months before JonBenét's murder. She was just a little girl. And the impact of her loss only grows stronger as one touches what remains of what she created.

(Left) JonBenét's handwriting. © John Ramsey. (Right) Christmas tree cutouts by JonBenét. © John Ramsey.

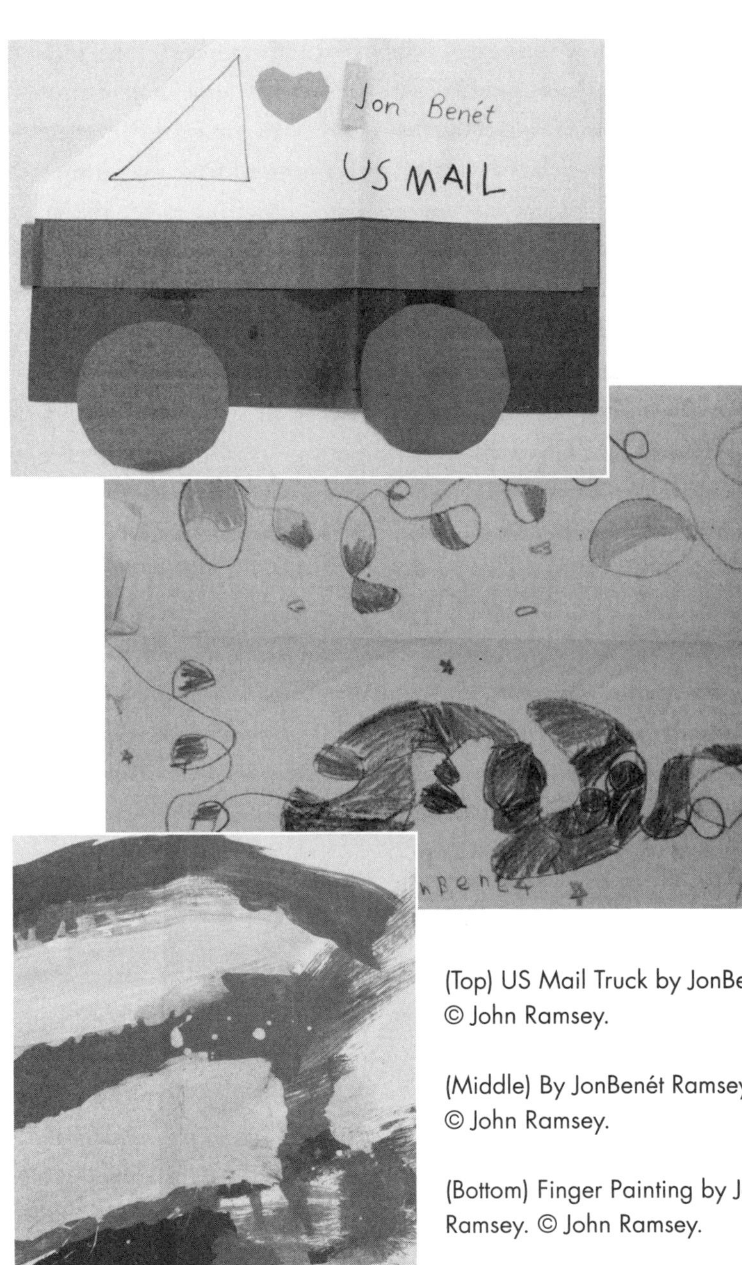


(Top) US Mail Truck by JonBenét. © John Ramsey.

(Middle) By JonBenét Ramsey. © John Ramsey.

(Bottom) Finger Painting by JonBenét Ramsey. © John Ramsey.

A big sack filled with Beanie Babies including turkeys, pigs, giraffes and a lamb sits abandoned on the floor. JonBenét's dad searches through them with care. Toys and kid stuff, a pair of baby pajamas and other clothing emerges. He studies the packed-away pictures from so very long ago. As he looks at what is left, John says, "This is just a fraction of what we lost because of the incompetence and stupidity of the investigation. This is what's left of our child." And he turns away for a brief moment to compose himself.

Never again would his little girl find the contentment of a job well done, the warmth of the summer heat, the determination of building sand castles on the beach, the happiness of playing with other children just like her.

No one would ever call her "Mom." Her lifetime lasted just six years, four months and twenty days.

In the years since his daughter's death, John Ramsey has stated "it was a mistake to have JonBenét in the pageants."

JonBenét's Beanie Babies. © John Ramsey.

"I was persuaded at the time by how much she enjoyed it," he said. "I didn't realize that this might be where her killer found her."

"She was too young," he added, "and even though we emphasized that her talent was what was important in her participation, and she loved doing it, this wasn't what was the most positive for her with the emphasis on looks and make-up. Patsy and JonBenét were doing it just for fun. Looking back, I was not pleased with the competitive environment in that many of the parents there seemed desperate for their child to win and that was quite different than why I believe Patsy and JonBenét were participating."

The anti-public sentiment about child beauty pageants has increased internationally with, in some cases, harsh consequences. In January 2014, the French National Assembly passed a law that banned child beauty pageants as part of a larger package of women's rights initiatives. The new law, which stated that girls under the age of thirteen were no longer allowed to participate in beauty pageants in France, included a carefully detailed description of "child beauty pageants." There is a criminal penalty for violating the ban. Child beauty pageants have been banned in the Russian city of St. Petersburg as well, and some Russian lawmakers have sought a nationwide ban. Meanwhile in Australia, activists have protested against an American company that has brought its competitive style of child beauty pageants to the city of Melbourne.

CHAPTER 16

# MONTHS FOLLOWING—1997 TO 1998

JonBenét in hula skirt on family vacation. © John Ramsey.

## CHRONOLOGY

**January 1997 to February 1997—The Ramseys are in Boulder living with friends.**

**February 1997 to June 1997—The Ramseys live with Glen and Susan Stine[1] until they leave Boulder for Charlevoix, Michigan.**

**June 1997 to Fall 1997—The Ramseys live in Charlevoix.**

**Fall 1997—The Ramseys move to Atlanta.**

"EVERY DAY BEGAN WITH ANGUISH," said Patsy. "That's just one of the words I can think to use. We had seen our daughter dead, murdered, and they were terrible images we couldn't forget. It was this kind of raw dread filled with nightmares and reality."

With so many fingers pointed at them and the media surrounding them, John and Patsy Ramsey were emotionally battered. "That's why the attorneys were such a blessing," Patsy added.

On January 13, 1997, the tabloid *Globe* published six autopsy and crime scene photos related to the Ramsey murder investigation that had been stolen from the photo lab that had processed them. A technician from the photo shop was arrested and charged with theft. So was his accomplice, a private investigator and former employee of the Boulder Sheriff's office. The technician, Lawrence Shawn Smith, and PI Brett Sawyer were ordered to apologize to the Ramseys and spent three days in jail. The *Globe* was forced to return most of the photographs, but was never charged with a crime.

John remembers the day he found out the photos of JonBenét's autopsy had been stolen and were going to be published. He and Patsy had promised each other they would never look at their daughter's autopsy photographs.

"I can't describe the assault of emotion," John said. "I hadn't protected her when she was murdered, and now I wasn't protecting her most terrible moments in the autopsy."

When John told Patsy about the photographs, they both "cried and cried." "It was such helplessness and despair," he said.

Both parents, but especially Patsy, lived in fear of the killer coming back.

John's Journal:

> *We keep our curtains pulled. Our doors and windows are locked. Going anywhere takes a major organized and planned operation. All the time, we don't know if the killer is posing as part of the group with the media.*
>
> *On one occasion we are being aggressively tailed and I pull into the police station, having alerted them that we were coming. The brazen photographer pulls in right behind us. And backs up and blocks the exit. The police come out and arrest him and we get a police escort to our destination. It's very unnerving, particularly when you remind yourself that the person could in fact be the killer and not a photographer.*
>
> *We get people coming to the door, claiming to have information that can be helpful in solving the case. They're tabloid reporters.*

Burke was home-schooled by his parents and friends for a few weeks after his sister was murdered. His parents were terrified that the killer would come back and concerned that school would be an easy place to find their son. John and Patsy soon realized, though, that Burke needed to be with his classmates amid the normal routine of school.

That's how the "Burke Watch" began. John, family friends and attorneys met with the school principal and district officials to discuss additional protection for Burke if he were to go back to school. At first, a detective was hired by the Ramseys to monitor their son at school.

Then school parents volunteered to be in the school all day to watch over Burke in his classes. The "Burke Watch" began in February 1997 and continued each day until school ended for the summer in June.

The Ramseys had moved in with their friends, Susan and Glen Stine, in February 1997. Stine and other friends felt the family was unable to cope alone, yet needed to stay in Boulder to help with their daughter's murder investigation. Susan Stine, as well as another woman who remained friends with Patsy after the murder and defended her, were each referred to in a Boulder Police Department report as "One of Patsy's pit-bulls [sic]." (BPD Report #1-1021.)

"I never in my life have felt as bad or as devastated as they were," Susan said. "John would get up and get dressed. Patsy would try to get up and be strong for Burke, and once he went to school, she would collapse. She was numb for such a long time. Sleeping was the best, because she could get it out of her head while she slept. John would just sit and stare at whatever was on television, whether it was children's programming or anything else."

"It's not something I can describe. It was not really living," Patsy would say later.

During the Ramseys' four months with her family, Susan Stine said dinner became the focal point of the day and offered a way to return to routine. Everyone would try to pump themselves up for the kids. But in the first few months, John and Patsy had to be instructed to do basic things like set the table. They had to be reminded to put the silverware, glasses and plates on the table while others cooked and organized the meal. Everyone would meet in the dining room, a traditional room with a red, blue and rose-colored rug, a cozy gathering place.

Susan would plan dinnertime conversation to include something positive or funny. She would ask her son and Burke to look through books to find jokes and would usually have a few to tell of her own. But Patsy would rarely last through dinner.

"She'd just wear down after an hour, and either John or I would put her to bed," said Susan.

According to a family friend, "Patsy was a 'limp doll' when at the Steins [sic]." (BPD Report #1-1019.)

Other friends remember the desperation in the aftermath of JonBenét's murder. The Ramseys' close friend and business attorney, Mike

Bynum, has said it's still difficult for him to even think about it. Bynum recalled one of his visits to the Stine home, when Patsy woke up from a nap and called for Burke but her son didn't answer because he'd gone outside to play.

"She became so hysterical it was painful to watch," Bynum said. "She was screaming for him and her face was contorted with horror and we were all running to find out where he was. When they found him playing outside with an adult supervising, Patsy just hugged him and cried. It was very painful to see when she didn't know even for that one minute where he was."

Even now, Bynum gets emotional thinking about how terrible John and Patsy's grief really was. "It was so awful," he said. "They could pull it together for a few minutes and then would just break down crying. When you think about them collapsing on the floor of their friend's house the night after her body was found and falling asleep there, it is just so horrifying to me."

The lack of privacy continued with reporters knocking on the Stine family's front door. "They were even searching through our garbage," Susan said, "so I poured liquid fish fertilizer in it just to give them pause. The fertilizer is beyond nasty smelling."

During the months that the Ramseys spent at the Stine home, the churn of publicity and speculation around JonBenét's murder continued.

In February 1997, two officially designed leaks hit the Ramseys with such a double-publicity-story-punch that some within the Boulder District Attorney's Office and the Boulder Police Department were deeply troubled by them. Even though JonBenét's pediatrician, the Boulder County Coroner, an expert from Denver's Children's Hospital and the Director of the Kempe Child Abuse Center in Denver had stated there had been no ongoing sexual abuse of the child (BPD Reports #9-110, #26-182), two new stories were deliberately put into motion just when momentum on the case publicity had begun to abate. The stories were about incest. One insider who was part of the plan to leak these stories to the media wondered years later if this should have been done.

"We're better than to do this, but we did," he said. According to this source, a small but consistent number of people were involved with continual calculated leaks from both the Boulder District Attorney's Office and the Boulder Police Department, and "they did a lot of damage." This source was highly placed in the Ramsey murder investigation.

The first story:

**February 20, 1997**, (*Daily Camera*)
POLICE EYE OTHER DAUGHTER'S DEATH

It was a cruel leak. John's oldest daughter, Beth, and her fiancé were killed in an auto accident in January 1992, when their car was hit by a semi-trailer truck on a wintry road in Illinois. The article stated that the Boulder Police Department had asked for a copy of Beth's autopsy and interviewed some of Beth's friends in case she had mentioned to them any problems she'd had with her father. They actually interviewed twelve friends and acquaintances, traveling to at least four different cities to do so and generating fourteen related police reports. (BPD Reports #1-455, #1-521, #5-3589, #1-397, #1-520, #8-80, #5-2638, #1-424, #1-457, #1-459, #5-2169, #1-472, #1-525, #1-527.) Two close friends of Beth's interviewed were asked by the BPD and told them there was "no indication of sexual impropriety in the family." Others said they didn't know. This part of the investigation led nowhere, other than to leaked headlines.

The implied accusation that incest had led to JonBenét's murder was spread further in the days following the publication of the *Daily Camera* story on multiple talk shows and blogs. *CBS Evening News* even broadcast the story. Such "coverage" was suggestive, misleading and only served to further distract from the investigation of a child's murder.

The second story:

**February 27, 1997** (*Daily Camera*)
EX-MISS AMERICA INTERVIEWED TWICE IN RAMSEY INVESTIGATION

This leak, published just one week later, made it clear what the finely tuned incest publicity campaign against John Ramsey had been designed to accomplish. According to this article, the Boulder Police Department had interviewed Marilyn Van Derbur Atler of Denver about the Ramsey case. A graduate of the University of Colorado in Boulder who was crowned Miss America in 1958, Atler was described by the *Daily Camera* as "an outspoken victim of incest." This was due to Atler's long history as an advocate for incest and child abuse survivors who spoke out publicly about her own personal story of alleged abuse by her father. Boulder DA Alex Hunter verified publicly that he had also spoken with Atler about the Ramsey case.

Following the publication of the February 27 *Daily Camera* story, other newspapers as well as television and radio stations interviewed Atler extensively, contributing to public speculation that she had been contacted by the BPD and the Boulder DA's Office because both had reason to believe John Ramsey was guilty of incest and, for that reason, had likely been involved in his daughter's murder. Such conclusions made sense to many, especially when the *Daily Camera* reported that "Boulder city spokesperson Kelvin McNeill confirmed that Atler met with detectives as a 'noted expert in several areas that may or may not be of interest to our investigation.'"

"You've made the worst accusation you can make about a father," said Patsy's attorney, Pat Burke. "That was unforgiveable. They were jerks for having done this."

John's attorney, Bryan Morgan agreed. "It was repulsive beyond words."

At the start of a nationally broadcast press conference in February 1997, Boulder District Attorney Alex Hunter walked firmly to a podium and looked at the assembled media and their lights, cameras and recorders. He paused, then said, "This may not be a good sign that I already need water."

Hunter then continued with, "As I watched the dawn arrive this morning, I was doing my workout, which you don't allow me to do anymore midday, and I had the local morning paper, the two Denver papers, to see what had transpired about this case overnight."

Reporters looked at each other in amazement. This was a live national news conference about the unsolved death of a six-year-old child and its myriad investigative problems, and the DA was starting off with a joke and a chat about his exercise habits. It was in such moments that DA Hunter revealed how out of sync he was with the seriousness of the Ramsey murder investigation. Even though he did eventually change his message to one that was more appropriate for a somber news conference, his initial performance was a strange thing to witness. "It's very Alex-in-Boulder," remarked one local Boulder reporter to another reporter.

The battles that Ramsey attorneys were waging with the Boulder Police Department and the Boulder District Attorney's Office were continual and troubling. For example: In a previously undisclosed March 4, 1997, defense letter to BPD Chief Tom Koby, John Ramsey's attorney, Bryan Morgan, asked why Koby's detectives had used certain questions and made particular statements "during witness interviews." Morgan said several of the Ramsey witnesses who had been questioned by the Boulder Police Department had relayed concerns to the Ramsey attorneys related to the slant of the BPD detectives' questions. Morgan said the "statements and allegations by detectives were untrue and designed to smear the Ramseys." Such questions included:

"Do you know the Ramseys have named you a suspect in their daughter's murder?"

"Do you know anything about an affair John Ramsey had in Amsterdam?"

"Is John Ramsey having an affair?"

"We've heard that John Ramsey has a split personality; that he can be very quiet and then blow up?"

"Why won't the family support John Andrew Ramsey's alibi?"[2]

No prior knowledge or foundation had existed to support the use of such questions in these interviews. These types of questions also would not lead to the development of accurate information and further the search for new evidence in the case. In short, they were not valid.

Bits of information and misinformation related to the murder of JonBenét Ramsey continued to ricochet from one media outlet to another. Even details that were wrong—or perhaps deliberately calibrated as a false leak in order to achieve a certain impact—lost nothing in velocity as they traveled.

One such story was repeated so often it created an international sensation and a basis upon which many people decided the Ramseys had indeed been involved in killing their daughter.

The story came from police "sources" and was initially reported in the *Rocky Mountain News* by reporter Charlie Brennan. It hit driveways and front porches the morning of March 11, 1997:

> SNOW AT RAMSEY HOUSE LACKED FOOTPRINTS: ABSENCE OF TRACKS AMONG FIRST CLUES THAT LED POLICE TO SUSPECT MEMBERS OF FAMILY

"That is one of the earliest details that caused investigators to focus their attention on the slain girl's family, police sources said."

Yet, according to several different sources of information, the south sidewalks and patio of the Ramsey home were clear of snow on the morning of December 26, 1996.

The following portion of a Boulder Police Department search warrant affidavit dated March 1997, states what the second officer on the scene, Sergeant Paul Reichenbach, saw regarding snow and grass and footprints. He was the first law enforcement officer to search outside the Ramsey home:

> Sergeant Reichenbach states in his report that he had arrived at the Ramsey home at approximately 0600 hours on December 26, and that he had examined the exterior of the Ramsey home as well as the yard. Sergeant Reichenbach noted that the air temperature was approximately 10 degrees Fahrenheit. Sergeant Reichenbach noted in his report that there was a very light dusting of snow and frost on the exposed grass in the yard outside the Ramsey home. Some of the grass and yard was covered with snow from previous snowfalls and this snow was described as being crusty and measuring one-two inches deep.
>
> Sgt. Reichenbach states that he saw no fresh footprints in any of the snow or in the frost on the grass. (BPD Search Warrant Affidavit, March 1997.)

The concentration of this portion of the search warrant affidavit is on snow and frost in the "grass and yard." The sidewalks and driveway are not mentioned in the portion of the affidavit obtained. But they are in this BPD police report:

"Sgt. Reichenbach does not believe there was snow on the sidewalks or driveway." (BPD Report #5-3916.)

In Detective Linda Arndt's original police report about activities at the Ramsey home on December 26, 1996, she wrote:

"Sgt. Reichenbach said there was a light dusting of snow on the ground when he arrived at the Ramsey residence. Sgt. Reichenbach did not notice any footprints or other tracks in the snow. Sgt. Reichenbach personally checked the exterior of the Ramsey residence." (Detective Linda Arndt—Date of Report 1-8-1997.)

But what about the sidewalks? There was no mention of them in this report, either.

Exterior crime scene photographs were taken that Thursday morning, according to police records. One detective on the case told me he and an attorney from the Boulder District Attorney's Office had seen the photographs from that morning and they showed no snow on the driveway or southern sidewalks.[3]

John Ramsey's attorney, Bryan Morgan, said he and John were shown a photograph by police from the morning of December 26 during an interrogation. The photograph was taken early that morning, they were told, and showed the south entrance and the south door of the home, the round patio outside John's home office and the driveway on the west end of the house. The sidewalks and driveway in the photos were dry and had no snow on them, according to both Morgan and Ramsey.

JonBenét had ridden her new Christmas bicycle on the dry south-side patio, according to separate statements from each of her parents. Because the porch had been dry the afternoon of December 25, her bicycle left no tracks near the grated window well located above the broken window that some would later consider a possible entry point for an intruder.

Documents obtained from two local weather reporting stations in the Denver metropolitan area said there was "no precipitation" in Boulder overnight from December 25 to December 26. At the time, the closest weather information was from Jefferson County Airport, which is located approximately fourteen miles from Boulder.[4]

A meteorologist interviewed by the Boulder Police Department said if there had been any snow overnight from December 25 to December 26, "the snow probably would not have stuck to the pavement because of the high daytime temperature because the pavement would tend to hold the heat in." (BPD Report #26-263.) He was referring to the temperatures on Christmas Day and on the next day, December 26, 1996. Another meteorologist told the BPD "there was insufficient information to tell what the condition of the ground would have been around the Ramsey residence on December 25, 1996." (BPD Report #1-1100.)

In the only judicial review of the evidence to date, US Court District Judge Julie Carnes analyzed the evidence during depositions in a civil trial and, in March 2003, wrote a 93-page report that concluded, "Contrary to media reports that had discredited an intruder theory based on the lack of a 'footprint in the snow,' there was no snow covering the sidewalks and walkways to defendants' home on the morning of December 26, 1996." (SMF 139; PSMF 139 *Wolf v. Ramsey*, Judge Julie Carnes.)

Therefore, a person walking along these paths would have left no footprints.

When I interviewed *Rocky Mountain News* reporter Charlie Brennan about his "footprints story," he said he did "not regret doing the March 1997 story." From what he knew at the time, "it was correct." He said, "I thought my police sources believed it to be true." The story was published two and a half months after the murder of JonBenét Ramsey. The police sources, if they were intimately involved in the case, would have known that the south sidewalks had been dry the morning of December 26, 1996. Brennan did not get the other side of the story from the Ramseys or from their attorneys before publishing his article.

As with so many other leaks from inside the Ramsey murder investigation, the "no footprints in the snow" leak served the essential purpose of keeping the public in step with the Boulder Police Department's theory that JonBenét's murder had to have been an inside job.

And the false report became an urban and international legend.

In February 2011, fourteen years after JonBenét's death, CNN reported incorrectly that one of the details in the case that had pointed to the Ramseys was the "fact" that there had been "no footprints in the snow" outside the Ramsey home on December 26, 1996.[5]

Boulder District Attorney Alex Hunter knew he had big troubles with the Ramsey case. He liked to talk, muse and try ideas out on some people, including reporters. To me, he'd say it was off the record for now, but gesture and with a smile say, "But you can use it in ten years, if there isn't a trial by then."

"I don't know how to get through to Commander Eller and his detectives," he said to me in one 1997 conversation. "They are so stuck on their Ramsey theory, and I'm not seeing it yet either way. There isn't enough for a case." But then he would vacillate and tell others that either Patsy or John should be the focus of the case.

The spectacle was affecting Hunter's reputation, and that was something he wouldn't tolerate. His strategy was to consult with some "top nationally known guns" to help in the investigation. In February and March of 1997, Hunter also decided to hire his own detective to work with his attorneys and with the Boulder Police Department.

Interviews began with the goal of finding that detective. Investigators from the BPD and the Boulder DA's Office were so alienated from each other, however, that they wouldn't even sit near each other when interviewing prospective candidates for the new job. Retired Denver Homicide Lieutenant Tom Haney remembers walking into a conference room for his interview. "The district attorney people were huddled up on one end of the room and the police detectives were on the other end, and they weren't talking," Haney said. The two agencies weren't headed into distrust and dislike, they were already there.

Ultimately, the two agencies couldn't reach a consensus about the new hire despite interviewing thirty people who had applied for the job. Finally, one of the BPD detectives suggested retired Detective Lou Smit, who had worked homicides for thirty years with the Colorado Springs Police Department and the El Paso County, Colorado Sheriff's Department. In 1995, Smit had also solved the high-profile child kidnapping and murder case of Heather Dawn Church. Heather had been thirteen years old when she was kidnapped in 1991 from her home at night in an area known as Black Forest north of Colorado Springs. Her dad had been the main suspect. Smit found a fingerprint on a window screen where the suspect had entered the home and kidnapped, then killed, Heather. Robert Charles Browne confessed and was sentenced to life in prison. Brown also confessed to killing a total of forty-eight people, but that was never proven. Only a portion of Heather's skeleton was ever recovered.

Even though Smit hadn't applied for the job in Boulder, Hunter hired him at the suggestion of the BPD detective and with the approval of the Boulder Police Department. He also expected the plainspoken cop would be a huge help in the Ramsey investigation. Hunter counted on things getting better. He wrote a letter to Smit defining his assignment as "concentrating the totality of his energy and ability on inventorying and organizing and analyzing the investigative file developed by the Boulder Police Department concerning the investigation into the murder of JonBenét Ramsey." (BPD Report #30-446.)

"I felt from what I had read and knew about the case, none of it first-hand, that someone in this family was guilty," Smit would later say while reflecting on his first days at his new job in March 1997. "But after spending months organizing the police files, the evidence just wasn't there. I also made a point to befriend the Ramseys to get to know them better. It's how I worked as a detective on at least a hundred cases; to get as close to the suspects as I possibly could to get information and perspective for the case. One morning, the Ramseys saw me outside their old home. They stopped, talked and we even prayed together. You can learn a lot that way, and I needed to get to know them better. As the months went on, I continued to review and coordinate evidence from police reports. I became convinced it didn't point to the Ramseys. It pointed to an intruder. My theory wasn't popular with the Ramsey case investigators."

Smit quickly became somewhat of a pariah with BPD detectives on the case because of his belief in "following where the evidence pointed and getting friendly with the Ramseys." "Sources" leaked that he had prayed with the family outside the former Ramsey home, suggesting this had affected his objectivity. He was publicly ridiculed by an anonymous police source who leaked that he was a "delusional old man." But others came to his defense, especially other detectives who agreed that praying with possible suspects can be a clever way to get close to them and gather information from them.

It was on Wednesday, April 30, 1997, that Boulder Police Department officials first interrogated John and Patsy Ramsey. The courthouse was surrounded by media for the anticipated "formal interviews," which were in fact interrogations, questioning with targeted suspicion. Even so, no pictures of the couple were taken. They avoided the media by arriving in a van that had no windows and entering an underground garage used by the Boulder Sheriff's Department, where the interviews were to take place. The courthouse and the sheriff's department were in the same building.

It became apparent that the BPD was most interested in questioning Patsy Ramsey by the amount of time spent on the two separate "formal interviews" (as the BPD and DA described them) or "interrogations" (as

Ramsey attorneys described them) conducted that day. The Boulder Police Department's focus on John and suggestions of possible incest related to the case had gone nowhere, and John was interrogated for approximately two hours. But Patsy was interrogated for six and a half hours. A representative of the Boulder Police Department and of the Boulder District Attorney's Office as well as an attorney and investigator for either John or Patsy Ramsey was present at each separate interrogation.

On May 1, 1997, the day after their "formal interviews"/"interrogations" with BPD officials, John and Patsy gave their second joint interview with the media. Just as the Boulder Police chief had done for his first public question-and-answer interview, the Ramsey attorneys had handpicked specific local reporters to meet with their clients.

The conditions of the interview were kept mysterious. The journalists were told where it would be held just forty minutes before the interview began. They were instructed to keep that information secret until after the session had been completed. The reporters had to use a password in order to gain entry into a hotel conference room. They understood that they would not be allowed to ask questions about the facts of the case or about the Ramsey interrogations with police that had taken place the day before. Television, still cameras and other recording devices were already in place, and photographers were allowed in with the selected reporters. There were three television reporters, three print reporters and one radio reporter in attendance. The Ramsey attorneys explained that they had chosen this format for an interview with the Ramseys in order to "ensure some privacy and to limit the media circus."

The reporters were seated in the conference room first, and then the Ramseys walked in and were seated facing them. John and Patsy seemed determined and sad as they answered all the questions asked of them. The interview lasted thirty minutes.

I was one of the television reporters asked to participate in this interview. My television station, KUSA TV, broadcast the entire interview live within thirty minutes after it had ended, and I reported on it at that time and in later newscasts. Newspaper reporters printed the interview in its entirety. Such approaches helped ensure that the viewing and reading public could make their own decisions about the case by seeing or hearing the complete interview.

In June 1997, the Ramseys moved out of the Stine home and went to their summer retreat in Charlevoix, Michigan. They had already bought a home in Atlanta, where they would live beginning in the fall.

Charlevoix provided a good change for them, and the town embraced them. The Ramseys had long-time friends there who would sustain them through the summer and offer help and comfort. It was a familiar and bright and sunny place, and the distance from Boulder helped. But they were still, according to Patsy, "very sad, lonely, and afraid." "The tabloid people were all over the town following us and trying to get pictures," she said.

John's Journal:

*It was going to be very hard in Charlevoix because we had so many happy and fun memories there with JonBenét. Plus we knew the media would be relentless in their pursuit of us there. The media is indeed all over Charlevoix.*

Patsy was visiting garage sales one day with Burke. This pastime always became a treasure hunt for them, and a friend of Burke's was also along that day. Burke liked to find old toys and games, and Patsy occasionally found something special, too. On that day, however, they were being stalked by a photographer from the tabloids. When Patsy drove up to the photographer and asked him to leave them alone, he immediately started snapping pictures and shouting, "Fuck you, fuck you." Swearing at people is a ploy used by some tabloid reporters and photographers to provoke a negative reaction. They do this to get the angry picture that will sell lots of copies when featured on a front page under a headline such as "GUILTY MOM."

The following excerpt from John Ramsey's journal is from September 1997:

> *Returned to Atlanta. The media was at our house within 30 minutes of arrival. I hope this isn't a sign of things to come. Later I look back through my charge cards, and compare when I use them and when the media shows up. I find one card that, when used, coordinates with the arrival of the media. They must be paying someone on the inside of the charge card company.*
>
> *Met with security engineer in Atlanta. Discuss needs. We want to make sure home is lit well enough so that no one can hide in cars or bushes. Some even climb trees to try to get a better view of us. Astonishing and worrisome.*
>
> *Security analyst later shows me pictures of a hidden camera site he discovered, apparently installed by the tabloids at JonBenét's grave site.*

Hidden camera installed in utility pole which had a view of JonBenét's grave site. © John Ramsey

When they moved to Atlanta in the fall of 1998, John and Patsy entered a post-traumatic stress treatment program at Emory University to "desensitize" them to the events surrounding their daughter's murder. Both had received extensive grief therapy, but they were struggling. Each of them talked to a counselor at Emory and took a specific anti-depressant as part of the treatment, which also involved weeks of therapy sessions. At these sessions, each had to repeat over and over what had happened December 26, 1996, when they found out JonBenét was missing, and then dead. John has said it seemed as though they did this hundreds of times, but in reality it was much less. It was "tough," he said, "but we had to find a way to recover enough so we weren't still crying every day and could be good and effective parents to Burke, and this is what we chose." Patsy said simply, "It was something we had to do to survive."

Patsy and John had each, at various times, discussed killing themselves. The difficulty of living in this world without their daughter and the excruciating memory of how she was killed and what they had seen overwhelmed them. Yet they would always reach out to each other and decide why they would instead choose living. It was because of each other and their children.

John's Journal:

*Life difficult to go on with. Burden is almost too heavy. Melinda calls. That lifts my spirits. I am blessed by three wonderful living children.*

Three things centered their lives. They knew their children needed them, they had each other for support and they had their beliefs. It became enough to live for.

"Besides," Patsy said, "there was no way we were going to leave any stigma for the police to capitalize on in terms of who killed our wonderful daughter."

Time healed, but only somewhat. They longed for the little girl who had given them so much joy. "I want her with me," Patsy would say. "I want her with us."

John's Journal:

*Patsy is very depressed and expresses the view that everyone has rights except us. We discuss immigrating to New Zealand. I know it's hard for her, but it happens all throughout history. Oppressed people leave their homeland for a better place.*

More than nine months after the murder of JonBenét Ramsey in October 1997, Boulder Police Chief Tom Koby moved to replace BPD Commander John Eller on the Ramsey case. He chose BPD Commander Mark Beckner, who had worked on the case since its first weeks. Commander Beckner would be promoted to the position of Boulder Police Chief in June 1998.

Boulder DA Alex Hunter was privately "delighted." He and his investigators hadn't gotten along with Eller. They'd felt he'd disguised his lack of homicide experience with stubbornness and cantankerous ultimatums. "I remember one day," said Bill Wise, Hunter's First Assistant DA, "Eller actually pounded his fists on the table in the room where we were meeting. Pounded his fists and said we had to do it 'his way.'"

Hunter has said he remembers this instance as well. "He was furious with us. We were trying to help. To get this case going in the right direction together with the police department. He wanted it his way and that was it. I wonder if my jaw dropped when he pounded his fists. In a way, it made me want to laugh, but it was such a serious situation."

Eller's supporters who'd been in the room at the time thought he'd had "balls" by standing up to DA Hunter. For some of them, Eller's behavior provided a boost in morale, though ultimately it would make no difference.

Commander Beckner set out to get the investigation organized. He made a "to do" list for his detectives that consisted of the deliberate steps that were needed on a homicide case, especially this case. Beckner, according to Detective Lou Smit, was "trying to bring order and process to the case, which was really needed." Smit had spent the past seven months organizing and cataloguing the evidence, including police reports, photographs and DNA.

The Ramseys and their attorneys were anticipating that Beckner would take the investigation in a different direction and seriously consider an intruder theory. On December 5, 1997, however, they found out this would not be the case.

The infamous "umbrella of suspicion" term related to the Ramsey murder investigation had been used by Boulder DA Alex Hunter months before, but during a press conference in early December 1997, it was the focus of the event. At the start of Commander Beckner's first meeting with the media since taking charge of the Ramsey investigation, the scene was dramatic. The eight BPD police detectives still involved in the case stood in a half circle on the raised stage behind Beckner as their new commander reviewed with reporters what the detectives had accomplished in the weeks since he'd assumed charge.

It didn't take long for reporters to ask if the Ramseys were suspects. "What I will say is that we have an umbrella of suspicion," Beckner said. "People come and go under that umbrella. [The Ramseys] do remain under an umbrella of suspicion, but we're not ready to name any suspect."

Years later, Alex Hunter would regard the use of that phrase by himself and others as "unfortunate." Boulder Police Department officials never removed that label, however, and so the Ramseys have lived under this "umbrella of suspicion" for nearly twenty years.

John's Journal:

*I am concerned because I'm sure GE will view me as a liability because of all the nastiness that has been going on in the media. What they will do is not certain to me, but I'm sure they are wondering that themselves. They've got to be saying he's a guy that runs a good business but based on the media reports is one strange guy—We need to get rid of him. Another example of our lives being destroyed by a ruthless and dishonest media.*

In December 1997, General Electric fired John Ramsey from his job at Access Graphics after a buy-out of the company.

Late into the night of May 31, 1998, media satellite and live trucks began claiming their spaces outside the University of Colorado at the Boulder Coors Events Center. June 1 was going to be a big day in the Ramsey case, and members of the media were ensuring they got not only a place to park but a good viewing position, especially given the jammed conditions and what was expected to be a huge amount of coverage. There would be crowds of law enforcement officers inside and reporters with accompanying lights, cameras, cables and microphones attracting the curious outside.

On June 1, 1998 the Boulder Police Department was scheduled to present its case to multiple law enforcement agencies. And while the BPD had publicly announced the session, they'd also made it clear that this was an invitation-only event. Police officers, district attorneys, pro bono attorneys, outside experts hired by the DA, prosecutors from the Colorado Attorney General's Office, agents with the Colorado Bureau of Investigation and agents from the FBI's Child Abduction and Serial Killer unit were among the invited. Boulder Police Department officials hoped the presentation would pressure Boulder District Attorney Alex Hunter into calling for a grand jury in the Ramsey case.

Afterwards, there would be a private question-and-answer session inside among invited participants. Following that session, even though it had presented only one side of the investigation as conducted by the Boulder Police Department, those in attendance would reveal a general disagreement on whether the BPD had proven its case.

That afternoon, when the session was completed, Commander Beckner went outside with his officers to talk with the media. Reporters asked him about his "umbrella of suspicion" comment from the December 1997 news conference six months prior. "There are certainly fewer people under the umbrella of suspicion now," he said, adding, "the umbrella is not quite so big." He also stated, "I have an idea who did it. Yes."

When Beckner had finished, it was DA Hunter's turn at the microphone. As he had at past press conferences related to the Ramsey investigation, Hunter misjudged the seriousness of the occasion and started his comments with: "This is the kind of weather that brings us all here. How many of you are from out of state?" After a brief pause, Hunter went on to talk about the possibility of a grand jury being convened, saying he hadn't made a decision on this yet.

Eventually, Adams County District Attorney Bob Grant, not Hunter, would publicly answer many of the questions about the case from the perspective of the Boulder District Attorney's Office.

# CHAPTER 17
# *VANITY FAIR*

John and Patsy in Michigan. © John Ramsey.

SOME BROADCASTERS, TALK SHOW HOSTS AND THEIR GUESTS, newspaper editorial writers and the public said that in her January 1, 1997 CNN interview, Patsy Ramsey, who was on anti-anxiety drugs at the time, did not look like a grieving mother. And according to BPD Detective Linda Arndt's police report regarding the events of December 26, 1996, a report that included second-hand information (i.e., hearsay), one Boulder Police Department officer noted to another that the Ramseys weren't "acting right." (Detective Linda Arndt—Date of Report 1-8-1997.)

This statement by Arndt was contradicted, however, in multiple then-unreleased and still-confidential BPD officer statements and reports. The speculation that the Ramseys weren't "acting" like grieving parents because they had somehow been involved in the murder of their daughter continued to be leaked to the media for months. In September 1997, it was explored in painstaking detail in a controversial *Vanity Fair* article[1] written by Ann Louise Bardach.[2]

Journalists use the first paragraph of an article to grab readers by including in it enticing, or even explosive, information that makes them want to read more. Bardach used that technique in the first paragraph of her *Vanity Fair* article about the Ramsey case:

> Subsequently, French [first responding officer] told colleagues that he had been struck by how differently the two parents were reacting. While John Ramsey, cool and collected, explained the sequence of events to him, Patsy Ramsey sat in an overstuffed chair in the sunroom sobbing. Something seemed odd to French, and later he would recall how the grieving mother's eyes stayed riveted on him. He remembered her gaze and her awkward attempts to conceal it—peering at him through splayed fingers held over her eyes.

In the second paragraph of the article, Bardach wrote about Officer French not finding JonBenét's body:

> French told fellow officers that he felt awful that he had not discovered it in his search of the house. For months he berated himself as he relived every moment of his hours there. While Patsy Ramsey had wept inconsolably, a dry-eyed John Ramsey had paced incessantly. Later, French recalled that the couple had barely spoken to or looked at each other. Though they were faced with the most calamitous tragedy of their lives, he did not see them console each other. But it was the image of Patsy weeping and watching him that haunted French, especially after he learned that she had been sitting directly over the spot—less than 15 feet below—where her child's body lay.

The details from the article about Patsy "peering at [Officer French] through splayed fingers held over her eyes," and "watching him" quickly went international on wire services and in newspapers, on radio, on the Internet and in television broadcasts. Repeatedly broadcast and re-published, these details played a key role in fueling public opinion against Patsy, especially since initial statements of other BPD officers, and of French himself, that countered these claims had not been released. Most people were reading in newspapers and hearing in television and radio broadcasts personal reflections from one police officer that were not supported by as-yet-unpublished official police records. According to one reporter covering the Ramsey murder investigation, the prevailing sentiment related to the Ramseys among several in the Boulder Police Department and some in the Boulder District Attorney's Office was that they were "uncaring, cold and unnatural in their feelings."

Nowhere in the initial Boulder Police Department reports or excerpts of officer interviews obtained since 1997 does Officer French refer to Patsy Ramsey as "peering at" or "watching" him on the morning of December 26, 1996.

In fact, French says just the opposite about the family's emotions that morning in a later formal interview that was also kept confidential for some time: "Officer French thinks the Ramseys are acting appropriately at the scene." (BPD Report #5-3851.)

That statement is from the formal interview with Officer French conducted by two senior BPD officers on January 10, 1997.

French made several other statements about the Ramseys' behavior during that same formal police interview that were consistent with how emotional each parent was on the morning of December 26, 1996:

"Patsy is loosing [sic] her grip at the scene." (BPD #5-3851.)

"John Ramsey would break down and start sobbing at the scene." (BPD #5-3839.)

"Every time the phone rings, Patsy stands up and just like takes a baseball bat to the gut and then gets down on her knees and she's hiding her head and crying as soon as that phone rings and it's like a cattle prod." (BPD #5-3859.)

Statements from family friends to police are consistent related to Patsy's behavior:

"Patsy was literally in shock. Vomiting, hyperventilating." (BPD #5-433.)

"Patsy cries all the time." (BPD #1-640.)

"During the initial ransom demand time Patsy was hysterical, just absolutely hysterical." (BPD #5-230.)

"She is hyperventilating. She is hallucinating. She is screaming. She was hysterical. John was pacing around. [Close family friends] were trying to keep Patsy from fainting. She was vomiting a little." (BPD #5-404.)

"I thought Patsy was going to have a heart attack and die. I thought she was going to kill herself." (BPD #5-437.)

The police reports from that day continued with the same types of descriptions of Patsy's and John's emotional states. These were obtained from the JonBenét Ramsey Murder Book:

In the second paragraph of her *Vanity Fair* magazine article, Ann Louise Bardach included another statement that was contradicted by police reports and WHYD statements:

"Later, French recalled that the couple had barely spoken to or looked at each other. Though they were faced with the most calamitous tragedy of their lives, he did not see them console each other." In the second paragraph of Bardach's article, she says that French recalled the couple barely speaking to one another. This, too, was contradicted by police reports. French had said in his January 1997 formal interview with senior BPD police officers: "John Ramsey does do some touching of Patsy at the scene." (BPD Report #5-3844.)

And: "One of the victim advocates who was present on the scene said, 'In fact, Patsy and John had been in the formal dining room together for some time holding each other or talking . . .' I [didn't] know they were in there alone together." (BPD Report #5-2630.)

In a separate formal debriefing of the second officer on the scene, Sergeant Paul Reichenbach supported French's initial police debriefing with regard to how Patsy was acting emotionally that morning: "Sgt. Reichenbach felt Patsy was a complete emotional mess." (BPD Report #5-3917.)

Detective Linda Arndt provided more details in her report about Patsy that supported the initial statements provided by French and Reichenbach that Patsy was very emotional that morning:

> [Patsy] was sitting on a chair in the sitting room. This room is located at the southeast corner of the house on the first floor . . . Patsy spoke softly when she talked to me. At times Patsy seemed to be staring off into the distance. Patsy seemed to have a vacant look, and seemed dazed. Since Patsy was situated in a room at some distance from the den, I had limited contact with her. I asked Ofc. French to remain with Patsy. I did ask Patsy a few questions and was able to receive some information.
>
> While I was talking to Patsy she would repeatedly start crying. Patsy would be unable to speak. Patsy repeatedly asked, "Why didn't I hear my baby?" . . . Patsy looked physically exhausted. Patsy would close her eyes, but was not able to rest or sleep. Patsy seemed to be much less focused when I spoke with her. Patsy seemed to have a far-off look in her expression. Patsy's thoughts were scattered and it was difficult to get her to stay focused on one thought. Patsy would collapse in tears and repeatedly asked why had she not been able to hear her baby. (Detective Linda Arndt—Date of Report 1-8-1997.)

After JonBenét's body was found, Detective Arndt also wrote about Patsy:

> Patsy Ramsey appeared to be swooning and I was concerned for her health. The paramedics did physically check Patsy Ramsey. The paramedics did not examine nor touch JonBenét. I was told that Patsy Ramsey was obviously very distraught, however she physically did not need to have medical attention. The two paramedics cleared the scene after Patsy was checked. (Detective Linda Arndt—Date of Report 1-8-1997.)

The *Vanity Fair* article also included criticism of John Ramsey via a quote from Boulder District Attorney Alex Hunter: "As for John Ramsey, whom [Alex Hunter] referred to as an 'ice man,' he wondered aloud whether 'someone as smart as Ramsey would write such a long note.'"

The magazine article also said this about John Ramsey: "A Ramsey friend who met the elder Ramsey [John's father] in the mid-80's [sic] recalls, 'He was very cold, like John was with everybody.'"

And included this quote from a Ramsey business associate, Mike Glynn, with whom the article stated John Ramsey had "a close relationship": "But John could really get angry. I saw this on a few occasions involving business. Shouting and threatening. His eyes bulging like you cannot believe. It seemed like Jekyll and Hyde."

John has disagreed that Glynn was a friend, saying he was an acquaintance, and added that Glynn's statement was "simply not true."

"I don't shout or threaten," he said. "It's not my nature."

In her police report regarding December 26, 1996, Detective Linda Arndt was also critical of John's behavior that morning: "When I talked briefly with John Ramsey during the morning of Dec. 26 he was able to carry on a conversation and articulate his words," Arndt wrote. "John Ramsey had smiled, joked, and seemed to focus during the conversation." (Detective Linda Arndt—Date of Report 1-8-1997.)

Recently John responded to Arndt's report and said it was "untrue" that he would have joked when his daughter was missing. He says he was "dazed and numb" that morning. According to the Boulder Police Department and the WHYD Investigative Archive, the people with John at that time only emphasized his grief when they were interviewed by BPD officers: "During the initial contact [one friend] had during the ransom demand period of time, he stated that 'John Ramsey was not only visibly distressed he was absolutely, just the pain that John was feeling was just palpable. I could feel it. This was John in a way I've never seen him before. He was absolutely at the end of his rope. He just put his head in his hands and cried and shook, you know.'" (BPD Report #5-234.)

Hours after John found JonBenét's body, a friend said, "John wailed, pounded his legs, sank to knees on the floor . . . completely transported by grief." (WHYD Investigative Archive.)

Other friends describe John as "wailing, pounding legs, collapsing on floor, holding his family Bible." (WHYD Investigative Archive.)

Sergeant Paul Reichenbach's statements also differ from the statements made by Detective Arndt in her January 8, 1997 report and by Officer Rick French as quoted in the *Vanity Fair* article. The following note was included in reports on Reichenbach's formal debriefing: "Sgt. Reichenbach did not think John Ramsey said anything that was odd." (BPD Report #5-3918. "Sgt. Reichenbach spoke very little to John Ramsey, but he [Ramsey] seemed composed except for when he told someone his daughter was kidnapped during a phone conversation." (BPD Report #5-3917.)

The *Vanity Fair* article also stated that when John carried JonBenét's body upstairs and laid her down as Detective Arndt instructed him: "'What was interesting was when Ramsey brought the body upstairs he never cried,' relayed a source present at the time. 'But when he laid her down, he started to moan, while peering around to see who was looking at him.'"

The information about John "peering around" is not in the January 8, 1997 report filed by Detective Linda Arndt, the person in closest physical proximity to John Ramsey at that time.

The article by Ann Louise Bardach published in the September 1997 issue of *Vanity Fair* magazine also contained factual errors:

• "The [close family friends] were awakened by John Ramsey, who told them to hurry right over."

According to police reports and Patsy Ramsey, Patsy placed the phone calls to friends that morning.

• "Ramsey decided that his wife should have her own lawyers, and he retained Patrick Burke and Patrick Furman."

John and Patsy didn't hire their own lawyers. Mike Bynum, John's business attorney and friend, did without the knowledge of the Ramseys.

• "Why would a grieving couple go on national television while refusing to speak to the police?"

This speculation on the part of Bardach referred to the January 1, 1997 appearance of John and Patsy Ramsey on CNN. And yet the Ramseys had already talked with investigators from the Boulder Police Department. They have said they would have talked to the police as much as the police wanted them to that Thursday afternoon after their daughter's body was found, except Boulder Police Department officials did not ask them to continue being interviewed at BPD headquarters. In fact, BPD officials did not give the Ramseys any direction that afternoon, which is why they went to a friend's home.

• "The Ramseys have been provided with copies of all 'the most sensitive critical police and detective reports' as well as reproductions of both the ransom note and the 'practice' note found the same day."

Provided by an unnamed source who supposedly had "first-hand knowledge of the investigation" and "said that a flow of privileged, confidential information critical to a case against the Ramseys has been leaked from the D.A.'s office to the Ramseys' lawyers with the efficiency of a sieve," this information gave the impression that the Ramseys had been given significant amounts of material within the first six months of the investigation into the death of their child. This was simply not true.

With regard to the ransom note, Detective Linda Arndt gave the Ramsey attorneys a copy of the ransom note on her own authority without approval of the Boulder Police Department. Bardach mentioned this fact later in her article.

Regarding the other documents, the article also stated that "the Ramseys gave in to separate interviews, but they held fast to their demand for a copy of the entire police file."

According to Patsy's attorney, Pat Burke, however, the Ramseys' attorneys never asked for the entire police file, and never would have. "That wasn't reasonable," he said.

Prior to the first Boulder Police Department interrogations of John and Patsy on April 30, 1997, "portions of police reports from the first day" were given to the Ramseys' attorneys. Case documents show that Pat Furman, Patsy's other attorney, signed for thirty-two pages of police reports relating only to what had happened the morning of December 26, 1996. Case documents detail the page numbers of the reports supplied to Furman on April 21, 1997.

According to attorney Burke, "only prior statements the Ramseys had made to police were given to us as a condition of the interrogations scheduled for April 30. For perspective, in Colorado, persons appearing before a grand jury have the right to prior statements before they testify. We wanted to ensure BPD and the DA's office weren't setting traps by misquoting what was in the actual prior Ramsey statements."

• "On December 29, the family flew to Marietta, Georgia in a private jet piloted by John Ramsey, for JonBenét's funeral."

This incorrect information was taken from an equally incorrect *Rocky Mountain News* article published more than eight months earlier.

• "The ligatures around her neck and right wrist were, investigators say, 'very loose,' consistent with staging."

This was wrong. According to the autopsy report, the rope was "embedded" in JonBenét's neck. The Boulder County autopsy report was released to the public in August 1997, weeks before the *Vanity Fair* article was published. The coroner's report could easily have been used for fact-checking.

• "John Ramsey's children from his first marriage . . . arrived at the Ramsey house at 7:55PM on December 26."

According to multiple Boulder Police Department reports, John Ramsey's children arrived at the Ramsey home at 1:30 p.m.

• "Lou Smit offered the theory that a grown man had sneaked through a broken window so narrow that even [Boulder District Attorney] Hunter discounted the possibility."

The window was also mentioned in the article in this quote attributed to an anonymous "investigator":

• "'[N]o one but a small child or midget could have crawled through that space.'"

According to video from the WHYD Investigative Archive, however, Detective Lou Smit and a Boulder detective both crawled through the window in question to see if they could get through, and did. The videotape of Smit climbing through the window can be viewed online.

• "'The only time I ever saw John really lose his temper was about Patsy and money,' says Marino. 'He would throw the credit cards on his desk and say, "She's gonna spend every last penny I make."'"

This quote was attributed to Jim Marino, described by Bardach as an old friend whom John Ramsey hired to work at Access Graphics.

According to John, this allegation was "totally false."

"Money wasn't a problem," he explained. "Patsy was aware the budget wasn't unlimited. I would never say that about her." John has questioned Marino's other quoted perceptions of him and his family in the article, adding that while Marino was an acquaintance, he would not have known details about their personal life. Ramsey said he'd hired Marino at Access Graphics after a motorcycle accident had left Marino disabled, and he called Ramsey and asked for a job. "I hired him partly out of compassion," John said, "and he ended up being a heck of a good salesman."

- "Most stunning, according to some experts, was the revelation that the child had evidently been 're-dressed' after her murder. JonBenét's parents told investigators that she was wearing a red turtleneck pajama top when they put her to bed. She was found in a white one."

Evidence in the case included fibers from the "white" top found on JonBenét's bed sheet that supported Patsy's statement that her daughter was wearing a white top when she was put to bed that Christmas night. Furthermore, such a discrepancy in what a murder victim was wearing at the time of a murder and what others say the victim was wearing does not automatically point to any sort of re-dressing on the part of the killer.

Complete police records from the Ramsey murder case were not then, nor are they now, public record. The erroneous information Bardach reported would have had to have been leaked to her by the Boulder Police Department or the Boulder District Attorney's Office. Ex-detective Steve Thomas has admitted in a sworn legal deposition and in his book that he was a source for Bardach. One of many, he said.

After the Ramsey attorneys expressed outrage at the *Vanity Fair* article, BPD Chief Tom Koby demanded polygraphs of the primary detectives on the case to find out who had leaked to Bardach. Those polygraphs never happened. Chief Koby was not in good stead with his officers, and the police union pressured him to back down from having the polygraphs done.

On September 16, 1997, when *Vanity Fair* published the Bardach article, Chief Tom Koby sent a letter to Boulder Chief Deputy District Attorney Pete Hofstrom, apologizing for statements attributed to BPD officers in the *Vanity Fair* article. (BPB Report #90-241.)

Three days after Bardach's article was published, Chief Koby sent a letter to Ramsey defense attorneys Bryan Morgan, Hal Haddon and Pat Burke in response to a letter from them demanding an investigation into the information published in the article. Koby stated in his letter that there was no evidence the Boulder Police Department had authorized or condoned any improper releases of information. (BPD Report #90-243.)

Also on that same day, September 19, 1997, the interim City Manager of Boulder, Chris Japenski, wrote to Ramsey attorney Pat Burke in response to Burke's request for an investigation, saying the city "will not investigate" to find the source for the *Vanity Fair* story. (BPD Report #90-245.)

Twelve days prior to Bardach's article on the Ramsey murder investigation, on September 4, 1997, limited information had been released from *Vanity Fair* about the upcoming piece. At least forty-four newspapers and wire services throughout the country published this information, guaranteeing a great readership for the article.[3]

In early February 2012, when Ann Louise Bardach learned that official case records refuted some of her reporting about the homicide of JonBenét Ramsey, she responding by stating that she did not remember a lot about the story because she hadn't kept up with it. She added that, for her, "This is just another murder case and I've covered many murder cases and I know for a lot of people this [Ramsey case] is their whole life. I don't have a dog in this fight."

She also defended her reporting for the article. "We went through a variety of lawyers and fact checks representing *Vanity Fair* from various aspects. There were one hundred reporters on it," she said, "and everybody was working with their sources, but I know that no one compares to the level of fact-checking that we did. So that's all I can tell you."

# CHAPTER 18
# HANDWRITING ANALYSES

EXEMPLAR #5 - PARAGRAPH 1 A

**KNOWN PATSY RAMSEY OPPOSITE HAND**

Please take the time to listen carefully to what I have to say. We are one of a group of individuals that represent a small foreign company. We are a faction of the parent group who are located in another country. We respect your situation and would like to serve your needs and desires particularly since we will profit too. Ar

**KNOWN JOHN RAMSEY OPPOSITE HAND**

Line #

Mr Ramsey,

Listen carefully! We are a group of individuals that represent a small foreign faction. We respect your business but not the country it serves. At this time we have your daughter in our possession. She is safe and unharmed and if you want her to see 1997, you must follow our instructions to the letter

(Top sample) Patsy's opposite or left-hand writing test supervised by Boulder Police.

(Bottom sample) John's opposite or left-hand writing test supervised by Boulder Police.

## CHRONOLOGY

*Boulder Police Department Handwriting Analysis Process*

**December 26, 1997—Boulder forgery detective initially examines the Ramsey ransom note at Boulder Police Department headquarters.**

**January 1997—The Ramsey ransom note goes to the Colorado Bureau of Investigation for examination. CBI Examiner Chet Ubowski will ask for five handwriting tests from Patsy Ramsey over a five-month period.**

**October 1997—Boulder police detectives consult three other handwriting analysts for their opinions on the Ramsey ransom note.**

*Ramsey Attorneys Handwriting Analysis Process*

**January 1997—Ramsey attorneys receive a copy of the Ramsey ransom note from Boulder Police Detective Linda Arndt.**

**January 1997—Ramsey attorneys hire two handwriting experts, Howard Rile, Jr., and Lloyd Cunningham.**

**May 1997—Handwriting analysts Rile and Cunningham give a presentation to the Boulder Police Department and to Boulder District Attorney Office investigators that indicates Patsy did not write the note and explains why.**

BOULDER POLICE DEPARTMENT DETECTIVE LINDA ARNDT, on her own initiative, gave the Ramseys' attorneys a copy of the ransom note found in the Ramsey home within the first two weeks of the investigation of JonBenét's murder. The Ramsey attorneys immediately hired two nationally known handwriting experts. Meanwhile, BPD officials sent a copy of the ransom note to the Colorado Bureau of Investigation. CBI handwriting analyst Chet Ubowski spent ten months studying the note and gave Patsy Ramsey five separate handwriting tests before the BPD sought other outside opinions. The note is approximately 372-words long.

For contrast, the first ransom note in the 1932 kidnapping of Aviator Charles Lindbergh's baby boy was 58 words in length. The child was taken from his second-floor bedroom in the family home in Hopewell, New Jersey. The ransom note, left in a small white envelope, was written in cursive and riddled with spelling and punctuation errors.

> Dear Sir!
>
> Have 50,000$ redy 2500 in 20$ bills 1500$ in 10$ bills and 1000$ in 5$ bills. After 2-4 days we will inform you were to the deliver the Mony. We warn you for making anyding public or for notify the polise the child is in gute care. Indication for all letters are singnature and 3 holes.

Two months and thirteen ransom notes later, the Lindbergh baby was found dead in a shallow grave. His skull had been broken. Richard Bruno Hauptmann, a carpenter from the Bronx, was arrested and convicted after being tracked by the type of money he'd used to pay for ransom note delivery. A handwriting analyst testified in Hauptmann's trial that the suspect had written all of the ransom notes. Hauptmann was electrocuted in 1936.

Handwriting analysis was first admitted into court in England in 1792. It was deemed to be unscientific by some and since then has had a checkered history of admittance into court as evidence. While expert handwriting testimony is currently allowed in Colorado state courts, it is not admitted in all states or in all courts in the United States.

The accuracy of handwriting analysis is impacted by the fact that, until the 1990s, most students in the US were taught how to write in the Palmer Method, so they share similar handwriting characteristics. While the Palmer Method has continued to be taught, the D'Nealian style was also introduced in US public schools in 1978.

The trend toward admitting handwriting in court in the United States is increasing, but there are still limits. One high-profile trial in which handwriting analysis was presented as evidence was the 1997 Oklahoma City bombing trial in Denver. (BPD #30-656.) The bombing had destroyed the Alfred P. Murrah Federal Building in Oklahoma City in

June of 1995, killing 168 people, including 19 children. In February 1997, defense attorneys representing accused bomber Timothy McVeigh filed a motion asking that handwriting analysis be excluded because it was "junk science." Federal Judge Richard Matsch rejected that request, ruling the results of handwriting similarity and dissimilarity tests would be allowed.

Judge Matsch's decision underscored the fact that, while handwriting analysis is not as widely used, or accepted, as DNA, it may provide possible investigative information, or be used as an indicator of likelihood. Boulder District Attorney Alex Hunter told a few members of his staff and some reporters that he was "very interested" in Judge Matsch's ruling and followed the progress of the motions in federal court, adding that he wanted to know more about the validity of handwriting analysis and the likelihood of a judge allowing it in court for a possible trial in Boulder.

The length of the Ramsey ransom note was theorized to be an advantage for law enforcement because of the number of words it contained. The theory stated that a writer of such a long ransom note would normally be unable to consistently disguise their own handwriting throughout the entire length of the note. Handwriting experts have stated that the Boulder Police Department should have been able to get a relatively clear picture of who might or might not have written the Ramsey ransom note just by looking at the laborious way it moved along.

There were several initial theories that emerged about the Ramsey ransom note and when it was likely written. The first and most prevalent theory was that Patsy wrote the note as part of a staged cover-up after she'd killed her daughter because JonBenét wet her bed. A second theory suggested that somehow nine-year-old Burke was involved in his sister's death accidentally, and the ransom note was part of a staged cover-up by his parents. A third theory was that John had been molesting his daughter, she was mortally injured, and he wrote the note as part of the cover-up. A fourth theory was that the killer had been in the home before Christmas Day, taken Patsy's tablet, written the ransom note elsewhere and then brought it back into the home with him when he was prepared to commit the crime. Or that the killer carried a copy of the words to be used in the note into the home, and then re-copied them onto a tablet in the Ramsey home while the Ramsey family was at a friend's dinner party.

The first samples of the Ramseys' handwriting were given to the Boulder Police Department that Thursday morning, December 26, before JonBenét's body was found. The samples came from notepads the family kept in their home and had been written in the days and weeks leading up to the murder.

When John gave the notepads to the police, he also wrote at the top of one of the notepads at their request.

On Saturday, December 28, two days after JonBenét's body was found, John, Patsy and Burke Ramsey met with a BPD detective to give handwriting samples. These samples were given at the friends' home where the family was staying and were supervised by BPD Detective Linda Arndt. Melinda and John Andrew Ramsey, JonBenét's half-sister and half-brother, also gave handwriting samples that day. It was the only time the two half-siblings would do so.

John Ramsey gave Boulder Police Department officials handwriting samples on three separate occasions: on December 26, 1996, when he wrote at the top of the white notepad that contained his and Patsy's handwriting; on December 28, 1996 and on January 5, 1997. Burke provided one sample to police. Patsy gave five handwriting samples to the police: on December 28, 1996 and on January 4, February 28, April 12 and May 20, 1997. All of the Ramsey handwriting samples were provided voluntarily.

During these handwriting tests, experts asked the family members to write out the words from the ransom note several times with both their right and left hands, using a typed copy of the ransom note as a guide. The original note was not present during the handwriting tests.

The handwriting sessions included writing the ransom note over and over again. John and Patsy have since said this process was "traumatizing and immobilizing." Over and over again, they had to read and write the taunting words of the person who had killed their daughter.

Experts also analyzed samples of John and Patsy's handwriting from prior to December 26, 1996. This is called "normal or historical" handwriting. Handwriting analysts from both the prosecution and the Ramsey side quickly eliminated the possibility that either John or Burke Ramsey had written the ransom note.

Supposedly "confidential" information about the December 28, 1996 DNA and handwriting tests in which multiple members of the Ramsey family participated, including Patsy, was published in the *Rocky Mountain News* three days later on Tuesday, December 31. The handwriting tests and the leaks about them became another study in media manipulation. It also built the case that members of the media were not using sources from each side for handwriting expertise in their published stories. The headline for that story read, in part:

> OFFICIALS GET SAMPLES OF HAIR, BLOOD, WRITING FROM RAMSEY, WHO HAS QUIT TALKING TO POLICE

That same article stated that samples were taken from some Ramsey family members, "but not from her [JonBenét's] mother." Again, that's despite the fact that there was a BPD report from Saturday, December 28, 1996 that gave the times of the DNA testing for the Ramsey family, including Patsy.

As previously noted, the information published in that *Rocky Mountain News* article was wrong. Patsy gave both DNA and handwriting samples on Saturday, December 28. The incorrect information was provided to the *Rocky Mountain News* by a police spokeswoman.

On March 4, 1997, in an attempt to quell growing anti-Ramsey publicity, the Ramsey legal team decided to be pro-active and announce that Patsy had taken her third handwriting test. This tactic didn't work, however. Instead, it was countered by anti-Patsy backlash via a "sources say" leak in a March 8 *Daily Camera* article with the headline:

> RANSOM NOTE AUTHOR LIKELY WAS FEMALE, SOURCES SAY.

According to a US Secret Service handwriting expert, stating that a ransom note written in block-style printing must have been authored by a female constitutes speculation.

Through March 1997, there were more anti-Patsy articles published in *The Gazette* in Colorado Springs ("RAMSEY PROBE FOCUSES ON MOTHER'S WRITING") and in the *Rocky Mountain News* ("HANDWRITING POINTS TO PATSY RAMSEY").

This information was also leaked by law enforcement officials. At the time, however, the Boulder Police Department had only consulted with the CBI handwriting analyst and had not yet received any definitive results from him.

There was more publicity in March 1997 from "sources" who said police were examining the Ramseys' vacation home in Michigan for more of Patsy's handwriting samples.

The Ramsey attorneys hired two handwriting experts. The Boulder Police Department eventually consulted with four.

The first person to seriously study the handwriting in the Ramsey ransom note for the Boulder Police Department was Chet Ubowski with the Colorado Bureau of Investigation. While a Boulder detective trained in the examination of questioned documents had looked at the note on the morning of December 26, 1996, it was later determined that the original note needed to go to someone with more experience.

Ubowski began examining the Ramsey ransom note in January 1997. His last handwriting sample from Patsy Ramsey was taken on May 20, 1997.

Ubowski's conclusion: There is evidence which indicates that the ransom note may have been written by Patsy Ramsey, "but the evidence falls short of that necessary to support a definite conclusion."

"Detectives were hoping . . . to get an unequivocal opinion from the Colorado Bureau of Investigation examiner, which they, of course, never got," said Pat Burke, Patsy's attorney. "They should have simultaneously been consulting other experts. Then, the CBI investigator wouldn't give the conclusion they wanted about Patsy Ramsey's handwriting. Law enforcement couldn't get the definitive conclusion that Patsy wrote the note, because, obviously she didn't write the note."

In October 1997, when it became clear that Ubowski's opinion about whether Patsy had written the Ramsey ransom note would be inconclusive, police reports show that BPD officials began consulting other handwriting experts.

According to one police report, two Boulder detectives reviewed the credentials of various work document examiners and selected the US Secret Service and specialists Edwin Alford and Leonard Speckin to conduct additional comparisons between Patsy Ramsey's handwriting and the handwriting found in the Ramsey ransom note. (BPD Report #1-212.)

The US Secret Service is recognized as having one of the foremost questioned-document laboratories in the world. Secret Service examiner Richard Dusak was chosen to analyze the Ramsey ransom note for the Boulder Police Department. Yet Dusak's analysis was never released until now. It was also never leaked to the media. His conclusion was a stunner. Secret Service Examiner Richard Dusak concluded that Patsy Ramsey never wrote the Ramsey ransom note: "No evidence to indicate that Patsy Ramsey executed any of the questioned material appearing on the ransom note."

The two other handwriting analysis experts consulted by the Boulder Police Department came to similar conclusions regarding the Ramsey ransom note:

Examination of the questioned handwriting and comparison with the handwriting specimens submitted "has failed to provide a basis for identifying Patricia Ramsey as the writer of the letter." (Private Document Examiner Edwin Alford, Jr.)

"I can find no evidence that Patsy Ramsey disguised her handprinting exemplars. When I compare the handprinting habits of Patsy Ramsey with those presented in the questioned ransom note, there exists agreement to the extent that some of her individual letter formations and letter combinations do appear in the ransom note. When this agreement is weighed against the number, type and consistency of the differences present, I am unable to identify Patsy Ramsey as the author of the questioned ransom note with any degree of certainty. I am however, unable to eliminate her as the author." (Private Document Examiner Leonard Speckin.)

The Ramsey defense attorneys hired two document examiners shortly after they were given a copy of the Ramsey ransom note by Detective Linda Arndt in January 1997. They chose two nationally recognized handwriting experts based on their biographies. Those experts immediately began examining the copy of the note and would continue to analyze it prior to their grand jury testimonies in 1999. Over the two-year span, these experts' opinions only got stronger in discounting the Ramseys as the writers of the note. Both experts eliminated John and believed it highly unlikely that Patsy had written the ransom note:

> In my judgment, the evidence argues very strongly for a writer other than Mrs. Ramsey. (Forensic Document Examiner Howard C. Rile, Jr.)

> [T]here were no significant individual characteristics, but much significant difference in Patsy's writing and the ransom note. (Forensic Document Examiner Lloyd Cunningham.)

So certain were the Ramsey defense attorneys of their handwriting experts that in May 1997, they invited investigators from the Boulder District Attorney's Office and the Boulder Police Department to a presentation conducted by their two analysts. This was an unusual move by the attorneys. The two handwriting experts were allowed to look at the original note the morning of their presentation. Attorney Pat Burke said he and the other Ramsey attorneys were "trying to get the police to become more open-minded."

But the case detectives in the meeting (including Detective Steve Thomas), who were focused on Patsy as the killer, didn't budge. They stayed with their Colorado Bureau of Investigation analyst and his eventual conclusion that Patsy Ramsey "may" have written the note, even though the CBI analyst said "the evidence falls short of that necessary to support a definite conclusion."

The two Ramsey experts and two of the experts consulted by the Boulder Police Department in 1997 concluded that Patsy Ramsey did not, or probably did not, write the Ramsey ransom note. The other two police experts consulted by the Boulder Police Department concluded that she could not be included or excluded as the writer of the ransom note.

According to the Ramsey attorneys, "Patsy should have been eliminated as a suspect because the almost-uniform consensus from the most qualified handwriting experts was, and is, that Patsy Ramsey hadn't written the note."

Then there was a study of the actual language, phrasing and words in the Ramsey ransom note that led, in one instance, to a peculiar sequence of events.

Donald Foster, PhD, of Vassar University was a professor of English literature and self-professed forensic linguistic analyst. During his foray into the Ramsey case, Dr. Foster had the distinction of giving opposing "expert" opinions about the author of the ransom note to each side, both to the Ramseys and to the Boulder Police Department, within nine months.

In June 1997, Foster wrote an unsolicited and rather surprising letter to Patsy Ramsey saying he knew that she had not written the ransom note.[1]

"I know that you are innocent—know it, absolutely and unequivocally. I would stake my professional reputation on it—indeed, my faith in humanity." (Dr. Donald Foster letter to Patsy Ramsey 6-18-1997.)

Patsy and her attorneys never responded to Foster's letter but kept it as they kept all correspondence related to the case.

Months later, when the handwriting battle appeared lost for the prosecution, District Attorney Alex Hunter began looking for help analyzing the words in the ransom note. He heard that Dr. Donald Foster was an expert in language linguistics. On January 16, 1998, Foster was told that he was being retained by the Boulder Police Department. (BPD Report #1-505.)

Two months later on March 26, 1998, after a "careful study" of handwriting documents of Patsy and John Ramsey that had been submit-

10:06 06/25/'97 RAMSEY 6165471244 PAGE 02

VASSAR COLLEGE
POUGHKEEPSIE - NEW YORK 12601
Department of English

URGENT AND CONFIDENTIAL

Vassar College Box 388
18 June 1997

Donald W. Foster
Jean Webster Professor of Dramatic Literature

Mrs. Patricia Ramsey
112 Belvedere Ave
Charlevoix, MI 49720-1411

Dear Mrs. Ramsey,

This, first of all: I am terribly sorry for your irremediable loss. JonBenét was a remarkably charming and talented little girl, and I believe that you were an ideal mother, wise, protective, caring, truly devoted. I have no adequate words of consolation for your bereavement, or for its attendant horrors. I am sorry also to hear of your illness. I hope you that will overcome your cancer, not only for your own sake, but for Burke's. It must be hard to find the will to carry on, and the road ahead will be terribly difficult for you both. Your remark that you will soon be with JonBenét worries me--I urge you to find the strength, deep within your soul, to endure, not just for your sake and his, but for JonBenét's. If you succumb to your sorrow and illness, Burke may be lost at sea for the rest of his life, JonBenét may never receive justice, and the person who tortured and killed her will remain free to kill again.

I know that you are innocent--know it, absolutely and unequivocally. I would stake my professional reputation on it--indeed, my faith in humanity. But first, a word about my credentials (this comes from a sense of urgency, not immodesty): I have acquired some fame and prominence as an expert text analyst (true) and "computer expert" (not so true). I used to undertake such work only for myself or for fellow scholars; more recently, for attorneys (defense and prosecution alike) and investigative journalists. Most recently, I have been assisting the Prosecution

Portion of unsolicited letter to Patsy from Vassar professor she didn't know saying he knows she didn't write the ransom note. He was later hired by BPD and said she did write the ransom note.

ted to him by the Boulder Police Department (BPD Report #1-1509) and nine months after he'd sent his letter to Patsy proclaiming that she could not have possibly written the ransom note, Dr. Foster told Hunter that he was sure Patsy Ramsey had written the ransom note based on his examination of the language in it.

At this time, however, Dr. Foster failed to disclose to the Boulder District Attorney that he had not only previously and "unequivocally" concluded that Patsy was innocent, but had written to her that he was so certain she had not written the ransom note that he "would stake his personal reputation" on that conclusion.

In Dr. Foster's elaboration of his opinion for Boulder law enforcement officials, he went so far as to say that it was not possible that any individual other than Patsy Ramsey had written the ransom note. He announced his conclusion to a group of investigators from both the Boulder District Attorney's Office and the Boulder Police Department. Law enforcement officers in attendance said some detectives stood up and cheered and clapped when Foster ended his presentation.

After Foster had given his presentation, a prosecutor in the Boulder District Attorney's Office told John's attorney, Bryan Morgan, about the BPD's "new and expert" language analyst, and the expert's conclusion that Patsy had written the note. He concluded by stating that, due to this new development, the BPD's case against Patsy was gaining momentum.

At that point, it would have been easy for the Ramsey defense attorneys not to tell the Boulder District Attorney's Office about Foster's letter to Patsy in which he stated that he knew she was innocent. The Ramsey attorneys knew that if they withheld that information, it would eventually be publicly disclosed that Foster had duped Boulder law enforcement officials, and that disclosure would cause substantial embarrassment for the police and for the prosecution. Yet the Ramsey attorneys told the attorneys at the District Attorney's Office about Foster's 180-degree decision because Morgan stated, "We still wanted them to consider someone other than the Ramseys as their suspects and we thought this show of good faith would help." Foster was subsequently dropped from the BPD list of expert witnesses and hustled out of Boulder.

When I wrote to Dr. Foster in 2010 asking for an explanation of his opinions, he replied only after I had sent five e-mails to him. He said he couldn't comment on his complete reversal because of a confidentiality agreement he had signed with the Boulder Police Department. However, that confidentiality agreement hadn't covered the letter he'd written to Patsy Ramsey stating that he was certain she had not written the ransom note. Still, Dr. Foster refused to comment and thanked me for "understanding."

# CHAPTER 19

# THE CASE— BOULDER POLICE DEPARTMENT

Overview of Boulder from hill to the east of the city. The city is nestled in a valley. © Dan Weaver.

THE ROCKY MOUNTAINS with all their majestic heights have a thousand different moods that change with the time of day, the angle and intensity of the light, the weather, the season. The Rockies can be vividly serene, welcoming and beautiful. They can also turn menacing, hurling down violent storms that sometimes spin into tornados and rake the eastern plains of Colorado. Winter blizzards and spring storms can bring many feet of snow, creating havoc from the side streets of Front Range towns to Denver International Airport.

Boulder is very much defined by the Rockies, and not solely as a matter of topography. Along with the city's signature Flatirons, which rise just to the south and west of Boulder, the Rocky Mountains play a large role in the town's identity, giving it a Magic-Kingdom sense of isolation that allows residents to perceive themselves as the beneficiaries of a multifaceted grandeur. The great peaks all around, the nearby forests, and the tumbling, clear mountain creek that bisects the city all contribute to the general understanding among residents that they live in a special place.

Beyond that commonly shared assumption, Boulder is also defined by a liberalism typical of most university towns. To live in Boulder and embrace this outlook is one thing, but to be on the outside looking in or to live in Boulder and fundamentally disagree with a liberal point of view can lead to conflicts and tension on numerous levels. In outside circles, the city had been labeled the "People's Republic of Boulder" due to long-held public opinion that the people who live here consider themselves to be enlightened, are self-absorbed and/or overly concerned with environmental issues, and prefer not to interact with those who do not share their particular outlook.

The Boulder Police Department has long operated in a community often perceived by officers as politically out of touch with the nuances of law enforcement. Boulder government leaders do not always seem willing to work with the BPD to accomplish its goals and do not always show public appreciation for BPD efforts by pursuing charges and trials when arrests are made.

There is a common understanding in the metropolitan Denver area that you have to be from Boulder in order to successfully do business in Boulder. In the mid-1990s, this undercurrent affected every one of the police officers who worked in Boulder, and yet were not from Boulder.

Virtually all Boulder Police Department officers lived outside city limits at that time because they simply could not afford housing prices in town. Since the late 1970s, Boulder's growth rate cap limiting the number of new residential units that could be built in the city annually had contributed to skyrocketing housing costs. To some extent, the fact that the city's police patrolled streets in neighborhoods where they couldn't afford to live reinforced the disconnect they felt with the townspeople. The people who lived in Boulder weren't their neighbors.

As with every police department, BPD had its own culture, and it was one of being outsiders who were isolated and lacked support in the town they were sworn to protect. In early 2002, after several years of small riots on the University of Colorado campus during which college students dragged their old sofas off their porches and set them on fire to protest or celebrate something, the Boulder City Council showed its true colors. Instead of going after the students with arson or criminal mischief charges as the BPD would have preferred, the Boulder City Council simply passed an ordinance forbidding upholstered furniture from being outside, including on a porch. The officers at the Boulder Police Department were stunned.

That thought process has continued. In early 2014, a Boulder City Councilwoman suggested researching if licensed dogs in Boulder should be required to get a DNA test. The reason? To explore any left-behind canine waste in order to determine which pet owners are not picking up after their dogs in public areas.

In the mid-1990s, the BPD worked in what Boulderites considered to be their safe "little town." A few weeks before the Ramsey murder, Boulder Police Chief Tom Koby had actually warned people to please not leave their keys in their cars because vehicles had been stolen right out of driveways.

Yet at that time Boulder was also the home of high-tech companies, government labs, and a major university with a Nobel Prize winner on staff. One requirement of being hired by the Boulder Police Department was to have a college degree. Until 2001, BPD was organized differently than most others. Under the Boulder police union contract, officers regularly rotated through the various units including patrol, traffic, and investigations, an arrangement that effectively denied officers the ability to gain the expertise and experience they needed to perform their jobs in any department well. Since the Ramsey murder, that structure has changed in order to allow officers longer periods of time in individual units.

Some of the officers who worked for the Boulder Police Department in December 1996 have said that the department's culture and its attitude toward the city and its inhabitants affected the first steps taken on the Ramsey murder investigation. Initially, Boulder Commander John Eller wanted to be cautious and considerate with the Ramseys. According to an officer inside the department who was involved in the case, Eller had no homicide experience but was aware of the political risks involved when wealthy people found themselves at the center of a horrendous murder investigation.

In the first six hours following Patsy Ramsey's 911 phone call, when the case was effectively bungled and law enforcement did an about-face from sympathy for the parents to suspicion, the out-of-touch atmosphere at the BPD and the fact that the police were operating in isolation had a dramatic impact on the investigation. Meanwhile, BPD officials' initial decisions to not personally respond to the media and public about the case helped fuel the building media frenzy. Speculation reigned.

Boulder Police Chief Mark Beckner and former Chief Tom Koby declined requests to be interviewed about the Ramsey murder investigation for this book. Retired Adams County District Attorney Bob Grant, however, agreed. Adams County is in the northeastern greater Denver metropolitan area. Grant was term-limited out of office in 2005 after fourteen years as district attorney. Since then, he has served as executive director with the Colorado District Attorney's Council and serves on the board of directors of CASA, court-appointed special advocates. CASA recruits and trains volunteers to assist and represent abused and neglected children in court and other places. Grant was involved in the Ramsey case at the request of then Colorado Governor Roy Romer and Boulder District Attorney Alex Hunter, who was told point-blank by Romer to avail himself of outside help.

"I and three other district attorneys were asked to review the case, be able to consult with Alex and his team and to provide expertise to analyze the investigation. I also dealt with the media and was readily accessible for perspective," Grant has said. "The four of us met with Boulder Police for their presentation on the case and to consider and coordinate a possible grand jury."

Grant is a straightforward and blunt Scots-Irishman who is well known for his many media appearances related to the Ramsey case. As a district attorney, he was all law and order, and defense attorneys who worked with him still speak of him with nostalgia. They liked his tough yet consistent way of dealing with them. Grant was candid, a trait that has stayed with him into retirement.

"There was a lot of distrust between Boulder Police and the District Attorney's Office when the Ramsey murder happened," Grant said. "There is always the possibility of that disconnect in police/prosecutor relations, but there the connection between the two was a festering problem that continued to need attention. Police and prosecutors have to be vigilant about maintaining communications. There are always going to be disagreements, but there has to be a way to air those disagreements productively, and there wasn't in Boulder at that point."

Some law enforcement officers thought that Boulder District Attorney Alex Hunter's constant plea bargains on charges coupled with the documented lack of trials in Boulder represented a form of liberal permissiveness that put "getting along" ahead of getting the end results that the police felt their efforts merited.

"The reputation of the Boulder District Attorney was that he didn't try cases," said Grant. "They had this plea bargain deal where they'd make a deal before charging. 'We won't file this charge, but we will file this charge' kind of thing. The police hated it. But Alex had his finger on the pulse of his community. He understood the community, the voters and the jurors. His decisions were right for the Boulder community, but often didn't seem right to the Boulder Police Department."

While BPD officials didn't trust Hunter as a matter of course, Boulder prosecutors were deeply concerned with the police department's flawed efforts that began on the first day of the Ramsey case and impacted almost every aspect of the investigation.

That privately held opinion was made very public in early 1997, when Boulder First Assistant District Attorney Bill Wise went before the Boulder County Commissioners to ask for money to hire an experienced homicide detective and a full-time deputy DA exclusively for the Ramsey murder investigation. During his presentation, Wise publicly criticized the BPD investigation of the case. In the volatile atmosphere already created by the Ramsey investigation, Wise's public criticism of the Boulder Police Department poured gasoline on the embers and created a heated blowback from the BPD. Wise was subsequently removed from the case, and retired Colorado Springs Homicide Detective Lou Smit was hired.

At this early stage in the Ramsey murder investigation, District Attorney Hunter did not have criminal investigators in the true sense. According to a detective familiar with the structure of responsibilities in the Boulder District Attorney's Office at the time, Hunter's investigators conducted criminal background checks and made phone call checks, but they were not on-the-scene investigators.

Grant would not give an opinion about who he thinks killed JonBenét Ramsey. "I was never able to convince myself that it was an inside job with Patsy, John or Burke being responsible. And I was never able to convince myself that it was an intruder."

He said detectives from the BPD had theorized that one or both of JonBenét's parents had killed her. In a scenario painted by Grant with input from former and current police investigators, one can grasp why members of the Boulder Police Department believed as they did:

- From the BPD's viewpoint, the people who had been inside the home at the time of the murder would necessarily be the first suspects. This reflects standard procedure in a homicide investigation.

However, some of the Ramsey case detectives broke a basic rule of conducting a homicide investigation by not following the evidence. Instead, BPD officials decided that their primary suspects were John and Patsy Ramsey and then looked primarily for evidence that fit that theory. (WHYD Investigative Archive.)

- BPD officials were concerned about contradictions in John and Patsy's separate statements about what happened early on Thursday, December 26, 1996. Such contradictions included Patsy not remembering whether she saw the ransom note or JonBenét's empty bed first, and John and Patsy not knowing whether one or both of them went to Burke's bedroom. (WHYD Investigative Archive.)

Ramsey attorneys insisted that Patsy and John Ramsey had both been in shock when they spoke with different Boulder Police Department investigators about these events, and that some contradictions in their statements from that morning were to be expected. Certain that BPD officers had made errors in citing information from their clients, the Ramsey attorneys also asserted that if BPD officials had taken charge immediately after JonBenét's body was found and conducted formal interviews with John and Patsy at that point, they would have obtained a clear picture of what had transpired. The attorneys also pointed to details related to when Patsy saw the note and her daughter's empty bedroom that had been described concisely in Detective Linda Arndt's police report, which states that Patsy saw the ransom note first and then went to her daughter's room.

- Confusion also existed as to whether the blanket on which JonBenét's body was lying when her body was found by her father had been wrapped around her loosely or tightly. If it had been wrapped tightly, this would have signified to experts that someone had been trying to take care of JonBenét after she was killed. This would also signify to the police that at least one of the parents had been involved in the murder. In a July 1998 interrogation of John Ramsey by Chief Deputy District Attorney Mike Kane, who had

> been appointed to the position by Colorado Governor Roy Romer's Special Council, and Homicide Detective Lou Smit, who had been hired by Boulder DA Alex Hunter after an extensive vetting process, more was revealed about how JonBenét's body had been positioned in relation to the blanket. John's attorney, Bryan Morgan, and an investigator with his office, David Williams, were with John during the interrogation.

According to the transcript, when questioned by Lou Smit about the blanket, John answered that it "was crossed in front of her as if someone was tucking her in." He also said with additional questioning that his daughter's arms had been outside the blanket and raised above her head, and her feet had been uncovered. Further on in the interrogation, when questioned once more about the blanket, John said, "It was like an Indian papoose." This information was leaked to the media and only hardened the law enforcement's determination that the Ramseys had been involved in their daughter's death, because the killer had tried to take care of JonBenét after she'd been killed.

At the time, the Ramsey attorneys asserted that how the blanket was situated could also have indicated that the sexual predator who had killed JonBenét had shown brief remorse and tried to take care of her after she'd died. They added that any blanket theories represented "guessing" by Boulder Police Department officials and asked why John Ramsey would have incriminated himself when he'd been the only one to see how his daughter had been wrapped when he discovered her body? They also noted that a "papoose-style" of wrapping a child in a blanket sometimes encloses the feet as well, which in this case hadn't been covered.[1] The attorneys concluded that there were just too many assumptions being made related to the blanket, that John had been in shock, and that no factual basis existed that would allow anyone to conclude anything about the blanket. Lou Smit later said he believed the blanket had been tossed loosely around JonBenét's body.

- "John Ramsey said he'd read a story to both Burke and JonBenét out in the sitting room until 10:30 pm on Christmas night." (Officer Rick French, Date of Formal Interview 1-10-1997.)

Officer French wrote this in his first police report. Detective Arndt's report said that John had read to JonBenét and Burke and then gone to bed. Both reports contradicted later police information that stated John Ramsey had carried JonBenét to bed when the family first arrived home that night, and John played briefly with Burke before they each went to bed.

- The Boulder Police Department initially suspected John of incest, but there was no prior evidence for that, according to JonBenét's pediatrician, the coroner and the specialist he brought in from Children's Hospital in Denver, and the director of the Kempe Child Abuse Center. Other family suspects were considered, but when those didn't work out because of lack of evidence, police focused on Patsy Ramsey. Some BPD investigators theorized that Patsy had flown into a rage over JonBenét's possible bedwetting or something else, struck JonBenét, mortally wounding her, and then staged a cover-up that involved the torture, sexual assault and death of her daughter. Others imagined Burke had somehow injured his sister, and his parents covered up for him. Burke weighed 68 pounds as recorded in his medical records from August 1996, four months before his sister's murder. (WHYD Investigative Archive.)

- BPD officials also suspected that the alleged cover-up had involved Patsy Ramsey writing the ransom note inside her home. The note and the practice page containing the words "Mr. and Mrs. /" had been written on the tablet that belonged to Patsy. The pen used to write the note was found in the home. According to retired Adams County District Attorney Bob Grant, BPD considered the existence of the practice note to be one of the most incriminating indications that the murder had been an inside job.

From the Ramseys' point of view, however, the presence of the practice note revealed that the killer 1) had been brazen enough to use what he could find in the house to write the ransom note on the premises before killing their daughter, or 2) had been in the house before, possibly during the home's recent and extensive renovations, and removed items including the pen and Patsy's tablet, which he used to write the note outside the home and then replaced in the home before killing their daughter.

- Some BPD investigators speculated that the couple, or one of them, had staged the apparent disruption around the southwest window well and the open basement window with the suitcase under it after their daughter had been killed. They did not think an intruder had gotten into the house that way.

The window well and the possible evidence around it formed the basis for much contentiousness and bitterness related to the Ramsey murder investigation. Questions arose related to whether the state of the window well on Thursday, December 26 signified that an intruder had been present at any point during the night before. A lot rested on the answer to this question, which still hasn't been resolved due to differing opinions among experts on spiders and spider webs and how long it takes for a spider to construct a web. (BPD Reports #1-1106, #5-3339, #1-1108, #1-1109.)

Both an intact spider web and spider web strands were found in the window well the evening of Thursday, December 26. According to Jim Kolar, who studied the case evidence in the mid-2000s as part of his role of chief investigator for the Boulder District Attorney's Office, an extensive police videotape was made of a walk-through of the Ramsey home on the night of December 26, after JonBenét's body had been removed and the police re-entered the home for further investigation. In the videotape, a spider web is shown in the left-hand lower corner of the center window of the three-paned window that sits below the southwest window well. This is the same window that was found open the morning of December 26. The operating theory among Boulder detectives was that the intact spider web proved the killer had not climbed into the house by that window because that particular spider web would have been disturbed if that had been the case.

But according to reports from three different BPD officers, at least one spider web inside that window well had been disturbed. On Friday through Monday (December 27–30), those officers noticed spider web drag lines coming from the grate covering the window well and going down into the window well space. (BPD Report #1-1363.) According to one of those officers, these findings would indicate "that a spider web was disturbed." But others disagreed.

Later tests conducted by the Boulder Police Department also revealed that it would have been possible for an adult to climb through the center pane of the three-paned window into the basement, although others have long argued against this possibility. John Ramsey found this window open the morning of December 26. Styrofoam packing peanuts also seemed to have been brushed into the right and left window well spaces away from the center window, possibly indicating that someone had moved such debris in order to enter the center window, a possibility that would support an intruder theory. Other packing peanuts were also on the basement floor.

Yet it did not appear at the time that the dirt on the window sill at the center window had been disturbed. That finding casts doubt on the intruder theory. Or does it? Given the quality of the photographs taken by the BPD of the window in question, some say it is difficult to ascertain whether or not the dirt had been disturbed and therefore impossible to conclude whether anyone had gone into or out of that window based on these photos.

To further complicate issues related to the southwest window well, green foliage that had grown at the edge of the window well's grate was found folded over and underneath that grate. The folded foliage was still fresh when it was examined in the days after December 26, indicating the grate had recently been lifted and closed, according to Detective Lou Smit.

BPD Detective Carey Weinheimer also investigated the window grate and the material under it. According to excerpts from his report in the WHYD Investigative Archive, Weinheimer stated his observations:

Left, center, and right window well. Courtesy Boulder Police and Boulder County District Attorney.

Window grate from west-facing window. Lifting the grate and climbing through the basement windows below was one of the theories for how an intruder could have gotten into the home. Courtesy Boulder Police and Boulder County District Attorney.

"The weight of the grate crushed and traumatized the plant material under it. The plant will not just grow under the grate naturally." (BPD Report #1-1142.)

While the Ramsey attorneys were convinced there were other ways inside the home including unlocked windows and doors, they also believed the one video photo of a spider web did not preclude the possibility that an intruder had entered the home through the southwest window well. Explanations were also needed for the suitcase, the comfort items found inside the suitcase, the folded-over foliage under the grate, and the leaves and white Styrofoam peanuts that had been pushed away from the center window, and also found in the basement. When the Ramsey attorneys consulted experts on spiders, however, they also found contradictory information.

- Police said the layout of the home was confusing. According to Bob Grant, Boulder investigators questioned how an intruder could have gotten around so easily, particularly in the basement.

John and Patsy routinely left lights on in the first and second floors at night. They had done so on the night of December 25, 1996, a fact confirmed by two different neighbors. Furthermore, an unknown number of construction workers had roamed the house during recent extensive renovations. At least a thousand people had been inside the home during a Boulder Christmas Tour in 1994, when "the Ramsey residence was part of the Historic Society home tour" and "the Ramsey residence had numerous people tour the house as part of the tour." (BPD Reports #5-3919, 5-3920.) Plus, the Ramseys' attorneys believed an intruder could have secretly entered the home several times before because of the couple's careless security that left the alarm system unarmed and doors and windows often unlocked. It was also possible that an intruder at times could have stayed in the basement crawl spaces.

- Boulder Police Department officials noted that the broken paintbrush used to make the garrote to strangle JonBenét had come from within the house and was one of the brushes Patsy used for painting and sketching. (BPD Report #2-9.)

The Ramseys' attorneys said the paintbrush could have been removed covertly from the home and made into a garrote before the murder by an intruder who had broken into the home secretly and frequently.

- BPD officials thought the Ramseys had demonstrated guilt by hiring attorneys, especially because they'd hired separate attorneys. (WHYD Investigative Archive.)

But the Ramseys did not take the initiative to hire attorneys. Mike Bynum, John Ramsey's business attorney and friend who hired the attorneys for the family, has said he did so without specific permission. "It is a common misperception that people are guilty if they hire attorneys," he said, adding, however, that "if you're innocent, it's all the more reason to hire an attorney."

With regard to the concern that the Ramseys had hired separate attorneys: according to Colorado Rules of Professional Conduct as passed by the Colorado Bar Association, since both John and Patsy Ramsey were possible suspects, they had to be represented by separate attorneys.

- The lack of Ramsey interviews, formal interviews and interrogations were considered to be extremely suspicious and frustrating, according to police investigators. (WHYD Investigative Archive.)

"They did do interviews with Boulder Police," Bryan Morgan, John's attorney, explained. "But the police didn't release that information. It was BPD's responsibility to conduct interviews in a timely manner. They had plenty of opportunity the Thursday JonBenét was reported missing and did interview her parents. Then when her body was found, they should have gotten tremendous amounts of information from Patsy and John by taking them to the police station for individual interviews. But the police didn't know what to do. By the time we were fully involved, which was a week after [JonBenét's body] was found, the hostility and focus on the Ramseys being guilty of killing their daughter was so strong that we had to build numerous safeguards into the process; which in the weeks following were beset by game-playing and delays by Boulder investigators."

Morgan continued, "[The Ramseys] didn't ever have to do interviews with the police. They wanted to. Both the police and the defense attorneys were then later involved in delaying the interviews because of what was perceived as a built-in bias against the Ramsey family."

- Both the Boulder Police Department and the Boulder District Attorney's Office were also concerned about the timeline of the digestion of food found in JonBenét's body during the autopsy, and whether such a timeline would help prove who gave the food to her . . . and likely killed her. For nearly a year, these officials assumed that the material in the murdered child's stomach had consisted of pineapple only based on an open bowl of pineapple found on the kitchen table in the Ramsey home the following morning and a mention of pineapple in the coroner's report. (BPD Report #70KKY, #71KKY.)

Boulder police and/or the coroner did not seek out expert opinion or analysis of the contents of JonBenét's stomach/intestine until ten months after her autopsy, when the BPD approached experts at the University of Colorado in Boulder in October 1997. (BPD Report #1-1156.) In late December 1997, the BPD received a report from these experts stating that grapes, grape skins and cherries had been found with pineapple in JonBenét's body. (BPD Report #1-1349.) These foods are commonly included in most cans of fruit cocktail.

All the experts consulted by both the BPD and the Ramsey attorneys disagreed on how long it would take to partially digest the fruits, stating a wide variety of time requirements. One doctor told Boulder Police Department officials that the pineapple, grapes and cherries could have been eaten even the day before her body was found. (BPD Report #26-193.) A forensic coroner consulted in the case told me that "the food would have been in the stomach/intestine within 30 minutes, but digestion of the food would have stopped if she were traumatized by a stun gun or a blow to the head. There is no evidence as to who fed her the fruit."

- The BPD asserted that urine found in JonBenét's underwear had come from her wetting her bed. This also led to the theory that Patsy had become upset about JonBenét's bedwetting and hit her daughter, setting a deadly sequence of events into motion. The bedwetting issue was continually discussed in the early weeks of the investigation as a key to the police theory that one or both of the Ramseys had murdered their child. The housekeeper was quoted as saying that she had changed the sheets from those found on the bed three nights earlier. (WHYD Investigative Archive.)

However, the Ramseys' attorneys said no, JonBenét did not wet the bed the night of December 25, 1996, adding that the urine in her underwear most likely was caused by the trauma of a stun gun, her strangulation, the blow to the head or her death. Police reports also make it clear that JonBenét did not wet the bed that night. Evidence admitted into police custody (BPD Reports #44, #45, #46 #47, #48KKY, #2-7, #50KKY, #2-18) from the sheets, pillow and bedspread that had been on JonBenét's bed showed that forensic analysts had found fibers from her bed clothing on her sheets, indicating that they hadn't been changed, according to Detective Lou Smit. At least one crime scene photo reportedly showed sheets from JonBenét's bed in the dryer just outside of her room. Patsy said clean sheets were often left in the dryer until they needed to be used again.

JonBenét's family members have always insisted that her bedwetting was not a big deal, and Patsy has said she was never angry with her daughter about such accidents, but concerned for JonBenét, who was embarrassed by them when they did occasionally occur.

- BPD officers who worked the case were deeply and adversely affected by JonBenét's participation in child beauty pageants and wondered what kind of parents would encourage their child's participation. One high-ranking officer, upon seeing JonBenét's pageant picture for the first time, said "she looked like a whore." He would not allow his name to be used for this book. But such an attitude affected some BPD detectives' perceptions of John and Patsy Ramsey. The pictures and videos of JonBenét's participation in the pageants also helped drive the publicity about the murder. Many in the public judged her parents harshly for allowing or encouraging their daughter's participation in the child beauty pageant circuit, which was underscored by the endless broadcasting of video of JonBenét in pageant contests. (WHYD Investigative Archive.)

JonBenét's family and the Ramseys' attorneys have always insisted that JonBenét was an active little girl who wanted to be in the pageants and enjoyed them as much as she enjoyed other fun activities.

- Boulder Police Department officials noted that fibers from Patsy's clothing were on her daughter's clothes and insisted that indicated she'd carried her daughter to the basement to kill her. (WHYD Investigative Archive.)

The Ramseys and their lawyers maintained that Patsy could have left fibers on her daughter when she hugged JonBenét good night on December 25th or the next day when Patsy held her daughter's dead body, especially since Patsy had the same clothes on then. There are also other fibers on JonBenét's clothing that police were not able to identify, according to Detective Lou Smit and police reports. (BPD Reports #1-77, #26-187.)

- BPD officials were suspicious that Patsy was wearing the same outfit on Thursday morning that she'd worn the night before. They suggested that she hadn't had enough time to change or simply forgot to change because she was so busy staging the crime. (WHYD Investigative Archive.)

The Ramsey team has always argued that theory was ridiculous. If Patsy had tortured and murdered her daughter while wearing those clothes, and was clever and meticulous enough to do all that staging, why wouldn't it have occurred to her to change her clothes in order to hide any possible DNA evidence? They also said that, from a woman's viewpoint, it wouldn't be that unusual to wear a special holiday outfit two days in a row when planning to visit different family and friends.

- BPD officials believed the Ramseys did not act as though they were innocent. Individually, Patsy and John Ramsey acted very differently the morning their daughter was reported missing, according to Detective Linda Arndt's police report, which included hearsay from one officer to another.

But actual police reports and interviews from officers who witnessed the Ramseys' behavior that morning indicated that JonBenét's parents "acted appropriately." (BPD Report #5-3851.) BPD officers interviewed dozens of people, including business associates, teachers and friends across the country, about the Ramsey family, and the comments these people provided were overwhelmingly positive. At the time, Boulder Detective Steve Thomas said, "It seems the theme that's being portrayed is [that] John and Patsy were ideal parents, Christian people. It has been difficult at best during this investigation to uncover anyone that can offer any other perspective on the Ramsey's [sic]." (BPD Report #5-5026.)

Despite these findings, Detective Thomas formed an opinion very early on regarding the Ramsey murder. Eventually he would resign from the Boulder Police Department and, while the case was still active, would co-author a book in which he stated his belief that Patsy Ramsey had killed her daughter. As mentioned, Thomas was sued by the Ramseys about his book and his publisher paid damages.

- Then there was the hugely problematic ransom amount. The FBI quickly discerned that the ransom amount, $118,000, was an unusual number. Why not $100,000? Why not $150,000? Why choose that particular figure? Was it because a Bible on a nightstand next to John and Patsy's bed was turned to Psalm 118? (BPD Report # 1-1017.) The Ramseys said they'd kept that bible turned to a passage in that scripture because it provided peace and strength and gave them comfort.

Was it the amount close to John Ramsey's work bonus (BPD Report #5-797) of $118,117.50? According to the Ramseys' attorneys, the Boulder Police Department had learned about the work bonus coincidence in the first few days of the investigation from Ramsey investigators. The fact that John Ramsey's bonus had been for slightly more than $118,000 didn't make sense, said the attorneys, but that didn't seem to make any difference to the BPD, which soon leaked the information about the ransom amount matching the amount of John's bonus to the media.

Those who disagreed with the police theory related to John Ramsey's bonus didn't think the Ramseys would be so dumb as to use that amount if they had indeed written the ransom note. During the morning that JonBenét was reported missing, the Ramseys indicated to BPD investigators that they, too, were confused about the curious amount of the ransom demand. John said his tax returns were openly sitting in the kitchen, and pay stubs were kept in his unlocked desk at home. Both reflected a recent bonus of $123,000, which after taxes equated to slightly more than $118,000. (BPD Report #5-797.)

The amount of $118,000 was also similar to an amount noted in a case involving two separate people who were fired at Access Graphics, according to police reports. (BPD Reports #5-3295, #5-3488, #5-4809.) In one case, $118,000 was the amount a former employee had been ordered by a judge to repay to Access Graphics after that former employee was convicted of altering account statements in order to steal from the company. (BPD Reports #5-3295, #5-795.) That information was never leaked to the media.

- Another factor that deeply troubled BPD officials had to do with the fact that the killer had seemed to have no fear of discovery. This understanding immediately pointed to an insider or at least to a family-involved crime. (WHYD Investigative Archive.)

Those who disagreed with this theory said simply that it's difficult to predict the behavior of an intruder who is a psychopath or a pedophile, especially one who could have waited in a home for a family to return while writing a ransom note and planning to kill an innocent child. Such proponents of the intruder theory assert that an average person's fear is not the same as that of a predator or a psychopath, especially when one is dealing with an organized psychopathic killer.

- Additional suspicions arose when the autopsy of JonBenét revealed that she had been strangled at least twice, possibly both times with the garrote while she was facedown. The coroner/medical examiner found carpet fibers from the basement on her face and rope marks on her neck that supported this conclusion. Some Boulder

Police Department officers said that such findings indicated JonBenét's parents wouldn't have been able to cope with their daughter looking them in the eyes while they killed her. (WHYD Investigative Archive.)

Those who disagreed with this police theory argued that it was a matter of convenience for an intruder to use the garrote while his victim was facedown. According to military experts and homicide investigators, the common method of using a garrote is to loop it over the neck from the back, causing pressure and using leverage on the front of the neck to strangle.

- In the ransom note, the phrase "and hence" was used. In the Ramsey family's 1997 Christmas card, a year after JonBenét's death, the phrase "and hence" was also used. (BPD Report #33-1851.) In the point of view of BPD officials, this was an uncommon phrase suspiciously repeated.

The Ramseys stated that they did not know why they'd used the phrase in their Christmas card, but added that they might have become subconsciously familiar with it from having to copy the ransom note so many times in handwriting sessions for police and in later grief therapy sessions.

- BPD investigators were very curious about a black eye that the Ramseys' son, Burke, got in May 1997, five months after his sister had been killed. School teachers reported it to Boulder Police. Some BPD officials suggested that this might have been an indication of ongoing child abuse in the family. (BPD Reports #5-3147, #5-3369.)

Police reports documented how Burke said he'd gotten the black eye: "Burke Ramsey came to school with a black eye and he said that he got it playing baseball with his mother and she had thrown the baseball at his eye and he had gotten a black eye." (BPD Reports #5-5261, #1-1586.)

- Most Boulder Ramsey case investigators do not think the killer used a stun gun on JonBenét, although they searched the home for one and for other possible evidence, even taking apart a fireplace grate in their search. There is still no explanation for the two different sets of similar, evenly spaced round marks on JonBenét's body. A chief investigator with the Boulder District Attorney's Office in the mid-2000s later stated that the marks or abrasions shown on JonBenét's body in autopsy photos matched protrusions from the bottom of her brother's toy railroad train tracks. The train and tracks were set up in the basement.

Detective Lou Smit, who was a proponent of the stun gun theory, as were the Ramsey attorneys, suggested that someone with a stun gun could have incapacitated JonBenét in her bed and quietly carried her away, thus supporting an intruder theory. A family member would not have needed a stun gun, he surmised.

- At least one Boulder detective questioned why the Ramseys would have put the December 25, 1996 death date on their daughter's headstone if they hadn't known exactly when she died. The coroner had never stated an exact time of death, but it was presumed that JonBenét died around midnight on December 25 or in the early morning of December 26. (WHYD Investigative Archive.)

John Ramsey has said that he deliberately put December 25 as the date of JonBenét's death because it was Christ's birthday, and he wanted people to understand the outrage of her murder on that date. John added that he also chose the last day he and JonBenét's mother and brother spent with her when she was alive.

- Boulder police consulted audio experts because they speculated that they had heard Burke Ramsey's voice in the background of Patsy's 911 call the morning the ransom note was found. That would contradict John and Patsy Ramsey, who had said their son was still sleeping when Patsy placed that call. While Burke Ramsey did say in a statement that he'd pretended to be asleep when his parents came into his room that morning because they were so upset, according to his parents, he was still upstairs when Patsy placed the 911 call. (WHYD Investigative Archive.)

The 911 tape allegations went nowhere. Boulder Police Department officials were never able to play them clearly for those who gathered for their formal presentation to other law enforcement officials in June 1998.

- Since JonBenét's murder, there has not been a similar crime. This fact led one Boulder detective to privately state, "How could it be an intruder if there was never another crime like it?" (WHYD Investigative Archive.)

There is precedent for notorious killers who simply stopped killing, however.

One Ramsey attorney has pointed to the case of Wichita's serial killer Dennis Rader. Rader tortured and killed ten people between 1974 and 1991 and sent taunting letters to the media and police. He was self-proclaimed as BTK or "Bind, Torture and Kill." In 1991, he stopped killing and all communications from him stopped. For thirteen years, the police and public knew nothing. However, in 2004, he began writing letters publicly again. Through new evidence, police arrested Rader a year later in 2005. A church deacon, he eventually confessed to the ten murders.

In San Francisco in 1968 and 1969, the Zodiac Killer terrorized the city, claiming that he'd killed seven people. He would send letters to newspapers describing each crime and naming the victims. As far as authorities know, he stopped killing in late 1969 and has never been identified.

The Ramsey attorneys have also said that any intruder smart enough to come up with the complicated staging involved in the Ramsey murder would change the way he commits other crimes. Or, they added, it's possible that the killer just stopped killing, is in prison and never had his DNA taken, or is dead.

- Even though matching foreign DNA of a white male had been found on different pieces of clothing that JonBenét wore and on her body, some BPD officials considered this either an accident or a coincidence. (WHYD Investigative Archive.)

The defense responded to that by saying, "What else could it be other than the killer's DNA which doesn't match John and Patsy or their family?"

John's Journal:

*We also offer to pay for the extensive DNA testing that is desirable, but very expensive. I imagined later how confused the police must have been if their prime suspects were offering to pay for the serious part of the investigation. All a scheme to throw them off track, they apparently think. What a bunch of idiots.*

Shortly before Detective Lou Smit died in the summer of 2010 from colon cancer, he entreated those who visited him in hospice to not give up on the Ramseys and their case.

"It's as simple as getting the DNA from the right person," he said. "This is a DNA case now. No matter which way it goes, you have to get around that DNA. The answer is there."

- Some Boulder Police Department detectives were suspicious of two of Patsy's receipts from a Boulder hardware store in early December 1996 that each included a price of $1.99. The hardware store did not itemize then, but black duct tape was sold for $1.99 at that store. (BPD Report #1-792, #1-947, #1-948, #1-897, #1-876.) There were several other charges on the receipt. In Georgia, a sales clerk at a major hardware store reported that Patsy Ramsey had asked for "assistance in locating duct tape," leading detectives assigned to the case to do "a hand search of approximately 20,000 register receipts . . . and they did not find any matches to a

Colorado or Georgia driver's license in the name of Patricia Ramsey." (BPD Report #1-984.) The clerk said Patsy had been in the store between December 7 and December 14, 1996. (BPD Report #1-513.) Yet BPD officials also "couldn't find a register tape for a register for which they believed the witness [clerk] would have been working." (BPD Report #1-809.)

- Boulder police searched extensively to find evidence that one of the Ramseys had bought the type of rope or cord used on JonBenét. They went through thousands of receipts at hardware stores in Atlanta (BPD Report #1-984) and Boulder, then went through a hand search of records in Athens, Georgia, and found nothing conclusive connecting the family to the tape or rope. They did find three $2.29 charges from December 2, 1996 on Patsy's credit card, but the charges were not itemized, and there were several other charges on that receipt. (BPD Report #1-1117.) That amount of $2.29 matched the price listed for white rope purchased at a hardware store that was similar to the rope used in the murder. BPD detectives also found "visually" similar rope at the Boulder Army Store and at McGuckins Hardware, and from a neighbor's garbage can; the neighbor reported that the rope had been used on packages mailed to his home. (BPD Reports #1-513, #1-606, #1-779, #1-792, #1-983, #1-1114, #1-851, #1-885, #1-1125, #1-889.)

With regard to these Boulder Police Department searches, Ramsey attorney Pat Burke said, "They're guessing. These were costs in 1996 where pricing included a large number of items for sale for the less expensive $1.99 and $2.29. The prices then were far less expensive than they are today. It's a good example of the police trying to stretch to find anything to arrest the Ramseys. They didn't find it with these price checks or comparisons."

- The Boulder Police Department also suspected the Ramseys due to unexplained and/or troubling evidence in or near the Ramsey home, or on JonBenét's body:

- A shoe imprint from a Hi-Tec brand of work boot was found in the basement storage room imprinted in mold growing on the floor. It did not trace back to the Ramsey family. All investigators who had been in the room had their shoes tested. There was no match to that size of Hi-Tec boot to the Ramseys or the police investigators (BPD Reports #1-1576, #1-1594.)

- Additional, partial shoe impressions were found near JonBenét's body in the basement storage room and on the toilet tank cover in the basement northeast bathroom. (BPD Report #1-1518.) The Colorado Bureau of Investigation agent investigating these footprints has said that the FBI could never match them to anyone or any brand. (BPD Reports #3-165, #1-1518.)

- An unidentified pubic hair was found on the white blanket that had partially covered JonBenét's body. (BPD Reports #1-1440, #3-128.)

- John Ramsey noticed (and has said he reported to BPD investigators) the presence of a scuff or drag-type mark on the wall underneath the open window in the train room, where the suitcase was found. (BPD Report #1-65.) The scuff mark was noted in later police reports. (BPD Reports #1-101, #1-90.) (BPD Report # 5-421.)

- There was glass and debris from outside the home on top of the suitcase and some debris from outside on the basement floor.

- Some BPD officers stated that John Ramsey had failed to look at, or tell BPD investigators about, the suitcase and open window in the train room. Yet a reference source in a police report noted that John Ramsey had been observed going into the basement, where he found the train room window open and closed it. (BPD Report #5-2733.) One of John's friends also said that he noticed that the basement train room window was open and reported this to BPD investigators.

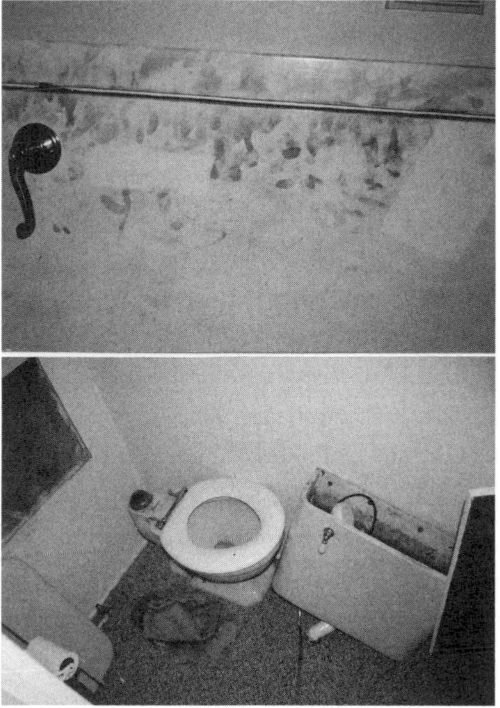

Northeast basement bathroom where an additional partial shoe impression was found on the top of the toilet cover. This area was investigated for possible entry into the home. Courtesy Boulder Police and Boulder County District Attorney.

- A stain on JonBenét's body initially labeled by police as semen (BPD Report #3-15) in later weeks was proven to be a blood smear. The untrue "semen" information, however, was leaked to the media.

- JonBenét's body had been wiped off. The autopsy report stated that, under specific lighting, the remains of some sort of liquid could be seen on her body. (WHYD Investigative Archive—Autopsy.)

- A rope was found inside a brown paper sack underneath a bed in the guest bedroom next to JonBenét's bedroom. This was the room that John Andrew had used when he was home from college.

The rope and brown paper sack did not belong to the Ramseys. (WHYD Investigative Archive.)

- Small pieces of material from the brown paper sack were found in JonBenét's bed and in the coroner's body bag that had been used to transport her. (WHYD Investigative Archive.)

- Brown cotton fibers were found on JonBenét's body, the paintbrush, the duct tape and the rope ligature, according to Detective Lou Smit. These fibers were not identified. Smit was a proponent of the intruder theory and considered the Ramseys innocent. He suggested that these fibers could have been from brown cotton work gloves.

- Two pieces or flakes of white paper were found on JonBenét's cheek. The Colorado Bureau of Investigation completed a microscopic examination of the paper and concluded they were from different sources. (BPD Report #3-40.)

- The suitcase found under the basement window had been used occasionally by John Andrew, who was attending nearby University of Colorado. At the time of JonBenét's death, he was in Atlanta visiting his mother and sister for Christmas. While these facts were not disputed, the purpose of the items found inside the suitcase was questioned. The suitcase contained a pillow sham, a duvet and a Dr. Seuss book, all belonging to the Ramseys. (SMF 146; SMF 146 *Wolf v. Ramsey* deposition—Judge Julie Carnes.) It has been suggested that the killer could have used these items to possibly "comfort" JonBenét.

- Fibers from the same sham and duvet were found on JonBenét's shirt when her clothing was examined. (SMF 147; PSMF 147 *Wolf v. Ramsey* deposition—Judge Julie Carnes.) The Ramsey attorneys asserted that this finding indicates that, at some point, JonBenét or her killer had had contact with those items.

- Fibers from the basement carpet, but no fingerprints, were found on a baseball bat found just outside the Ramsey home. The bat was considered a possible weapon that could have been used to fracture JonBenét's skull. John, Patsy and Burke all said the bat didn't belong to them. (WHYD Investigative Archive.)

- A heavy flashlight, similar to the type of flashlights carried by many police officers, was found on the counter in the Ramsey kitchen. It, like the baseball bat, was considered a possible weapon that could have been used to hit JonBenét and fracture her skull. (BPD Report #3-145.) The flashlight and its batteries were fingerprinted, but no prints were found. The outside of the flashlight and the batteries inside had been wiped clean, according to an investigator. The Ramseys said the flashlight wasn't theirs. (For several months, the flashlight couldn't be found, according to one person working on the investigation. It was finally discovered in police evidence storage when the new commander on the investigation ordered a resorting and documentation of all Ramsey articles.) (WHYD Investigative Archive.)

- Forensic examiners found JonBenét's blood on her Barbie Doll nightgown, which was found next to her body in the basement storage room. (JonBenét Ramsey Murder Book Index.)

- Fibers from the rope used to strangle JonBenét were found on her bed. (JonBenét Ramsey Murder Book Index.)

- Investigators discovered dark animal hairs on JonBenét's hands. These hairs did not match any items tested from inside the house. (JonBenét Murder Book Index.)

- An examination of the duct tape by the FBI discovered a black beaver hair stuck to the duct tape. (BPD Report from FBI #1-1140.) The FBI also found human hairs and fibers on the duct tape. (BPD Report #3-205.)

- Open doors were found in the home the morning the kidnapping was reported. (BPD Report #5-419.)

- A piece of blue paper was found outside next to the southwest window grate with a Boulder woman's name on it. There was also a reference to a New Year's Eve party. (BPD Reports #26-125, #5-4812.)

- An unidentified palm print was found in the storage room door area. (JonBenét Ramsey Murder Book Index.)

- Patsy Ramsey's palm print was found in the storage room door area. (WHYD Investigative Archive.)

- "Leaf and white Styrofoam packing peanuts consistent with leaves and debris found pooled in the window-well were found on the floor under the broken window." (SMF 136; PSMF 136 *Wolf vs. Ramsey* deposition—Judge Julie Carnes.) Such items were also "found in the wine-cellar [storage] room of the basement where JonBenét's body was discovered." (SMF 134; PSMF 134 *Wolf v. Ramsey* deposition—Judge Julie Carnes.)

- On December 24, 1996, in the morning hours, a neighbor who was also a personal friend of Boulder Detective Linda Arndt "observe[d] a dark blue Astro van parked across the street" from the Ramsey home. (BPD Report #1-98, Source.) On December 25 at 10 a.m., the same neighbor "observed a dark blue Astro van traveling north bound [sic] on 15th Street in the 700 block and stopped [sic] in front of the Ramsey home." (BPD Report #1-98,

Source.) On December 26, 1996, the same neighbor "may have seen [a] dark blue Astro van parked in the same general location near front of Ramsey home." (BPD Report #1-98.) On May 21, 1997, Boulder Sheriff Homicide Detective Steve Ainsworth "determined a blue van parked across the street from the Ramsey residence on the morning of December 26, 1996 belonged to friends of the Ramseys." (BPD Report #26-80.) There was no tie-in with the blue van on Christmas Day, when it was spotted twice. There was also no indication that "the friends" with the van visited the Ramseys on Christmas Day.

- Some items used in the murder were not found in the home:

- Police never found an unused section of the rope used to bind JonBenét. (WHYD Archive.)

- The roll of black duct tape vanished. Only a torn-off section covering her mouth was left behind. It had been torn on both ends, according to crime scene photos. The killer either took the roll of tape out of the home, disposed of it in some manner or only brought or had the amount of tape used. (WHYD Investigative Archive.)

- Seven blank pages from the middle of the tablet used to write the ransom note that were also ripped out of the tablet were never found. Detective Smit regarded them as possible practice pages for the ransom note because of their original location in the tablet.

- The unused portion of the paintbrush that was part of the garrote was not found. (WHYD Investigative Archive.)

- Police never determined what weapon was used to fracture JonBenét's skull and whether it came from inside or outside the home. (WHYD Investigative Archive.)

- Investigators never located a stun gun or an object that definitely caused the marks on JonBenét's skin. (WHYD Investigative Archive.)

- The cloth or fabric used to wipe off and clean up JonBenét's body was never found. (WHYD Investigative Archive.)

- The liquid used to clean and wipe off her body was never found. (WHYD Investigative Archive.)

- No other beaver hairs were found in the home, except for the one on the duct tape. (WHYD Investigative Archive.)

- There were no hairs in the home that matched the animal hairs found on JonBenét's hands. (WHYD Investigative Archive.)

- Items matching the brown cotton fibers on JonBenét, the paint-brush, duct tape and ligature were not found elsewhere in the home. (WHYD Investigative Archive.)

- The two different bits of paper found on JonBenét's cheek were not matched to anything inside the home. (WHYD Investigative Archive.)

So how were all those items removed from the Ramsey home?

By mid-1998, residents of Boulder were pressuring their police department and district attorney's office to get the hordes of media with their negative publicity out of Boulder. Eighteen months after the murder of JonBenét Ramsey, however, that would not happen because, according to one attorney familiar with the case, nothing had worked well enough in the investigation to provide enough evidence to build a foundation for a prosecution.

Former Adams County District Attorney Bob Grant has said that, given a choice, he'd much rather have been a defense attorney than a prosecutor on the Ramsey case. He said he didn't ever expect there to be a prosecution and called it a "very difficult" investigation.

In spite of continuing problems with the Boulder Police Department, Lou Smit supported them publicly in July 1998. When John Ramsey was interrogated again by the prosecution side with Michael Kane and Lou Smit present, Smit (whom the family trusted) told John he understood John's concerns about his family being targeted. He also, however, stood up for the Boulder Police Department, telling John, "I know there's been a lot of focus on you, but I looked at every one of those reports. There's been a lot of [police] work done in other ways. And I know from your perspective it seems like that . . . but they have done a lot of work."

Two months later, though, Smit resigned from the Boulder DA's office with a public letter saying the case was focused in the wrong direction—on the Ramseys.

# CHAPTER 20
# ADDITIONAL EVIDENCE

Picture from hired Santa Claus McReynolds to Burke at the 1996 Ramsey Christmas party. Front and back.

MYSTERY TRUMPS FACT in the case of JonBenét Ramsey's murder.

Parts of the JonBenét Ramsey Murder Book Index and the WHYD Investigative Archive offer a compilation of ominous and detailed facts and evidence ranging from excerpts of interviews with registered sexual predators to notations about bagels. "The victim advocates left the residence to get bagels, brought them back and served them to individuals in the residence with some fruit," says one part of the WHYD Investigative Archive.

This material also offers an organized and invaluable summary of: data and quotes from police reports; portions from formal police interviews of officers involved in the Ramsey murder case; interviews with witnesses from the morning of JonBenét's disappearance; lists of evidence collected; crime scene photographs; summations of interviews with family, friends, neighbors and acquaintances of the Ramseys; notes on the emotional conditions of John and Patsy and their children; a compilation of possible evidence found and admitted into BPD custody; detailed lists of people who could be called as witnesses and why, in case of a trial. There's also a list of all the officers in the Boulder Police Department who were involved in the case and brief summaries of their participation. Interviews with key people in the case over the years and their perspectives are also included. Innumerable clues point in every direction, and there is factual data that is irreplaceable. While most of the material is based on documentation, some is just plain strange.

For example, the unusual connections with Santa Claus.

At every Christmas party at the Ramseys, the home was filled with several Christmas trees, lots of presents, decorative angels, a myriad of colors coming from brightly lit and shining decorations, holiday excitement, lots of little kids and Santa Claus.

"This was the best of times with children," Patsy observed. "I wanted to continue their excitement and wonderment. It was just plain fun. We [had] met a lot of parents whose children went to school with Burke and JonBenét, and so we invited them and their children, too. It was magical. What I loved the best, I think, was the laughter of the children."

For two years at the Ramseys' annual Christmas children's party, Santa Claus was Bill McReynolds, a retired University of Colorado journalism professor hired by Patsy to play the part. But behind the jolly Santa was a chilling story.

On December 26, 1974, twenty-two years before JonBenét was reported kidnapped on December 26, 1996, the nine-year-old daughter of Janet McReynolds, the wife of Bill McReynolds, was kidnapped. (BPD Report #1-568, Source.) Janet's daughter and a friend were taken to an unknown location, where Janet's daughter was forced to watch her friend being sexually molested. Both children were then released. Two years later, Janet McReynolds wrote a book that became a play in which a girl is sexually assaulted and tortured in a basement. The victim in the story later dies in a hospital. (BPD Report # 1-645.)

Is all of this linked to JonBenét's murderer or just a macabre coincidence?

The Boulder Police Department investigated McReynolds as a suspect because they found pornography in his possession and because of the similar events that had happened to his step-daughter. (BPD Report #1-580.) No pornography was ever found in the Ramsey home, according to two separate housekeepers and police investigators. (BPD Reports #5-983, #5-1331, #5-2164.)

Police took hair and handwriting samples from both Bill and Janet McReynolds. Their DNA did not match the foreign DNA left behind on JonBenét. The police also did not consider McReynolds a viable suspect because of his weakened physical condition from recent heart surgery and because one of his lungs had been accidentally punctured and partially removed. (BPD Reports #1-376, 1-576.) McReynolds and his wife moved away from Boulder after JonBenét's murder because of rumored suspicions that he might have been involved. He died in 2002 from a heart attack.

Then there is the statement from the mother of a friend of JonBenét's. The woman said that on Christmas Eve day in 1996, JonBenét said Santa had told her he was going to make a secret visit to her after Christmas. (BPD Reports #1-1874, #26-144, #1-41, #1-162, #1-204, #1-304, #1-2622, #5-297, #5-371, #5-2202) Could that Secret Santa have been the killer and someone JonBenét knew? Another mother also stated to BPD investigators that JonBenét had told a playmate about a Secret Santa. (BPD Report #1-1149.)

With regard to physical evidence found at or near the Ramsey family's home and noted in the archives, Boulder Police Department officials remain unsure whether some of it was related to the case:

- Two BPD detectives who had "measured the three crawl spaces in the basement of the Ramsey home" (BPD #1-137) found an unidentified canvas bag in one of the crawl spaces. (BPD Report #2-16.) That would support those who believed an intruder could have hidden in one of the three Ramsey home crawl spaces.

- An earring was found by a BPD police officer along the curb directly in front of the Ramsey home a day after JonBenét's body was discovered. (BPD Report #2-16, #1-104.)

- A broken Christmas ornament was found in the wine cellar storage area where the Ramseys stored some of their Christmas decorations and where JonBenét's body was found. (BPD Report #3-143.)

- A red pocket knife was discovered near the broken ornament. (BPD Reports #2-17, #1-104.)

- A neighbor who lived a few homes away from the Ramseys found a latex glove in her trashcan in the alley. (BPD Report #1-1924.) She didn't know how it had gotten there. (Latex gloves are used by law enforcement officials to avoid contaminating evidence with their fingerprints.) The glove, if part of the case, could have been used by an intruder. Or it could have been discarded there by a BPD officer. (BPD Report #2-37.)

- A neighbor reported "someone dropped off a high-tech [sic] hiking boot on New Year's Eve in the front of home on the front walk." (BPD Report #1-1221, Source.)

- Boulder Detective Jane Harmer contacted that same neighbor and "received a high-tech [sic]hiking boot and cord." (BPD Report #1-1221.)

- According to Colorado Bureau of Investigation reports, no fingerprints were found on the black duct tape that had covered JonBenét's mouth, on the broken paint brush or on the black felt-tip pen suspected to be the instrument used to write the ransom note. (BPD Report #3-45.)

- On February 13, 1998, photos of a bound and gagged Barbie doll that was left in the yard of the Ramsey residence were sent anonymously to the Boulder District Attorney's office with a letter postmarked Hickory, North Carolina. (BPD Report #33-1874.)

Near the time of JonBenét's murder, there were reports of suspicious activity in the Boulder area that also may or may not have been related to the crime:

- In November 1996, a man was reported to be exposing himself outside High Peaks Elementary where JonBenét and Burke Ramsey went to school. (BPD Report #5-3153.)

- On November 16 and December 8, 1996, two separate people in Boulder with no known connections to the Ramseys reported to police what sounded like someone knocking on their basement windows. (BPD Reports #21-60, #21-62.)

- Between December 12 and December 25, 1996, police investigated a series of home break-ins in the northwest part of Boulder on a case called "The Midnight Burglar." Police did not relate the burglaries to the Ramsey case. Most of the residents were home and sleeping during the break-ins. The burglars, who usually took jewelry, credit cards and cash, were able to enter fourteen homes, most of which were occupied, without discovery. (WHYD Investigative Archive.)

- Three days before Christmas 1996, a congregation member at the Ramseys' church reported to police that another attendee had said to him, "Don't you just want to strangle her?" The congregation member had felt the man was referring to JonBenét Ramsey, who was at the church with her mother at the time. The churchgoer said he had seen the attendee near the Ramsey home the previous summer. Police later learned the man who had made the report was on heavy anti-psychotic medication. (BPD Report #5-1942.)

- The Sunday before the murder, a man representing himself as a process server arrived at another man's home in Boulder, told the absent man's girlfriend "these aren't bad papers, they're good papers," and added, "he'll want them." The alleged process server never returned. The absent man's mother, who was also at the home, envisioned that the alleged process server had been casing the home. (BPD Report #21-63.)

- On Christmas Day 1996, someone inside a Ramsey family friend's home noticed that a Jaguar convertible drove by that home at least five times. The Ramseys joined close friends for dinner inside that home on Christmas Day night. (BPD Report # 26-125.)

- That same evening, a Ramsey neighbor saw a person outside the Ramsey house. The person was described in a police report as a "tall thin blond male wearing glasses [and] thought to be John Andrew." (BPD Reports #1-690, #5-690.) It was later established by the Boulder Police Department that John Andrew Ramsey had been in Atlanta for Christmas with his sister and mother at the time. Another police report states that "an unknown neighbor supposedly saw a person outside the door of the Ramsey house (during the night)." (BPD Report #1-771, Source.)

- Another Ramsey neighbor "stated that she heard one loud incredible scream [that] was the loudest most terrifying scream she had ever heard. It was obviously from a child and lasted from three to five seconds at which time it stopped abruptly. She thought surely the parents would hear that scream. The scream came from across the street south of the Ramsey residence." It happened "between midnight and two AM" the morning of December 26, 1996. (BPD Reports #1-1390, #1-174, #1-175.) This neighbor lived across the street and one home south of the Ramseys. The scream was first reported publicly, and then a BPD detective interviewed the woman, who said she actually heard it on January 3, 1997.

Another neighbor who lived south of the Ramsey home contacted a BPD detective on December 31, 1996 because of the scream the first neighbor had heard. This neighbor said she had also heard a scream. She was interviewed on February 26, 1997. (BPD Reports #1-174, #1-481, #1-1548.)

A separate BPD report stated that, "According to Burke, he woke up at about 11:30 [p.m. on December 25, 1996] because he heard the water heater squeaking a little. Did not hear any screams." (BPD Report #5-100.)

Audio experts hired by the Ramsey defense attorneys conducted tests inside the Ramsey home and concluded a scream from the basement "would not have been heard" on the third floor but could have been heard by a neighbor because an exterior basement vent could have amplified the sound. (WHYD Investigative Archive.)

The intruder theory related to the murder of JonBenét Ramsey needed an explanation for how someone might get into the house. Evidence that might provide such an explanation includes:

- John and Patsy Ramsey had given several keys to subcontractors (BPD Reports #1-6505, #1-1264), friends and neighbors (BPD Report #1-1104), most of which were not returned. The Ramsey family did not keep an accurate count of the keys they gave out. Several Boulder Police Department reports indicate that investigators talked with more than thirty-five people outside the family about whether they had keys to the home. (JonBenét Ramsey Murder Book Index.)

  Also: "Patsy Ramsey while preparing for the tour of homes openly told a variety of people where a key was hidden outside the home under a statue." (BPD Reports #5-3920, #5-3921.) The key was not found during a check for it after JonBenét's murder.

"There are literally hundreds of people who have been through that house." (BPD Report # 5-421.) In a reference to the Ramsey Home Tour—Christmas 1994, another police report states, "About a thousand people went through her house that weekend." (BPD Report #5-331.) "1994, December—The Ramsey home was on a Christmas tour with house captains in charge of the volunteers. There were approximately 10 volunteers every hour in the house. Printed flyers are in the basement with the names of all the domestic help people." (BPD Report #1-203.)

- The Ramsey housekeeper plus a long-time babysitter both said the family left some doors unlocked and never used the alarm. (WHYD Investigative Archive.)

- The Ramsey housekeeper did not remember anything about the broken glass in the train room, the scuff mark on the wall or cleaning up glass underneath the broken window. (BPD Report #1-1068.) (BPD Reports #1-101, #1-90 re: scuff mark on the wall.) The housekeeper's husband "supposedly washed the windows at Thanksgiving time and supposedly went down in the basement and washed the basement windows." (BPD Report #5-29.) "Last time [housekeeper's husband] was there was around Thanksgiving. Cleaned all of the windows inside and out." (BPD Report #5-607.)

In the months following the Ramsey murder, tip line phone calls to the Boulder Police Department resulted in many leads. BPD officers considered most of them false.

- Several people claiming to be psychic called the telephone tip line with tips ranging from "Sam did it" (BPD Report #1-1535) and the "parents are involved" (BPD Report #1-1678) to the "possible involvement of [a] John Andrew look-alike and a female." (BPD

Report #25-92.) BPD officials were unable to determine who "Sam" might be.

- An unidentified female called Boulder District Attorney Alex Hunter's home phone in October 1997 and left a message saying, "I did it" and "I want to confess." (BPD Report #26-244.)

- An inmate incarcerated in the Federal Penitentiary in Atlanta wrote the following to the Boulder Police Department:

> Detective you do not have a family member or a terrorist killer here. You have a very specialized pedophile. He is sadistic and he is a killer who only preys on young girls. It's obvious to me. I've been there but hidden to others. (BPD Report #8-141.)

Atlanta is where John and Patsy Ramsey had spent most of their married lives.

This was information typical of the Ramsey case: unusual, possibly connected, and impossible to definitively attach to the case.

# CHAPTER 21
# PUBLIC REACTION

Wanted flyers of John Ramsey posted throughout Boulder in 1997. It was never discovered who made and posted them.

TO SOME, WHAT IS EXPRESSED AS SELF-RIGHTEOUS INDIGNATION can be received as the cruelest of attacks. By early 1997, John and Patsy Ramsey had become fair game for anyone with access to a computer, a telephone or any other vehicle through which they could voice their opinion to the media or general public.

On March 4, 1997, a local radio station disc jockey from KBPI erroneously told his audience "an arrest had been made in the murder" in reference to the Ramsey case. He later said this had been a prank and not true, but his statement provoked enough interest that newspapers as well as television and radio stations immediately reacted. A new barrage of chaos occurred with the Ramseys once again enduring requests for interviews, knocks on the door of the home in which they were temporarily living and visits to Burke's school by members of the media.

On March 13, 1997, the *Daily Camera* newspaper published a story with the headline:

"A 10-foot-by-25-foot mural presenting three beauty pageant portraits of JonBenét Ramsey beneath the words 'Daddy's Little Hooker' sparked anger and controversy at the University of Colorado this week."

John Ramsey felt sucker-punched. "I just didn't understand how something so terrible to our daughter's memory could be considered as an art project displayed on the university campus." He wrote a letter to the art student explaining his feelings about his daughter's death but said he never received a response. The art student, a CU senior, had told the *Daily Camera* that he created the mural in order to expose child pageants. "This is a rich and powerful family and they're manipulating all the resources for their benefit," he added. The University of Colorado Fine Arts Department said the artwork fell under the constitutional protection of the First Amendment so they would not remove it, though it was eventually taken down.

In 2011, the art student was an editor for Middle Eastern issues and the principal editor with an information technology company when he responded to my 2011 request for an interview about his "Daddy's Little

Hooker" mural. I asked if he considered that the mural had been appropriate and fair. His reply included the following excerpt:

> I lived several houses down from the Ramseys prior to the murder and I saw JonBenét frequently when I walked to university. She was a young girl who played and ran around like any other six-year-old. So like everyone, I was shocked when I learned of the murder. But that shock turned to disgust when the images of her pageantry life began to emerge. I found it increasingly difficult to reconcile two images in my mind: JonBenét innocently riding a tricycle outside her house, and her being dolled-up by her parents with makeup and suggestive clothing. My instinct told me there was something deeply troubling in that family. Whether or not one of the parents was involved in the murder, I am convinced the way they paraded JonBenét around as a beauty queen was a key factor that led to her demise.

"Amplifying that belief was the core justification for my art project," he added. "Although it came off as hurtful and sensational to some, I believe it was an appropriate artistic response to the array of issues that the murder provoked."

Negative publicity and hostility against the Ramsey family continued to grow. On May 8, 1997, the *Daily Camera* reported that fake reward posters for John Ramsey were being posted around the city:

"The fliers —patterned after a reward advertisement—began appearing on kiosks downtown . . ."

In June 1997, a man named James Thompson (aka J.T. Colfax) started a fire in the Ramsey family's empty home by igniting paper and pushing it through the attached mail slot next to the front door. (BPD Report #1-996.) He then reported himself to police. Thompson also admitted to stealing the original log-in page with JonBenét's information from the mortuary where her body was taken. (BPD Report #1-996.)

In August 1997, someone phoned in a report to the Charlevoix, Michigan, police station saying John Ramsey had committed suicide. The family was staying in Charlevoix until their eventual move to Atlanta. When Charlevoix police went to their home, Patsy came to the door. They told her, "We have a report that John committed suicide." Patsy wasn't concerned, answering simply, "Oh no, he's fine. He just left to go down to the lake." The police then went to the dock to check on John and told him what had been reported. They apologized and were "very considerate," John later said. It was impossible to track the source of the call, but the false report spread quickly on the Internet and into the mainstream media. Friends and family called that day, frantic because they had been asked by the media if John had killed himself. John would later state that he imagined "a tabloid reporter phoned it in just to create a stir again in the case." The "suicide story" was reported the same day that JonBenét's full autopsy was released, reporting in detail how she'd been killed.

In October 1998, JonBenét's tombstone at her burial site was defaced after Boulder District Attorney Alex Hunter announced there would be no indictment following grand jury proceedings related to the case. Painted on her gravesite were the words "No Justice in the USA."

According to employees of a fire station located near JonBenét's gravesite, a tabloid news organization had tried to bribe employees of the fire station for information on when the Ramseys visited the site. The fire department employees said "no" and told the family of the attempt.

Local and national gossip shows on television and radio, columns in mainstream newspapers and, of course, the tabloids, continued to howl and hate. Some hosts significantly boosted ratings and profited off the killing of a child by making sure JonBenét's murder remained an everyday sensation. While this momentum couldn't be supported by factual information in the Ramsey case, that hardly mattered. Anti-Ramsey tirades beat on with whatever would entice, contributing to the ratings of any media outlet that would carry them.

National network evening news coverage of the murder of JonBenét Ramsey began on Tuesday, December 31, the day JonBenét was buried in Atlanta.[1] CBS and NBC introduced the case to the nation. Both described JonBenét as a "young beauty queen" or as a "six-year-old beauty queen." This was the most common manner in which all four networks would introduce her through the fall of 1997. National newscasts continually aired video of JonBenét performing in pageants. In some cases, television shows slowed the video down in order to exaggerate her movements while she performed, and some national tabloid television shows added suggestive music to the videos.

By calling her a "beauty queen," the media allowed the public to easily categorize JonBenét Ramsey not as a six-year-old, but as a more suggestive child beauty contestant. This shorthand helped the networks sell the JonBenét updates to viewers and prompted less compassion for the dead little girl. It also suggested that JonBenét had been somehow responsible for drawing interest to herself, and perhaps even unwittingly drawing in her own killer. This reasoning runs along the lines of asking a sexual assault victim what she was wearing when she was attacked, which suggests that the victim may have "brought this on herself" or even "asked for it."

When the media's coverage of the Ramsey murder case first began, the Boulder Police Department was criticized publicly for botching the case. But that coverage was not nearly as dramatic and lasted for only weeks. Simultaneously, BPD officials began leaking details implicating John, Patsy, Burke or John Andrew Ramsey in the case, causing the victim's family members to become instant media targets.

To add to the growing media circus around the Ramsey murder investigation, most "experts" booked on talk shows and quoted in newspaper columns related to the case were anti-Ramsey and not involved in the investigation in any way. Little verification of the accuracy of statements made by such "experts" was done, creating an open forum for uninformed opinions. The hosts interviewing such experts on broadcast shows would also slip in damaging buzzwords like the "secret room," one of the rumored names for the storage room where JonBenét's body was found, in order to influence listeners and keep them coming back for more.

The constant smears and false charges against the Ramseys piled on top of each other in several different public formats. In the years 1997 and 1998, the 24-7 media cycle was still new, and show hosts were scrambling to fill their programs with material that would pull in ratings on a daily basis. The listeners and viewers of these shows didn't always understand that such broadcasts constituted entertainment, where anything goes, and not news, where accuracy is normally verified. And in their race to salvage dropping circulations in the wake of the advent of 24-7 broadcast media shows, newspapers across the country followed suit by reporting every new detail related to the high-profile case that was getting so much time on the airwaves.

In November 1997, Geraldo Rivera held a live several-day mock trial involving so-called witnesses who were not formally involved in the Ramsey murder case. The "jury" was composed of Rivera's television audience as well as officials who were not part of the murder investigation in any way. At the end of the mock trial, the "jury" found the Ramseys "liable for the wrongful death" of their daughter.

At the time of this mock trial, no one had been charged or arrested in the Ramsey murder case, and the parents of JonBenét Ramsey were presumed innocent. Yet Rivera created a public spectacle that in a sense "convicted" the parents of killing their daughter.

Rivera did not return requests for comment.

According to Al Tompkins, Senior Faculty for Broadcast and Online at the Poynter Institute for Media Studies, a preeminent leadership organization and journalism think tank that teaches excellence and ethics in journalism, there is no place for mock trials like the one held by Rivera.

"It has nothing to do with journalism," Tompkins said. "And there's no place for it in our judicial system. There's no function in turning crime into an entertainment show. It's ultimately harmful to the people involved and to the process of justice. I don't see any value in doing something like that."

Fourteen years after the murder of JonBenét Ramsey on November 16, 2010, *Denver Post* columnist and television critic Joanne Ostrow wrote a piece about reality shows. In the article, Ostrow referred to a reality show that featured "JonBenét look-alikes" without saying the show was about child beauty pageants. JonBenét had been murdered in a vicious and sadistic way. Fourteen years after her death, her name had become a toss-away line synonymous with child beauty pageants.

Ostrow later explained in a January 27, 2012 email why she used the term "JonBenét look-alikes."

"I believe you are referring to something I wrote about cable network TLC giving up its reputation as the 'Learning Channel' and becoming something low-brow," Ostrow wrote, "'a repository for families with 19 kids, hoarders, polygamists, and Jon-Benét look-alikes.' I referred, as millions of TV viewers know, to '19 Kids and Counting,' 'Hoarding: Buried Alive,' 'Sister Wives,' and 'Toddlers and Tiaras.' The hyper-sexualizing of children in beauty pageants, depicted on 'Toddlers and Tiaras,' is a deeper subject than I was treating in that TV column."

I wrote back: "JoAnne: My question is if you feel it is appropriate to use the term 'JonBenét look-alikes' for contestants in a child beauty pageant?"

Ostrow's response: "I don't feel the need to comment further."

The tabloids were the most savage as they spread over their covers lurid JonBenét headlines and pageant photographs. Small disclaimers were hidden on the inside pages of many of these publications, saying the JonBenét photographs on their covers had been "altered" with added eyeliner and mascara, darker shades of lipstick on her mouth and blush on her cheeks.

Some of the photos purporting to be JonBenét and Patsy weren't even them, but people made up to look like them. But the magazines didn't clarify the substitutions.

Examples of these tabloid headlines included:

LITTLE BEAUTY ABUSED MONTHS BEFORE MURDER?
(*Globe* January 28, 1997)

BROTHER, 10, MAY KNOW WHAT REALLY HAPPENED TO JONBENÉT
(*Star* June 3,1997)

BEAUTY QUEEN'S BROTHER HOLDS KEY TO MURDER
(*The National Enquirer* June 3, 1997)

DA'S SHOCKING OUTBURST: Inside mind of DA: JonBenét Dad did it—but he'll get away with it
(*Star* November 25, 1997)

I HEARD JONBENÉT DIE! Neighbor's stunning testimony: JonBenét's chilling screams filled my ears
(*Globe* November 25, 1997)

GRAND JURY TO CHARGE: MOMMY KILLED JONBENÉT
(*The National Enquirer* January 26, 1999)

JONBENÉT MOM BRAGS YOU'LL NEVER PROVE I DID IT
(*The National Examiner* September 28, 1999)

JONBENÉT: SHOCKING POLICE FILES
(*Star* October 5, 1999)

EXPOSED! SHOCKING SEX & BOOZE PARTIES IN JONBENÉT'S HOUSE
(*Star* October 19, 1999)

John's Journal:

*I stop by the newsstand to get something to read and staring me in the face is the Globe Tabloid with JonBenét's picture on it with the headlines: Mother bought "murder weapon." "11-year old-son hides evidence." What a disgusting cancer we have allowed to prosper in our society! I take the papers and bury them behind the rack. This stuff hurts and it outrages me that people like this with no morals or*

> *ethics are allowed to profit by exploiting the tragedy of a child with bald-faced lies. All under the umbrella of the first amendment and the legitimate media who have set a respectable standard.*

With regard to such coverage, Patsy said, "John shields me from most of the publicity, but occasionally I see a tabloid with our daughter's photograph on the front, and I just can't breathe, you know, for a few seconds."

# CHAPTER 22

# RAMSEY ATTORNEYS— PERSONAL PERSPECTIVES

Ramsey family in canoe. © John Ramsey.

## CHRONOLOGY

**2010 – 2011—The Ramseys' attorneys participated in several interviews for this book in which they discussed their personal perspectives. Their comments are utilized throughout. They have never spoken publicly about their personal perspectives.**

## PEOPLE IN THIS CHAPTER

Patrick J. Burke—Patsy Ramsey's attorney

Michael Bynum—John Ramsey's business attorney and friend

John Eller—First Boulder Police Department Commander in charge of the Ramsey case

Lee D. Foreman—A partner in the Haddon, Morgan & Foreman firm who worked part-time on the Ramsey case

Pat Furman—University of Colorado law professor and attorney who joined with Pat Burke in defense of Patsy Ramsey

Harold (Hal) A. Haddon—One of John Ramsey's defense attorneys and a partner in the Haddon, Morgan & Foreman firm

Saskia A. Jordan—Attorney in the Haddon, Morgan & Foreman firm who worked part-time on the Ramsey case

G. Bryan Morgan—John Ramsey's primary defense attorney and a partner in the Haddon, Morgan & Foreman firm

John's Journal:

*September 7, 1997*

*I had difficulty sleeping last night. I'm becoming very concerned about finances . . .*

*September 8, 1997*

*Talked to Bryan about reducing the cost of lawyers. We have been running about $175,000 per month and I need to get it down to*

*$50,000/mo. to sustain our finances for awhile. Bryan tells me that he, Hal and Pat are in this for the duration and getting paid for their time is not an issue. These are fine people who are at the top of their field and I'm grateful for their dedication. How many of us would work for free because we were so dedicated to our work. Not many, I suspect.*

SO DEEPLY DID JOHN AND PATSY BELIEVE that the Boulder Police Department's investigation into their daughter's murder was dangerously inept that they spent a huge amount of money, $175,000 a month for several months, on their own defense attorneys, plus their own investigators, to try to find the killer of their daughter.

So deeply did the Ramsey attorneys come to support the innocence of John and Patsy Ramsey that they've worked for more than eighteen years on this case without being paid. Less than a year into the investigation in September 1997, Hal Haddon, Bryan Morgan and Pat Burke began working for the Ramseys for free. Partner Lee Foreman and future partner Saskia Jordan worked part-time on the case to help the other attorneys. The firm's investigators also worked on reduced salaries. For some of them, this was a serious hardship.

There are two types of government attorneys working in our system of criminal justice. One is the prosecutor, the chief legal representative for the government responsible for presenting a case in a criminal trial against an individual accused of breaking the law. The other is the public defender.

Public defenders protect the rights of the accused. Their clients are people who can't afford to hire an attorney. Among those they represent are the indigent, the powerless and the disenfranchised who have no place to turn for representation other than to lawyers who are provided to them for free by the court system. Many young attorneys turn to public service and become public defenders or prosecutors because such experience provides tremendous training due to the large number of cases assigned and the significant amount of time these types of lawyers spend in court. One former public defender told me he wanted the job because he believed helping those who couldn't protect themselves was a "righteous" thing to do. Haddon, Morgan and Foreman were former public defenders. Burke was a former prosecutor who became a public defender.

Just as public defenders have a distinct mindset, so do prosecutors. They, too, see their work as a higher moral calling. State prosecutors represent the people of the judicial district in which they serve. They have duties to everyone in the criminal justice system including the victims, law enforcement agencies, the public and the accused. Their duties include being open-minded, yet decisive. They exercise tremendous power in deciding who should be prosecuted and for what crimes and who should be punished and how severely. They also wield the power of the office to protect the public and vindicate the victim. Prosecutors provide recommendations for compassion and discretion for some people and severe punishment for those they deem are too dangerous to continue living in our society.

Started by Hal Haddon and Bryan Morgan in 1976, the firm of Haddon, Morgan & Foreman launched with a team of former public defenders as its original partners. The experiences and mindsets of these former public defenders carried over into their law firm. They seemed to have a built-in radar for those who needed their help most.

By 1996, Haddon, Morgan & Foreman had successfully represented the Eisenhower Tunnel contractors, Kiewet, on bid rigging; later in 2000, Qwest on possible criminal charges for insider information; controversial author Hunter Thompson on a sexual assault charge and a five-year-long case on the Cold War nuclear weapons research, development and production facility known as Rocky Flats and their contractors, Rockwell International and later Boeing, that resulted in a congressional investigation. The law firm also won a case in which they represented the University of Colorado related to patent fraud, and they defended professional basketball player Kobe Bryant on sexual assault charges in a case that was ultimately dismissed. The Haddon, Morgan & Foreman firm is nationally recognized.

Bryan Morgan had worked in the Denver Public Defender's Office for several years before he and Hal Haddon formed their own law firm in the mid 1970s. Morgan is described by his peers as extraordinarily smart, personable, utterly and painfully honest and loyal to his clients. He has described the Ramsey case as "a complete whirlpool . . . Things had been set into motion and were inevitably circling their way toward a certain conclusion even at the very beginning."

Attorneys do not usually make decisions on the guilt or innocence of their clients quickly, and sometimes never. In this case Morgan noted, "After two days with John Ramsey, [I knew] he could not possibly have done what they say happened to this child. I believed this with every instinct I had."

Hal Haddon started in the Public Defender's Office in Jefferson County, Colorado, in 1970, then moved to the Denver Public Defender's Office and was eventually the chief trial deputy of the State Public Defender's Office. Haddon is considered an "attorney's attorney." He's the attorney other lawyers hire when they need legal counsel, and he's considered unparalleled intellectually. Haddon also cares deeply about his clients.

Haddon came into the Ramsey case a week later than Morgan. He determined that both John and Patsy Ramsey were innocent early on. "After the first interview with John and Patsy, they did not fit as anything other than terribly emotionally injured parents," he said. "The way their daughter was killed was consistent with parents who fly into rages and sometimes hurt their children. They did not then nor now strike me as people who would be physically assaultive with their children. John raised five children without physically disciplining them. You have to by necessity make decisions on what your clients tell you, and your instincts. I've been wrong on both sides of those questions before. I always re-evaluate my clients constantly. My very strong first impression is that these are not the kind of people who would hurt their child; certainly not in the ways she was savaged. That faith in them has not wavered."

Pat Burke was the counter to Morgan and Haddon with his prosecutorial mind. He's also the consummate Irishman. He is effusive, tough when he needs to be, and totally devoted to the system of law and the people he represents. He had worked as an assistant city attorney in the Denver metro suburb of Lakewood and was an assistant attorney general for Colorado. He then changed roles to become an assistant federal public defender in the District of Colorado.

Pat Burke had been invited to join Haddon, Morgan & Foreman as a partner beginning in 1997. This fact hadn't been announced publicly because of minor details still to be worked out, but once Pat Burke became Patsy Ramsey's attorney, he could not join the firm because that would have resulted in a conflict of interest. Patsy's attorney until she died in 2006, Pat Burke still protects her interests related to the case as well as those of her son, Burke.

Pat Burke said that he approached the case with an open mind, as did the other Ramsey attorneys. He soon had taken measure of his client. "There was nothing bad about Patsy Ramsey. She was smart, nice, good mom, good wife, good daughter, good sister and intelligent student. She basically was a wonderful all-around decent human being." You can hear the affection when Burke speaks about Patsy. Their attorney-client relationship also developed into that of two trusted and respected friends. Patsy relied completely on Pat's advice and counsel. He, along with only a few others, held her up when she broke down.

Bynum, John's business partner who originally hired the Ramsey defense attorneys, was the head of a highly respected Boulder law firm. He retired from the legal profession in 2002 and went on to other business ventures. He said that one reason he hasn't gone back to the practice of law is his disillusionment with what he calls "a total betrayal by the legal system" in the Ramsey case. "The Ramseys lost their daughter [and] their reputation, and the criminal justice system did nothing," said Mike Bynum, still disheartened.

In April 2010, Bynum, Haddon and Morgan met with John Ramsey and me to talk about the case, now well into its second decade. While Patsy's attorney, Pat Burke, was in court and could not attend this meeting, he was candid and forthcoming in later interviews. Taken together, all of these interviews represented the first time the Ramsey attorneys had ever spoken publicly about their insights and perspectives on the case.

The Haddon, Morgan & Foreman firm's style is low key. They work within the system, assure confidentiality and do not try cases in the media. This is the same approach taken by Pat Burke.

"We've been criticized a lot for not engaging more with the media," Haddon said. "That was a zero-sum game because the media had decided very early on they wanted this to be the next O. J. media sensation. I'd never seen anything like it before. I decided not to divert our attentions to playing the media game as opposed to doing what lawyers ought to do: preparing to gather and analyze the facts and determine what the legal implications are. I could have taken one hundred media calls a day, but it [would have been] to the detriment of doing whatever I could for the Ramseys."

Haddon normally speaks in a calm voice, but when discussing the Ramseys he was exactingly soft spoken. Even though the attorneys kept the family from being indicted by the Boulder district attorney because of their relentless insistence that he adhere to the law, Haddon carries a heavy burden because he and the others were unable to repair the family's reputation. His measured cadence reflected his deliberate control while talking about extraordinarily difficult circumstances that still affect him greatly.

Throughout the case, the attorneys prepared as though, at any moment, a Ramsey family member would be charged. They hired handwriting experts, organized an investigative staff, conducted hundreds of interviews. They tried to be as ready as they could to defend their clients without the benefit of knowing what information the police had. Since the Ramseys had not been charged or arrested, their lawyers weren't given access to such material. The Ramsey lawyers knew, however, that the case was focused on one or both of their clients. They prepared for trial as best they could without the benefit of "discovery," the legal requirement that the prosecutor must provide all evidence to the defense after an arrest has been made.

Within weeks of JonBenét's murder, the Ramsey lawyers hired a public relations representative to handle the onslaught of media requests for information on the case. Haddon reflects, "I think, in hindsight, it was a mistake to hire anyone to deal with the media because the media simply took that as an excuse to postulate that they were somehow being manipulated. But the media storm that consumed this case began really before any lawyers were fully engaged."

The Ramsey lawyers all agreed the most frustrating part for them was the fact that there was very little they could do make things "right" for their clients because of certain police officers and one or two prosecutors who actively leaked information, most of it false, to the media in order to set in motion the whisper and rumor campaign that terrified the family.

Well into the investigation, Morgan recalls making an appointment for Haddon and him to talk with Boulder District Attorney Alex Hunter about the leaks to the media. "I told Alex I knew he couldn't control the police leaks, but the District Attorney's Office was leaking erroneous information as well, and Hal and I were considering filing a lawsuit against the District Attorney's Office and Boulder Police regarding leaking false information." Both attorneys remember Hunter saying, "I could make a pretty good witness for you on that." Morgan added, "It was an outrageous acknowledgment by the DA, yet he still wouldn't discipline those in his office who were leaking. So the news leaks continued. With that kind of response, we, as attorneys, felt anything we tried to do to change things was futile; but we still had to try."

Haddon admitted that he continues to have a lot of anger about the Boulder Police Department.

"There was and is this maniacal belief that they're right," he said. "They can never acknowledge what they did to this family. They won't acknowledge that what they did was evil."

The Ramsey lawyers had a two-fold problem. They deeply mistrusted the commanders in charge of the investigation as well as all but a few of the attorneys in the Boulder DA's Office. And the feelings were reciprocated. While there is always a natural animosity between prosecution and defense in any case, such natural animosity was like a campfire compared to the forest fire of dislike and mistrust that three important entities in this case—the Boulder Police Department, the Boulder District Attorney's Office and the Ramsey defense attorneys—had for each other. From their perspective, Ramsey lawyers believed that BPD investigators, hell-bent on tailoring evidence to fit John and Patsy's actions into their killer theory, were framing their clients.

This relationship in particular had settled into open animosity the second day after JonBenét's body was found, when the police commander in charge of the investigation, John Eller, demanded that the Ramseys give an interview at police headquarters or he wouldn't return their child's body to them. That threat lingered and smoldered and was never forgotten by the Ramsey attorneys.

When they were interviewed for this book in April 2010, each of the Ramsey attorneys was clearly emotional still about this case. Haddon was somber and seemed to try to keep his frustrations with how the investigation was conducted hidden. Bynum had a difficult time when attempting to speak of the past.

Morgan, his eyes brimming with tears, apologized to John Ramsey about something that had bothered him for so many years. He told John that he (Morgan) should have given the results of JonBenét's autopsy to John alone, instead of to the entire family, especially the finding that JonBenét had been sexually assaulted.

"I remember your reaction when I told you," Morgan said. "You had no idea she had been sexually assaulted. I saw the look of disbelief on your face and how completely stunned and overcome by grief you were at that moment. And I'm so sorry I told you that way, John."

Ramsey nodded, and then froze in the memory of that long-ago moment. After an extended pause, as he seemed to sort through the layers of pain once again, he looked across the room at Morgan and responded, "It's OK, Bryan. There was no right way to tell me. You did the best you could."

Despite the frustration they felt and their clients' raw anguish, the Ramsey attorneys all remained dedicated, in part, they said, because of the character displayed by John and Patsy throughout the investigation. They said the case was critically important for them personally.

"It's a lawyer's highest calling to represent somebody who is innocent, who is demonized," said Haddon. "I don't get attached to many clients, but I love [the Ramseys]. I appreciated then and now [that] they had more dignity in the face of outrage than anyone could have expected a human being to have."

CHAPTER 23

# COLORADO GOVERNORS

(Top left) Colorado Governor Roy Romer, (Top right) Colorado Governor Bill Owens, (Bottom) Colorado Governor Bill Ritter.

## CHRONOLOGY

1987 to 1999—Governor Roy Romer, a three-term Democrat, was governor when JonBenét Ramsey was murdered in 1996. He chose not to run for a fourth term.

1999 to 2007—Republican Governor Bill Owens served two terms, from 1999 until 2007, and was term-limited out of office. He was in office during the continuing Ramsey investigation.

2007 to 2011—Democratic Governor Bill Ritter served one term and chose not to run for a second term. Ritter had been a Denver district attorney in 1998 when he was appointed by Governor Romer to serve on a task force to advise Boulder District Attorney Alex Hunter on the Ramsey murder investigation.

## PEOPLE IN THIS CHAPTER

Trip DeMuth—Worked on the Ramsey murder investigation as a deputy district attorney in Boulder. The district attorney task force advising DA Hunter told him that Demuth must be taken off from the case. He was removed by Hunter.

Troy Eid—Governor Owens's chief legal counsel who served on the Governor's District Attorney Task Force to determine if there would be a special prosecutor. Eid later became US Attorney in the District of Colorado.

Bob Grant—Adams County district attorney who was one of four district attorneys advising DA Hunter under Governor Romer's mandate.

Hal Haddon—One of John Ramsey's attorneys.

Peter Hofstrom—Worked on the murder investigation as the chief deputy district attorney in Boulder. The Governor's Task Force advising DA Hunter advised him that Hofstrom be removed from the case. He was removed by Hunter.

Alex Hunter—Boulder County district attorney

Bryan Morgan—John Ramsey's lead attorney

**Ken Salazar—Colorado attorney general who served on the Governor's Task Force to determine if there would be a special prosecutor. Salazar later became a US senator from Colorado and then Secretary of the Interior under the Obama administration from 2009 to 2013.**

**Lou Smit—Retired Colorado Springs homicide detective hired by Boulder District Attorney Alex Hunter with approval from the Boulder Police Department in order to increase experience, neutrality and professionalism on the case.**

IT WAS INEVITABLE that the Ramsey murder investigation would become the hottest political currency in Colorado. Eventually it resulted in Boulder District Attorney Alex Hunter removing two of his attorneys from the case: the chief deputy DA, who was his second-in-charge, and a deputy district attorney working with others on organizing and analyzing Boulder Police Department reports.

As weeks turned into months and months into years, the investigation into the brutal death of JonBenét Ramsey developed into a grim deadlock with pressure on all sides from higher-ups to stop the incessant bickering and resolve the case once and for all. It became a political liability for those who didn't try to fix it, as reflected by the several newspaper editorials asking that the governor become involved.

Governor Roy Romer (1987–1999) wanted to "fix the mess" of the investigation that was reflecting badly on Colorado. Romer's dilemma was compounded when, in August 1998, Boulder Detective Steve Thomas, who had resigned while on medical leave, venomously blasted the investigation. "I believe the district attorney's office is thoroughly compromised," Thomas said. A central "Patsy did it" proponent, he shared his resignation letter with the media. It was dated August 6, 1998, which would have been JonBenét's eighth birthday. "It is my belief the district attorney's office has effectively crippled the case," Thomas wrote. "The time for intervention is now."

Shortly afterward, Detective Lou Smit, who supported the intruder theory in the case, resigned on September 20, 1998 with a letter of explanation: "They [the BPD] are just going in the wrong direction and have been since day one of the investigation," Smit stated.

Romer had already sought advice from several people about what he should do to bring the fractured investigation to a satisfactory conclusion by controlling the infighting in Boulder and bringing the killer to justice. He ultimately asked for input from four experienced Denver-area district attorneys who made up his appointed Governor's District Attorney Task Force.

Romer said, "I listened carefully to what [my] district attorney advisers told me because all four were experienced and successful prosecutors." Two of those district attorneys, Bob Grant and Bill Ritter, agreed there were three options. One was to appoint the attorney general in Colorado to act as a special prosecutor in the case. They quickly dismissed that option, however, because the attorney general's office did not necessarily have the expertise or the time. The second option was to remove the Boulder district attorney from the case and appoint a special prosecutor from a metro-area district attorney's office, assuming the special prosecutor would have some neutrality. The third option: bolster the Boulder district attorney's staff with experienced outside prosecutors and leave the Boulder DA in place. Unfortunately, "bolstering" the staff evolved into "removing" the current staff from the case.

"Governor Romer made the final decision," said Grant, the Adams County district attorney at the time. "I advised him I thought the better of the options was to bring in new attorneys for the Boulder district attorney's office and to not appoint a special prosecutor. I made my recommendation on the fact that I felt it was important to keep the case in Boulder. But it was the governor's decision."

Then Denver District Attorney Bill Ritter recommended the same, because he felt a special prosecutor involving a Denver-area district attorney "would be a very significant undertaking for any prosecutor's office. One that I felt my office couldn't undertake because we had so many cases and weren't staffed to take this on." Ritter felt the best solution was to bring in new attorneys.

Romer gave Boulder DA Hunter a Hobson's choice: call for a grand jury in Boulder and remove two of his attorneys from the case, or be removed himself and replaced by a special prosecutor.

Hunter found out about the change in his role in mid-August 1998, when he walked into a meeting with the Governor's District Attorney Task Force with a smile on his face, apparently believing he was in charge and could "use a little advice," according to First Assistant DA Bill Wise. Hunter walked out of the meeting silent and withdrawn.

"It was him or them," said Wise, who had waited outside the meeting room for Hunter, as had Chief Deputy DA Peter Hofstrom, who would be taken off the case. "He had no choice but to fire his own people from the case, receive continuing advice from the Governor's District Attorney Task Force and hire their recommendations for the three new attorneys who would be in charge of the grand jury."

In making their recommendations, Grant and Ritter took sides: both advocated for new attorneys, which meant removal of DA Hunter's people, Peter Hofstrom and Trip DeMuth.

"I have great respect for both Peter and Trip, but it is important to remember this was the first homicide in 1996 in Boulder, and it did strike me that there was a different level of homicide experience in the new prosecutors who would be brought in," Ritter said. "It was about the experience level needed to take on a high-profile homicide case. There needed to be a different skill set . . . In my mind, the most important thing was to staff this case and staff it appropriately. How do you staff it? How do you staff it so you have the most competent prosecutors to investigate a high-profile homicide that was gaining international attention? And, in my mind, ultimately, that was done."

Ritter, who would later become governor of Colorado, selected two of the three new prosecutors who would take over the Ramsey murder case. He chose one from his office and advised DA Hunter on another. Grant selected one from his office. The prosecutors who were chosen had district attorney backgrounds and, by nature of their jobs, had worked closely with police in the past on homicide cases.

The two attorneys removed from the case who had worked in the

Boulder DA's office, Peter Hofstrom and Trip DeMuth, were considered by the Ramsey lawyers to be capable and fair. Boulder police commanders had determined just the opposite about them, however, complaining that the prosecutors were unfairly helping the Ramseys and their attorneys. Both prosecutors helped organize and coordinate incoming evidence from BPD police officers. And neither automatically accepted the "Ramseys did it" theory favored by the Boulder Police Department.

Both Hofstrom and DeMuth had been involved in the Ramsey murder investigation since the afternoon of the first day after the discovery of JonBenét's body. One had been on the scene. The other advised BPD officials. Their removal from the case took their experience of the investigation with them.

For the Ramsey lawyers, the decision to switch prosecutors on the case was devastating. Morgan remembers being called to Chief Deputy DA Hofstrom's office. "Peter was very quiet and told me, 'This will be the last time I can talk to you about this case. We've been removed from this case. Trip and I.'" Hofstrom continued, "I want you to know that Trip and I are very comfortable with what we've done on this case."

Morgan said he was "stunned, because to me, Peter was the firewall, standing firm regardless of the politics. I don't ever remember being lower in my life. Pete Hofstrom and Trip DeMuth were honest and straightforward. But no array of facts could get the Boulder Police Department to change their devil theory that the Ramseys were guilty.

"The problem was never with the prosecutors," Morgan added. "They were knowledgeable and completely informed of the facts. The problem was with the investigators, mainly the Boulder Police Department, because of their unrelenting bias against the Ramseys."

When Morgan objected publicly about the removal of the two attorneys, the counterattack against him in the rumor/gossip arena stated that Morgan was a close friend of Chief Deputy DA Peter Hofstrom, and therefore neither Hofstrom nor Morgan could deal with the case objectively.

Defense attorney Hal Haddon said about the decision, "Alex Hunter wanted everyone to get along, and I give him a lot of credit, at least until

Peter Hofstrom and Trip DeMuth were purged. That's when prosecutors who were pro-police and thus anti-Ramsey were put in place. Up until then, Alex had wanted to do the right thing, not the expedient thing."

What wasn't being said was that a special prosecutor could have brought in his own investigators, instead of using BPD investigators, by borrowing detectives from other jurisdictions or getting approval to hire detectives from outside Boulder. This would have had the effect of starting over inside both the district attorney's office and the police department and ensuring more of a clean sweep with regard to the Ramsey murder investigation.

"Changing the police agency was on the table from the beginning," Grant later recalled. "Governor Romer was concerned with police and the DA's office. Legally, though, he could only appoint an attorney general or a special prosecutor. The governor did not have the right to replace the local law enforcement agency. The police agency has to ask for assistance, which they had initially refused to do, or a special prosecutor could replace the police investigators.

"Hunter was still the district attorney on the Ramsey case under the new agreement. The new prosecutors did not ask to have police replaced, or Hunter did not agree to have them replaced." Grant added, "Governor Romer understood his options. And it was very clear that Alex Hunter understood the governor's options. Romer decided his special district attorney task force would appoint experienced prosecutors. Hunter knew what it meant."

As Ritter has put it, "Hindsight is 20-20 about changing the police on the investigation." At the time he supported part of the deal in "bringing in a retired Denver police lieutenant who had vast homicide experience and would assist on the police side of the case." That retired Denver homicide detective was Tom Haney. According to BPD and DA investigators who were present at private meetings with Haney, the former Denver investigator voiced his opinion at such meetings that the Ramseys had been involved in their daughter's death. Haney has said that's not true, that he was neutral. He added that he had refused a job offer from the Ramsey defense attorneys as an investigator very early in the case because, as he told them, he wasn't able in his mind to switch from "homicide detective to defense investigator."

In September 1998, a grand jury was seated on the Ramsey case. The three newly appointed attorneys, who had replaced the two DA attorneys removed from the case, were actively running the new grand jury. The four district attorneys from the Governor's Task Force, including Grant and Ritter, were sworn in as officers of the grand jury and acted in an advisory capacity. Boulder District Attorney Alex Hunter was also in the grand jury room for every session but did not run the hearings.

In 2010, former Governor Romer talked about the "no choice" he had given Hunter. "I felt this was the right decision then, and I believe it still is."

The Ramsey case percolated on low until October 13, 1999, when DA Hunter announced the Boulder grand jury had reached its decision, and Hunter had decided there would be no indictment. The grand jury had reviewed evidence related to the investigation over a period of thirteen months.

At that point, Governor Bill Owens entered the fray. In office since January, Owens involved himself in the case by vaulting into the constituency of people who wanted John and Patsy Ramsey tried and found guilty of the murder of their daughter. He pushed this agenda with incendiary remarks that gained him valuable national airtime again and again, providing him with exposure that served to redeem his political career in the eyes of many who had followed a very close gubernatorial election in Colorado the previous fall.

Owens announced that he would consider a special prosecutor for the case and soon appointed a committee composed of prosecutors, the attorney general and a Colorado Supreme Court judge to advise him about his options.

John and Patsy Ramsey were desperate to talk with that committee. "We wanted a special prosecutor," they each said at different times, adding their belief that continuing the investigation with someone outside

Boulder would increase the likelihood of finding their daughter's killer.

While the committee was making its decision, the main defense attorneys, Burke, Haddon and Morgan, sent a letter to the governor. They had spoken with one of the committee members, Colorado Attorney General Ken Salazar,[1] who had said he was concerned the committee process might be viewed as a media event and wanted to assure Haddon that he was objective. In that conversation, Haddon reiterated that the Ramseys were willing to cooperate and meet with the committee. Salazar recommended that the Ramsey attorneys contact the governor.

In their letter to the governor, Burke, Haddon and Morgan wrote: "The Ramseys '(plural)' would be willing to meet with that group." The letter continued by stating there were "very capable detectives who worked on the case and who did not share the Boulder Police view that the Ramseys were involved in their daughter's murder" and suggesting that these detectives also talk with the committee.

According to Hal Haddon, "Attorney General Salazar said that while he was a member of the group, [Governor Owens's counsel,] Troy Eid[2] was the person to whom these requests should be conveyed." On October 15, 1999, Haddon called Eid and, when he got Eid's voice-mail, left a message that reiterated what the letter from his firm to the governor stated.

Eid wrote back to Haddon, saying he understood only John Ramsey had offered to talk with the committee and not Patsy, and that Haddon had been "inaccurate." Regardless, the committee did not ask John, Patsy or the recommended BPD detectives to talk before them. It heard only what the grand jury heard.

As an investigative reporter for KUSA-TV in Denver at that time, I spoke with Governor Owens about whether he would talk with the parents of JonBenét Ramsey. I told him I was aware both of them wanted to talk to him. The governor told me there were considerations I was not aware of, and he wouldn't discuss sitting down and talking with the Ramseys.

I also spoke to Patsy in a phone conversation she wanted kept off the record at the time. She told me, "Both John and I are begging our attorneys for us to talk with the governor or his committee. They agree.

But the governor won't talk with us. I don't understand why he won't."

The explanation of why John and Patsy were not called to talk with the committee came from the governor's attorney, Troy Eid, who served on that committee. "We looked at no new evidence whatsoever. That was not our role," Eid has said. "The Governor appointed a Special Prosecution Task Force that, among other things, double-checked what DA Hunter did and, based on a review of the admissible evidence his office collected, did not find probable cause to believe his office had erred by not charging someone with a crime. It would be an extreme injustice for a Governor and the State Attorney General to undo a local DA's decision unless that DA had engaged in misconduct. The Governor appointed some of the state's most respected legal experts—including the retired Chief Justice of the Colorado Supreme Court—to determine independently whether Hunter erred in not prosecuting based on the admissible evidence his office had collected. The task force determined that there was no probable cause for Hunter to charge either the Ramseys or anyone else, in connection with this terrible crime. The Ramseys were not called before the task force because they did not testify before the grand jury." Yet Detective Lou Smit, who eventually did testify before the grand jury, was not asked to testify before the Governor's Special Prosecution Task Force even though he asked to. The decision on who would appear before the committee was made by the Governor and Eid, according to two of the committee members.

In an October 27, 1999 news conference, Governor Owens said "no" to appointing a special prosecutor to the Ramsey murder case. During the news conference, which reporters had expected to be a basic question-and-answer session, Owens took a surprising tack, using the force and credibility of his office to launch a full frontal assault on John and Patsy Ramsey and their right to be presumed innocent.

"Quit hiding behind your attorneys," Owens said, speaking directly into the microphones and looking straight into reporters' cameras. He was talking to the Ramseys through the assembled media. "Quit hiding behind your public relations firm. Come back to Colorado and work with us to find the killers in this case, no matter where that trail may lead."

Ramsey attorney Haddon was furious. "Owens was not qualified, was uninformed and simply decided to publicize himself in a case where he became another person victimizing these tragic people," he said. "Except that he had the powerful platform as the Governor of Colorado. It was a cynical ploy to get national television exposure, which he got, by pandering to public sentiment."

While the Ramsey defense attorneys did hire a public relations firm at the beginning of the case "to handle the media onslaught," that contract ended in 1997, almost two years before Owens criticized the Ramseys for it.

In his October 1999 news conference, Governor Owens also claimed, "The killers in the case made some very serious mistakes." He did not flinch at using the plural word "killers." It was easy for people to translate "killers" to "Ramseys."

On the CNN television show *Larry King Live* on the same night of the news conference, King asked Governor Owens whether he was "impressed by the statement of Lou Smit, who said that he thinks they're not guilty at all." Owens responded that the evidence Smit presented, including "a so-called stun gun," had been investigated and "unfortunately, dismissed." Adams County DA Bob Grant publicly contradicted the governor, stating "That's not true" with regard to the stun gun being "dismissed" as potential evidence.

A few days later, Owens continued his attack via the October 30, 1999 issue of *Rocky Mountain News,* which stated, "Gov. Bill Owens continued firing barbs at the parents of JonBenét Ramsey on Friday, saying a meeting with John Ramsey would have allowed a 'prime suspect' to influence his decision whether to appoint a special prosecutor . . . It would have been wrong to grant the Ramseys a meeting, said the governor, because John Ramsey would have wanted a hand in deciding whether a prosecutor should be named—and if so, who that person might be.

"'Mr. Ramsey is considered to be a prime suspect. It would be very inappropriate to meet with him.' Owens said."

This was the first time a public official had referred to John Ramsey as a "prime suspect." It also represented a dramatic change in the reason why the governor and his task force did not meet with the Ramseys as explained by the governor's attorney, Troy Eid.

On November 1, 1999 on KOA Radio, the governor said to a commentator in a discussion about the Ramseys: "If they're innocent, they're sure not acting like they are."

State legislators and attorneys criticized Governor Owens publicly for his ongoing comments related to the Ramsey case. District Attorney Bob Grant, who had been on Governor Roy Romer's District Attorney Task Force, declared that it was "totally inappropriate for the Chief Executive of Colorado to be placing blame on anyone."

Several newspaper columnists wrote commentaries critical of Owens that ran with headlines such as this one in the *Rocky Mountain News:*

OWENS PLAYING TO A TABLOID NATION

Defense attorney Haddon noted that the governor was "inaccurate" in saying that only John Ramsey had wanted to meet with him. "Both John and Patsy wanted to meet with Governor Owens and his committee," he said.

Five months later in March 2000, Owens continued his media campaign in an interview with ABC's *Good Morning America.* "There was substantial new evidence in October and there's even some new evidence in the last couple of weeks," Owens said, refusing to divulge any details about such new evidence.

Then Boulder Police Chief Mark Beckner discounted the governor's statements about new evidence, saying the governor was likely referring to ongoing FBI laboratory tests of evidence. "I have not spoken to the governor in the last couple of weeks," Beckner said. He added that he had spoken to the governor only "occasionally" since the October 1999 news conference.

Owens also argued live on television with ABC's Barbara Walters, saying she hadn't been tough enough during an exclusive interview with John and Patsy Ramsey. He also cited two male anchors who might have been tougher on the Ramseys than Walters. The criticism created more national attention.

Owens's stature during this period continued to grow. In 2002, *National Review,* a conservative magazine founded by William F. Buckley, named him "Governor of the Year." Owens was mentioned as a potential GOP presidential candidate. He was a rising star in the Republican Party, and his strong stance against the Ramseys represented political gold. The former governor is currently a national and international business adviser living in Colorado.

Owens declined to be interviewed for this book. He did agree, however, to respond to the following questions from a longer list of questions that had been emailed to him:

1. The Ramseys and their attorneys asked if they could talk with you and your commission about the decision so you would have their input. Why didn't you talk with them?

2. In retrospect, do you believe you should have taken such an active role as a governor, but not as a law enforcement investigator, in criticizing the Ramsey family in this unfortunate murder case?

3. I have quotes from people involved in the case saying you were "interfering in the case for publicity to gain national attention." Do you believe that is accurate? If you believe this is not true, why did you make the statements previously mentioned, criticizing the Ramseys and strongly suggesting their guilt?

4. In 2008, former Boulder District Attorney Mary Lacy issued a document clearing John, Patsy, Burke and other Ramseys of the murder based on new DNA evidence. What is your reaction to that?

Part of Owens's response follows. Owens did not answer any of the specific questions, but focused instead on the qualifications of the people on his advisory committee.

> Paula—the statement (below) will be all I have to say on the issue. Best, Bill
>
> I stand by the statements made as the Governor of Colorado into the tragic murder of JonBenét Ramsey. As Governor, I worked with former Colorado Attorney General Ken Salazar to convene a Special Prosecution Task Force to advise me as to whether a special prosecutor should be appointed, as provided by Colorado law, in connection with the criminal investigation into her murder, which was and remains the most high-profile such investigation ever conducted in our state. The members of the Task Force were all designated as Special Attorneys General by Mr. Salazar in order to ensure that their deliberations, and the advice they ultimately gave me collectively and as individual experts, would remain strictly confidential.
>
> After meeting with the members of the Task Force and being briefed on their findings, I decided not to appoint a Special Prosecutor in this case. While there was a tremendous amount of evidence collected in this case, the difficulty of ultimately achieving a conviction or convictions led me to believe that such an appointment would not be productive.

# CHAPTER 24
# RAMSEY GRAND JURY

Boulder District Attorney Alex Hunter surrounded by media as he walks to the podium to announce his decision on the grand jury and Patsy and John Ramsey. Courtesy photographer Andy Cross (staff credit), the *Denver Post*, October 19, 1999.

## CHRONOLOGY

**September 1998—Ramsey grand jury begins.**

**October 19, 1999—Boulder District Attorney Alex Hunter announces his decision on whether he'll go to trial after the grand jury makes its confidential decision.**

## ADDITIONAL PEOPLE IN THIS CHAPTER

**Ramsey grand jury specialist Michael Kane— headed a team of two attorneys and directed the activities of the grand jury.**

**Retired Homicide Detective Lou Smit—hired by the Boulder District Attorney's Office in March 2007 to work on the Ramsey case.**

IN 2012, BOULDER DISTRICT ATTORNEY ALEX HUNTER'S First Assistant District Attorney, Bill Wise, told me the grand jury had voted to indict both Ramseys, but he remained uncertain of the exact charges. Wise had been removed from the case and so was not bound by a secrecy oath. He said he had been told about the decision from someone who had participated in the grand jury process. While all participants involved in the grand jury had taken an oath of secrecy, after several years a few of them talked privately to certain reporters. They said they had voted to return two indictments each, including child abuse resulting in death, against both Ramseys.

The story broke in January 2013, reviving the fervor about the Ramsey family that would lead to the eventual release of the grand jury indictments.

*The Los Angeles Times* was among several media outlets throughout the country to report the information that January. *The Times* published the story on its web page with an opinion poll that asked "Should the prosecutor have pursued charges against JonBenét Ramsey's parents?"

The results of the opinion poll: YES 76 percent; NO 24 percent.[1]

The interest in the story remained. So did the bias against John and Patsy Ramsey.

The indictments from the grand jury were officially released on October 25, 2013 by a Colorado Senior District Court Judge after a lawsuit was filed asking that they be released.

There is a distinct difference between a grand jury and a criminal trial. In a criminal trial, both the prosecution and the defense present their cases. In a grand jury, only one side is presented: the prosecution. Denver Defense Attorney Craig Silverman says, "A grand jury can be a rubber stamp. It goes wherever the prosecution wants it to. The overused cliché, 'You can get a grand jury to indict a ham sandwich' is accurate." Those testifying before a grand jury can have an attorney with them, but those attorneys cannot confer with their clients during the proceedings. The prosecutors shape, question and determine who testifies and what direction is taken in interviews, and usually lead grand jurors where they want them to go. The speculation related to the Ramsey case was that the new prosecutors were organizing to indict one or both of the Ramseys based on their efforts to prevent some witnesses from testifying.

In the fall of 1999, when the indictment was returned and still confidential, Boulder District Attorney Alex Hunter had a choice on whether or not to accept the grand jury's decision.

Looking out the door from inside the courthouse on October 13, 1999, just minutes before he would make his announcement on whether John or Patsy Ramsey would be charged in their daughter's murder, Boulder District Attorney Alex Hunter was absorbing what lay before him, which he later described to me. He saw at least one hundred reporters and at least as many photographers, backed up by satellite trucks with their massive dishes pointed into the blue sky. He noted an extraordinarily beautiful fall afternoon. He took a deep breath to calm himself. He had already told a disappointed police chief and selected detectives of his decision, and he mused about it once again. Boulder Police Chief Mark

Beckner was "extremely disappointed we weren't going to trial against Patsy and John," Hunter later acknowledged privately.

Hunter and the three prosecutors on the grand jury had been in lengthy discussions about what to do about the grand jury's decision. These were the prosecutors Hunter had been ordered to accept by Governor Romer because of their experience. That order had resulted in Hunter having to fire his own two deputy district attorneys on the case. The new prosecutors had been very involved in the reasoning on charges. They and Hunter had decided there wasn't enough evidence to go to trial and convict Patsy and John Ramsey. As one defense attorney has explained to me, "A person can only be tried and acquitted in criminal court once [i.e., one time] on a case. It's our system of justice. It's called double jeopardy. Presumably, without enough evidence against the family, they felt it was a bad decision to move forward."

Part of this reasoning may have involved consideration of the possibility that if the Ramseys were indeed guilty, more evidence could some day surface that could lead to a conviction in court. At this point, however, no such evidence existed.

So Alex and the three attorneys who had led the grand jury opened one of the courthouse doors that afternoon. Reporters surrounded them and asked questions as they began the long walk across the courthouse yard to the makeshift podium and microphone that had been set up for them. Later, Hunter would say he'd always remember the crowds of people waiting for him to speak on that day in October 1999. But most of all, he'd remember the actual walk to the microphones. His three grand jury prosecutors were Lead and Chief Prosecutor Michael Kane, Denver Chief Deputy District Attorney Mitch Morrissey and Adams County Chief Deputy District Attorney Bruce Levin.

Hunter turned to the reporters who had crowded the courthouse parking lot and said, "The Ramsey grand jurors have done their work extraordinarily well, bringing to bear all their legal powers, life experiences and shrewdness."

Then he added, "We do not have sufficient evidence to warrant filing charges against anyone who has been investigated at the present time."

Some of the grand jurors were working people, some were students and some were not working. They were described as a pyrotechnical worker, an accountant, a retired outdoorswoman, a part-time nutritionist, a one-time county probation office worker, a business manager, a former Naval officer and firearms expert, a woman who worked for a non-profit organization, a woman who had a real estate license, a former utility company service technician, a woman who took night classes and a man working on a doctorate in chemical engineering.

The grand jurors had studied and heard testimony from September 1998 to October 1999 with four months off during that time. They had gone to the Ramsey house and individually reviewed any areas they wished. They listened to the testimony of police detectives, DNA and other scientific experts, handwriting analysts and Ramsey friends and family before coming to their conclusion.

The day of Hunter's electrifying announcement, Patsy and John Ramsey were secluded at a close friend's home in Boulder with two of their attorneys, Bryan Morgan and Pat Burke. Everyone in the room sat transfixed in front of the television, waiting for the news conference to begin, wondering what would happen next. For John and Patsy, their grief for their murdered daughter had become so enmeshed with what they believed was persecution by the Boulder Police Department as well as prosecution by politicians, the media and the public that a powerful collection of emotion threatened to sweep them away. The pending press conference represented a decisive moment when they would learn what their future held as it had been determined by a grand jury. They stared at the television as if their lives hung in the balance, which they, in fact, did.

"If there was an indictment, I wanted to make sure there was not a mob scene when they turned themselves in," Morgan said. "I wanted to do that privately, and that's why I kept them where no one knew where they were."

When Hunter made his announcement, Morgan rose from his chair, went outside and wept, releasing at least some of the tension he'd endured through the years of fighting for the Ramseys.

What struck Morgan, and what he remembers to this day, is that John followed him outside after the televised news conference, touched Morgan's shoulder as he choked away tears, and said, "Thank you, Bryan." As Morgan recalls, "It meant a lot."

In order to ensure the secrecy of the location of the Ramseys that day, Hal Haddon was not in Boulder with John, Patsy and attorneys Burke and Morgan. While Morgan remained with the Ramseys for most of that day, Burke was in and out of the home where John and Patsy were staying, fully aware the grand jury outcome could go either way. "We were prepared to turn them in, but enter the court house through a different entrance to give them some dignity," Burke said. "That's why we were close by or with them."

Haddon was in his Denver office, watching the news conference on television. When Hunter made his announcement, Haddon did not smile. He did not gloat. A huge sense of relief swept through his body. He was exhausted and felt deep inside that it wasn't over for the Ramseys. He couldn't believe that it was over. He took some time that night to breathe in the lack of indictment. Then he tried to think about what was next. He felt their enemies would not give up. And they didn't.

Even though the workings of a grand jury are, by law, confidential and are supposed to remain that way, some secrets leaked out. People saw each other going in to testify and they did not always remain silent. The list of those who testified and what they said is still under confidential seal, but it is known that two of John's children from his first marriage, John Andrew and Melinda, testified. Regarding his testimony, John Andrew has said, "Grand jury prosecutor Michael Kane and I really butted heads during my testimony." Burke Ramsey also testified. In the beginning of the grand jury hearings, several police officers testified as well.

Patsy and John had formally asked in a letter that they be subpoenaed to testify, but the grand jury prosecutors, with whom that decision rested, refused their request. Without subpoenas, the Ramseys were also unable to review their prior interviews and interrogations with the Boulder Police Department and the District Attorney's Office. Their defense attorneys had said that since their clients were targets for the grand jury, it was too dangerous for them to testify without reviewing their former testimonies. So the Ramseys didn't testify for two reasons: they were not subpoenaed, and they didn't have access to former statements they had made to members of the Boulder Police Department and to investigators with the Boulder District Attorney's Office.

Susan Stine, a close family friend of the Ramseys, did testify. "It was very clear to me that the prosecutors were out to get the Ramseys," she said. "That's how their questioning was shaped. Their questions were filled with facts and evidence that the police and prosecutors should have already known wasn't accurate."

On January 21, 1999, investigator Lou Smit wrote a letter to the grand jury foreperson after he was told he would not be called to testify before the Ramsey grand jury:

> My name is Lou Smit, a retired detective previously assigned to the JonBenét Ramsey case who resigned from the case in September 1998. I was hired by Alex Hunter in March 1997 to assist his office in organizing and analyzing the case materials presented to his office by the Boulder Police Department. During the 19 months spent in Boulder, I worked very closely with D.A.'s Trip DeMuth and Peter Hofstrom. Together we examined all aspects of this case.
>
> I have been in law enforcement for 32 years, have been involved in over 200 homicide investigations and have worked many high-profile cases in Colorado. I was hired because of my experience and background. I take my work very seriously and truly desire to seek justice not only for JonBenét but her parents as well.
>
> I resigned because I do not agree with others in authority, that John and Patsy Ramsey killed their daughter. I see evidence in the case of an intruder, and I cannot in good conscience assist in the prosecution of people I believe to be innocent.
>
> That is why I am writing you this letter. I would respectfully

request that I be called to give testimony before the Grand Jury to provide an "intruder" side of the story. Please take the time to consider what I have to say while evaluating the evidence and making such difficult decisions regarding an indictment in this case.

I have prepared a presentation, which would take about eight hours of the Grand Jury's time.

Respectfully submitted,
Lou Smit
Retired Detective

The response to Smit's letter was brief. Within a month, the principal grand jury prosecutor, Michael Kane, and Boulder District Attorney Alex Hunter wrote Smit a letter under grand jury seal, which meant the letter could not be publicly released. That letter, dated February 11, 1999, said that Lou Smit's request to present his "intruder theory" to the Grand Jury had been denied.

Hunter and Kane weren't finished. After they sent the letter to Smit, they then sought a court order to bar Smit's testimony. Why?

Hunter has told me he "absolutely will not talk about anything to do with the grand jury and Lou Smit. People might think it's unreasonable, but that's just what they're going to have to think. I won't talk about it."

Kane has also declined to be interviewed about the case.

Smit persisted in trying to appear before the Ramsey grand jury, challenging Kane and Hunter in court at his own expense. He finally won and succeeded in testifying. Smit wouldn't talk about his actual testimony because of grand jury secrecy rules, but said he'd "never been treated more terribly" by prosecutors.

Smit's experience mirrors that of handwriting analyst Howard Rile, who had been hired by the Ramsey attorneys at the beginning of the case. After his grand jury appearance, he hired an attorney to ask if he could testify again, because he felt the treatment he'd received from the prosecutors of the grand jury had been aggressive and confrontational. His request was refused. Rile had testified that he was very close to eliminating Patsy Ramsey as the writer of the ransom note.

By the spring of 1999, the grand jurors who had entered the courthouse as strangers to each other walked outside as a group. They appeared relaxed, exchanging small talk and smiles. The media was set up across the street watching, under court order to stay 100 feet away. Reporters peered anxiously at the jurors, looking for any clues, any signs that might telegraph their inclinations. Nothing came back, except perhaps a comfort or agreement among the jurors, which might signal that they were coming to a decision. Only a few reporters noticed.

The grand jury decision did not ease the pressure against the Ramsey family. District Attorney Hunter "tried to make up for his lack of indictment," according to one of his advisers. The day after the announcement that the parents would not be indicted, Hunter, his advisers and Boulder Police Chief Mark Beckner held another news conference and vowed to carry on the investigation. "We are not going to quit the investigation," Hunter said, adding that Patsy and John were still suspects.

Ramsey attorney Hal Haddon had been correct on that long fall afternoon. It was definitely not over. The suspicion of the Ramsey family continued unabated.

In 2013, John Ramsey commented on the grand jury's decision, which he had learned when it had been first leaked: "As we prepared for the grand jury results in 1998, we had been warned by our attorneys that the system was broken and even though it wasn't right, we should expect to be indicted for murder. And so that was what we were prepared for. We never knew other than what was publicly announced about the results of the grand jury. When we subsequently learned that the grand jury indicted us for child abuse because we were in the house and should have protected our child, it was a very deep hurt because nothing could have

COUNT IV (a)

On or between December 25, and December 26, 1996, in Boulder County, Colorado, Patricia Paugh Ramsey did unlawfully, knowingly, recklessly and feloniously permit a child to be unreasonably placed in a situation which posed a threat of injury to the child's life or health, which resulted in the death of JonBenet Ramsey, a child under the age of sixteen.

As to Count IV (a), Child Abuse Resulting in Death:

A TRUE BILL

Signature Redacted

NO TRUE BILL

Forman

COUNT VII

On or about December 25, and December 26, 1996 in Boulder County, Colorado, Patricia Paugh Ramsey did unlawfully, knowingly and feloniously render assistance to a person, with intent to hinder, delay and prevent the discovery, detention, apprehension, prosecution, conviction and punishment of such person for the commission of a crime, knowing the person being assisted has committed and was suspected of the crime of Murder in the First Degree and Child Abuse Resulting in Death.

As to Count VII, Accessory to a Crime:

A TRUE BILL

Signature Redacted

NO TRUE BILL

Foreman

Indictments against the Ramseys by the Boulder Grand Jury. Boulder District Attorney Alex Hunter did not do as the grand jury recommended. He did not charge/indict the parents.

COUNT IV (a)

On or between December 25, and December 26, 1996, in Boulder County, Colorado, John Bennett Ramsey did unlawfully, knowingly, recklessly and feloniously permit a child to be unreasonably placed in a situation which posed a threat of injury to the child's life or health, which resulted in the death of JonBenet Ramsey, a child under the age of sixteen.

As to Count IV (a), Child Abuse Resulting in Death:

A TRUE BILL

Signature Redacted

NO TRUE BILL

Forman

COUNT VII

On or about December 25, and December 26, 1996 in Boulder County, Colorado, John Bennett Ramsey did unlawfully, knowingly and feloniously render assistance to a person, with intent to hinder, delay and prevent the discovery, detention, apprehension, prosecution, conviction and punishment of such person for the commission of a crime, knowing the person being assisted has committed and was suspected of the crime of Murder in the First Degree and Child Abuse Resulting in Death.

As to Count VII, Accessory to a Crime:

A TRUE BILL

Signature Redacted

NO TRUE BILL

Foreman

been further from the truth. I would have given my life in an instant to protect JonBenét and certainly wish I could have done so."

The indictments are numbered IV (four) and VII (seven), "which indicates the grand jury prosecutors presented at least seven different alternative legal theories of the parents' possible involvement in JonBenét's murder," one current defense attorney with considerable grand jury experience has said. He added, "The indictments do not name the identity of the person or persons who killed JonBenét and do not list the facts that support the conclusions."

In October 2013, when a judge ordered the indictments released, then Boulder District Attorney Stan Garnett wrote a Guest Commentary in the *Daily Camera* about the indictments that emphasized the accomplishments of the Boulder District Attorney's Office and its then current strict adherence to the law. He also added about the grand jury charges: "I asked my appellate staff to review them and was told they related to charges for which the statute of limitations had run years ago. My staff evaluated the Ramsey case to determine if there was any charge for which the statute of limitations had not run and for which there was conclusive evidence. Because there was none, we focused on other cases."[2]

# CHAPTER 25
# FEDERAL JUDGE RULING

IN THE UNITED STATES DISTRICT COURT
FOR THE NORTHERN DISTRICT OF GEORGIA
ATLANTA DIVISION

ROBERT CHRISTIAN WOLF, Plaintiff,

v.

JOHN BENNET RAMSEY and PATRICIA PAUGH RAMSEY, Defendants.

CIVIL ACTION NO 1:00-CV-1187-JEC

Page 90

In sum, plaintiff has failed to prove that Mrs. Ramsey wrote the Ransom Note and has thereby necessarily failed to prove that she murdered her daughter. ) Moreover, the weight of the evidence is more consistent with a theory that an intruder murdered JonBenét than it is with a theory that Mrs. Ramsey did so. For that reason, plaintiff has failed to establish that when defendants wrote the Book, they "in fact entertained serious doubts as to the truth of the publication." St. Amant v. Thompson, 390 U.S. 727, 731 (1968); Hemenway v. Blanchard, 163 Ga. App. 668, 671-72, 294 S.E.2d 603, 606 (1982). Accordingly, the Court GRANTS defendants' motion for summary judgment as to plaintiff's libel claim.

(Top) Front cover of Federal Judge Julie Carnes's decision. (Bottom) Summary of Federal Judge Julie Carnes's decision.

## CHRONOLOGY

March 2003—Judge Julie E. Carnes, United States District Court for the Northern District of Georgia, 11th Judicial District, writes a 93-page ruling dismissing a defamation case against the Ramseys before trial.

THERE IS ALWAYS A BACKGROUND BUZZ on any day of a high-profile criminal trial. People arrive early to get a seat, and everyone has their own agenda, whether they're a cop, reporter, attorney or interested observer. There is a familiarity among the regulars who have been following the trial, and when the defendant enters the courtroom, most glance their way. What is the posture, the facial expression and the demeanor of the person on trial? What are they wearing?

As events proceed, detectives wait in the hallway to be called to testify, and there are also witnesses for the defense, depending on how far along the trial is. The prosecutor is focused on the next step, where the case will go. The defense attorney is doing the same. Both are wondering what, if anything, the other has that they haven't anticipated. This is their chance to bring it all out, to present to the best of their ability their side of the case and question the witnesses from the other side.

Had the Ramseys gone to a criminal trial—which is what Boulder Police Department officials wanted—it would have been a huge media event, just as the O. J. Simpson trial was in 1995. But Boulder detectives could never make a case that was substantial enough for a criminal trial that the Boulder DA and the three appointed outside prosecutors would support.

The Ramseys did go to court, but not because they were ever arrested on criminal charges. They filed nine slander and libel lawsuits against various media organizations. Eight were settled out of court in favor of the Ramsey family, with substantial financial settlements, although the exact amounts of the settlements remain confidential. The ninth lawsuit was settled in favor of the defendant, but the Ramseys did not pay any damages.

Two additional defamation cases were filed against John and Patsy Ramsey by people who felt they were unfairly named as possible suspects in the couple's book, *The Death of Innocence,* which was published in 2000. One case was settled with no damages awarded. The other suit, *Wolf vs. Ramsey*, was dismissed before trial, but the evidence that came out in that suit created a reliable blueprint for what might have transpired had there been a criminal trial.

Robert Christian Wolf filed the lawsuit, and key information was revealed by three people from whom investigators took depositions: former Boulder Detective Steve Thomas, who had resigned from the BPD and written a book accusing Patsy Ramsey of killing her daughter; Boulder Police Chief Mark Beckner, who began investigating the case within three weeks of when JonBenét's body was found; and retired Detective Lou Smit. Smit's job of documenting incoming police reports and evidence had convinced him the Ramseys were innocent.

All three men testified under oath in depositions and answered questions for attorneys on both sides of the case. A deposition is held to gather basic facts and to establish baseline information before a trial. It provides a way to discover more information from probable witnesses. There is no criminal court cross-examination with depositions.

In March 2003, Federal Judge Julie Carnes wrote a rare analysis defending the Ramseys after reviewing all the pre-trial depositions in the case. She dissected the testimony and dismissed the case before trial. For clarification, the plaintiff was Robert Christian Wolf. The defendants were John and Patsy Ramsey.

"In sum, plaintiff [Wolf] has failed to prove that Mrs. Ramsey wrote the Ransom Note and has thereby necessarily failed to prove that she murdered her daughter. Moreover, the weight of the evidence is more consistent with a theory that an intruder murdered JonBenét than it is with a theory that Mrs. Ramsey did so," Judge Carnes wrote.

Before she noted the evidence for her ruling, Judge Carnes revealed her guidelines for judging the evidence or "material facts." The judge considered the statements of facts where the Ramseys and the plaintiff agreed. When looking at a list of facts and evidence where they didn't agree, Judge Carnes said she ruled in "the light most favorable to plaintiff"—i.e., Mr. Wolf, the person suing the Ramseys.

The text from Judge Carnes provides a unique perspective into the case from someone not involved in the Ramsey investigation. She did not live in Colorado (the jurisdiction for the *Wolf vs. Ramsey* case was in

Atlanta) and had not been exposed to the publicity overload related to the case that had been experienced by residents of Colorado. The judge's job was to be an impartial, neutral, legal observer in reviewing the testimony before trial. Some of the judge's conclusions are as follows:

> Plaintiff, however, contends that Mrs. Ramsey did not go to sleep the night of December 25, but instead killed her daughter and spent the rest of the night covering her crime, as evidenced by the fact she was wearing the same outfit the following morning . . . He further posits that Mrs. Ramsey authored the Ransom Note in an attempt to stage a crime scene to make it appear as if an intruder had entered their home . . . Plaintiff theorizes that, at some point in the night, JonBenét awoke after wetting her bed . . . and upon learning of the bed-wetting, Mrs. Ramsey grew so angry that an "explosive encounter in the child's bathroom" occurred, during which tirade, Mrs. Ramsey "slammed" JonBenét's head against "a hard surface such as the edge of the tub, inflicting a mortal head wound." Plaintiff has provided no evidence for this particular theory.
>
> . . . The above theory is merely speculation by plaintiff as to what might have motivated Mrs. Ramsey to act so violently toward her daughter.
>
> Crime scene photos taken the following morning do not indicate that JonBenét's bed was wet or suggest that the sheets to the bed had been changed . . . Urine stains, however, were reported to have been found on JonBenét's underwear and leggings that she was wearing when her body was discovered . . . Thus, at some point after going to bed, but before being murdered, JonBenét urinated in her clothing. The evidence does not indicate whether this occurred in her bedroom, the basement, or during the route between the two rooms.
>
> Plaintiff [Wolf] further contends, based again solely on Mr. [ex-Detective Steve] Thomas's speculation that "Mrs. Ramsey thought JonBenét was dead, but in fact she was unconscious with

her heart still beating . . ." Mr. Thomas then surmises that "it was that critical moment in which she had to either call for help or find an alternative explanation for her daughter's death." . . . Plaintiff then speculates that Mrs. Ramsey chose the latter route and spent the remainder of the night staging an elaborate cover up of the incident.

. . . In Mr. Thomas's scenario then, rather than being grateful that her child was alive, Mrs. Ramsey nevertheless decided to finish the job off by fashioning a garrote from one of her paintbrushes, looping the cord around the girl's neck, and then choking JonBenét to death . . . Plaintiff notes that the fact JonBenét was "choked from behind" is consistent with the murder being committed by someone who knew JonBenét and did not want to look at her face while killing her.

After murdering her child and staging the crime, plaintiff opines that, to cover her tracks, Mrs. Ramsey must have taken the items used in the staging out of the house, "perhaps dropping them into a nearby storm sewer or among Christmas debris and wrappings in a neighbor's trash can." . . . Indeed, the sources for the duct tape and cord used in the crime were never located, nor sourced . . . to the defendant's home. Plaintiff claims that Mrs. Ramsey next placed the Ransom Note in a place "where she could be sure to 'find' it.

Judge Carnes noted in her report that Mrs. Ramsey "disputes" the plaintiff's recitation of facts. The judge details what Patsy Ramsey's version of the events in question. Then, Judge Carnes turned her attention to John Ramsey:

Plaintiff contends Mr. Ramsey probably first grew suspicious while reading the Ransom Note that morning, which surmise is again based solely on the opinion of Mr. Thomas . . . Plaintiff speculates that upon examining the Ransom Note, Mr. Ramsey "must have seen his wife's writing mannerisms allover [sic] it, everything

> but her signature . . ." Upon determining that his wife was involved in JonBenét's disappearance, plaintiff [sic] surmises that Mr. Ramsey chose to protect his wife, rather than to facilitate the capture of his daughter's murderer . . . Mr. Ramsey asserts, however, that he never once suspected his wife to be involved in the crime.

Later in her ruling, Judge Carnes returned to Thomas's description of how Patsy Ramsey killed her daughter:

> JonBenét's body was bound with complicated rope slipknots and a garrote attached to her body . . . The slipknots and the garrote are both sophisticated bondage devices designed to give control to the user . . . Evidence from these devices suggests they were made by someone with expertise using rope and cords, which cords could not be found or "sourced" within the defendant's home . . .
>
> No evidence exists that either defendant knew how to tie such knots.
>
> [O]ther fiber evidence supports an inference that some of these items from outside the home were, at one time, in the second floor area near JonBenét's bedroom. That is; fibers consistent with those of the cord used to make the slipknots and garrote were found on JonBenét's bed. (SMF 168; PSMF 168.)

The judge again took issue with ex-detective Thomas's testimony concerning the digestion rate of pineapple, which was found in JonBenét's stomach. "Relying solely on the testimony of Mr. Thomas, who has no apparent expertise as a medical examiner, plaintiff fixed the time of death at around one a.m. 'suggested by the digestion rate of pineapple found in the child's stomach.' . . . The coroner's report does indicate that a vegetable or fruit matter consistent with pineapple was found in JonBenét's stomach during the autopsy . . . The report, however, does not establish a time of death based on the digestion rate of the unidentified matter." The other fruit matter, grapes and cherries, was not discussed in the judge's report.

Judge Carnes went on to describe "a series of events . . . that severely compromised the crime scene." She then detailed some of the noteworthy mistakes the police made the morning JonBenét was reported missing.

Judge Carnes also cited her reasons for disqualifying one handwriting expert for the plaintiff and partially disqualifying the second one. Neither the defendants nor the Boulder Police Department had consulted these handwriting analysts during the initial stages of the case. The second expert, who was partially disqualified by the judge, was eliminated because: "The Court, however, has concluded that [the handwriting examiner] cannot properly testify that he is certain that Mrs. Ramsey was the author of the Note."

The following excerpts are from several pages of comment about the ransom note from Judge Carnes:

> At first blush, and even without an appraisal of the handwriting, the Ransom Note seems to support plaintiff's argument that the kidnapping was a hoax set up by someone in the house. It is an extremely long and detailed note of over three pages. Moreover an examination of the notepad on which the note was written indicates that the writer had attempted some earlier drafts of the note. In addition, the writer had apparently not even brought his own materials, but instead had used a note pad and felt marker from the Ramsey's [sic] home. These facts suggest that the killer had not come prepared with a ransom note already written, as one would expect a diligent kidnapper to do. Further, one does not assume that an intruder, intent on beating a hasty retreat, would take the time to practice writing a note or to write a long, detailed note. These assumptions then might suggest that someone in the house contrived the note.
>
> Defendants have argued, however, that it is just as plausible that the killer had been hiding away in the home for many hours, waiting for the household to go to sleep, before he sprung into action. That waiting time would have allowed him the leisure to write a note. Further the length of time that it took to practice and write the note could also conceivably undermine a notion

> that Mrs. Ramsey wrote it. Under plaintiff's scenario, Mrs. Ramsey was working quickly to create a staged crime scene before her husband and son awoke. Given those time constraints, and presumably a desire to provide as little handwriting as possible for purposes of future analysis, she arguably would not have written such a long note. Accordingly, the existence of this peculiar, long Ransom Note does not necessarily favor, as the killer, either an intruder or Mrs. Ramsey.
>
> During the investigation, the Boulder Police Department and the Boulder District Attorney's Office consulted at least six handwriting experts. All of these experts consulted the original Ransom Note and original handwriting exemplars by Mrs. Ramsey. Four of these experts were hired by the police and two were hired by the defendants. All six experts agreed that Mr. Ramsey could be eliminated as the author of the Ransom Note. None of the six consulted experts identified Mrs. Ramsey as the author of the Ransom Note. Rather, the experts' consensus was that she "probably did not" write the Ransom Note. On a scale of one to five, with five being elimination as the author of the Ransom Note, the experts placed Mrs. Ramsey at a 4.5 or a 4.0. The experts described the chance of Mrs. Ramsey being the author of the Ransom Note as "very low."
>
> The fact that there may be similarities between the two [Mrs. Ramsey's handwriting and the Ransom Note] hardly constitutes persuasive evidence that Mrs. Ramsey actually wrote the Note. Without that proof, plaintiff cannot show that Mrs. Ramsey was the killer.

In the "Investigation of the Murder" portion of the ruling, Judge Carnes discussed the qualifications of the Boulder Police Department investigators, saying that they "had limited experience in conducting a murder investigation . . . Commander John Eller was primarily responsible for the investigation, which was his first murder investigation . . . One lead detective assigned to the case, Steven Thomas, had no prior experience with a murder investigation and had previously served as an undercover narcotics officer . . . Finally, the officer who took charge of the investigation in October 1997, Mark Beckner, also had limited homicide experience."

The judge also discussed the role of the media in the case:

> Pursuant to the FBI's suggestions that the Boulder Police publicly name defendants as subjects and apply intense media pressure to them so that they would confess to the crime, the police released many statements that implied defendants were guilty and were not cooperating with police . . . In addition to official police releases, many individual officers also released information about the investigation without official authorization, some of which disclosures were highly confidential and potentially undermined the investigation.

She discussed cooperation by the family as well:

> During the course of the investigation, defendants signed over one hundred releases for information requested by the police and provided all evidence and information requested by the police . . . Upon request, within days after the murder and in the months that followed, defendants provided the police with historical handwriting samples and supervised written exemplars . . . Defendants also gave hair, including pubic hair, and DNA samples to the police . . . Despite widespread criticism that defendants failed to cooperate in the murder investigation, defendants note that they agreed, on at least three occasions, to be interviewed separately by representatives of the police or the Boulder County District Attorneys Office.

Judge Carnes also ruled on "Evidence in Support of the Intruder Theory," writing:

[A]fter a half-decade investigation into the murder of JonBenét Ramsey, and [a] year-long grand jury investigation, no plausible evidence proves Patsy Ramsey had anything to do with the murder of her child. Every prosecutor to examine this case agreed that no charge or crime should have been brought against (defendants).

Certain undisputed evidence of how defendants' house was found on the morning of December 26 is also consistent with the intruder theory of the crime. For example, the lights were on in the basement, when first searched at approximately 6:15 a.m. that day . . . In addition, the butler's door to the kitchen was found ajar that morning . . . Defendants note that the butler's door was only a short distance away from the spiral staircase where the Ransom Note was found and within plain view of where the pad of paper used for the Ransom Note was found . . . Moreover, contrary to media reports that had discredited an intruder theory based on the lack of a "footprint in the snow," there was no snow covering the sidewalks and walkways to defendants' home on the morning of December 26, 1996 . . . Hence, [a] person walking along these paths would have left no footprints.

Defendants further aver that the undisputed physical evidence is not consistent with an "accidental killing" followed by staging . . . but instead is more consistent with a theory that the intruder subdued JonBenét in her bedroom and then took her to the basement, where she was sexually assaulted and subsequently murdered. First, JonBenét's body was found bound with complicated and sophisticated bondage devices, namely neatly-made rope slipknots and a garrote designed to give control to the user . . . The parties agree that such devices necessarily were made by someone with expertise in bondage . . . While it is certainly possible that defendants possessed such unusual and specialized skills, there is no evidence that establishes this fact. Obviously, if defendants lacked the skills to fashion the bondage device, then it necessarily had to be an intruder who crafted the implement.

Of course, plaintiff's primary theory, taken from Detective

Steve Thomas's book, is that Mrs. Ramsey murdered her daughter and staged the scene. According to this theory, Mr. Ramsey becomes complicit only the next day, after the Note was discovered, when he realized that the handwriting on the Note was his wife's . . . Under this proposed timeline, he would not have been involved in making the bondage device.

Although most of Detective Smit's conclusions derive from his analysis of physical evidence, he has also testified that he has been unable to find any motive for defendants to murder their daughter . . . Absent from the defendants' family history is any evidence of criminal conduct, sexual abuse, drug or alcohol abuse or violent behavior . . . In addition, there was no evidence that JonBenét's bed was wet on the night of her murder.

Defendants point to evidence from the autopsy report indicating that a stun gun was used on JonBenét . . . Because it is logical to assume that JonBenét would struggle against an attacker she did not already know, the use of a stun gun helps to explain why no evidence of a struggle was found in any of the bedrooms in defendants' home. Further, defendants state that they have never owned nor operated a stun gun . . . In addition, no stun gun was ever located at defendants' home, nor is there any evidence that defendants have ever owned such a gun. Further, the parties agree that a stun gun could be used and not heard in other rooms of a house.

Plaintiff does not agree that a stun gun was used, however, arguing that the evidence establishing the same is inconclusive. Yet although plaintiff disputes that a stun gun was used in the murder, he has failed to produce any evidence to suggest what caused the burn-like marks on JonBenét.

Admittedly, it is not unprecedented for parents to kill their children, sometimes even brutally. Yet plaintiff's theory of the motivation for the crime—that Mrs. Ramsey accidentally hit JonBenét's head on a hard object, presumed she was dead, and then tried to stage a hoax kidnapping—seems at odds with his

> belief that although Mrs. Ramsey later became aware that JonBenét was alive, she nonetheless proceeded to garrote, torture, and sexually assault her child. If Mrs. Ramsey had accidentally hit her child's head, one would think that, upon becoming aware that the child was still alive, the mother would have been just as likely to call an ambulance, as to commit a depraved torture/murder of the child.
>
> Detective Smit states JonBenét was a "pedophile's dream come true". . . JonBenét received considerable public attention as "Little Miss Colorado" and through several beauty pageants in which she participated . . . On December 6, 1996, three weeks before the murder, she was in the Lights of December Parade, an event thousands of people attended.

When she threw out the lawsuit, Judge Carnes faulted the Boulder Police Department and former detective Steve Thomas and censured the plaintiff's attorney, Darnay Hoffman.

Judge Carnes explained only once why she wrote the ruling. In 2009, in an article for *The National Law Journal,* "Fulton County Daily Report," she commented on the Ramsey case, saying the media "had played the story very differently."

"What it teaches," she added, "is that drawing broad information based on very limited and selective evidence is a very dangerous thing to do."[1]

On January 1, 2009, Federal Judge Julie Carnes was promoted to Chief Federal Judge of the United States District Court for the Northern District of Georgia.

Patsy and John Ramsey read the decision and were encouraged. Patsy said, "Finally someone in authority at the highest level knew we didn't kill our daughter." John reflected, "I wonder if it will make a difference with Boulder police and cause them to rethink their theories about us." Years later he added, "It didn't make a difference to them. They were still after us as our daughter's killers."

# CHAPTER 26
# WHO?

Hi-Tec boot print found in wine/storage cellar next to JonBenét's body. Courtesy Boulder Police and Boulder County District Attorney.

ONE OF THE MOST PERPLEXING MYSTERIES about the killing of JonBenét Ramsey is the absolute dichotomy between the style and length of the rambling ransom note and the seemingly precise, methodical way in which the six-year-old was tortured and killed.

Who would write a note that was two and a half pages long, possibly using quotes from movies about kidnappings, who wasn't particularly sophisticated, yet included words like attaché with the accent correctly placed? Who would also have shown no great anger in the note, and why would they write it at all if in fact no actual kidnapping was planned?

Who would make a garrote with unusual knots and use it to slowly strangle a child to unconsciousness, taking every last breath from her and then bringing her back, only to strangle her a second time? And was the garrote used both times? Something was pulled so tightly that it not only left two different rope furrows/ligatures in the skin on her neck, but left the rope embedded in her neck.

Who would sexually penetrate a six-year-old with a wooden object? Who would hit her so hard in the head that a portion of her skull caved in and an 8.5-inch crack was left in her skull and would have left her with only minutes to live according to two coroners on the case?

What was the motive? Was it a sexual homicide, a kidnapping gone wrong, an accident or a genuine kidnapping attempt? Why was JonBenét tortured and killed? Only the killer likely knows.

(The profiles and psychological background of the possible killers in the different scenarios presented in this chapter come from discussions and interviews with psychologists, forensic psychiatrists, forensic coroners, behavioral specialists, profilers and homicide investigators.)

Let's look at the strongest possibilities of who that killer might have been by looking at what evidence is known. Some evidence is presented here for the first time:

## SCENARIO #1
## PATSY RAMSEY KILLED HER DAUGHTER, JONBENÉT

Patsy was tired and in bed. It had been a long and fun Christmas Day, but her family had arrived home late, and they all needed to be up early for a trip to Michigan. John, who had taken a sleeping pill after playing with Burke and putting their son to bed, was asleep in bed beside Patsy.

Patsy heard JonBenét cry out for her. She knew she was the one who needed to get up to attend to her daughter, but getting out of bed was almost more than she could bear. She became angry. Finally, she got up and went to JonBenét's room to see why her daughter was crying.

At this point, something happened that led Patsy to become enraged with her daughter.

A variety of possible situations in this scenario have been considered by law enforcement officials since JonBenét was found murdered. But the case evidence never supported most of those initial theories. According to one theory, JonBenét had wet her bed, and Patsy lost control and eventually murdered her daughter because of her daughter's accident. That theory was questioned for various reasons, including the fact that it was contradicted by evidence—including the presence of fibers from JonBenét's clothing on her sheets that indicated those sheets (which showed no sign that a child had recently urinated on them) had not been changed during any kind of cover-up attempt.

Did Patsy learn John was assaulting their daughter that night and hit her daughter for this reason? Not according to the evidence. JonBenét's pediatrician, the coroner and a colleague of the coroner with firsthand knowledge of JonBenét's physical condition all said there had been no ongoing sexual abuse. JonBenét's teachers also reported no signs of suspected physical or sexual abuse.

What about the pineapple, grapes and cherries found in JonBenét's stomach during her autopsy? Discussions about when JonBenét had eaten these foods and how long it had taken her to digest them ran rampant in the months following her murder. Did Patsy become so furious over something to do with JonBenét and the food she'd eaten that she hit her daughter? A small bowl of pineapple was found in the Ramsey kitchen on the Thursday morning of JonBenét's disappearance. The bowl had Burke's and Patsy's fingerprints on it. Patsy would later tell Boulder Police Department investigators that she had not fed JonBenét pineapple at any time on Christmas Day or that evening, and that her sleeping daughter had been taken out of the family's car and put to bed upon their arrival home Christmas night. Patsy also said that JonBenét and Burke were allowed to get food from the refrigerator whenever they were hungry, so she may not have known about JonBenét getting such a snack. After JonBenét's autopsy, many different estimates on how long it would take to digest the fruit were offered, but no definitive answer was provided.

So, in the theory that Patsy killed her daughter, she became so outraged that she struck JonBenét with some sort of heavy, blunt object or pushed her daughter with such force that JonBenét hit her head on something hard enough to cave in part of her skull and cause an 8.5-inch crack in her skull. The skull fracture, however, did not break her skin and couldn't be seen until her skull was exposed when the autopsy was performed.

After harming her child so seriously that she believed she may have killed her, the theory continues, Patsy became at once horrified and devastated and yet cold and detached. In a flash frame of reality, she realized she was not willing to lose everything and must do something drastic in order to ensure that didn't happen. She knew her life and family would all vanish if JonBenét was indeed dead. Yet Patsy didn't want to go to prison, and she didn't want her husband to leave her. A smart woman, she decided to think through a way to blame her daughter's death on someone else. But who would that be? The only people in the home were John and Burke. So it had to be someone from the outside, she reasoned . . . an intruder who had been after JonBenét. Better yet, someone who had broken into her family's home and kidnapped JonBenét. By staging things to look like an intruder had killed her daughter and even dumping her daughter's body outside their home, Patsy could convince everyone, including the police, that she'd had nothing to do with her child's death.

At some point during that night, this theory continues, Patsy wrote the ransom note, peppering it with lines from various action movies. Critics of this scenario have said it was unlikely Patsy would know quotes from these movies because she and her husband did not go to movie theaters; they had told the police this fact, and their friends had supported it. Furthermore, all the movies found in the Ramsey home had been made for children. Boulder Police Department investigators had even checked movie rental stores and learned the Ramseys had never rented any of the action movies featuring quotes consistent with those used in the ransom note.

Why did Patsy write a ransom note that included phrases that very likely came from thriller movies? How long did it take her to write it, or was the note premeditated and written several days before? If she wrote the note beforehand, why had she planned ahead to hurt and kill her daughter? Why did she leave a partially finished greeting in the tablet and tear out seven pages after that greeting and then the three pages for the ransom note? Had she been practicing in those seven missing pages? Investigators determined the number of pages that had been torn out because of the page tears at the top of the tablet, including those that matched the tears at the top of the ransom note pages.

Only one fingerprint was found on the ransom note, and that was later traced to a police investigator, so Patsy must have worn some sort of gloves to hide her fingerprints and DNA while she wrote the note. While no expert involved in the case was ever able to identify Patsy as the note writer, the theory that asserts her guilt also suggests she was so crazed from the pressures of her daughter's death or near-death that she became a different personality, a development that affected her handwriting to the degree that it wasn't easily recognizable by experts. Some Boulder Police Department investigators operated on this theory in the late 1990s, and still do.

To summarize this theory, Patsy was shocked by the initial harm she'd caused to her child but able to think through a complicated plan to take what she thought was her dead daughter out of her home to abandon her. When she realized that JonBenét was still breathing, Patsy once again became furious (instead of relieved) and realized her plan to dump her daughter's body somewhere wouldn't work. Somehow Patsy determined that she must muster the strength to finish what she knew at this point was inevitable, because her daughter was either going to die or be terribly damaged, and there was no reason to further destroy her family over this.

At this point, Patsy's actions under the scenario that she killed her daughter became even more bizarre. She made a garrote using rope that was never found in her home. How many people even know what a garrote is? Devising one would surely be a deliberate and time-consuming act for anyone, especially a distraught parent. The garrote used to kill JonBenét was considered unusual by those who studied it, including a knot expert from the Royal Canadian Mounted Police, especially due to the slipknots it contained. Could that mean that the person who had made it was not an experienced killer, because an experienced killer would have kept it simple? While at least one homicide expert has suggested this possibility, who can explain the reasoning of this killer's mind?

The Boulder County Coroner described the garrote and the rope used to make it in his official report: "Tied loosely around the right wrist, overlying the sleeve of the shirt is a white cord. At the knot there is one tail end which measures 5.5 inches in length with a frayed end. The other tail of the knot measures 15.5 inches in length and ends in a double loop knot. This end of the cord is also frayed.

"Wrapped around the neck with a double knot in the midline of the posterior neck is a length of white cord similar to that described as being tied around the right wrist. This ligature cord is cut on the right side of the neck and removed . . . The posterior knot is left intact; extending from the knot on the posterior aspect of the neck are two tails of the knot, one measuring 4 inches in length and having a frayed end, and the other measuring 17 inches in length with the end tied in multiple loops around a length of a round tan-brown wooden stick which measures 4.5 inches in length . . . Blonde hair is entwined in the knot on the posterior aspect of the neck as well as in the cord wrapped around the wooden stick. The white cord is flattened and measures approximately ¼ inch in width. It appears to be made of a white synthetic material."

According to homicide experts and profilers and testimony from retired homicide detective Lou Smit, garrotes are used in murder and sexual bondage activities. A garrote can be as simple as a wire or rope looped around the neck from behind a person to pull the head back and, as both hands pull on the wire or rope, tighten pressure on the front of the throat. The first *Godfather* movie, released in 1972, showed a garrote used as a method of killing, and garrotes have been used in other movies as well as television series since then.

The rope garrote used to kill JonBenét was described by some as complex and by others as simple. It had a loop with a slipknot at the back of its open noose portion so it could be tightened at the back of the neck. Then the garrote rope extended to the wooden paintbrush stick, where several tight loops were made around the stick in order to strengthen it and allow for more pressure against the child's neck. Another slipknot was made at the bottom of those loops on the stick. The knots were used to alternately loosen and tighten for strangling. What kind of person would make a garrote and then use it as described?

Evidence also showed two distinct furrows in JonBenét's neck, one with a rope still embedded in it, leading the coroner to state that there had to have been at least two instances of near strangulation. According to a forensic psychiatrist, such findings indicate JonBenét suffered through an excruciatingly painful and torturous death, and her killer was not only cruel but sadistic.

This theory continues to suggest that, at some point, Patsy would also have had to sexually penetrate her daughter with a broken-off portion of her paintbrush forcefully enough to cause her to bleed. None of Patsy's DNA was found on any part of the garrote, rope or duct tape. Nor was anyone's.

With her dead daughter's body on the floor of the basement storage room alongside JonBenét's favorite nightgown, according to this theory, Patsy then had to stage not only a kidnapping but a cover-up of a gruesome murder.

Considering the stressful situation and all she'd already been through that night, Patsy must have made her next decisions with impressive exactness and thoroughness. First she wiped her daughter's body with an unknown and never-found substance to ensure she hadn't left any of her own DNA behind. She then left a boot print from a Hi-Tec shoe next to her daughter's body and tossed some personal items next to it, too. She also left a partial footprint (with a different shoe) nearby on the floor of the storage room and on the northeast basement bathroom toilet lid.

Patsy then unlocked various doors and windows in her home so they would be considered possible entry or exit points for "her intruder." Back in the basement, she went in the storage room where her son's train set was kept and adjusted the window that John had broken the summer before so it also looked like another possible point of entry. She even moved debris in the window well to the sides so it appeared as though the center section of the three-paned window had been entered. But she forgot to make marks on the window sill to make it look like a person had entered there. How did she move the debris inside the window well without making marks on the window sill? And how did she lift the heavy basement window well grate and mash the grass underneath it, just as evidence indicated, so it would look like the grate had been recently opened?

Patsy then collected some of her daughter's belongings, including a duvet cover. Prior to putting everything in a suitcase often used by another family member, she returned to the storage room to rub the duvet cover on her daughter's clothed body in order to leave fabric evidence behind on both JonBenét's clothing and on the duvet. This, she must have theorized, would indicate that the kidnapper had planned to take her daughter away inside the suitcase.[1] The duvet placed in the suitcase with other items, Patsy then moved the suitcase next to the broken basement window in the train room.

Patsy would have had to make a long scuff mark on the basement wall underneath the broken window and scatter pieces of window glass and outside debris on top of the suitcase to add credibility. She also moved material from the window well into the storage room and into the northeast basement bathroom.

Back upstairs, this theory continues, Patsy washed the wet sheets on JonBenét's bed and put them in the dryer. She then remade JonBenét's bed with new sheets, carefully pulling the covers back halfway and throwing her daughter's pillow onto the end of the bed to disguise the scene. She also somehow made sure to leave fiber evidence from JonBenét's clothing on the clean changed sheets she'd just put on the bed. She left the washed sheets in the dryer. The sheets in the dryer would become possible evidence of Patsy's assumed motive for attacking and killing her daughter because JonBenét had wet her bed. While some would speculate that fiber evidence on the bed indicated the sheets hadn't been changed, others would insist the evidence showed the sheets had been very cleverly manipulated.

Eventually, the theory continues, Patsy realized she had to get rid of some of what she had used to kill her daughter: the rope, the duct tape, part of the paintbrush, anything she could think to grab. Or maybe she was methodical enough to see what she had left in the basement, and that's what she took. She had to have left home to go somewhere, unseen, through the dark cold of the frigid December night, in order to get rid of at least part of the evidence. How did she decide what to take out of her home? Where did she dump it? Did she use a car, go down the alley or go down the front walk?

Soon, her adrenaline waning, Patsy must have realized she was exhausted. Though she was also aware that she had just brutally tortured and murdered her daughter, Patsy maintained her determined detachment that wouldn't let reality in, at least until she got up the next morning.

Only then did Patsy Ramsey release her emotions over what she had done and begin to emerge back into her regular life, confident that she had, in her delusional mind, saved her family.

This theory concludes by asserting that Patsy was so smart that—after finding the ransom note she'd planted on the back staircase of her home, screaming for her husband and checking on her son with him and then calling 911—she immediately called family friends to come to her house, not because she needed their emotional support, but in order to add to the confusion in the home.

She also cleverly remained in character by telling police investigators some time later that "Whoever left the note knew I always came down those staircases in the morning." (BPD Reports #5-402, #5-9999.)

If Patsy killed her daughter, this theory holds that true evil exploded openly during those brief hours in the middle of the night between December 25 and December 26, 1996. Patsy Ramsey, a savage psychopath, during those hours was alternately enraged and cruelly detached. Only after returning to bed and finally getting some sleep did her "normality" surface at some point, returning her to her everyday persona, allowing her to hide in the open, her evil side never to appear again.

## SCENARIO #2
## JOHN HELPED PATSY KILL JONBENÉT

In this slightly modified scenario, after Patsy hurt her daughter and began to believe she'd killed her, Patsy ran upstairs to her husband and frantically awakened him. Somehow he sorted through her incoherence, began to understand that Patsy was certain she had killed their daughter, and ran to JonBenét, finding that she was still alive. Instead of calling for an ambulance to help his daughter, however, he decided her condition was so devastating that she wouldn't survive and it was more important to save his wife by killing his daughter and then helping Patsy cover up what she has done.

How did they come up with a kidnapping scheme? John asked Patsy to write a ransom note, took JonBenét to the basement and destroyed her there, using sexually based acts as part of the kidnapper staging. John and Patsy did this solely to save their way of life. They rehearsed their story and finalized the staging during the rest of the night while their dead daughter lay on the concrete floor of a dingy basement room, arms above her head, a blanket casually covering part of her body.

This theory was developed by some Boulder investigators shortly after the murder of JonBenét despite the fact that John Ramsey had discovered his daughter's body, thereby ruining the staging he and his wife had supposedly so carefully devised. Why wouldn't John have instead allowed his friend, who was with him during the search, discover JonBenét, thus not interfering with the elaborate staging he and Patsy had created? The two men were in close proximity to each other at that moment. John could have easily pointed his friend toward the storage room where he'd left his daughter's body. Or would he have considered that action too contrived?

What are the odds that two psychopaths who had been married for sixteen years suddenly had their perversions surface at the same time, leading them to brutally kill their daughter and then attempt to return to a normal life? Were they in strict survival mode? Where did they dispose of the items used in the murder that were never found? How did they decide to stage a kidnapping and then torture and murder their daughter? Those are just some of the considerations that must be successfully addressed in order for this theory to work.

"Psychopaths are all about control and winning," Eric Hickey, PhD, a criminology consultant and an expert in psychopathic personalities, has said. He was describing the personality of a psychopath without drawing any analogy to the Ramsey murder. "They are very good at manipulating. They are expert liars and charming. They are narcissistic and completely absorbed in themselves and satisfying their own needs. Psychopaths are users. They use people to gratify their personal needs and have no empathy, shame or remorse. Psychopaths don't have fear and they have a higher intelligence. Ted Bundy was a classic psychopath." A serial killer executed in Florida in January 1989, Ted Bundy raped and killed a twelve-year-old girl and killed two sorority sisters. He never confessed to the number of women he killed, but he was suspected of killing more than thirty in several states including Colorado, where he was jailed but eventually escaped.

## SCENARIO #3
## JOHN DISCOVERED PATSY HAD KILLED JONBENÉT AND COVERED FOR HER

The day after Christmas, according to this theory, John realized Patsy had been involved in his daughter's death. To save his wife and since his daughter was already dead, John decided to keep the terrible secret of what actually happened and to trade any justice for his daughter for his wife's sake so together he and Patsy could continue on with their way of life. In this scenario, Patsy had tortured and killed JonBenét and completed all the staging herself.

## SCENARIO #4<br>BURKE RAMSEY WAS INVOLVED IN HIS SISTER'S MURDER

In this variation, Burke fatally hurt his sister in some kind of accident, and his parents decided they must ruthlessly cover up for him.

Burke was nine years old when two Boulder Police Department detectives interviewed and tape-recorded him on the morning of JonBenét's disappearance without his parent's permission. That would not be an unusual procedure, according to one homicide expert who added that he would have insisted neither parent be present when the child was interviewed. A child psychologist representing the Boulder County Department of Social Services also interviewed Burke on January 8, 1997. A third interview occurred in Atlanta, when two detectives questioned Burke with his attorney present. All of these interviews were taped. None of his interrogators detected that Burke might be lying about his sister's death and his lack of involvement in it. The Boulder Department of Human Services (Social Services) went even further, stating in their March 1997 Evaluation of the Child report related to Burke Ramsey that, "From the interview it is clear that Burke was not a witness to JonBenét's death."

The theory that Burke was involved was not considered seriously for very long, but talk radio speculated about it and tabloid headlines and bloggers advanced the idea enough for the rumor to spread internationally. Law enforcement leakers in Boulder did nothing to discourage such rumors, which continued to resurface for months on slower news days.

## SCENARIO #5
## AN INTRUDER KILLED JONBENÉT[2]

When the Ramsey family came back the night of December 25, 1996 from their Christmas dinner at a friend's home, an intruder was already hidden in the guest room next to JonBenét's bedroom. Evidence has shown that unidentified rope left in a sack was found underneath the bed in that room.

He had what he needed. He'd written the ransom note, made the garrote and left the suitcase in the basement, out of the way. Did the idea for the note come to him from watching action movies, most involving kidnappings? Had the language used in those movies matched the message he wanted to get across in his note? He had planned and prepared for weeks or months, and he'd been in the house before. He listened to John and Patsy put their daughter to bed. Patsy then went to the third floor master suite to bed, while John played with Burke for a few minutes on the other end of the house on the second floor.

He was excited—thrilled, really. He waited until the home was quiet and everyone was asleep.

Then he approached JonBenét's bedroom on the thick plush carpet. His footsteps were silent. He used a stun gun to incapacitate his six-year-old victim and bound her mouth shut with duct tape. JonBenét had been so tired from days of Christmas excitement that she'd been sound asleep in her bed.

He carried her downstairs to the basement. The suitcase, packed with a few items to help keep JonBenét comfortable, was ready to go. Perhaps he'd planned to take her out of the home inside the suitcase along with the duvet and other items. Or he'd known he was going to kill his victim in the basement and escape alone, and the suitcase was just staging.

Whatever his original intentions, apparently something went wrong with his plan. Why else would he have struck JonBenét on the head so hard? If a stun gun was indeed used, why else would it have been used twice, leaving two sets of marks? Maybe JonBenét woke up and struggled, or her kidnapper couldn't fit her in the suitcase. Either way, he struck her on the head with a weapon and knocked her out, and/or he shocked her again with the stun gun.

Then he continued his rampage. He slipped the garrote over JonBenét's head and pulled, choking her unconscious. He pulled down her long johns and assaulted her with part of a paintbrush handle. He tightened the garrote again. The little girl died from the combination of a blow to the head and strangulation, according to the coroner who did her autopsy.

JonBenét's killer left her body in a dark storage room. Her hands had landed above her head, or perhaps he'd posed her that way. He tossed the blanket over her and left her Barbie nightgown next to her on the floor. He paused over her body, and his weight sunk into the dirt and mold, leaving either a clear footprint or a partial one, or he had someone with him as the two separate footprints found in that room didn't match. Would he have been clever enough to bring an extra unmatched shoe for that extra footprint? When did he take the time to leave a footprint on the basement bathroom toilet, or was that footprint made when he broke into the house through the bathroom?

Finally, JonBenét's killer pushed the makeshift door of the storage room open and then shut and dropped the latch above the door into place. He picked up what he wanted to take, left the ransom note on the circular staircase and left the house.

In such a scenario, what might have been the motive? Why would someone do this?

Retired detective Lou Smit, who considered pedophilia and psychopathic personality for a motive, has suggested that the killer likely watched JonBenét for months, and what he saw was not what anyone else saw. Others saw a cute little girl at school, playing, maybe in the neighborhood or in a pageant, maybe with her mother at the grocery store. He saw someone he had to have. He wouldn't say no to his own addiction. He was angry, desperate and selfish. Society would label him a pedophile. In his world, he wanted children sexually, and didn't care, really, whether it was considered right or wrong. He would find a way to have what he wanted. His need did not touch a conscience because he didn't have one.

Experts have also speculated that JonBenét Ramsey's killer could have been a pedophile, a psychopath or both.

Kidnapping from a home is rare but not without precedent:

Many remember Elizabeth Smart of Salt Lake City. Elizabeth was fourteen years old on June 5, 2002, when she was abducted from her home at night. Elizabeth lived in a large home, like JonBenét. She was part of a loving family. Her mother, father and five siblings were in the home, asleep. Elizabeth and her younger sister slept in the same bedroom. Her kidnapper came into the home and forced Elizabeth to go with him. Her sister was too terrified to go for help for two hours.

For nine months, Elizabeth Smart was assaulted and kept from her family while living with her kidnapper, Brian David Mitchell, and his wife, Wanda Barzee. The couple was homeless and panhandled and preached on the street. Mitchell had seen Elizabeth when he was hired off the street to do odd jobs around the Smart home. He came back six months later and kidnapped Elizabeth from her bed in the middle of the night.

Elizabeth was effectively brainwashed with daily abuse and threats against her family. She was eventually rescued when a Good Samaritan reported seeing Mitchell, his wife and possibly Elizabeth, to the police.

Mitchell had a history of sexual crime. He's now serving life in prison. His wife plea bargained with federal prosecutors and got fifteen years in prison. The prosecutors said going into the Smart home was high-risk behavior. Like the Ramsey killer in the intruder theory, Mitchell cared about nothing except satisfying his own needs, according to Salt Lake City investigators.

The kidnapping and murder of Heather Dawn Church in September 1991 showed pre-planning, surveillance and violence. Thirteen-year-old Heather lived near Colorado Springs in an area called Black Forest. She was babysitting her little brother that night when an intruder removed a screen in the home, entered through an open window and kidnapped her. Authorities had no leads for two years until her skull was discovered several miles from her home.

Robert Charles Browne had lived just down the road from Heather Church and coveted and stalked her. He confessed to her murder in 1995, when a fingerprint from the window screen matched one taken after he was convicted on motor vehicle theft and burglary charges in Louisiana. That was the only physical evidence in the case. While Browne said he had strangled Heather or broken her neck, law enforcement never knew for sure how she died because the rest of her body was never found.

Browne was sentenced to life in prison without parole. He later wrote to investigators that he had killed others. Detective Lou Smit was on the cold case team that finally solved Heather Dawn Church's murder. Credit was given to Smit for finding her killer. Smit described Browne as a "violent sexual predator, pedophile and psychopath."

Thirteen-year-old Dylan Redwine disappeared November 19, 2012 from his father's home in Vallecito, Colorado. He was staying with his father on a court-ordered visit. His mother and father were divorced. His father said he last saw Dylan at home while he went out to run errands. When he got home, he said, Dylan was gone. That was the Monday before Thanksgiving weekend. In June, 2013, parts of the boy's remains were found in a high-mountain range near Vallecito by law enforcement officers involved in one of several searches. The parents blamed each other for Dylan's death, but law enforcement officials as of this writing say they have no suspects.

If the perpetrator in the Ramsey murder case was not a pedophile, perhaps the motive to kill JonBenét was anger and jealousy of John Ramsey and his seemingly ideal life and family. Renowned former FBI profiler John Douglas suggested this possibility when he was first hired by the Ramsey team. Nowhere in the ransom note was JonBenét mentioned by name. The focus of the note was on John. So, an alternative motive could have been hatred or resentment of John. Perhaps the killer was someone who had suffered an imagined slight by Ramsey, someone who obsessed about such things and refused to forgive John. Seen in this light, the ransom note becomes a taunting puzzle. The writer of the note used it to build upon his outrage and continue to build upon his grievances enough to plot a complicated way to get his revenge. His resentment escalated, nourished by his sadistic plan to torment John Ramsey by attacking his beloved daughter.

Douglas was criticized by some in the media who learned through law enforcement leaks that he'd made the decision that the Ramseys were not involved in their child's murder after having only been briefed by the Ramsey attorneys. Yet, according to Douglas as well as the Ramsey attorneys and an attorney at the Boulder District Attorney's Office, he had also talked with Boulder Police Department officials and with attorneys in the DA's Office.

Of course there is a third possible motivation for choosing the Ramsey family to victimize, and it's possibly the most terrifying suggestion because it's random. The killer may have chosen to break into the Ramsey family home and attack their daughter without knowing anything about them. Instead, he simply chose this family as his target because he wanted to assault and kill or needed a victim to kidnap.

The Polly Klaas case is one example of a seemingly random, violent murder. Though her murder had been planned, it had involved no cover-up, staging or elaborate and extensive planning.

On October 1, 1993, Richard Allen Davis, who had been paroled from prison only three months before, broke into the Klaas home through a window. Twelve-year-old Polly was having a slumber party that night with some friends at her small home in Petaluma, California, near San Francisco. Davis had been seen loitering around the home that day. His plan was short term, organized and involved only those present in the home. He entered the house and, while Polly's mother was asleep in a nearby room, tied up Polly's friends and took Polly out of her home while holding a knife against her neck.

Davis had an extensive criminal history of kidnapping and violence against females. On December 4, 1993, he confessed to kidnapping and killing Polly Klaas and led law enforcement officials to her body. He was convicted of kidnapping, first-degree murder and committing a lewd act.

According to California Supreme Court transcripts, a clinical therapist and psychologist testified that Davis had antisocial disorder and sexual sadism. A psychiatrist who testified had diagnosed Davis with avoidance personality disorder, antisocial personality disorder and schizoid personality disorder. Basically, they said, Davis enjoyed hurting others and inflicting both physical and emotional pain. He was also a very organized offender. Richard Allen Davis was sentenced to death and, in January 2013, was denied all but one of his appeals by the California Supreme Court. He currently remains on California's death row.

Such depravity was also portrayed in the kidnapping of a child in Lake Tahoe, Nevada. The eleven-year-old girl was on her way to school in June 1991 near her home when she was grabbed, thrown into a vehicle and stun gunned. For eighteen years, her abductor, Phillip Garrido, and his wife, Nancy, kept the girl prisoner in an extensive rundown backyard compound.

From the moment the girl was captured, Garrido began raping her. She had two daughters while in captivity, both fathered by Garrido. With his wife's help, Garrido kept their three prisoners locked away in a life of unimagined hell.

Garrido was a registered sex offender who had been convicted of rape and was on parole. During the eighteen years following the kidnapping, parole officers visited his house sixty times and saw the young woman and eventually her daughters, but did not investigate.

Garrido's prisoners were finally rescued following his attempt to get a permit to sell a "book" that was actually a four-page essay he'd written about religion and sexuality. Two employees at the University of California, Berkeley events office grew suspicious of Garrido and the girls who had stopped by their office with him and reported their suspicions to police. Garrido was forced to bring his "children" in for a parole check that resulted in his three victims being rescued in August 2009. Garrido was sentenced to more than 400 years in prison. His wife got more than 30 years.

There was shock and horror when neighbors rescued three young women in Cleveland in May 2013. The three had disappeared in kidnappings that occurred between 2002 and 2004, when they were fourteen, sixteen and twenty years old. Each had accepted a ride from a part-time school bus driver, Ariel Castro, when he kidnapped them. They were found in his local neighborhood home. One of them had a six-year-old child fathered by Castro. One of the girls knew the kidnapper's daughter. It was unclear whether Castro had known the other two girls before he took them. The three women were kept mostly in the basement of Castro's rambling two-story house. There was confusion in the neighborhood about the kidnapper because he had seemed, as one neighbor told reporters, to be just like the rest of them. But Castro had beaten, starved and sexually assaulted his captives at various times. He was not one of them.

In July 2013, Ariel Castro pleaded guilty to kidnapping and sexual assault in order to avoid the death penalty. He was sentenced to life in prison, plus 1,000 years. Part of his plea agreement included signing over the deed to the house where he had kept the three girls. The house was torn down in August 2013. Castro committed suicide by hanging himself in prison the next month.

In 2005 in Coeur d'Alene, Idaho, Joseph Edward Duncan III kidnapped an eight-year-old girl and her nine-year-old brother from their home. He had targeted the family without knowing them. Duncan first killed the two young children's older brother and mother and their mother's fiancé. He then kidnapped and sexually traumatized the two and finally killed the boy in front of his sister.

The little girl was rescued after being spotted with her abductor seven weeks later at a local restaurant.

Duncan was a convicted sex offender who later confessed to other killings. The majority of his victims were children. He had spent most of his life in prison. In 2008, he received three death penalties. He told the jury in one of the death penalty sentencing stages of his trial, "You people really don't have any clue yet of the true heinousness of what I've done . . . My intention was to kidnap and rape and kill until I was killed, preferring death easily over capture."

On October 5, 2012, ten-year-old Jessica Ridgeway of Westminster, Colorado, was kidnapped on her way to school. Parts of her body were identified just days later on October 10 in an open space area near her home. Her body had been dismembered and mutilated. Seventeen-year-old Austin Sigg, who was interested in mortuary science and enrolled in a nearby junior college, was arrested on October 23 after he confessed to his mother and she called the police. Experts and research indicate that it is unusual for someone of Sigg's age to so violently destroy a body. Sigg pleaded guilty to fifteen counts, including first-degree murder and sexual assault of Jessica and an attack on a female jogger in May 2012. That woman had been able to fight Sigg off after he tried to disable her with a rag saturated with a chemical over her mouth. "Evil is apparently real. It was present in our community on October 5, 2012," the judge said when he sentenced Sigg after the teenager had pleaded guilty. Sigg got life in prison, plus an additional eighty-six years to be served consecutively.

On October 28, 2013, in Aurora, Colorado, a white, blonde male broke or cut the screen off an eight-year-old girl's first-floor bedroom window, opened it, grabbed her and pulled her outside. She screamed, and her father ran out of the house to find she had escaped from the man. He saw the man's car drive away. The next day, then Aurora Police Chief Dan Oates was quoted in *The Denver Post* as saying, "We think there's a predator out there." Police believed this had been an attempted "stranger" kidnapping. They charged a twenty-six-year-old man for the attempted kidnapping on November 1, 2013. By then, John Stanley Snorsky was already in jail on theft charges. He pleaded guilty to first-degree burglary and second-degree kidnapping in September 2014, when he was sentenced to thirty years in prison as part of a plea agreement.

No one will know the mindset of JonBenét Ramsey's killer until that person is caught, and maybe not even then. "Why?" is the question most easily asked and agonized over. It is also the most difficult to answer.

One of the questions still unanswered is how JonBenét's killer became so familiar with the Ramsey home. This question contributed to the widespread belief that her family had been involved in her murder. Yet in the case of Elizabeth Smart, her kidnapper came back to her family's large home to kidnap her several months after being hired to work there for part of one day.

Early in the Ramsey murder investigation, investigators surmised that JonBenét's killer had been someone who knew the house well, knew the Ramsey family's plans and possibly had a key to the Ramsey home in their possession. At first, such reasoning pointed to family members as likely suspects, but soon other intruder possibilities were suggested.

The Ramseys were careless about their home security. They'd given out keys to friends and to people working on their lengthy home renovations. One key, hidden outside in front of their house, turned up missing. An intruder without a key also could have entered through an unlocked window or door. The family never set their security alarm.

Part of the intruder theory includes the belief that the killer had been in the home not once but several times and therefore had little fear of being caught. It's also possible that the killer had browsed through the family's belongings, including John's pay stubs or tax returns showing information about his $118,000-plus bonus.

The Ramsey family also spent their summers in Michigan and often traveled to visit friends in Georgia and other states. The intruder could have wandered the home during one of these family trips earlier in 1996. It's interesting to note that such an intruder could also have known about the unusual set-up with the house's doorbell and its phone. As the Ramseys had told friends and neighbors, the doorbell was connected to the telephone, so if you rang the doorbell and heard the telephone inside keep ringing, you knew no one was home.

Questions about missing items that had apparently been used to torture and kill JonBenét also led to suggestions by experts that the killer would have brought with him his own personal "crime kit" with the tools he needed and taken most of them back out of the house with him. Law enforcement investigators use the term "crime kit" when referring to the survival pack of tools and weapons that a criminal might bring along in order to limit the possibility that anything is left to chance.

Patsy Ramsey kept her day planner in the kitchen and also jotted reminders down elsewhere in her home, so it's possible an intruder would have known of the family's plans to be out of their home on the evening of Christmas 1996. He could have taken the notepad and the paintbrush used for the garrote shortly before Christmas Day, writing on the notepad and fashioning the garrote at his leisure outside of the home. While Patsy was organized in her daily planning for her family, she was casual about keeping her house organized. She wouldn't have missed the paintbrush and may have assumed she'd misplaced the tablet, according to John Ramsey.

If an intruder did indeed kill JonBenét, he would have been called an "organized offender" by law enforcement officials because of his elaborate planning. He was able to either lie in wait for the family to return the evening of December 25, or enter after they were asleep because of his familiarity with their home. He was also apparently able to cope with the unexpected.

If JonBenét Ramsey's killer had been a true psychopath, he could have walked among the Ramseys and their friends undetected. According to experts, psychopaths copy others in their everyday behavior by watching them closely. They also view themselves as being smarter than most, especially law enforcement.

It's possible that while JonBenét's killer ultimately wanted her, he also gained enormous satisfaction from his meticulous planning to either kidnap or torture and murder her.

The murder of JonBenét Ramsey was a unique crime, out of the norm for even the most experienced homicide detectives. There are no valid national statistics on the use of garrotes in child murders.

## POSSIBLE SUSPECTS

On February 13, 1997, Boulder District Attorney Alex Hunter held a news conference during which he addressed the killer directly. "I want to say something to the person or persons that committed this crime," he said. "You have stripped us of any mercy that we might have had in the beginning of this investigation.

"The list of suspects narrows," he also warned. "Soon there will be no one on the list but you. We will see that justice is served in this case, and that you pay for what you did."

Hunter's statements were made on the advice of behavioral advisors who had conceived that such a challenge might cause the killer to react in some public way. Right after the news conference, Patsy called Hunter to thank him for his perseverance and message to the killer. That phone call confounded Hunter and his advisors. As Hunter said privately, "The message was designed [for] and directed at Patsy."

On February 14, 1997, one day after Hunter's direct statement to the killer, twenty-six-year-old Michael Helgoth committed suicide at his home, according to a Boulder County Sheriff's report. Helgoth worked for his aunt and uncle in a salvage yard in Boulder and lived with them. He was estranged from his mother and father. In Helgoth's bedroom, detectives found a pair of Hi-Tec shoes similar in size to the footprint that had been left in the basement where JonBenét's body was found. Helgoth also had a stun gun and a 9mm pistol.

Helgoth's hands were swabbed for gunshot residue (GSR), but the sheriff's office never tested the gunshot residue swabs to see if the deceased man had fired the weapon used to kill him, because Helgoth's death was considered a suicide. According to experts, a GSR test cannot determine whether someone fired a gun, only that the person was in the vicinity when the weapon was fired.

The on-call Boulder Police Department detective when Michael Helgoth's suicide was reported was a sex crimes investigator, not a trained homicide investigator.

Serious questions were raised by some of the Ramsey investigators about whether Helgoth had actually killed himself. They said photos from the investigation showed Helgoth would have been in an awkward position to shoot himself in the chest.

Michael Helgoth's Hi-Tec boots found after his suicide. Courtesy Ramsey Defense attorneys.

Boulder Police Department officials tested Helgoth for DNA and said it didn't match the foreign DNA found on JonBenét Ramsey's body.

One man, forty-one-year-old teacher John Mark Karr, confessed to the slaying of JonBenét Ramsey in August 2006, nearly ten years after the murder, saying to the media: "I was with JonBenét when she died." Karr's criminal history included jumping bail in California on a 2001 child pornography charge. Following his "confession," he was arrested in Thailand and transported back to Boulder. He had e-mailed about the case for four years to a University of Colorado professor. But Karr's DNA didn't match the DNA found on JonBenét's body, and several investigators who talked with him said he did not know basic and key information about the murder scene. Charges were dropped, and Karr willingly appeared on several talk shows at the time. While he has not been further pursued by law enforcement, Karr continues to correspond with some who are searching for answers in the murder of JonBenét Ramsey and continues to reveal more information related to the case.

Another man who was investigated because his wife had been fired from Access Graphics told me he was retested for DNA in 2011 by Boulder Police Department investigators. Detective Lou Smit had come up with the theory about this man being a possible suspect because of the signature on the ransom note. That signature, "S. B. T. C" matched the initials of the first names of three of this possible suspect's family members. But his DNA did not match the forensic evidence found on JonBenét's body, according to Boulder police. For this reason, his name is not being used in this book.

Another person briefly considered as a possible suspect was Chris Wolf. His ex-girlfriend turned him in to authorities, saying he disappeared the evening of December 25, 1996, came back early in the morning, washed the clothes he was wearing, took a long shower and then was fixated on the Ramsey case. She said he was capable of violent behavior. His handwriting was reportedly more similar to the ransom note than the handwriting of any of the others who had been tested. John and Patsy named Wolf as a possible suspect in their first book, leading Wolf to sue the Ramseys for libel in the defamation case eventually dismissed before trial by Federal Judge Julie Carnes in Georgia.

Wolf's DNA did not match the DNA found at the scene, according to Boulder Police Department officials. His ex-girlfriend, according to one detective, was obsessed with the idea that he had killed JonBenét. Ten years after the murder, she hired her own handwriting expert and a publicity firm to hold a news conference, saying her ex-boyfriend's handwriting had many characteristics that matched the writing in the ransom note.

The photographer who took some professional photographs of JonBenét was also suspected and tested for DNA comparisons. He was arrested in the fall of 1998 for walking nude down the main street of a small town in eastern Colorado. When apprehended, he told law enforcement, "I didn't kill JonBenét." He was also not a DNA match.

These are just a few of the people whom the Boulder Police Department and the Ramsey defense team have investigated. According to the Colorado Bureau of Investigation, 165 people in Boulder County in 1996 and 1997 were registered as sexual offenders.

# CHAPTER 27
# DNA

COLORADO BUREAU OF INVESTIGATION
LABORATORY REPORT

LAB CASE NUMBER:D96-4153 SECTION:DNA TESTING
AGENCY NAME: CO0070100 - PD BOULDER
OFFENSE: 0902 - HOMICIDE - WILLFUL KILL-FAMILY
INVESTIGATED BY: DET. THOMAS TRUJILLO SUBMISSION DATE: 123096

* SUSPECT(S): AKA:/ R/S D.O.B:
RAMSEY, PATSY W/F
RAMSEY, JOHN W/M

* VICTIM(S):
RAMSEY, JONBENET W/F

Kathren M. Brown Dressel
EXAMINED BY/ KATHREN M. BROWN DRESSEL, LABORATORY AGENT/CRIMINALIST
DATE COMPLETED/JANUARY 15, 1997

Front cover of CBI DNA Report

## CHRONOLOGY

January 1997—Colorado Bureau of Investigation releases some preliminary DNA information to the Boulder Police Department.

February 1997—BPD officials send DNA for testing to Cellmark Diagnostics in Maryland.

May 1997—Cellmark Diagnostics DNA test results reveal "no surprises" as they are similar to the CBI results.

July 2008—Boulder District Attorney Mary Lacy clears the Ramsey family based on advanced DNA "touch" testing from the Bode Technological Group.

February 2015—Former Boulder Police Chief Beckner does his first extensive interview related to the Ramsey murder investigation on the Reddit website.

IT'S THIS SIMPLE ABOUT THE DNA in the JonBenét Ramsey murder case:

In a new and advanced "touch DNA" test conducted in 2008 on JonBenét's clothing, two new areas of DNA were found on two spots on the inside of the waistband of her long johns. The waistband represented a previously untested area. The newly discovered DNA matched the 1997 DNA collected from her panties. The 2008 test had been conducted on the request of Boulder District Attorney Mary Lacy.

In 1997, two different agencies consulted by the Boulder Police Department had tested foreign DNA that had been found in three places: mixed with blood in JonBenét's panties and under her fingernails on both hands. The three samples that were tested twice in 1997, although weak, had indicators that they matched each other. All the samples had been taken from the same unknown male and excluded individual members of the Ramsey family.

In 2008, Boulder District Attorney Mary Lacy hired the Bode Technology Group in Virginia to analyze the untested areas on JonBenét's clothing with the new, advanced "touch DNA" technique. Bode Technology Group in Virginia had performed DNA tests in thousands of criminal cases and helped identify criminals, terrorists and victims of war and natural disasters. In 2008, the lab found that the newly unidentified DNA in the Ramsey case *matched* the unidentified DNA that had been collected from a different area of JonBenét's clothing and tested in 1997. None of this DNA matched anyone in the Ramsey family; not John, not Patsy, not their children or immediate relatives.

District Attorney Lacy had worked in the Boulder DA's sex assault unit before she was elected DA in 2001.

After Lacy was elected, she took the Ramsey case away from the Boulder Police Department and moved it into her own office. Because of her prior experience as an attorney in the Boulder DA's office who handled sexual assault cases, Lacy (with her investigators) considered whether there were any other places the killer could have left evidence on JonBenét's clothing. They reasoned that the killer would have used his fingertips and perhaps shed skin cells when he pulled down JonBenét's long johns in order to sexually assault her. This was the reason why they had two places on the inside waistband of her long johns tested.

"We became aware last summer that some private laboratories were conducting a new methodology described as 'touch DNA,'" Lacy wrote in a letter to John Ramsey that was dated July 9, 2008. "The Bode Technology laboratory was able to develop a profile from DNA recovered from the two sides of the long johns," she continued. "The previously identified profile from the crotch of the underwear worn by JonBenét at the time of the murder matched the DNA recovered from the long johns at Bode.

"Unexplained DNA on the victim of a crime is powerful evidence. The match of male DNA on two separate items of clothing worn by the victim at the time of the murder makes it clear to us that an unknown male handled these items," Lacy explained. "Despite substantial efforts over the years to identify the source of this DNA, there is no innocent explanation for its incriminating presence at three sites on these two different items of clothing that JonBenét was wearing at the time of her murder."

The three sites Lacy was referring to were two spots on the left and right sides of the inside waistband of the long johns tested in 2008 and one site in JonBenét's underwear, which was first tested in 1997. The DNA found under JonBenét's fingernails in 1997 was not mentioned in the 2008 comparison.

Lacy acknowledged, "There will be those who will choose to continue to differ with our conclusion. But DNA is very often the most reliable forensic evidence we can hope to find, and we rely on it often to bring to justice those who have committed crimes."

DNA has become an incredible indicator. It cannot identify the perpetrator of a crime, only confirm the identity of the person belonging to the DNA, but that is usually what is needed to identify and convict a suspect.

Boulder Police Chief Mark Beckner issued a statement in 2008 on the "trace" DNA results found by District Attorney Lacy that seemed to indicate that a stranger had killed JonBenét Ramsey: "This is a significant finding. The police department has continued to look diligently for the source of the foreign DNA, and to date, we have compared DNA samples taken from more than 200 people," Beckner said. "Finding the source of the DNA is key to helping us determine who killed JonBenét."

Still, rumors denouncing the new DNA findings swirled.

On February 21, 2015, nearly two decades after JonBenét was killed, former Boulder Police Chief Beckner, who had retired in 2014, answered questions in an extensive question-and-answer interview on the website Reddit.com. This interview represented the most that Beckner had ever talked publicly about the Ramsey murder case. It is important to understand that Beckner had more continuing influence on the case than any other law enforcement officer. He was working on the case within three weeks of JonBenét's murder. He was appointed commander of the Ramsey investigation in the fall of 1997. He was appointed Boulder Police Chief in the fall of 1998 and guided the case as police chief for nearly sixteen years.

In the Reddit Internet interview, Beckner speculated on possible sources of the DNA in ways that reflected the mantra of some Boulder investigators who'd been on the case for most of the past eighteen years when he said: "Manufacturing process is one. Interactions with other people is another. Intentional placement is another. Belongs to an intruder is another. Yes, you can often tell where DNA comes from. In this case, it is small enough that it is difficult to tell. CBI [Colorado Bureau of Investigation] thought it was either sweat or saliva." Yet the DNA samples had been significant enough to fit the stringent FBI Combined DNA Index System or CODIS format for inclusion of DNA.

Three days after the Reddit question-and-answer interview went live online, Beckner did a case-changing complete public reversal on his DNA comments, according to a February 24, 2015 article published in the *Daily Camera* newspaper in Boulder. In that article, Beckner is quoted as saying, "I think the only thing I would emphasize is that the unknown DNA (from JonBenét's clothing) is very important. And I'm not involved anymore, but that has got to be the focus of the investigation. In my opinion, at this point, that's your suspect."

This 2015 comment was the first time Beckner had ever acknowledged a direct link from the DNA to a suspect in the Ramsey murder. Prior to this, Boulder Police Department rumors had asserted that the DNA was *not* key to solving this murder.[1] In essence, what the former chief said meant: *the DNA does not match the Ramseys, so they are not suspects in the murder.* Only the *Daily Camera* picked up and published this case-changing statement.

Those who officially researched it considered the foreign DNA weak, but the DNA profile contained sufficient alleles and met the rigid criteria for inclusion in the FBI's CODIS.

The CODIS program is a national computerized data bank operated by the FBI that stores DNA profiles of convicted and charged offenders or unknown profiles from criminal incidents. It is accessible to law enforcement officials for comparison purposes and for entering DNA profiles as long as such profiles have been approved for admittance by the FBI based on certain criteria. In order to be admitted into CODIS, DNA must be identified by forensic analysts to have eight to thirteen physical locations of genes on alleles.

When a DNA profile submitted by law enforcement "hits" or matches a DNA profile in the CODIS database, the FBI notifies the submitting agency so additional testing and comparisons can be done of the subject who has been identified.

As of March 2016, the National DNA Index contained more than 12,253,681 offender profiles, 2,292,478 profiles of people arrested and 690,220 forensic profiles. While CODIS has produced more than 325,615 hits assisting investigations, the foreign DNA found on JonBenét Ramsey is one of the 500,000-plus forensic profiles with no DNA match, so far, in CODIS.[2]

According to DNA experts, there could be several reasons why no match has been found in the JonBenét case. One reason is untested rape kits, an issue that was investigated in a series of reports in *USA TODAY*:

"In the most detailed nationwide inventory of untested rape kits ever, *USA TODAY* and journalists from more than 75 Gannett newspapers and TEGNA TV stations have found at least 70,000 neglected kits in an open-records campaign covering 1,000-plus police agencies—and counting. Despite its scope, the agency-by-agency count covers a fraction of the nation's 18,000 police departments, suggesting the number of untested rape kits reaches into the hundreds of thousands . . . The records reveal widespread inconsistency in how police handle rape evidence from agency to agency, and even officer to officer. Some departments test every rape kit. Others send as few as two in 10 to crime labs."[3] Since the *USA TODAY* investigation was published, several legislative jurisdictions in the US have passed mandatory legislation requiring time limits on the testing of DNA, including in rape cases.

The National Institute of Justice said in 2015 that it is "unknown, nation-wide" how many untested DNA and DNA sexual assault kits exist in the US.

Other possible reasons why no match has been found with regard to the DNA in the JonBenét Ramsey case involve state requirements on who must give DNA samples. Due to a lack of uniformity among states on who is required to give DNA, some people convicted of crimes have never been tested.[4]

In 1988, Colorado became the first state in the country to require collection of DNA from sex offenders. Since April 2002, all convicted felons in Colorado, not just sex offenders, have been required to give DNA samples to law enforcement agencies. In September 2010, Colorado lawmakers expanded the law again to require that DNA from all charged felony suspects be uploaded into CODIS for comparison. If no felony convictions are filed against the suspects, the law allows their DNA samples to be destroyed after one year.

JonBenét's DNA saga began its "nothing is ever easy with this case" format with the results of the first testing on January 15, 1997. The Colorado Bureau of Investigation gave the results of its testing to the

Boulder Police Department. While the CBI results did not conclusively identify anyone, they did eliminate the Ramseys, provided the foreign DNA found all matched one person. The DNA results were publicized four months later, but not completely. An unnamed "source" leaked that the DNA tests were "not conclusive," even though the test results had eliminated the Ramseys and several of their friends as possible suspects.

The 1997 Colorado Bureau of Investigation DNA report concluded:

> The DNA profiles developed from [bloodstains from panties as well as from right- and left-hand fingernails from JonBenét] revealed a mixture from which the major component matched JonBenét. If the minor components contributed from [bloodstains from panties as well as from right- and left-hand fingernails from JonBenét] were contributed by a single individual, then John Andrew Ramsey, Melinda Ramsey, John B. Ramsey, Patricia Ramsey, Burke Ramsey, Jeff Ramsey, [etc.] would be excluded as a source of the DNA analyzed on those exhibits.

That document is still sealed.

Dr. Elizabeth Johnson from Thousand Oaks, California, is an expert in DNA analysis. She studied the 1997 CBI report at my request and concluded that the minor or foreign DNA tested at that time was "very weak." Dr. Johnson said there is an indication that the DNA from all three 1997 samples was from the same person. She added that, if the DNA from these samples was from the same person, it eliminated the Ramseys and their family members as contributors to the mixture.

As mentioned earlier in this book, despite the 2008 "trace" result findings, some law enforcement officials still do not believe those findings exonerated the Ramseys. Instead, some believe that this DNA could have come from law enforcement or medical personnel who had mishandled the evidence. Forensic analysts say it's possible that a "secondary transfer" could occur with "touch DNA." This occurs when a person touches a second person who then touches something else and leaves the first person's touch DNA or cell DNA in a strategic area. In the Ramsey murder case, several people involved in processing the new set of DNA, including "all" CBI and Denver Police Department lab people handling these items, were tested and cleared as possible contributors.[5]

Boulder County District Attorney Stan Garnett took office in January 2009 after District Attorney Lacy's terms were completed. At that time, he returned the Ramsey murder investigation to the Boulder Police Department. "There are persons in law enforcement, or who used to be in law enforcement, who believe that the Ramseys are guilty and they contact me from time to time," he said. "I tell them the same thing I tell everyone else: the Ramseys are presumed innocent and are entitled to be treated with that presumption. All I care about is the evidence and unless, at some point, I have sufficient evidence to charge someone in a court of law, where I will openly explain to a judge or jury my views of this case, I have no comment about the state of the evidence."

Garnett did talk extensively off the record, but at the time did not want to say more because "it's still an open case." "What I want to make sure I do," he added, "is to not say anything publicly that forecloses my ability to follow whatever evidence that may develop in the case in the future. I think I owe that to the public and that's what I've tried to do. I also understand the Ramseys are presumed innocent. They've been exonerated by letter by my predecessor, which really has no legal effect, but certainly emphasizes that they're presumed innocent . . . I will follow the evidence."

# CHAPTER 28

# BEHIND THE SCENES—TWENTY YEARS

John Ramsey during his mission to help the poor in India. © John Ramsey.

## CHRONOLOGY

**December 1996—JonBenét Ramsey is murdered.**

**January 2010—Boulder Police Department investigators search for John Ramsey and visit his son's home.**

**May 2010—BPD officials visit Ramsey's son, Burke, at Purdue University in Indiana.**

**September 2010—A story that Burke has talked with BPD officials is leaked to the media, and media coverage begins anew. The story was false.**

**October 2013—The Ramsey grand jury indictments are unsealed by order of a judge. The documents list two recommended charges by the grand jury against each of JonBenét's parents. Boulder District Attorney Alex Hunter had declined to charge either of the Ramseys with a crime in 1999.**

GUILT ERODES THE CONSCIENCE, for those who have one, no less than salt water over time works its corrosive effect against metal. Eventually, the culpable mind crumbles. Thirteen years after the strikingly brutal and unresolved murder of a beautiful, happy child in Boulder, Colorado, the idea that time could be on their side sustained a small group of police officers still working the JonBenét case. Suddenly, it seemed, they might be right.

The main police decision-makers had never been able to move off their primary working theory that one or both of JonBenét's parents had killed their daughter. Patsy's death in 2006 left John as the sole object of their fixation and their prime lead.

Almost a decade and a half after JonBenét's murder, some Boulder police officers became convinced that John Ramsey had disappeared. In January of 2010, they thought he couldn't handle the guilt over his involvement in his daughter's death any longer. Despite the new DNA evidence from 2008, which led Boulder District Attorney Mary Lacy to exonerate every member of the Ramsey family, some BPD detectives still reasoned that Patsy had been responsible for her daughter's death, and John had been complicit in it.

A number of BPD officers worried that their continuing surveillance of John Ramsey had grown loose and casual over the years. There was a near sense of panic about his vanishing that morphed into anger for some, and then into a sense of resolve to find John Ramsey and bring him to justice.

A few officers from the original 1996 investigating team were still working the case in 2010, which at the time was not yet considered a cold case. They remembered the horrific first days after the murder and how they'd felt a tremendous responsibility for finding the depraved and vicious killer who had mercilessly murdered a child on their watch. They also carried the knowledge that their department had failed to take charge that fateful day when JonBenét Ramsey's body was found in her home. They hadn't searched the house thoroughly. They'd allowed the crime scene to become grossly contaminated. They'd retreated back to headquarters, leaving one inexperienced detective at the home who allowed the father to discover, by himself, his daughter's body and remove it from the scene.

Now, more than thirteen years later, Boulder Police Department investigators had no idea where the father, their prime suspect, was. They asked themselves how they could have let this happen and became determined to keep the fact that they didn't know where he was a secret. They had to keep it quiet in order to avoid suffering more humiliation related to the case. Out of a sense of survival and in order to prove their resolute theory, these BPD investigators resolved to find the fleeing father and bring him back. "Find Ramsey because he knows what happened," one BPD officer said.

Meetings and hurried discussions were conducted, and the group decided on a strategy to find John Ramsey: they would pursue his family. Surprise them at their front doors. And in their quest for the father, BPD investigators trooped to his oldest son's home.

John Andrew Ramsey had been college-aged when his half-sister was murdered in 1996, old enough to experience the trauma of the police and the media pursuing his father and stepmother and him. Even though he had been in Atlanta for Christmas at the time of the murder, he, too, had been considered a suspect. John Andrew has said he remembers that well, but primarily he remembers his father's and stepmother's continuing anguish at being hounded as suspects, and their resignation that the police who had sworn to protect them and their family were focused solely on them as suspects and were not searching for the real killer of their daughter.

On the January night in 2010 when the doorbell rang at his home, John Andrew was out with his wife. Their children were under the care of a babysitter, who had been instructed not to let anyone in the house. The ringing and knocking continued; the Boulder police officers outside were insistent. Finally, they left a message with the babysitter for John Andrew. They told her it was urgent that John Andrew call his dad and have him contact Boulder Police Chief Mark Beckner. They needed to know where John was.

When the sitter told John Andrew about the visit, he didn't call the police; he e-mailed his father. John Andrew was furious. Why hadn't the police just called him? Why did they come unexpectedly after dark and frighten his babysitter? This was intrusive and harassing behavior, he concluded, the same type of tormenting behavior his family had endured for years.

The search was also continuing in another part of the country. John Ramsey's last known address had been in Little Rock, Arkansas, but he was no longer there. According to John, he'd left a forwarding address at his apartment complex and the manager would have given this information to the police if they had simply asked for it. Instead, BPD detectives asked police in Little Rock to knock on the door of a close friend of John's in order to find out where Ramsey was. Boulder police seemed to know a lot about John's personal life from their loose surveillance. Little Rock police cooperated. The friend later e-mailed John, saying the Boulder Police Chief was urgently trying to reach him. The friend added, "I trust this means a resolution in the case."

So, where was John? Had he fled the country because of his guilt, as some in the Boulder Police Department both feared and hoped?

Well, no.

At the time, he was in India on a religious service trip called Discipleship Training for Adults, part of a larger religious organization. The trip had been recommended to him by a missionary friend. He was in India for two months, still seeking direction in his life and striving to live and go on after losing two of his daughters as well as his wife, and providing service to poor communities in India.

Boulder Police Department officials could have easily found John Ramsey by calling one of his defense attorneys. Two lived right in the BPD's own town, two others a few miles away in Denver. Perhaps pride or concerns about giving a prior warning had prevented them from taking that simple step. According to sources, BPD officials had discussed taking that course but concluded the Ramsey attorneys would refuse to disclose John's whereabouts or would set conditions the police wouldn't be willing to follow.

Legally, the Ramsey family had very little protection. Law enforcement had described them for more than a decade as "suspects" and as being "under the umbrella of suspicion." Those terms condemned them to be viewed with suspicion, uncertainty, even hatred, especially as they lacked the legal protection they would have been given if they had been arrested and charged and thus allowed to see the evidence that the Boulder Police Department had against them.

When John Ramsey returned from his religious mission in the early spring of 2010, he received a letter from Chief Mark Beckner. In the process of moving back to Charlevoix, Michigan, John was as easy to find as he had been when the police were actively looking for him just two months before. Beckner asked that John keep his letter confidential and out of the media, and John honored that request. Beckner suggested in his letter that the two of them meet with no attorneys and no other police officers present. It was a "let's just talk about the case . . . just the two of us . . ." type of letter. In all the years following the murder and the turmoil afterward, the men had never sat together and talked alone.

Beckner wrote that he was sure John would like to know more about the investigation. "I know I would if I were you," the police chief added.

Ramsey considered that comment condescending and recent BPD behavior threatening. So he declined, saying he didn't trust the request, the Boulder Police Department or Beckner. He added, however, that he would consider speaking with Beckner if the police chief would answer some questions first. Beckner wrote back reiterating his request, but said he wouldn't answer John's questions unless they met alone and in person.

When Chief Beckner couldn't get his "sit-down" with John Ramsey, momentum related to the case seemed to stall out. The BPD officers on the case consulted with others and continued to discuss their options, and then someone suggested approaching John's other son, Burke, since John Andrew had not been cooperative. Just as they'd done with John Andrew, the BPD officers on the case decided not to give Burke a chance to say "no" by calling and asking to see him. Instead, they'd just drop in at his Purdue University apartment to see if there was something on his mind he'd like to talk with them about. Not all Boulder Police Department officers involved with the case agreed on this strategy. Some considered it to be the wrong thing to do. But the decision was made to go ahead.

In May 2010, three Boulder officers traveled to West Lafayette, Indiana, to visit, unannounced, Burke Ramsey in his college apartment. It was two months after Burke's dad had declined to meet with the BPD police chief, and more than thirteen years after Burke's younger sister had been murdered in the Ramsey family's Boulder home.

Burke was in his senior year at Purdue, where he was majoring in computer and information technology. It was finals week, and he was studying for his upcoming exams. In the middle of his study haze, there was a knock on the door.

Burke opened it, expecting a friend, and was surprised to see three police officers, two men and a woman. One man and the woman introduced themselves as Boulder police detectives and gave Burke their business cards. Burke has said he doesn't remember the third person identifying himself. That man was Sergeant Tom Trujillo, then the supervisor in charge of Burke's sister's murder investigation. Like Chief Beckner, Trujillo had worked the case since the first few days of the investigation.

The two detectives told Burke they were new on the case and asked if there was anything he wanted to know or tell them.[1]

"It's finals week," Burke told them, surprised when they didn't seem to understand the enormity of that fact. Later he would state, "I didn't have time to do anything but study and take tests. They were very polite and nice, but I [didn't] see why they flew all the way out there. Why were there three of them? It was a bit of overkill. Why didn't they call first or just call as opposed to traveling all that way? It wasn't that professional. If you want to do an interview, contact me. Don't just show up at my door." His answer was the same, regardless of where they suggested meeting to talk with him: "No thanks."

"Even if I wanted to do an interview, and I didn't, that was the wrong way to approach me," he said. "What were they expecting?" The police told Burke they'd be in town in case he changed his mind and wanted to talk with them.

Nearly fourteen years after Burke's sister had been killed, Boulder Police Department officers dropped by to find out if Burke wanted to talk about anything. In police jargon, this is referred to as a cold call. In this case, the BPD approved a 1,000-mile cold call with a price tag of more than $5,000, according to travel records.[2] The BPD officers had gambled that they'd surprise Burke and he would talk. But Burke has said repeatedly that he has nothing to say to, and nothing to hide from, the Boulder Police Department. He simply wonders why they tried to catch him off guard and intimidate him.

The story about Boulder police officers visiting Burke Ramsey was leaked and reported as exclusive news on KDVR, the Denver Fox 31 television station on September 21, 2010, four months after the visit took place. A mini-study in how false stories about the Ramsey case had spread so many years ago, the story became one of the most-viewed stories on the Fox 31 website. It was also wrong.

Reporter Julie Hayden broadcast that her exclusive story had come from "sources."

"Sources tell us Boulder detectives met with Burke and interviewed him in the past month . . . Nightside [the 10 p.m. Fox 31 newscast] has learned Boulder detectives have interviewed Burke within the past few weeks. Police aren't saying anything about what was asked or answered, but they probably had Burke go over events before he and JonBenét were put to bed that night. What, if anything, he heard that evening and what he saw that morning. They also could have talked with Burke about details of the family's life.

"Now, police aren't officially commenting at all, except to say JonBenét's murder remains an open, active investigation. But obviously . . . this is one of the few people in the house that night, one of the, you know, the brother. He has a lot of information and clearly something the police are going to keep trying to get."

ANCHOR—Julie, is he a reluctant witness, does he want to get on with his life and remain as normal as he can, or was he forthcoming?

HAYDEN—You know, I get the impression, and again this is the impression from sources, that he was willing to talk with police. When he was a little boy, his parents, understandably, kind of protected him from all of that. But, I think also, you know, you look at his Twitter's [sic] posts, his Facebook posts, this is a kid who's been under tabloid scrutiny, you know, most of his life. I think a great part of him wants to be just as normal as possible.

The report was broadcast without getting the other side of the story and without asking John, Burke or their attorneys if it was true.

Contrary to Hayden's report and sources, Burke was not interviewed by Boulder police at any point in 2010. When I called the reporter to talk about her story, Hayden said she would have to get permission from her news director to respond. When Hayden didn't call back, I wrote her an e-mail. Hayden then replied, saying she wasn't able to talk because of "internal policy changes."

The erroneous story built its own momentum and was reported over and over across the country, demonstrating the staying power of the Ramsey murder and the high level of interest it still commanded. This time, however, as the false story grew in strength and impact, it began to be corrected based on accuracy checks and double-source checks by some members of the media who were reporting on it.

On September 28, 2010, reporter and author Lawrence Schiller, who wrote the first book published about the Ramsey murder in 1999, appeared for an interview on *CBS This Morning.* CBS News had done its homework and called John Ramsey's civil attorney, Lin Wood, for the other side of the story.

ANCHOR—We called the Ramsey family attorney. He says that Burke has not been questioned, but your sources are telling you that police are trying to question him?

SCHILLER—I was in Denver yesterday by pure coincidence, and I called some people in Boulder, and they said the police have sent on their business cards and asked Burke, if time permitted, if he could get in touch with them.

ANCHOR—He was questioned and exonerated 14 years ago. Why would the police be trying to talk with him now?

SCHILLER—You have to remember, as you said, he was nine years old, a frail kid, not very large in size. His sister was younger. There's a lot of evidence that has still been unexplained over the years . . . Police are never going to give up on this case. There is no statute of limitations on murder.

ANCHOR—In other words, they may have discovered some new evidence that wouldn't necessarily then make this then nine-year-old a suspect, but he could possibly speak.

SCHILLER—That's correct. He was exonerated by DNA, by many, many methods that the police used at that point. But the question is, in his own mind now, this many years away, has he locked away the facts of this murder, has he in essence put it in a room, closed the door and doesn't want to think about it? So how helpful can he be? You know, just because questions are unanswered, that doesn't mean someone is withholding the answer.

The momentum on the Burke story continued to grow in the media.

On October 1, 2010, the *Daily Camera* in Boulder published an article that began:

> BOULDER POLICE CONDUCTING ADDITIONAL INTERVIEWS IN JONBENÉT RAMSEY CASE
>
> Boulder police are conducting a new round of interviews related to the 1996 JonBenét Ramsey homicide based on recommendations from an advisory committee that met in 2009 and pored over all the evidence.

This statement was countered, however, by two BPD detectives who said a task force (referred to in the article as an "advisory committee") met for only three days and didn't even begin to look at the evidence of the case. There was no poring "over all the evidence," they said. That would have taken months of full-time work. According to the detectives, the task force had recommended re-interviewing Burke Ramsey, yet more than a year had passed since the task force made that recommendation.

Six days after Lawrence Schiller's CBS interview, he was back on television, this time on ABC's *Good Morning America* show. Again, he discussed Burke Ramsey and reiterated his opinion of the Boulder Police Department's actions:

ANCHOR—Investigators are taking a new look at old evidence . . . reaching out for fresh interviews with witnesses who may help solve the six-year-old beauty queen's murder. Among them, JonBenét's 23-year-old brother, Burke. He was only nine when his sister was killed. A Ramsey attorney told a newspaper that a police detective recently met with Burke and gave him a card and said, 'If you want to talk to us, here's how you would contact me.'

ANCHOR—And for more on why this is happening and where the case goes from here, we are joined by investigative journalist Larry Schiller.

SCHILLER—. . . But you see, Burke was nine years old at the time. He was in the house, either asleep or awake, during some of these events. The most important thing is that those memories from a young child are put in a room in his mind, a door is closed, and then the room doesn't exist. But is there an element that now can trigger some of that and bring back some of it?

ANCHOR—Wouldn't you bring in psychologists, and not just have police interviews?

SCHILLER—No, I don't think at this point they're going to try to bring in psychologists. He was interviewed that way shortly after the murder in a room with a glass window in which his mother and other members studied his actions and so forth. I think it's a matter of can he corroborate something that they know about or that they suspect may lead them to a solution.

Factually, Patsy had brought her nine-year-old son to the human services interview in 1997, but was not allowed to watch it.

The day after Schiller's October 4 ABC *Good Morning America* interview, Fox News interviewed former Los Angeles police detective Mark Fuhrman, who was an author and Fox News contributor. In 1995, Fuhrman had been the focus of a publicity storm as a lead Los Angeles police detective when he testified in the O. J. Simpson trial.

ANCHOR—So now we understand they're conducting a new round of interviews based on recommendations of an advisory committee that's been looking into this. Do we have any idea what the new focus is?

FUHRMAN—Well, Megyn, I think the new focus might be that somebody finally read Steve Thomas's book, as the first lead detective after the first couple of days, and he was told to clean up all the mistakes. There's the first problem. There was never any doubt in Steve Thomas's mind that there was no intruder . . . that the person who took JonBenét Ramsey into the basement and killed her was in fact somebody who was in the household by permission or there with the approval of the parents and/or friends.

Fuhrman was wrong. Thomas was not the lead detective on the Ramsey case. Commander John Eller was in charge, then Commander Mark Beckner. Thomas was one of many detectives on the case. He was a narcotics detective with the Boulder Police Department who was borrowed from narcotics for the homicide investigation. He had no prior homicide experience. The Ramseys later sued him for libel when he named Patsy as her daughter's killer in his book. His publisher paid thousands of dollars and signed a confidentiality agreement to settle the lawsuit.

The interview continued:

ANCHOR—So who does that leave? Because you've got John and Patsy, who a judge in a civil suit many years later declared that not necessarily were the parents innocent of the crime, but she said the evidence is much more consistent with an intruder than it is with the parents having killed JonBenét. And then, her brother Burke, who was nine years old at the time, was reportedly cleared.

FUHRMAN—Well, let's not count too much on what juries say, especially a civil jury.

Fuhrman was wrong again. The case never went to trial, so no jury was ever involved. The federal district judge dismissed that lawsuit in its deposition stage with a 93-page summary that stated, in part, "The weight of the evidence is more consistent that an intruder murdered JonBenét than it is with the theory Mrs. Ramsey did so."

The following week on October 14, 2010 on the CNN news program *Anderson Cooper 360*, Cooper debriefed CNN Senior Legal Analyst Jeffrey Toobin and Reporter/Anchor Tom Foreman about the case and the latest development related to BPD officials wanting to talk with Burke Ramsey. Foreman reviewed the case and provided perspective. Toobin also offered some insights.

TOOBIN—The paradox of the current situation is you can sort of understand both sides. It is frustrating to the police, as it should be, to [not be able to] solve a crime that should have an answer. There are so many clues. There is such a limited universe of suspects.

COOPER—There are so many contradictory clues. That's what's so endlessly fascinating about the case.

TOOBIN—So you can see why they'd want to talk to Burke just because he's one of the handful of people who might have had some firsthand knowledge of what went on in the house. But on the other hand, you can certainly understand Burke's perspective, which is, "Go to hell. I've cooperated. I've done my best. My family's cooperated. This has been nothing but pain for us. I'm not going to tell you anything new that I couldn't have told you five, 10, 15 years ago," and I can certainly understand his perspective, too.

Toobin got it right. Burke Ramsey didn't offer up the blunt "go to hell," but he didn't respond to the offer to talk when confronted by the Boulder Police Department.

During this coverage of the Burke story, which ran through several mainstream news cycles, more reporters began to get it right. They covered both perspectives on the story, something that did not happen when the Ramsey murder story first broke in December 1996.

However, the tabloids did not.

On September 30, 2010, the *Globe* tabloid ran this headline:

CONFLICTING STORIES ABOUT "BOULDER PD QUIZZING BROTHER BURKE RAMSEY"

On October 25, 2010, the *Globe* ran another front-page story:

JONBENÉT MURDER SOLVED

The *National Enquirer, National Examiner* and the *Star* all had varying versions of information about Burke Ramsey. Six months after Boulder police officers made their cold call in Indiana and were told by Burke that he wouldn't talk with them, the *National Examiner* headlined its November 15, 2010, edition:

WHAT JONBENÉT BROTHER TOLD COPS!

These stories were broadcast or published throughout the world.

For nineteen years in the Ramsey case, too much fiction had been perceived to be fact. For some reason, exaggerations and false information about the Ramsey family were pervasive, starting as small disturbances but then spreading in an outward, expanding circle until they became entrenched myths. The lies spread much faster than the truth. The truth, John and Patsy Ramsey insisted, was that they and other members of their family were all innocent.

Fortunately, in the example of Burke and his 2010 encounter with the police, parts of this story began to be corrected via double-checking by some reporters. What was first broadcast on mainstream media by Fox 31 in Denver in the "Burke Interviewed by Police" piece was simply incorrect. Not only were the presented facts false, but they were accompanied by a heavy dose of speculation. During the episode of coverage through several news cycles that this story instigated, more fact than fiction eventually emerged as both sides of the story were actually covered. That hadn't happened in the early years of coverage of the Ramsey family. Instead, a staggering lack of wisdom had influenced most members of the media, from the field crews to their managers, all of whom seemed driven by the quest to be "first" when it came to reporting about this investigation rather than right.

During Burke's September–October 2010 media siege, he got another knock at the door. This time he was offered $20,000 from a tabloid for an interview, a deal he didn't accept. Eventually, after more than twenty calls from reporters, he changed his phone number. He also consulted his mother's defense attorney as he was forced to deal once again with the results of front-page and lead stories. "I can handle it, but I don't like it," he has said. "There's nothing more to say. I just worry for my dad and how hard it is on him."

A 2010 research study by professors from the University of Michigan and Georgia State University has shown that people are selective about the facts they accept and, when corrected about a misperception or inaccuracy, "corrections frequently fail to reduce misperceptions." In some cases, according to the study, those being corrected believe even more strongly in their misperceptions. This tendency, called "backfire," is related to how facts can do just that. "The general idea is that it's absolutely threatening to admit you're wrong," said Dr. Brendan Nyhan, one of the authors of the study.[3]

In Colorado, the backfire related to the Ramsey case still burns. In 2015, some people in positions of power remain convinced that Patsy Ramsey killed her daughter, just as others are convinced she did not.

Those who are convinced about the Ramseys' guilt point to the October 2013 judicial order that led to the unsealing of the Ramsey grand jury indictments. The grand jury had asked for child abuse resulting in murder, two charges each, against Patsy and John Ramsey.

All sides remain bitter. They dislike each other and argue over which side they're on and why, and the hapless case slogs on, year after fruitless year. And the person who actually tortured and killed six-year-old JonBenét Ramsey in her Boulder, Colorado, home at Christmastime in 1996 remains unidentified and unpunished.

CHAPTER 29

# JOHN AND BURKE RAMSEY, 2015

JonBenét ice skating. © John Ramsey.

FOR MUCH OF 2010 AND THE FIRST HALF OF 2011, John Ramsey lived in a rented doublewide trailer in a small high-desert town in Utah. It's what he could afford. For those who believe Patsy killed her daughter and that she got what was coming to her when she died an agonizing death from cancer in 2006, they could now believe the same for John.

What has his life been like since December 26, 1996, when he found his daughter's body in the basement of his home? More specifically, has he been punished by life? Has he gotten what was coming to him?

Whether or not you believe John Ramsey was involved in the death of his daughter, his suffering has been immeasurable. He has taken direct body blows of loss. But not, perhaps, in the manner that those who maintain he was involved in his daughter's murder would anticipate.

John spent 2010 and the first part of 2011 working in Utah with his former business attorney, Mike Bynum, for an Australian company. He has also worked for the same company, which has since been sold, in marketing and investor communications. In 2013, 2014 and 2015, John worked on real estate projects with Bynum. The jobs he's held since 2010 have represented the first full-time employment he's had since being fired in December 1997— one year after JonBenét was killed and at the height of the investigation of his daughter's brutal murder—as head of Access Graphics by its parent company, General Electric.

Even John can't explain how he has survived the grief and torture of his soul.

"I don't know if I have," he has said. "There are still days when it takes a lot of positive to get moving, to get going, decide what I'm going to accomplish that day, keep planning life." His three children help. So does his new wife, Jan, whom he married in 2011. He has a group of friends who are very loyal and have guarded John's and his family's well-being for all these years.

His oldest son is a protector. When his dad attended the funeral of Detective Lou Smit in the summer of 2010, John Andrew was always

| JonBenét | SUN | MON | TUE | WED | THUR | FRI | SAT |
|---|---|---|---|---|---|---|---|
| WALK JACQUES | ✓ | ✓ | ✓ | ✓ | ✓ | | |
| MAKE BED | ✓ | ✓ | ✓ | ✓ | ✓ | | |
| PLATE TO SINK | ✓ | ✓ | ✓ | ✓ | ✓ | | |
| PICK UP ROOM | ✓ | ✓ | ✓ | ✓ | ✓ | | |
| TIDY PLAYROOM | ✓ | ✓ | ✓ | ✓ | ✓ | | |
| PRACTICE VIOLIN / PIANO | ✓ P | ✓ P | ✓ P | ✓ | ✓ | | |

List of weekly chores for JonBenét. © John Ramsey.

close by to make sure everything went well for his father. Many people wanted to talk with John, to offer him understanding, support and thanks for his devotion to Lou Smit.

John Andrew, who is now married and has children, simply won't talk about the terrible events his family has experienced.

And he has a great deal of contempt for what the Boulder Police Department did to those close to him.

Like her brother, John Ramsey's daughter, Melinda, is married and has children. She also supports and protects her father. Unlike John Andrew, however, she will share private moments of her family's tragedy with those she trusts.

Perhaps due to what she's seen her family endure, Melinda seems to easily deflect the small things that cause angst to most others in daily life. When her kitchen flooded because her children had accidentally left the stopper in the sink while the water was running, she handled it with a shrug of her shoulders and a mop. She is glad her dad has remarried. She wants him to be happy and knows of his loneliness after Patsy died.

His marriage with Patsy had been very important to John. "I missed that goodness, that partnership and companionship. Within a good marriage, your spouse is your best friend. That certainly was what Patsy was. I missed that. I missed my best friend. After Patsy died, there was a companionship and love that I wanted to fulfill."

Patsy died in 2006 from a recurrence of her ovarian cancer. It metastasized again in 2002 in her abdomen and traveled to her brain. She had treated living as a gift. And while she considered that what had happened to her family shouldn't have to happen to anyone, she accepted that it had indeed happened to her. "There is always a way through the terrible things that happen in life," she said. As simple as that may sound, this attitude allowed Patsy to make every minute as positive as she could make it, even though there were times when she simply gave up trying. For the most part, however, Patsy Ramsey focused on the promise she felt for her family and herself. She said her goal was "to love my family," and added that "what didn't matter, wouldn't." She also said such a focus "takes a lot of constant thought."

After their daughter was murdered and before Patsy died, slowly, the Ramseys' life evolved into an appreciation for, and contentment with, what they had left. Though still hopeful that they would help find who had killed their daughter, they had learned not to let the need to do so devour them.

After eight years of Patsy being cancer-free, they cautiously believed she had won that assault. When Patsy was diagnosed with a recurrence of her ovarian cancer, she and John at first decided to treat it as "just an illness that could be controlled and [that] we would live with." The doctors at the National Cancer Institute treated Patsy initially. She had been their most successful ovarian cancer patient, the one who had lived the longest out of twenty-four other women who had undergone the experimental protocol for their cancer treatments in 1993. This time when Patsy underwent cancer treatments at the NCI, her cancer went into remission for a year, but then came back. Even the doctors at the National Cancer Institute couldn't help at that point, so the Ramseys went to an oncologist in Atlanta and Patsy had more experimental treatment there, which helped for nearly another year. She then continued treatments in Atlanta and in Charlevoix, Michigan.

In 2005, doctors found that Patsy's cancer had moved aggressively into her brain. A new laser surgery obliterated the tumors, but they came back. Friends in Charlevoix, Linda and Susan, would stay with Patsy at night in the hospital because of her confusion and terrible pain. Patsy said her pain from the cancer was like "a migraine times ten." What amazed her friends, they later said, was that even while they were taking care of Patsy, she would still ask how they were doing and try to take care of them.

Short months later, Patsy's oncologist leveled with John, saying "this really is the end for Patsy."

"The kindest, least painful alternative is to stop her treatments and enter into palliative care," the doctor said. "Continued treatments will make no difference in how much time she has left to live." John, his children and Patsy's family agreed with the doctor's recommendation, if only to end Patsy's suffering. Other doctors they consulted said there were really no other treatments left.

The Ramseys had already moved from Michigan back to Atlanta to live with Patsy's parents by the time the doctor suggested no more chemo, no more radiation. Everyone agreed to do what they could to make Patsy comfortable. The disease had started to affect her thinking. She still painted a little, and sometimes couldn't understand why a picture she had painted didn't make sense to her. She would often ask John when her next treatment was scheduled. "I'd never lied to her before, but I had to about the treatments," he said, "and that was impossibly difficult because we had always made decisions together." Letting his wife die with a measure of peace and comfort was all he could do, however.

"Patsy was never aware that I had decided to stop any further treatments," John said. "She wasn't alert and understanding at that point, and I didn't want to tell her we had given up. It seemed like that would have taken away her hope." John still agonizes over this decision. "I knew it was the compassionate thing to do, but it was the hardest decision I have ever been forced to make. We had fought for so long; it was very hard to stop and admit defeat, yet to continue to bombard her with chemo and radiation would have only made her last days very painful ones. Instead, we opted to make her final living as comfortable and peaceful as we could."

He doesn't remember his last words to her. He knows he can't count the times he told her he loved her in those last days and knows some of that got through to her. As she neared death, he knew it was coming because the doctors had told him what to expect. She died at about two in the morning. She opened her eyes, held them open for a moment, and then was gone. He was right there holding her. It was early on a Saturday morning, June 24, 2006. Patsy was forty-nine years old.

John and Patsy's son, Burke, was nineteen when his mother died almost ten years after his sister was killed. For all those years, members of the Ramsey family had worked very hard to keep Burke out of the spotlight. They'd wanted to give him as normal a childhood as they could after JonBenét's death.

I first met Burke with his father at a hotel in Atlanta in 2010, where we sat in a vast, quiet and private lobby. It was his first and as of this publishing, his only public interview.

Burke was twenty-three then, and wore an ever-present smile. His smile looks just like his mom's smile. When he hears that, he says thank you with a genuineness that is touching, clearly flattered. It's apparent that he deeply loves and respects his parents, and that he wants his dad to find peace.

What's happened in his life has been difficult. "Yeaahh," he said in a long, drawn-out response. "There's always something unexpected. Like the police showing up at my university without notice, or at graduation someone walked up to my dad and I saying, 'Oh you're JonBenét Ramsey's family. I've seen you on television.'" He said he worries about people he doesn't know, because it's possible they might be from the tabloids. The people who approach him about JonBenét are invariably kind, he added, but he would rather that his family not be defined by his sister's notorious death. I asked if he wonders why two of his sisters were killed and his mom died of cancer. "Sure," he said. "But there's nothing I can do about it. I don't know if it's bad luck. I don't know what to call it. You just deal with it, and you don't dwell on it."

He smiled throughout the conversation and admitted it's his way of dealing with an unpredictable, uncertain world. "I'm a pretty happy, easy-going guy. My mom taught me to always be upbeat and positive. She was a sweet lady. She helped make me who I am today."

So did his dad. "My dad taught me to be strong because he's been so strong through all of this," Burke said. "I follow his wisdom and kindness by his example. With both my parents, I valued their opinions and took their advice. I watched them go through all the challenges. My dad taught me how to fly, and I got my pilot's license." He turned and looked at his dad with pure admiration.

Burke had never talked publicly prior to this interview. But he agreed to speak this time because he and his father were both convinced that the surprise visits by Boulder police officers to Burke's apartment and John Andrew's home earlier in 2010 had been wrong. His father was particularly infuriated that, once again, his family was being harassed by the police. He was especially upset that, by confronting his son with no warning, they had drawn Burke back into the media spotlight after all this time.

Burke said he views his sister's murder not with anger, but with sadness and frustration, and he wonders how his life would have been different if she had not been killed or if the police had not targeted his parents. He's absorbed a lot through the years, warding off attacks directed against his mom and dad from so many directions. And he's learned to cope by burying some of it, leaving it alone.

He also said he remembers brother-and-sister stuff with JonBenét: playing in the back seat of their parents' car when they were driving somewhere, his little sister knocking over his elaborate LEGO creations while trying to help him with them, laughing on the beach with JonBenét and swimming with her in Michigan during their summer vacations. And he remembers not being able to go outside to play because the news cameras were there, and his parents didn't want pictures of him released to the public. He remembers their house in Atlanta being robbed, too, and news helicopters flying around overhead. He added, though, that his teen years were pretty normal.

There's a lot going on behind Burke Ramsey's smile. He has made choices and grown into a young man who seems to have found balance in his life.

About those early days after his sister was killed: "I was a little kid and didn't understand much," he said simply.

John Ramsey doesn't want anyone's pity. He believes it is his responsibility to tell the story about his little girl. He will not give in to hatred because he thinks it's a waste of life. He hopes that if he talks about JonBenét's murder, something he says may give an investigator a new lead or may prompt one person who knows something to make a phone call or send an e-mail that leads to an answer regarding his daughter's death. He becomes revitalized when a credible investigator expresses interest in investigating. Recently, a retired DA and a detective told him they'd like to become involved.

He won't walk away. The tears, the torment, the nights when he couldn't sleep and days when he anguished over nothing else but what he could do to find his daughter's murderer are less a part of his life now, but they still linger and always will. He understands that none of his family can escape the shadow of suspicion until JonBenét's killer is caught—or at least positively identified. He wishes "to clear their name" for the sake of his remaining children. He appreciates the strangers who come up to him when they recognize him and wish him well.

He still has the unusual in his life. He fought off a burglar who was trying to burglarize his home in the late 1990s in a struggle that caused him to suffer a detached retina that led to emergency eye surgery. A used SUV he'd bought from John Andrew was demolished in a collision while it was parked at an airport. Such things he greets with equanimity. What would have been a major ordeal for many is to him an inconvenience from which he simply moves on. John has dealt with so much that he's clear about what really matters and what doesn't. And he is now appreciating a fair share of normality and contentment.

John Ramsey now also has confidence in the futures of his children, and his current marriage has given him a companionship of peace. He enters most days resolved to accept whatever comes his way. He says he knows there will always be people who will never accept that he and Patsy are innocent, but that matters much less now than it once did. He understands fulfillment comes with loving those closest to him.

In order to survive, John has learned to search for and find joy in his own way, aware that the process is part of the resolution.

On July 21, 2011, John Ramsey remarried in Charlevoix, Michigan. The wedding was attended by a small group of family and friends at a converted dairy farm now designed to host special events. It was scheduled at seven in the evening, and by then the heat of the day had moved on, replaced by the gradual coolness of the night. John's three children and his new wife's two children were there, greeting guests as they arrived.

Happy grandchildren bounced around talking about the "biggest fish in the world" in a nearby pond and asking if they could have more cupcakes.

John and his new wife, Jan, arms entwined, entered the courtyard from a side door to say their vows to each other that summer evening in Charlevoix. Jan is a missionary's daughter who spent much of her early and teen years in Ethiopia. She is also a fashion designer and event planner whom John describes as "open, positive and energetic."

Unfortunately, some things never change. When the *National Enquirer* reported that John Ramsey had remarried, they quoted him as saying, "Patsy is smiling down from heaven," even though John never said that.

Fortunately, however, some good things continue as well. Each year, strangers still leave little gifts—dolls, angels, Christmas cards—on JonBenét Ramsey's gravesite in Atlanta on Christmas Day. On December 25, 2016, she would have been twenty-six years old.

Jan and John Ramsey at their wedding in July of 2011. © John Ramsey.

Among the items that belonged to JonBenét still kept by the family, is an unopened Christmas present for her from her half-brother and half-sister. It was meant for their Christmas celebration together with the rest of their family in Charlevoix, Michigan, later in the day on December 26, 1996. It has never been opened.

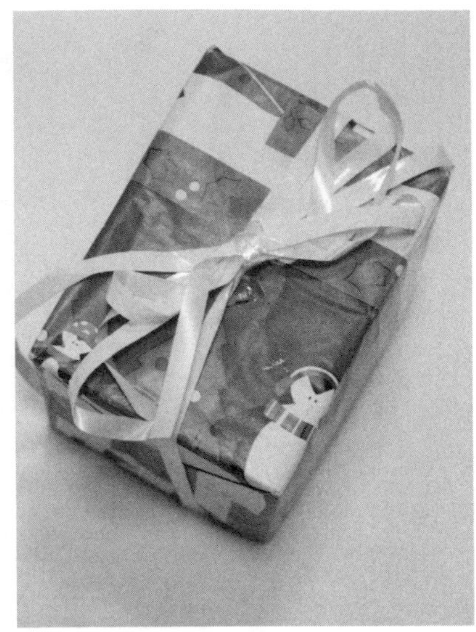

Unopened Christmas present to JonBenét for Christmas 1996. It's from her half-brother and half-sister, John Andrew and Melinda. It has never been opened. © John Ramsey.

As stated, according to the Colorado Bureau of Investigation, 165 people in Boulder County in 1996 and 1997 were registered as sexual offenders.

One of them, Gary Howard Oliva, was arrested in 1997 after police checked him out because of his status as a sexual offender. They found a shrine to JonBenét in his home. He became a suspect.

He was arrested again in June of 2016 in Boulder for sex crimes. Police confiscated his telephone, where they found numerous pictures of JonBenét, including autopsy photographs which he could have gotten from the Internet. Also on his phone were several pictures of child pornography. None involved JonBenét.

The Boulder Sheriff's Department lists twelve bookings for Oliva, mostly for failure to register as a sexual offender. It indicates the amount of time he continued to spend in Boulder. His DNA is not a match to that found on JonBenét. Oliva was fifty-three years old at the time of his June 2016 arrest.

# EPILOGUE I

ON FEBRUARY 21, 2015, former Boulder Police Chief Mark Beckner participated in an online interview on the website Reddit.com. His interview took place in an "Ask Me Almost Anything" session for a Reddit forum devoted to "Unresolved Mysteries." Taking part in this interview session was an unusual act for Beckner, who had avoided interviews during his tenure on the Ramsey case. Afterward, he told the *Daily Camera* "my impression was that this was a members-only type group . . ." "It was a misunderstanding and naivete on my part," that his Reddit interview would be published online unrestricted. Beckner said he participated because he didn't think the interview would be world-wide.

Mark Beckner was the longest-serving Boulder law enforcement officer involved in the Ramsey murder investigation. He began working the case three weeks after the murder by interviewing his own officers about reports they had filed, was commander on the case from October 1997 to June 1998, and was police chief from June 1998 to April 2014, when he retired.

This epilogue contains Beckner's written opinions on Reddit related to the investigation of the murder of JonBenét Ramsey and contrasts the former police chief's statements against information acquired by the author of this book through the collection and analysis of case file documentation.

Within days of his Reddit appearance, Beckner retracted the statements from his online interview that had referred to the DNA found on JonBenét's clothing in an interview with the *Daily Camera* in Boulder. On Reddit, Beckner had answered a request for "possible explanations" related to where the DNA found on JonBenét's clothing could have come from by listing possibilities such as "manufacturing," "intentional placement," and "interactions with other people" as well as "belongs to an intruder."

Three days later, in his new statement to the *Daily Camera,* Beckner disagreed with his *own* initial statements on Reddit and said the DNA found on JonBenét's clothing was the "key to solving the case."

"I tried to be honest and fair," Beckner told the newspaper, "and I think the only thing I would emphasize is that the unknown DNA (from JonBenét's clothing) is very important. And I'm not involved any more, but that has got to be the focus of the investigation. In my opinion, at this point, that's your suspect . . .

"The suspect is the donator of that unknown DNA, and until you can prove otherwise, I think that's the way you've got to look at it."

By February 24, 2015, the publication date of the *Daily Camera* article "Mark Beckner Opens Up about JonBenét Ramsey Case, Then Regrets It," Beckner had deleted all of his online interview answers from the Reddit website.

Created in 2005, Reddit is a social networking and news website through which registered community members can submit content such as text posts with direct links, making it essentially an online bulletin board system. Anyone can read what is posted. Typically, Reddit has more than 200 million unique visitors per month. It is ranked twenty-eighth in a list of the world's most-visited websites and ninth by Alexa, a web traffic analytics site. In 2015, Reddit was featured in a *Wall Street Journal* article about its successes.

Although Beckner retracted his answers on Reddit, the interview page as of this writing can still be found at the *Denver Post's* cached website: http://extras.denverpost.com/jonbenetAMA.html.

The only portions of the Beckner/Reddit interview used in this epilogue are those that contain substantial differences between the former police chief's stated opinions and the information about the facts of the case provided by Boulder Police Department reports and other reliable documentation such as court records. Reddit participant questions and Beckner's answers have been shortened or paraphrased as needed for brevity and clarity. Reddit participant names are not used.

These excerpts are included in this book because they illustrate the knowledge and mindset of one of the key leaders and longest serving law enforcement officers from the Boulder Police Department investigation into the Ramsey homicide case.

Beckner's second statement to the *Daily Camera* newspaper that the DNA found on JonBenét's clothing "has got to be the focus of the investigation" represented the "first public move away from the Ramseys as suspects" by anyone involved in the Boulder Police Department's investigation of their daughter's murder.

## INTRODUCTION

This portion of the Beckner Reddit session was posted above the interview.

In his introduction, Beckner described his background in a statement that included the following details:

Beckner: I am former Boulder Police Chief Mark Beckner. I worked in law enforcement for 36 years and headed the investigation into the JonBenét Ramsey murder. Past experience includes the following: Training Officer and Instructor, Investigator, Supervision, Liquor Code Enforcement, Hostage Negotiator, Traffic Investigation, Crime Scene Investigation, Professional Standards Investigator, Patrol Commander, SWAT Commander, Detective Commander, Personnel Management, College Instructor, Ethics Instructor, Criminal Justice Instructor.

**Author Comments:** While the former chief has lengthy experience, he did not list any homicide investigation experience in this summary of his career. Prior to being appointed head of the Boulder Police Department detective unit investigating the Ramsey murder in October 1997, Beckner had never run a homicide unit nor investigated a homicide case, which would have been critically important in understanding the Ramsey murder.

In sworn testimony for his video-taped deposition on November 26, 2001 for the civil lawsuit *Wolf v. Ramsey*, Beckner confirmed his lack of homicide investigative experience:

Ramsey Lawyer: Let me go back and make sure I've got . . . I believe I have this correctly. Prior to October of 1997 when you were placed in charge of the JonBenét Ramsey investigation, your experience in homicide investigation would have consisted of assisting in a couple of homicide investigations back in 1981 to 1983 where you did some interviews, the other you're not really familiar with in terms of recollection and then in one case sometime in the 1994 to '97 timeframe where you were the acting chief and therefore oversaw for a two-day time period the investigation into the homicide where the individual was shot in the chest when he opened the door?

Beckner: Correct.

Ramsey Lawyer: Have I now covered all of your homicide experience as a police officer prior to October of 1997?

Beckner: To the best of my recollection. (Deposition Pages 18-19.)

Ramsey Lawyer: And I don't mean this disrespectfully, but I guess you would agree with me that you weren't brought in to be in charge of the Ramsey investigation in October of '97 because of your experience in dealing with homicides?

Beckner: No.

Ramsey Lawyer: You would agree with me, wouldn't you?

Beckner: I would agree with you. (Deposition Page 20.)

**Perspective:** In November of 2011, retired New York Police Department Lieutenant-Commander and author Vernon Geberth wrote: "The supervisor of homicide should ideally have a homicide or investigative background as experience is a prime asset to appreciate and understand the dynamics of the investigative function. This does not mean a supervisor who lacks a homicide or investigative background cannot effectively supervise investigations. However, it does suggest there is a need for learning the investigative processes involved. Even for the experienced supervisor, managing investigations is an ongoing educational process."[1]

There was tremendous controversy in the media and among a few investigators over Beckner's lack of homicide experience when he was appointed to head up the investigation as the commander.

## QUESTIONS AND ANSWERS

In this section of the Reddit interview, Beckner answered specific questions related to the Ramsey homicide investigation posted by Reddit participants. Following are a number of these questions followed by Beckner's full or excerpted answers and the author's comments in response to those answers.

### 911 CALL

This question referred to rumors that words could be heard at the end of the tape of the 911 call phoned in by Patsy Ramsey early in the morning on December 26, 1996, hours before her daughter's body was found. According to such rumors, the voices of John and Patsy Ramsey were heard on the tape in addition to the voice of Burke.

Reddit Participant: It has been reported the dialogue at the end of the 911 tape was: Male: "We're not speaking to you!" Female: "Help me, Jesus. Help me, Jesus." Young Male: "Well, what did you find?" Do you believe this is valid, that those words were actually spoken?

Beckner: The words are difficult to hear and some claim they cannot hear them. After listening to the tape many times, I can tell you that I can hear what sounds like voices saying those words.

**Author Comments:** In July 2003, the Boulder County District Attorney's Office released audio copies of Patsy Ramsey's 911 call from December 26, 1996, and the tape aired publicly for the first time on the NBC network. NBC had experts analyze the tape to test the rumor that the Ramseys' son, Burke, could be heard in the background after Patsy Ramsey thought she had hung up the phone. NBC experts said no other voices could be heard on an enhanced version of the tape.

The confidential, mandatory Boulder County Department of Social Services interview with Burke Ramsey conducted in early 1997 revealed no information about his being in the kitchen with his parents when the 911 call was made. The interview, conducted by a psychologist appointed by Boulder Social Services, included questions provided by Boulder Police Department officials. Burke stated during another interview that he'd stayed in bed and pretended to be asleep when his parents came to his room to check on him that morning.

In a confidential group law enforcement meeting in June 1998, Boulder Police Department investigators presented their theory related to the Ramsey homicide. The 911 tape was part of the presentation, but investigators could not get the tape to play.

## RANSOM NOTE AND RANSOM AMOUNT

Reddit Participant: Do the police think the murderer sat in the house and wrote a long-winded note on the Ramsey's notepad before attempting to kidnap [JonBenét]?

Beckner: No, we do not believe someone wrote the note prior to attempting to kidnap JonBenét. Neither the [BPD nor] the FBI believe this was ever a kidnapping. It was a murder that someone tried to stage as a kidnapping.

**Author Comments:** There are some Boulder Police Department officers and FBI agents interviewed by this author who believe an intruder was the killer and the ransom note was likely written before JonBenét was murdered.

Reddit Participant: Is it true that the amount of ransom wanted was the same amount of John Ramsey's bonus check that year?
Beckner: As I recall, I believe that is correct.

**Author Comments:** The ransom note request was for $118,000.00. The amount of John Ramsey's deferred compensation bonus was $118,117.50. Ramsey investigators told Boulder Police Department officials about this development.

## CRIME SCENE

Reddit Participant: Did the original officer to respond report anything strange?
Beckner: Yes, quite a few observations seemed strange to him.

**Author Comments:** The actual Boulder Police Department report filed by the first officer on the scene, Rick French, is printed in Documents at the end of this book. It includes sections related to his arrivals and departures at the Ramsey home. The reader can judge whether French reported any "strange" observations.

Reddit Participant: Was urine found anywhere in the victims [sic] room[,] bathroom or on her clothes?
Beckner: Her clothes and bed appeared to be stained.

**Author Comments:** According to Detective Lou Smit, hired by the Boulder District Attorney's Office to work on the Ramsey murder case with the approval of the Boulder Police Department, JonBenét's bed sheets were not stained with urine. Only her clothing was stained. When the bed sheets on her bed were tested, they showed fibers remaining from the clothing she was wearing indicating the sheets had not been changed.

**Perspective:** One of the early Boulder Police Department theories in the case was that JonBenét wet the bed and one of her parents became enraged and hurt her. It underlines the importance of whether the sheets had urine on them or had been changed. They didn't and hadn't.

The Ramsey attorneys believed that her clothing was urine-stained because of the violence and trauma of her death.

Reddit Participant: Can you clarify the condition of the snow ground cover the morning the first officer arrived? Was it patchy or solid and were any footprints ever noted by the open window leading away?

Beckner: It was patchy from an older snowfall, but there was frost on the ground from the humidity and temperature that night. No footprints were observed near the window well or on the deck to JonBenét's bedroom.

**Author Comments:** Police crime scene photographs from that morning show no snow on the south side of the Ramsey home, where the window well in question and JonBenét's second-floor bedroom balcony were located. In addition, BPD reports stated that the police sergeant who reported on the outside conditions that morning did "not believe there was snow on the sidewalks or on the driveway." In October 1997, a BPD detective spoke with what is described as a "weather expert" who said "there was insufficient information to tell what the condition of the ground would have been around the Ramsey residence."

Reddit Participant: Regarding the intruder theory, can you comment on the point of entry, how an intruder might have gained entry and whether it is plausible?

Beckner: Most investigators do not believe there was a legitimate point of entry. It is unknown how an intruder may have gotten in. [Detective] Lou Smit always believed it was the basement window, but we did not agree with him, as the dust and spider web were undisturbed.

**Author Comments:** According to Boulder Police Department reports, there were several other ways into the Ramsey home, including unlocked doors, open doors, and unlocked windows. A list of ways into the home quoted verbatim from the JonBenét Ramsey Murder Book Index is provided in the main part of the book. The information was compiled directly from BPD reports. There are also investigators who believe an intruder could have gotten through the broken basement window because there were broken spider web strands hanging down inside the area and debris from the window well on the basement floor of the home. More of this theory is discussed in the book.

## JOHN RAMSEY

Reddit Participant: Is it true John Ramsey went down into the basement on his own a short time before he was asked to go down with his friend and search it by a police officer?

Beckner: That is according to what he told police.

**Author Comments:** John Ramsey told BPD investigators on the morning of December 26, 1996 that he had gone to the basement to look for his daughter because he didn't know what else to do. He then told police that he was concerned because he had found a broken basement window with a suitcase underneath it. Ramsey stated the police did not follow up at that time. This information is reflected in Boulder Police Department reports.

Others searched the basement. Officer Rick French, the first BPD officer on the scene that morning, said he first searched the basement when he arrived sometime after 6 a.m. He did not mention the "broken window and suitcase." He did write about the door where JonBenét's body was found: "In the basement I attempted to open the door leading to the area where JonBenét was ultimately found, but it was secured by a wooden latch above the door. The door opened inward and I was looking for access out of the house. Since the door could not have been used for that purpose, and it was latched closed, I did not open it." (Officer Rick French—Date of Report 12-26-1996 Time written: 2317—11:17 p.m.)

French wrote this part of his report slightly more than ten hours after JonBenét's body was discovered. Here's why these statements he wrote about the door are incorrect and misleading:

- The door opened outward only, not inward.
- French could not have known if there was an exit out of the room unless he opened the door and looked into the room to find out where it led. "I did not open it," he wrote.

Officer French gave even more contradictory and incorrect information about that critically important basement door in a formal debriefing two weeks later on January 10, 1997. According to the JonBenét Ramsey Murder Book Index, two senior officers reported: "Officer French finds the wine cellar locked." (BPD Report #5-3853.) (Date of Formal Interview: 1-10-97.)

"Officer French thinks the wine cellar door is nailed shut." (BPD Report #5-3854.) (Date of Formal Interview: 1-10-97.)

John's friend who arrived early that morning also searched the basement. He noticed the broken window and suitcase, says he moved the suitcase, and glanced into the storage room where JonBenét's body was lying. He didn't see her body, possibly because he was unable to find the light switch and possibly because of the left-hand wall in the storage room that blocked a full view of the room.

Later in the day, the only BPD detective left in the home, Linda Arndt, asked that same friend to take John and search the basement. It was at this time that John Ramsey found his daughter's body in a basement storage room.

## JOHN AND PATSY RAMSEY

Reddit Participant: The Ramseys being so distant towards each other just after their daughter has been kidnapped is very strange. Did you ask the FBI or any other law department is this normal?

Beckner: They rarely interacted and this did not seem normal given the circumstances. Lots of speculation as to why.

Reddit Participant: Can you comment on the emotional state of the parents when they were interviewed . . . ? Was there anything unusual?

Beckner: There were many things that investigators thought were unusual, including Patsy being upset at the first officer being in uniform and wearing a gun. Officers found that very strange given that her daughter was missing and allegedly kidnapped. The officers also noticed how distant John and Patsy seemed to be toward each other.

**Author Comments:** Several BPD reports contradict Beckner's statements that Patsy and John "rarely interacted" and seemed to be "distant" toward each other on the morning of their daughter's disappearance. Police officers on the scene stated in BPD reports that the Ramseys acted "normally for the circumstances." There is also much more information in the main body of this book on the Ramseys' emotions and interactions. The concerns raised by the first responding BPD officer showing up at the Ramsey's front door in uniform after parking a police car in front of their house when the ransom note had instructed that no police should be called, are also addressed.

## BURKE RAMSEY

Reddit Participant: What are your thoughts on whether Burke may know more than he has told?

Beckner: I'm not going to speculate on what Burke may or may not know. He was only 9 years old at the time. However, after a short initial interview that day (before we had many facts), Burke was only interviewed one more time and that was by a social services worker. We of course had many other questions we wanted to ask him as the investigation wore on, but were never given an opportunity to interview him again.

**Author Comments:** Beckner was wrong about the number of times Burke was interviewed related to his sister's murder and who interviewed him. The importance and relevance of the correct information reflects the cooperation of the Ramsey family about interviews with their son. Burke was interviewed four times during four years, and the circumstances of these interviews were different from what Beckner described. Those who actually interviewed Burke provide insight into the depth and credibility of those interviews by experienced experts:

1. Burke was interviewed the first time by a BPD detective in a tape-recorded session the day his sister's body was found, on December 26, 1996. Burke was questioned at his friend's home, where he was taken that morning so he could be away from the confusion at his own home. Neither of his parents was present during that interview nor were they asked permission for Boulder Police to interview their son.

2. Burke's second interview on January 8, 1997 was scheduled by the Boulder County Department of Social Services. A child psychologist, Dr. Suzanne Bernhard—not a "social services worker" as Beckner stated—was selected by Boulder County Social Services to conduct this interview. The interview was videotaped. Boulder Police Department officials had been allowed to prepare questions and submit them for Dr. Bernhard to ask Burke during the interview. BPD officers were also among those who were allowed to watch the interview through a one-way mirror. The Evaluation of the Child Report prepared by Boulder Social

Services following this interview stated: "From the interview, it is clear that Burke was not a witness to JonBenét's death."

3. A June 26, 1998 *Daily Camera* article entitled "Police Question JonBenét's Brother" stated that Burke was interviewed two weeks earlier in Atlanta by a detective from Broomfield, Colorado, a town 13 miles southeast of Boulder. The detective conducted the interview as a representative of the Boulder District Attorney's Office. Burke's Atlanta-based lawyer, who had negotiated the terms of the interview, was present. The interview took a total of six hours and was conducted in multiple parts from June 10 to June 12, 1998.

4. Burke testified before the grand jury that was convened in May 1999 to investigate his sister's murder. At the time, he answered questions from a number of sources. A Boulder Police Department liaison, Sergeant Tom Wickman, was present during the grand jury proceedings. He worked with the grand jury attorneys and, as a representative of the Boulder Police Department, would have submitted to those attorneys questions for witnesses, including Burke Ramsey. No cross-examination by Burke's attorney was allowed due to the rules of these grand jury proceedings.

Reddit Participant: Now that Burke is an adult, has anyone asked him to submit to an interview?

Beckner: Yes, we had two detectives fly out to meet with him at his residence to see if he would sit down and talk to us. He refused and later his lawyer told us not to contact him again.

**Author Comments:** The residence was Burke's apartment at Purdue University, where he was attending school. According to BPD records, two detectives and a sergeant flew to Burke's university to try to interview him without calling to ask first. The trip cost $5,000, according to information provided by the BPD via e-mail in response to a Colorado Open Records request.

Reddit Participant: Were you surprised at Burke's unwillingness to submit to an interview a few years ago?
Beckner: No, it was a typical Ramsey response.

**Author Comments:** This question also referred to the arrival of three BPD officers, two detectives and a sergeant, at Burke Ramsey's Purdue University apartment during finals week in his senior year of college. The police officers arrived unannounced, knocked on his apartment door and requested an interview. In a later interview with the author of this book, Burke said, "It's finals week. I didn't have time to do anything but study and take tests. They were very polite and nice, but I don't see why they flew all the way out there. Why were there three of them? It was a bit of overkill. Why didn't they call first or just call as opposed to traveling all that way? It wasn't that professional. If you want to do an interview, contact me. Don't just show up at my door." His answer to their request: "No, thanks."

Reddit Participant: Has BPD ever successfully obtained the medical records for Burke?
Beckner: No.

**Author Comments:** According to official documentation, the Ramseys signed more than 100 releases for records, including Burke's medical records. The Ramseys also supplied their son's medical records to Boulder Social Services, and the Boulder Police Department had access to them. The Boulder County grand jury, and thus the Boulder Police Department, also had Burke's medical records. BPD was also able to gain access to the Ramsey's pediatrician's safe deposit box where he stored both sets of records from each child. So BPD did have Burke's medical records.

## THE CRIME

Reddit Participant: What do you believe actually happened to JonBenét? Who do you think [was] responsible?

Beckner: We know from the evidence she was hit in the head very hard with an unknown object . . . The blow knocked her into deep unconsciousness . . . The strangulation came 45 minutes to two hours after the head strike, based on the swelling on the brain . . . While the head wound would have eventually killed her, the strangulation actually did kill her. The rest of the scene we believe was staged . . .

**Author Comments:** The former chief's statement that "The strangulation came 45 minutes to two hours after the head strike, based on the swelling on the brain" was not supported by the official autopsy report. According to the Boulder County Coroner's report of the autopsy for JonBenét Ramsey, "Cause of death of this six year old female is asphyxia by strangulation associated with craniocerebral trauma." Both injuries were the cause of death. The coroner stated privately he did not know which happened first, strangulation or the blow to the head, and that is what is reflected in his formal autopsy. There is no mention of swelling in the brain in the autopsy. There was a hemorrhage inside her head which was an indication to the coroner that she was still alive at the time of the massive blow because of the bleeding. The Boulder County Coroner's references to the head wounds sustained by JonBenét Ramsey included "area of hemorrhage" and "a contusion [that] measures 8 inches in length."

Beckner's statement that "The strangulation actually did kill her," is also unsubstantiated by the autopsy report. The Boulder County Coroner listed two causes of death in his autopsy: strangulation and head trauma. By law in Colorado, the coroner is the expert in the case.

Reddit Participant: Did you find any sign of a struggle at all?

Beckner: Other than her injuries, no.

**Author Comments:** According to the autopsy report, DNA was found underneath JonBenét's fingernails. This finding could have indicated that she had been involved in a struggle. There were also scratch marks on her neck that could have indicated that she struggled to loosen the garrote that was being used to strangle her.

Reddit Participant: Is there an earliest and latest time you can confirm as the time of death?
Beckner: We believe it was around 1:00 a.m.

**Author Comments:** The Boulder County Coroner did not list a time of death for JonBenét Ramsey in his autopsy.

The following question referred to the fact that JonBenét was dressed when her body was found by her father.

Reddit Participant: Does this mean the killer sexually molested her . . . and then dressed her back in her underwear and leggings?
Beckner: Yes.

**Author Comments:** It is not possible for Beckner to know or conclude that the killer removed JonBenét's clothing to assault her and then put her clothes back on her. Whoever pulled her leggings and panties down could have simply pulled them down, but not off, and then pulled them up when he was finished.

This statement followed the above question about the killer possibly replacing JonBenét's clothing after sexually assaulting her.

Reddit Participant: I guess there wasn't a time problem for the killer.
Beckner: The killer also took the time to find a pad and sharpie [sic] pen, write a 2.5 page ransom note, fashion a garrote and choke her with it, then wrap her in a blanket with one of her favorite nightgowns and place her in a storage room.

**Author Comments:** Here are reasonable alternate theories:

1. The killer was in the Ramsey home sometime or perhaps several times prior to Christmas Day, took the pad and the Sharpie with him, and composed the ransom note before he went back to the Ramsey home on Christmas with the other articles used in the murder, such as the rope and the duct tape. The Ramseys had several notepads and pens, so they may not have missed either. They were also careless about security.

2. The killer went into the home when the Ramseys were at Christmas dinner at their friends' home and rewrote the note from his own copy, using paper and a pen from the Ramsey home in the hours he spent waiting for the family to return.

## HISTORY OF SEXUAL ABUSE

Reddit Participant: Do you believe there was evidence of chronic sexual abuse with regard to JonBenét?

Beckner: Based on evidence of prior damage to her vagina and hymen, experts told us there was evidence of prior abuse. No way to really know if it was chronic.

Reddit Participant: [I have heard] the autopsy report . . . found evidence of sexual abuse prior to the night JonBenét was murdered . . . [that] there were injuries which had actually healed previously, indicating there was sexual abuse . . . prior to the crime. Is there any truth to this?

Beckner: Yes, there was evidence that would indicate prior sexual abuse.

**Author Comments:** Both of these answers from Beckner are false. No physician who examined JonBenét's body or consulted with the Boulder County Coroner said she had been sexually violated other than during the time period when she was killed. The coroner who conducted the autopsy wrote about her genitalia: "The upper portions of the vaginal vault contain no abnormalities. The prepubescent uterus measures 3 x 1 x 0.8 cm and is unremarkable. The cervical os contains no abnormalities. Both fallopian tubes and ovaries are prepubescent and unremarkable by gross examination."

The coroner, a forensic pathologist, was specifically trained in examining bodies in suspicious circumstances. The day of the autopsy, he called a medical specialist from Children's Hospital in Denver to help examine JonBenét's body. Both agreed that there had been penetration but no rape, and there was no evidence of prior violation. The Director of the Kempe Child Abuse Center in Denver, who was also consulted by the Boulder County Coroner, also stated publicly there was no evidence of prior sexual abuse of JonBenét Ramsey.

By Colorado law, JonBenét's primary pediatrician would have been prosecuted and lost his medical license if he had suspected any kind of sexual abuse during his time as her doctor and not reported it. According to him, no evidence of prior sexual assault had ever existed. He had examined JonBenét during Child Wellness examinations that included inspections of the genitalia. Four medical experts, including the Boulder County Coroner who performed the autopsy, all agreed there was no prior sexual assault. They were all involved in the case.

**Perspective:** In February of 1997 during two consecutive weeks, there were two damaging leaks indicating "incest" was what was being investigated. "Prior sexual abuse" would have to be accurate for these rumors to be true: First, there was a story about the Boulder Police Department checking into the death of John's oldest daughter in a car accident in 1992. The police were focused on whether friends of daughter, Beth, had ever talked of any sexual problems with her father. They found nothing.

The second story, one week after the first, is when Boulder County District Attorney Alex Hunter confirmed he was interviewing a former Miss America from Colorado, Marilyn VanDerbur Atler. She had gone public years before that she was a victim of incest allegedly by her father. The message for all who read it was that John Ramsey was being investigated for incest—sexually abusing his daughter JonBenét. There was "no prior sexual abuse" according to the three experts who consulted with the Boulder County Coroner, so there was no incest. It was an irresponsible action to suggest and rumor about John Ramsey.

## DNA TESTING

These questions referred to new DNA testing that led then Boulder District Attorney Mary Lacy to exonerate the Ramseys in 2008. It also referred to a book by Jim Kolar, who worked on the Ramsey murder investigation for one year in the Boulder District Attorney's Office.

Reddit Participant: Can you comment on the usefulness of the new DNA testing that apparently exonerated the parents? I read Foreign Faction by James Kolar, and he asserts that the DNA in no way exonerates them . . . I'd be very interested to see a rebuttal, if there is one."

Beckner: Sorry, I can't provide the rebuttal, as I agree with Jim Kolar. Exonerating anyone based on a small piece of evidence that has not yet been proven to even be connected to the crime is absurd in my opinion.

Reddit participant: What would be some examples of reasonable explanations for where the DNA could come from?

Beckner: Manufacturing process is one. Interactions with other people is another. Intentional placement is another. Belongs to an intruder is another. Yes you can often tell where DNA comes from. In this case, it is small enough that it is difficult to tell. CBI thought it was either sweat or saliva.

**Author Comments:** These answers about DNA are what Beckner retracted in the *Daily Camera* three days after his online interview session, as discussed earlier in this epilogue. Referring to the DNA findings he told the *Daily Camera,* "In my opinion, at this point, that's your suspect." Then, Beckner deleted his online interview including questions and answers.

The "small piece of evidence" that Beckner referred to in his Reddit answer was actually five different DNA samples taken from JonBenét's clothing and body, and three were substantial enough to be included in the FBI CODIS DNA databank. Those samples were also substantial enough to determine that they were all from the same unknown male, and not from any member of the Ramsey family.

In 1997, two different organizations (the Colorado Bureau of Investigation and Cellmark Diagnostics in Maryland) tested DNA that was found in three places on JonBenét: mixed with blood in her panties, under fingernails on her left hand, and under fingernails on her right hand. The three samples tested had indicators that they matched one another, and all the samples were from the same unknown male.

In 2008, a new and advanced DNA test (touch DNA) was used on JonBenét's clothing and two new areas of DNA were found, one on each side of the waistband of her long johns. The waistband was a previously untested area. Boulder District Attorney Mary Lacy hired the Bode Technology Group in Virginia, which used the new, advanced DNA technique. Bode concluded that the newly discovered 2008 DNA matched the 1997 DNA profile from JonBenét's panties and fingernails. This DNA matched no one in the Ramsey family; not John, not Patsy, not their children nor immediate relatives.

In June 2008, Boulder District Attorney Mary Lacy wrote a public letter of apology to John Ramsey and his family, clearing them of any involvement in JonBenét's murder because of the newly uncovered DNA evidence. Although she had already died of brain cancer in 2006, Patsy was included in the exoneration.

## WHO DID IT

Reddit Participant: If this case could be solved with your gut instinct as evidence, how would it be solved?
Beckner: Through a confession.

**Author Comments:** Beckner told the *Daily Camera* three days after his original Reddit interview, as part of his retraction of the DNA portion of that interview, the suspect would be found through a DNA match, not a confession.

## NEW INFORMATION

Reddit Participant: Is there any information not publicly available that, in your estimation, would be considered "huge" to followers of the case?
Beckner: There is some information that is not yet public, but nothing that would be considered huge or definitive.

**Author Comments:** For the first time ever, the reports of the Boulder Police Department officers and detectives who arrived on the scene first that day are released in this book. Whether the information in these reports is "huge" is up to the reader.

Information is also provided in this book related to the personal perspectives of the Ramsey attorneys from an interview with the author, and to the fact that those attorneys did not charge John Ramsey any fees after the autumn of 1997 because they felt the Ramseys were innocent and being railroaded.

This book also contains excerpts from John Ramsey's personal journal that were written over a period of eleven months beginning in January 1997, as well as excerpts from personal and sometimes emotional interviews conducted through the years with both John and Patsy Ramsey.

Finally, Burke Ramsey is interviewed for the first time publically.

While the author of this book considers all of the information included within its pages to be critical to a complete understanding of the very complex and often misguided investigation of the murder of JonBenét Ramsey, it is up to the reader to determine what, and whom, to believe.

# EPILOGUE II

TO THE PERSON WHO KNOWS, IF YOU ARE STILL ALIVE:

Isn't it time to tell someone what happened and why? What about the souvenir you took? You seem clever enough to divulge your story without being caught. So why don't you?

(Above) JonBenét's cursive signature. © John Ramsey. (Below) JonBenét at Statue of Liberty. © John Ramsey.

# NOTES

CHAPTER ONE

[1]The FBI, CBI, BPD and other law enforcement agencies contributed or wrote reports referenced in the Murder Book Index. They are listed as Boulder Police Department (BPD) Reports as there is no consistent delineation in the material obtained as to the originating agency. Only report numbers are provided.

CHAPTER TWO

[1]The time listed in the WHYD Archive from police records is 5:45, which is probably not accurate. Patsy reportedly did not call friends until after her 911 call was officially recorded as coming in to police dispatch at 5:52 a.m.

[2] WHYD Investigative Archive.

[3] Whitson's comments were made exclusively to this author for this book.

[4] National Forensic Science Technology Center, "Preliminary Documentation and Evaluation of the Scene," *Crime Scene Investigation—A Guide for Law Enforcement,* Revised September 2011.

[5] Ibid., "Turn Over Control of the Scene and Brief Investigator(s) in Charge."

[6] Ibid., "Conduct Scene 'Walk-Through' and Initial Documentation."

[7] JonBenét Ramsey Murder Book Index.

[8] Ibid.

CHAPTER THREE

[1]The entire ransom note with the original handwriting is reprinted in Chapter 4.

[2]Whitson wrote a book about the Ramsey murder case that he published in 2012. In his book, *Injustice*, he stated his belief that JonBenét was killed by a psychopath and not by her parents.

[3]National Forensic Science Technology Center, "Secured and Control Persons at the Scene," *Crime Scene Investigation—A Guide for Law Enforcement* (Revised September 2011).

CHAPTER FIVE

[1]The Ramsey wedding photos were not included in this book because we were unable to locate the photographer for permission to use them.

CHAPTER SEVEN

[1]Chris Dunker, "The anatomy of a drug investigation," *Beatrice Daily Sun* (February 1, 2013).

[2]National Institute of Justice, *A Guide to Death Investigation* (June 2011).

[3]Ibid., "Arriving at the Death Scene."

[4]Ibid., "Evaluating the Scene."

CHAPTER EIGHT

[1]Bureau of Justice Assistance, U.S. Department of Justice, "10 Things Law Enforcement Executives Can Do To Positively Impact Homicide Investigation Outcomes," (2013).

[2]*A Guide to Death Scene Investigation* (June 2011).

CHAPTER NINE

[1]Mike Byrd, "Written Documentation at a Crime Scene," Miami-Dade Police Department Crime Scene Investigation.

[2] In some places in the JonBenét Ramsey Murder Book Index, police report numbers were followed by the word "Source." These references are duplicated throughout this book.

[3]Department of Justice, "Evaluating the Scene," *A Guide to Death Scene Investigation* (June 2011).

[4]Ibid., "Collect, Inventory and Safeguard Property and Evidence."

CHAPTER TEN

[1]In his autopsy report, Boulder County Coroner Dr. John Meyer would not give a time of death for JonBenét Ramsey. Later, he wrote about speculation in media reports regarding the time of death in this case: "The time of an 'unwitnessed' death is very difficult to determine with any precision and, at best, is an estimate based on autopsy findings but also on investigative information." (Date of Report 8-13-1997.)

[2]http://www.encyclopedia.com/doc/1G2-3448300444.html.

[3]Visits numbered more than thirty, according to medical records listed by the Boulder Police Department and the Boulder District Attorney's Office.

[4]Children's Hospital Colorado Website, Bedwetting, Reviewed by Marcella

A. Escoto, DO (August 2015) https://childrenscolorado.org/nighttime-wetting. https://childrenscolorado.org/department of urology/bedwetting.

[5]The complete autopsy report is on the website for the book: www.wehaveyourdaughter.net.

CHAPTER ELEVEN

[1]Three metro Denver newspapers were studied from NewsLibrary.com and LexisNexis as part of research for this book: the *Daily Camera* (aka the *Boulder Daily Camera*), the *Denver Post*, and the *Rocky Mountain News*. All major national broadcast news archives at that time, which consisted of ABC, CBS, CNN and NBC, recorded at the Vanderbilt University Broadcast News Archives in Nashville, Tennessee, were also examined. Newspaper as well as television broadcasts dating from December 26, 1996, to January 1998, were analyzed as well. More recently, Denver's Fox 31 and national broadcasts were examined with regard to the 2011 coverage of Burke Ramsey. No complete and centrally located archive of all local television and local radio broadcasts from the 1996–1997 time period exists. For this reason, less extensive comparisons were made using these sources.

[2]Charlie Brennan, "Police Puzzle Over Girl's Slaying," *Rocky Mountain News* (December 28, 1996).

[3]NewsLibrary.com.

CHAPTER TWELVE

[1]"Interviewing vs Interrogation," Policetraining.net (April 2012)

[2]"Developing an Interview Strategy," PoliceLink, No date.

[3]"Interviewing vs. Interrogation," Policetraining.net (April 2012).

CHAPTER THIRTEEN

[1]Vanderbilt Broadcast Archives.

CHAPTER FOURTEEN

[1]Steve Thomas wrote a book about the Ramsey case that was published two years after he resigned from the BPD and while the investigation was still active and open. Thomas stated in his book that he believed Patsy Ramsey had killed her daughter, and John and Patsy Ramsey sued Thomas and his publisher for libel. Thomas's publishers were ordered to pay John and Patsy Ramsey damages. The case referred to here is not that case.

[2]WHYD Investigative Archive.

[3]In the mid-1990s, the name of this agency was the Colorado Department

of Social Services, but that name would soon change to the Colorado Department of Human Services. Both names used in this book refer to the same state agency. While the state agency oversaw county agencies, counties in Colorado managed local cases with considerable independence. The Ramsey case was handled by Boulder County Human Services.

CHAPTER FIFTEEN

[1]Pageant information was primarily obtained from Patsy and John Ramsey's first book, *The Death of Innocence.* Police documents, personal interviews and the Internet were also used as sources.

CHAPTER SIXTEEN

[1]The Stines have given permission for their names to be included in this book. This is why their names are not redacted throughout, as others are for privacy.

[2]WHYD Investigative Archive.

[3]WHYD Investigative Archive.

[4]The weather reporting stations for Boulder at that time were located at the Jefferson County Airport and in West Broomfield, a suburb in west Denver. Individual citizens fed into those weather reporting systems.

[5]WHYD Investigative Archive.

CHAPTER SEVENTEEN

[1]Vanity Fair, a monthly magazine about celebrities and newsmakers, had 1.228 million readers a year in 2015 (Source: Alliance for Audited Media, Snapshot Report – 12-31-2015). Wikipedia describes it as a "magazine of popular culture, fashion, and current affairs published by Conde Nast."

[2]Ann Louise Bardach worked as a contributing editor at *Vanity Fair* and has written for publications including the *New York Times,* the *Washington Post, Los Angeles Times, The Atlantic, New Republic* and *The Daily Beast.* According to her biography, she has appeared on several highly rated television news programs and has written several books.

[3]NewsLibrary.com.

CHAPTER EIGHTEEN

[1]The entire Foster letter is on the website for this book: www.wehaveyourdaughter.net.

CHAPTER NINETEEN

[1]Several Internet searches show the "papoose" style of wrapping a child in some cases covers the child's feet, but in other cases does not cover the child's feet. Also, some "papoose" photographs show the papoose does not cross over itself, but is lined up straight. Proponents of the theory that the manner in which JonBenét's body was wrapped indicates guilt on the part of the Ramseys should remember that John Ramsey found his daughter and at the suggestion of attorneys interrogating him, he used the word "papoose."

CHAPTER TWENTY-ONE

[1]Vanderbilt University Broadcast News Archives.

CHAPTER TWENTY-THREE

[1]Ken Salazar, a US senator from Colorado in 2005, was interior secretary for the Obama Administration from 2009 until he resigned in April 2013.

[2]Troy Eid was US attorney for the District of Colorado from 2006 to 2009.

CHAPTER TWENTY-FOUR

[1]There were no figures for the actual number of people who voted in the *Los Angeles Times* poll.

[2]The entire Garnett letter is on the website: www.wehaveyourdaughter.net.

CHAPTER TWENTY-FIVE

[1]The entire report of Judge Carnes is on the website for the book: www.wehaveyourdaughter.net.

CHAPTER TWENTY-SIX

[1]There are several precedents for bodies being carried in suitcases that can be found on the Internet. One example: In Geneva, Wisconsin, on June 5, 2014, two women's bodies were found in two different suitcases by highway workers. A security officer who was arrested for their deaths said he had met both women online.

[2]"He" is used in referencing a possible suspect based on DNA findings.

CHAPTER TWENTY-SEVEN

[1]Portions of the www.Reddit.com interview with former Chief Beckner are in Epilogue I of this book. Included is additional information from police documentation obtained by this author that in some cases contradicts what the

former chief wrote in that interview.

[2]CODIS—NDIS Statistics. Source: FBI, March 2015.

[3]Steve Reilly, "Tens of Thousands of Rape Kits Go Untested in USA," *USA TODAY* (July 16, 2015).

[4]Congressional Research Service, "DNA Testing in Criminal Justice: Background, Current Law, Grants, and Issues" (December 2012).

[5]WHYD Investigative Archive.

CHAPTER TWENTY-EIGHT

[1]WHYD Investigative Archive.

[2]Related travel records and expense reports for the three officers involved were provided via e-mail by the Boulder Police Department in response to a Colorado Open Records Act request.

[3]Brendan Nyhan and Jason Reifler, "When Corrections Fail: The Persistence of Political Misperceptions," *Political Behavior* 32(2) (2010): 303–330. Brendan Nyhan was then a Robert Wood Johnson Foundation scholar at University of Michigan. Jason Reifler was then Assistant Professor, Department of Government, Georgia State University.

EPILOGUE

[1]Vernon Geberth, Hendon Media Group: Law Enforcement Publications and Conferences. "Homicide Unit. . . and its Commander," *Law and Order*, (November 2011).

# AUTHOR'S NOTE

DETECTIVE LOU SMIT'S BATTLE with colon cancer was brief; eight weeks between diagnosis and his death in August of 2010. He remained committed to the Ramsey's innocence believing that an intruder, "a sexual predator," killed JonBenét.

During a visit with him shortly before he died, he clasped my hand from his hospice bed and looked at me with exhausted eyes. "You know, I'll know before you will who the killer is."

Lou was a man of strong religious convictions and his conclusion was that of the two alternatives, he would be going to heaven to spend his after-life there.

I smiled and replied, "Is there some way you'll be able to send a signal or sign of who the killer is?"

In his sincerest, but weakened voice, "I would, but I don't know what the rules are there yet."

There is a binder with Angels and Hearts on the cover. Inside are letters and pictures to JonBenét's parents from her school classmates. A friend had kept it for the family all these years and John had just found it and was looking at it for the first time.

The children who painted the pictures and wrote the notes to the family and JonBenét are now in their twenties, like JonBenét would be. They didn't understand what death or murder meant when they wrote their notes and drew their pictures. But their innocence adds depth to the portrait of the little girl they knew. Teacher and student names have been changed for privacy.

The bookbinder is covered with smiling gingham angels with wings and hearts. The book clasp is a heart. Inside, the colors red, yellow, green,

Binder with angels and hearts prepared for the Ramsey family by JonBenét's kindergarten class in 1997. It included drawings from her classmates. © John Ramsey

turquoise, orange and blue burst out of the pages. They are happy colors, just like those JonBenét used in her own drawings. There are rainbows and flowers and pictures of JonBenét.

"This is JonBenét holding a flower," writes a classmate, in a childish scrawl with a drawing of a red flower held by a girl in a turquoise shirt with blonde hair and a smile on her face.

Another drawing has a pink heart with JonBenét's name in purple and the words "JonBenét was my best friend. I rele mis her."

There are suns and houses and trees, and in every one of the pictures of JonBenét, she wears a smile. That's what her friends and teachers conveyed. She always smiled.

"JonBenét, JonBenét. I liked her a lot. She's an angel now up in the sky," from a friend who painted flowers and a happy JonBenét.

One of her teachers tells how JonBenét helped clean up a closet and shared a cupcake when they were short one at a birthday party. The teacher recalled sending JonBenét to the school nurse with a sick student. She was used to being around sickness because of her mother's cancer. To her, it was simply part of her life. She was kind, the teacher wrote, and

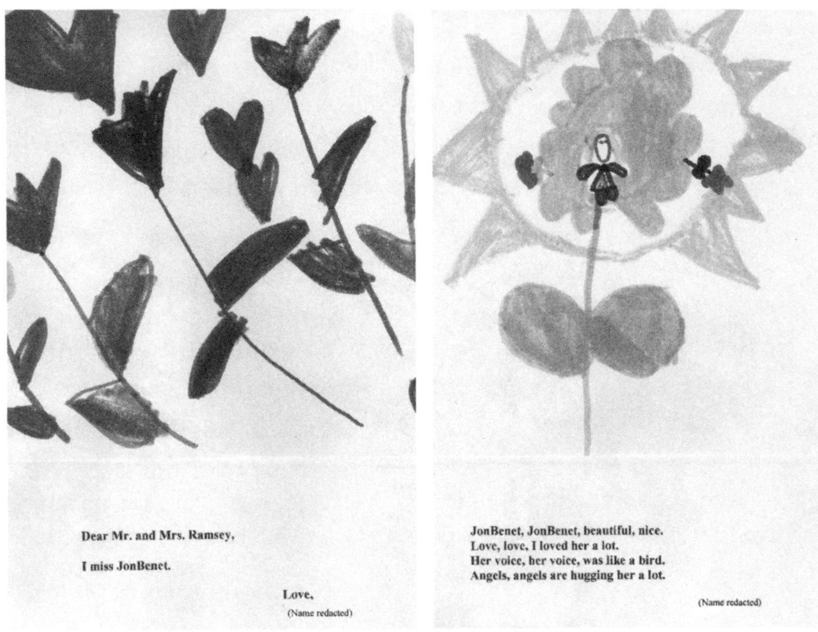


Drawings from JonBenét's classmates for the Ramsey family after her murder. © John Ramsey

Dear Ramsey Family,

It was a pleasure and a privilege to have JonBenet as a student in my class. She was truly an exceptional child. She was smart, hard working, artistic - but the quality that shone so brightly above everything else was her compassion and caring for others. It was a caring that went way beyond just being nice or having good manners. It was a reflection of the beautiful inner person of JonBenet.

At the beginning of the school year our coat closet was always a mess because there were no hooks on which to hang coats. The closet irritated me day after day. One day JonBenet came to me and said quietly, "I can fix it for you." She not only arranged the closet that day, but she "fixed it" on many more days without my asking, saying anything, or even remembering to thank her. When someone in the class needed to go to the nurse's office, she was often the person I asked to escort them because she was so good at helping people who were hurt or sick. JonBenet lived out her faith of serving others with a quietness, completeness and simplicity that few adults ever achieve.

JonBenet was able to accomplish so much in her life because she made decisions based on enthusiasm for life and caring for others. She wasn't afraid to tackle the dirtiest classroom job, or to sing in front of a group, or to help a child who was sick or hurt. The joy and love that she brought to those around her shows in the hearts of the children in the class. We will all miss her greatly.

As I look back on our time together, I realize now that JonBenet was the teacher and I was the student. I learned so much from her example about making compassion and caring for others a part of life.

Thank you, JonBenet, for teaching me that we don't have to wait to be in heaven to be angels. We can be angels in this life by how we live every day.

With Love, (Teacher name and signature redacted)

Kindergarten teacher's letter to Ramsey family about JonBenét.

always asked her classmate how she felt. JonBenét also assured the sick child that the nurse or their mom or dad would make them feel better.

Another teacher said once when she saw JonBenét walking down the hall "she gave me a wide smile, a bear hug and she stuck like glue and we walked down the hall together, her feet on my feet and arms around my middle, muddling along."

"Thank you, JonBenét, for teaching me that we don't have to wait to be in heaven to be angels," wrote another teacher.

Recently, John sat alone in a chair and opened the Book of Angels for the first time. He was reluctant because he was unsure how he would react. For many years now, he has tried to keep his emotions on an even keel. It's one of the ways he has survived the trauma. He finds it very difficult to be reminded in detail of the past. Still he feels he owes it to himself, his daughter, and JonBenét's classmates from so very long ago, to look at their work. He leafed through the binder slowly, running his hands across some of the pictures and silently mouthing the scrawled inscriptions.

"I had forgotten what joy there is with a six-year-old," he said as he looked at page after page of the sweetness that was in his daughter's life.

And then, he put his hand on his forehead and partly covered his eyes as they filled with tears.

In early 1997, I reported that two expert sources, one from the prosecution and one from the defense, said it was "highly unlikely" that John or Burke Ramsey had written the bizarre ransom note and "unlikely" that Patsy Ramsey had written it. The report created a big push-back from the then Director of the Colorado Bureau of Investigation. An employee in his agency was examining the note. The Director charged the report wasn't accurate and appeared on television and radio saying that no one on the prosecution side believed it was "unlikely" Patsy Ramsey had written the ransom note.

What followed was a reporter's classic dilemma—what to reveal and what not to reveal when "legitimate sources" are involved. I needed to honor my commitment of protection to the prosecution source, thus I was unable to vigorously counter the allegations. To do so would have exposed the source by inference. It is likely that source would have been fired had I continued to defend my reporting with sources from both the prosecution and defense sides on the handwriting in the ransom note.

The accuracy of that source was proven in late October of 1997, when the Boulder Police Department decided to get more than just one handwriting analyst's report. The BPD carefully expanded their pool of experts. An analyst for the Secret Service, considered among the world's leading document authorities, wrote in his report to the BPD that there was no evidence Patsy Ramsey wrote the note. She never was arrested with regard to her handwriting and the ransom note, because there wasn't ample proof and the Secret Service information has not become public until now. This is a behind-the-scenes look about the complexities in understanding the commitment of balanced reporting and the involvement with protection of a source that was part of this book.

In the early days after JonBenét's death, what no one outside the Ramsey inner circle realized were the hundreds of letters the family received internationally, expressing sympathy to them. It's a new perspective of the support they got from those who didn't know them. Some of those letters and cards were simply addressed to "The Ramsey Family" and were delivered wherever they were staying. An example:

> We believe you. We are praying for you and are so very sorry.
> (Name Withheld) Canada

There are two current law enforcement officers whom I consider very thoughtful and observant. They are former Boulder police officers who talked just briefly with me about the morale of some of the men and women in their department after the murder when they were still working there. "It was picking up their chins off the floor. It was trying to find the killer of a child. There isn't anything worse when we are supposed to serve and protect. It was reinforcing to them that there were very good officers in the department. It was telling them not to watch late-night television entertainment shows where there were skits making fun of Boulder police and their incompetence. It was getting them to believe in themselves again."

After the murder, a highly regarded homicide expert and then Denver Police Sergeant Jon Priest was asked to come to Boulder to teach basic Crime Scene Investigation for three months to every member of the department.

Those in law enforcement who made the decision to talk about the case for this book, but didn't want to be identified, have my great gratitude and respect. It was unnerving for some of them and many didn't want to go back to remembering that awful time in detail. But they did it mostly because they thought it was the right decision for them. In listening to them and rechecking their information, they were straightforward, forthcoming and insightful. They are the best in law enforcement officers—honest and honorable.

To the readers of this book, thank you for your time and comments. This is the best information that I could research and gather, but it's certainly not all of it. I was prompted to write this book because of curiosity about what I didn't know, even after reporting on the story for these many years. I began writing the book in mid-2009.

Those of you who are devoted to this business and have a passion for journalism deserve a thank you for staying with and continuing to do the best in tough times. Investigating and reporting what happens with accuracy is so important to our society. My best conversations were with a lot of you when hashing out what to include, what not to include and why, and I'm reminded how many truly committed people there are who do it right.

# ACKNOWLEDGMENTS

THERE WAS SIMPLY NO WAY TO WRITE THIS BOOK without help from many intelligent people who believed it was important to contribute and be heard for this project.

To Sandra Bond, my agent, and believer in the book. Thank you for your support through all the ups and downs of getting it published.

To Stephen White, best-selling fiction author of more than twenty novels on crime, who patiently shared his knowledge of the book business, including selling, writing, encouragement, and advice to a first-time book writer. Stephen, you are so important to me. Thank you.

Editors Marjorie Braman, news veteran Jim Trotter, and Karen Carter helped in so many ways. They were logical and supportive and awfully good with their critiques.

To readers Lisa Holste, Cindy Pena, Deborah Sherman, Chris Vanderveen and those who willingly took the time for expert opinion including Amber Raile, PhD, Communication, Erin Koterba, PhD, Psychology, Elizabeth Johnson, PhD, an expert in DNA. Joe Russomanno PhD, from Arizona State University and the Walter Cronkite School of Journalism and Mass Communication was of particular help. It was great to learn from all of you.

The research librarians consulted at the following libraries were incredibly helpful: The Norlin Library at the University of Colorado in Boulder and the Denver Public Library, in particular Research Librarian Ellen Zazzarino, and the Auraria Library in Denver and Research Librarian Louise Treff Gangler. The research librarians gave so much thought to how we could research and solve various questions on a case that still doesn't have many answers.

The University of Colorado Hospital Anschutz Cancer Pavilion

Outpatient Treatment Center and their nurses and patients do wonderful work. Thanks to those who let me be there and absorb the culture of cancer and talk with the nurses in telling me why they choose people with cancer. And thanks also to Dr. Pat Moran and the Rocky Mountain Cancer Center, Boulder Division, for their expertise with cancer and its treatment and in this case, treatment of Patsy Ramsey.

Tina Simms from New York got this whole thing started by believing in the book and proceeding to proactively help me find an agent. Thanks Tina for that phone call.

It was a delight to get to know and appreciate research and editorial assistants, Jaclyn Grossfield and Erin Maher who always had that one idea to make the book better.

Former Denver Chief Deputy District Attorney and current defense attorney Craig Silverman and Lynn Kimbrough with the Denver DA's Office, thank you for your informed opinions.

To those in the public, who, when they found out about this book, were willing to discuss what they thought about the case and why and whether they believed the killer was an intruder or a member of the Ramsey family: thank you. You taught me a lot.

Thanks to Kate Montgomery who understands negotiation and Emma Williams and Kristin Wamsley for your writing insights. Also, much appreciation goes to chapter readers Dennis, Nancy, Ann, Kathie, Rick, Tiffany, Brooke, Ashley, Liam, Sophia, Landon, Myles, Kittrin, Lily, Wyatt, and Holden.

To Susan and Sue, two very smart women who have strong points of view, a willingness to share concrete information, many documents to help the book, and who were never shy in sharing their opinions.

Thanks to Susan Baldacci and Ashleigh Walters for always being so supportive and also teaching me about social media.

More thanks to the district attorney people in several jurisdictions, police officers and sheriff deputies, and former FBI agents and FBI profilers who gave invaluable time and attention. Your fact and opinion were incisive and thoughtful.

New York City entertainment attorney Bob Stein was a smart and valuable partner during critical times in negotiations. Thank you, Bob, for your logical and honest advice. Attorney Steven Zansberg had just the right information to help the book immensely.

To Dave Cullen, author of *Columbine*, and the long conversations we had about journalism and journalists and what happened on this case and others. Dave brings me to journalists who understand dedication, working hard to get it right and why a free press (despite its many questionable moments) is so important. It takes courage on some of these stories, and the accuracy and time spent in getting the extra perspective is always worth it. The trust given to us by others who confide still leaves me somewhat awed. Thank you for giving the information that breaks through the bureaucracy and leads to the truth.

And a special thanks to Deborah Sherman and Dan Weaver for the friendship, their unwavering support and help. They were there from the beginning and always seemed to know when that supportive text or phone call was needed.

Thank you to my wonderful family, each and every one of you, for your support and patience.

To the readers: It is encouraging to meet so many people who simply want enough credible information to decide for themselves.

When the tragic happened in my own life, thank you to so many of you for helping me through and being there still. Time passes, the loss lessens, but doesn't end: Alan and Lani, Marc and Sydney, Mark and Kerry, Nancy and Dennis, Amy H. and Cortney M., Amy B. and Kristin W., Kathie and Rick, my family, and so many wonderful friends and colleagues.

Tommy Collier of Tommy Collier Productions is so good at what he does as was Greg Moore of the *Denver Post*. They helped immensely.

Thank you to publisher David Wilk.

Once more, thanks to you all. It was nice to meet or reconnect with you.

# DOCUMENTS

The following Boulder Police Department documents include information only from the morning of December 26, 1996, the day JonBenét's body was found.

The first report is written by the first police responder on the scene: Officer Rick French.

**FIELD REPORT**
**NARRATIVE AND SUPPLEMENT**

Page No. 3 | CASE NO. P96-21871

| DATE OF REPORT (mo./day/year) | TIME | COMPLAINANT-VICTIM |
|---|---|---|
| 12-26-96 | 1300 | Ramsey |

NARRATIVE

X-STOLEN D-DAMAGED R-RECOVERED

DESCRIPTION | SERIAL | UCR | VALUE (LOSS) | RECOVERED

NARRATIVE: I responded to 755 15th st. in the city and county of Boulder, Colorado at approximately 0555 hours on the 26th of December 1996 on a report of a possible kidnapping. Upon arrival I met with a distraught Patricia Ramsey and her husband, John. John advised me that their six year old daughter, Jonbenet, was missing and that their nine year old son, Burke, was asleep upstairs. John directed me through the house and pointed out a three page handwritten note which was laid on the wooden floor just west of the kitchen area. He told me that his wife had found the note on the bottom step of a spiral staircase which led to the upper levels of the house. (I'm uncertain about who moved the note.) The note advised the Ramsey's that their daughter was in the possession of a group of suspects and demanded a ransom of $118,000.00, to be delivered by a means detailed to them later in a subsequent telephone call.

I spoke with Mr. and Ms. Ramsey while Burke continued to sleep. Ms. Ramsey told me that she had gone into JonBenet's room at about 0545 hours to wake her in preparation for a short trip the family was to take later that day. She found Jonbenet's room empty and then discovered the note as she walked down the stairs. She immediately called the police.

A quick inspection of the interior of the house, as well as talking to Mr. Ramsey, indicated that there was no obvious signs of a forced entry or struggle. Mr. Ramsey told me that the house appeared to be locked up as it had been left. The Ramsey's have an alarm system inside of the house which was not engaged, as his normal for them. They have a small dog, but he had spent the night with a neighbor across the street, which is also normal. Both Mr. and Mrs. Ramsey stated they had not heard anything unusual during the night. As there was no initial refuting evidence I advised SGT Reichenbach that it was possibly an actual kidnapping and we proceeded to control the scene as such, with SGT Reichenbach paging advocates, detectives, and crime scene investigators.

Within fifteen minutes [redacted] and [redacted], and [redacted], all

12/87 BPD-8

Reporting Officer: R French No. 644 Supervisor Approval:

1 03

**BOULDER POLICE DEPARTMENT**
**FIELD REPORT**
**NARRATIVE AND SUPPLEMENT**

Page No. 4 | CASE NO. P96-21871

| DATE OF REPORT (mo./day/year) | TIME | COMPLAINANT-VICTIM |
|---|---|---|
| 2-26-96 | 2254 | RAMSEY |

NARRATIVE

X-STOLEN D-DAMAGED R-RECOVERED

DESCRIPTION | SERIAL | UCR | VALUE (LOSS) | RECOVERED

friends of the Ramsey's arrived at the house. By 0650 OFC Weiss and OFC Barklow were photograghing and fingerprinting areas of the house, and OFC Veitch had collected the ransom note. Reverend [redacted] of St. John's Episcopal church in Boulder came to the house at 0713, joining Victim Advocates [redacted] and [redacted] in the house with the others. Detectives Linda Arndt and Fred Patterson arrived at the house at about 0810 hours.

I was concerned with gathering information from Mr. and Ms. Ramsey. They told me that they had spent Christmas night with the [redacted], and that they arrived home at 2200 hours. Mr. Ramsey said he read to both kids for a short time and then they were in bed by 2230 hours. Ms. Ramsey said that Jonbenet had been dressed in white long underwear and a red turtleneck. Jonbenet's and Burke's bedrooms are separate and are located on the second floor of the three story house, with the master bedroom on the top floor. Jonbenet's bedroom has an access door to a second floor porch which was locked and undamaged.

As Mr. Ramsey made preliminary telephone calls to gather the demanded amount of money he told me that the only other people with keys to the house are their house-keeper, [redacted], and two relatives in Atlanta, Ga. Ms. Ramsey told me that [redacted] had spoken to her by telephone on the morning of the 24th and asked for a loan of two thousand dollars. [redacted] had called again later that day and seemed upset about an arguement with her sister, and she made plans with Ms. Ramsey to come by the Ramsey's house while they were out of town and pick up a check which the Ramsey's would leave for them.

When [redacted], Patricia Ramsey's mother, was advised by telephone of the incident, she asked that the officers on scene be told of [redacted] often commenting on how beautiful Jonbenet was and if Ms. Ramsey was concerned about her being kidnapped. Mrs. Paughs comments were relayed to me by [redacted].

Reporting Officer: R. French No. 644 Supervisor Approval:

12/87 BPD-8

FIELD REPORT
NARRATIVE AND SUPPLEMENT

Page No. 5 CASE NO. P96-21871

| DATE OF REPORT (mo./day/year) | TIME | COMPLAINANT-VICTIM |
| --- | --- | --- |
| 12-26-96 | 2317 | RAMSEY |

ATIVE

X-STOLEN D-DAMAGED R-RECOVERED

DESCRIPTION | SERIAL | UCR | VALUE (LOSS) | RECOVERED

These factors relating to ███ were given to DET Arndt and she began to develop background information on ███. Ms. Ramsey told me further that ███ ███ lived in Ft. Lupton with her husband, ███, and a 12 year old daughter, ███. Hoffman also has two adult daughters in their twenties, ███ and ███, and she rents the house she lives in from her sister. (Unknown name.)

Two other possible suspects were given by the Ramsey's. One was an ex-emplpyee who had been fired during the past summer, and had threatened to "bring down Access Graphics," Mr. Ramsey's business. His name is ███. Mr. Ramsey contacted his personnnel department to gather information on ███ for the detectives.

The second person mentioned was ███ (H: ███), who lives in Louisville. She was Jonbenet's nanny up until two years ago and had a very close relationship with her. This relationship was the only reason ███ was mentioned as the Ramsey's were trying to allow for all possiblities.

Between times of consulting with the detectives and the family I walked through the lower level of the house and the garage, looking for obvious evidence. Although somewhat messy due to the season the residence did not look out of order. In the basement I attempted to open the door leading to the area where Jonbenet was ultimately found but it was secured by a wooden latch above the door. The door opened inward and I was looking for access out of the house. Since the door could not have been used for that purpose, and it was latched closed, I did not open it.

Shortly after DET SGT Whitson arrived at the house, after 1000, I was released from the scene and went to the PD to begin the original report.

Just after 1300 hours I heard radio traffic concerning a 911 call and the discovery of a code black body at the residence, and I returned to 755 15th with OFC Morgan. I spoke with ███, and he told me that Jonbenet had been found in the basement by Mr. Ramsey while ███, ███, and Mr. Ramsey were looking through the house. Mr.

12/87 BPD-8

Reporting Officer: R. French No. 644 Supervisor Approval: 1 65

**FIELD REPORT**
**NARRATIVE AND SUPPLEMENT**

Page No. 6 | CASE NO. P96-21871

| DATE OF REPORT (mo./day/year) | TIME | COMPLAINANT-VICTIM |
|---|---|---|
| 12-26-96 | 2344 | Ramsey |

NARRATIVE

X-STOLEN D-DAMAGED R-RECOVERED

DESCRIPTION | SERIAL | UCR | VALUE (LOSS) | RECOVERED

████ told me that he had opened the door to that area earlier in the morning and had not seen Jonbenet's body inside. I secured the area around where Mr. Ramsey had laid the body and assisted in getting the family and friends out of the house to close the crime scene. I left the house for the second time at approximately 0345 hours, and OFCs Weiss and Schunk were securing the front and back, respectively.

Burke Ramsey was awakened by his father shortly after ████ arrived and he was taken to the ████ residence as soon as he was dressed. I did not speak to him other than to walk him to Mr. ████ vehicle. He seemed confused and was crying, and Mr. Ramsey again told me that he had slept through the night.

EVIDENCE: See PCR's concerning collection by OFCs Veitch, Weiss and Barklow.

CONCLUSION: Preliminary indications of the abduction of Jonbenet Ramsey from the residence give way upon the discovery of her body in the residence. A homicide investigation is begun and continued by detectives, with the reclassification of this incident to be forthcoming.

RF

should this be "1545" HRS?

12/87 BPD-6

Reporting Officer: Rick French No. 644 Supervisor Approval: ________

1 06

The following is a portion of the first report of the detective who was left alone by the other BPD officers on-scene about 10 a.m. that morning. The other officers were ordered to leave the Ramsey home and go back to the Boulder Police Department or off-shift. This report is from the morning of December 26, 1996, and continues through when JonBenét's body was found shortly after 1 p.m. that day. Detective Linda Arndt was the detective.

**Detective Supplemental Report: P96-21871**
**First degree murder**
**Det. Linda Arndt**
**Date of Report: January 8, 1997**

On Dec. 26, 1996 at approx. 0635 hours I received a phone call at my home phone number from Det. Sgt. Robert Whitson. Sgt. Whitson informed me that officers were on the scene of a reported kidnapping. The reported kidnapping had occurred at 755 15th St. located in Boulder, Boulder County, Colorado. JonBenet Ramsey, a 6 year old female, was reported to have been kidnapped from her home. JonBenet's mother had found a ransom letter inside the home at approx. 0550 hours this morning. JonBenet had last been seen inside her home at approx. 2200 hours on Dec. 25, 1996. There was no apparent forced entry to the residence. Other family members who were inside the home from the night of Dec. 25 through the morning of Dec. 26 had not been harmed. These family members included JonBenet's mother, father, and brother.

In the note left by the reported kidnappers, the author of the note stated the reported kidnappers would phone the Ramseys between 0800 hours and 1000 hours. Sgt. Whitson requested that I respond to the Ramsey address on 15th St. Sgt. Whitson was going to make attempts to have US West Communications place a trace on all incoming calls placed to the Ramsey home.

I went to the Boulder Police Dept. and obtained a hand held tape recorder as well as my notebook. I met with Det. Fred Patterson at the Boulder Police Dept. (BPD). Det. Patterson and I responded to the Ramsey address located on 15th St. While at the BPD, I briefly met with BPD Ofc. Karl Veitch. Ofc. Veitch informed me that he had the ransom note which had been left by the reported kidnappers. I requested that Ofc. Veitch make 3 copies of this note. This request was carried out. I retained possession of one of the copies of the note, another copy was given to Det. Patterson, and the third copy was placed in a seal envelope and left on my desk. I quickly reviewed the contents of this 3 page note. Det. Patterson and I then responded to the Ramsey residence. Prior to arriving at the residence we met with Watch III Sgt. Paul Reichenbach. We met with Sgt. Reichenbach at the rear of the Basemar shopping center at approx. 0755 hours. Sgt. Reichenbach personally provided us with the following additional information:

> After officers had been dispatched to this call, all further communication was done by telephone rather than radio traffic. The first officer on the scene was Ofc. Rick French. Ofc. French had told Sgt. Reichenbach that something didn't seem right. The 6 year old daughter of John Ramsey, JonBenet Ramsey, had been kidnapped from her bedroom sometime between approx. 2200 hours on Dec. 25, 1996 and 0600 hours on Dec. 26, 1996. A 2 1/2 page note had been found by JonBenet's mother. Demands in this note stated that $118,000 be paid to ensure the safe return of JonBenet. No police or law enforcement were to be notified, otherwise JonBenet would be

P96-21871 2

"decapitated." The 2 1/2 page note had been found by JonBenet's mother (Patsy Ramsey) at the bottom of a spiral staircase located in the house.

John Ramsey is the president of Access Graphics. This business is located at 1426 Pearl St. in Boulder. This business is very successful.

Sgt. Reichenbach said there was a light dusting of snow on the ground when he arrived at the Ramsey residence. Sgt. Reichenbach did not notice any footprints or other tracks in the snow. Sgt. Reichenbach personally checked the exterior of the Ramsey residence. Sgt. Reichenbach did not notice any signs of forced entry to the residence.

Sgt. Reichenbach had arranged through Boulder Regional Communications Center (BRCC) dispatcher [redacted] to have a trap placed on the Ramsey home phone number. The home phone number for the John Ramsey residence is (303) [redacted]. Dispatcher [redacted] had spoken with [redacted], an employee with US West Communications. The trap was activated and in place by the time Det. Patterson and I arrived at the Ramsey residence. Sgt. Reichenbach informed me that US West Communication would need a "letter of demand" on BPD letterhead within 48 hours, explaining the necessity for this trap.

Sgt. Reichenbach had informed us that Boulder County Sheriff's Dept. (BCSD) Dep. Scott Williams was a canine officer. Dep. Williams was notified that his services may be needed, and was placed on standby. Sgt. Reichenbach also suggested that if a bloodhound's services were needed, Aurora Police Dept. might be able to assist.

Det. Patterson and I arrived at the Ramsey residence at approx. 0810 hours. I personally met with BPD Ofc. Rick French. Ofc. French provided me with a synopsis of who was on the scene and what had already been done. BPD crime scene investigator Officers Barry Weiss and Sue Barcklow were also at the Ramsey residence. Ofc. Weiss was photographing the interior and exterior of the residence. Ofc. Barcklow was attempting to obtain latent fingerprints. Areas checked included: possible points of entry and exit to the residence; as well as the spiral staircase leading from outside JonBenet's bedroom to the first floor; and the door leading into JonBenet's bedroom. Ofc. French provided me with the following information:

Ofc. French told me that when he arrived he met with Patsy Ramsey, JonBenet's mother. Patsy was very upset and distraught and it was difficult for Ofc. French to obtain information from her. Ofc. French also spoke with John Ramsey, JonBenet's father. Ofc. French learned that the

1 10

P96-21871 3

Ramsey family had been at a friend's house on the late afternoon and evening of Dec. 25, 1996. They returned home at approx. 2200 hours on Dec. 25. JonBenet and her brother, Burke, went to bed shortly after the family returned home. John Ramsey had read to JonBenet after she'd gone to bed, and before she went to sleep. JonBenet had last been seen wearing a red turtleneck and white long underwear. Patsy woke up this morning and discovered the suspected ransom note at the bottom of the spiral staircase. Patsy originally thought that the note may have been left by the housekeeper. Ofc. French had been told that the Ramsey family had been planning to leave early this morning for Michigan. The Ramsey family has a home in upper Michigan. After Patsy discovered the note she went to JonBenet's bedroom. Patsy discovered JonBenet was missing.

Ofc. French told me there was no apparent forced entry to the Ramsey home. Ofc. French had checked the Ramsey home and had not detected any sign of JonBenet. Four friends of the Ramsey's had been notified by the Ramseys of JonBenet's disappearance and were currently at the house. The pastor from the Ramsey's church had also been notified and was also present at the house. BPD Victim Advocates had been notified and were also present inside the Ramsey home.

After I had briefly met with Ofc. French I met with John Ramsey. I informed John Ramsey that US West Communications had already placed a trap on incoming phone calls made to his home. I told Mr. Ramsey that I would also like to connect a tape recorder to the incoming phone line. John Ramsey gave me his verbal permission. I asked John Ramsey for the location of the phones in the house, on the first floor. John Ramsey showed me a telephone mounted on the wall at the west end of the kitchen, and a telephone located in the den. The den is located west of the kitchen. I connected the tape recorder to the telephone located in the den. I informed Mr. Ramsey that if the author of the suspected ransom note called, we would be able to tape record the conversation. John Ramsey was informed of my actions and gave his verbal consent. After the phone recorder had been connected to the telephone in the den, I instructed John Ramsey on the use of the tape recorder. John Ramsey told me that he would answer the phone for all incoming calls.

After the tape recorder had been connected to the telephone, I met with Patsy Ramsey. Patsy was sitting on a chair in the sitting room. This room is located at the southeast corner of the house on the first floor. Two of Patsy's friends were with her, [redacted] [redacted] and [redacted] [redacted]. Patsy spoke softly when she talked to me. At times Patsy seemed to be staring off into the distance. Patsy seemed to have a vacant look, and seemed dazed. Since Patsy was situated in a room at some distance from the den, I had limited contact with her. I asked Ofc. French to remain with Patsy. I did

1-2

P96-21871 4

ask Patsy a few questions and was able to receive some information. The following is information I received from Patsy:

Patsy had gotten up on the morning of Dec. 26, 1996 and had gone down the stairs from her bedroom to the kitchen. Patsy used the back (i.e. west) stairway. The back stairway consists of a spiral staircase leading from just outside JonBenet's bedroom to the northwest corner of the first floor of the house. At the bottom of this spiral staircase Patsy discovered a 3 page handwritten note. The note had been written on legal pad sized paper. Patsy said she originally thought the note might have been left by her housekeeper. After Patsy looked at the note and read it she ran to JonBenet's bedroom. JonBenet was missing.

I asked Patsy who had keys to her home. Patsy said the woman who was responsible for housekeeping at her home, [redacted], had a key to the home. I asked Patsy if the home had an alarm system and if the alarm system had been activated on the night of Dec. 25. Patsy told me that the home does have an alarm system, however it had not been used for awhile. Patsy did tell me that she believed the house had been locked when she and the rest of her family went to bed on the night of Dec. 25. Patsy said she had not received any suspicious phone calls nor hang up phone calls in the past few weeks. There had been no unwelcome solicitors nor suspicious persons at the Ramsey home in the past few weeks.

Patsy said that she, her husband, JonBenet, and Berke (her 10 year old son) had planned on leaving Boulder on the morning of Dec. 26. The family was going to fly to Michigan to spend time at their summer home. I asked Patsy who knew about this trip. Patsy said some of her close friends knew, and the housekeeper knew. Patsy had not arranged for the neighbors or anyone else to watch their home while the Ramsey family was in Michigan.

I asked Patsy if she could think of anyone who might be responsible for JonBenet's disappearance. Patsy told me that her housekeeper, [redacted], had asked to borrow money on Dec. 24. Patsy told me that she had had a Christmas party at her home on Dec. 23. [redacted] was supposed to clean up from this party on the morning of Dec. 24. Linda Hoffman had phoned Patsy on the morning of Dec. 24. Linda Hoffman asked Patsy if she could borrow some money. Patsy had said yes. Patsy told me she had loaned money to [redacted] in the past. [redacted] phoned Patsy again on the afternoon of Dec. 24. [redacted] was crying. [redacted] said she needed to borrow $2,000. Patsy thought the money was needed for dental repair for [redacted] and her family. Patsy told [redacted] that she would write a check for $2,000. Patsy said she would leave the check on the kitchen counter. Patsy told

1 2

P96-21871 5

me that ███████ was scheduled to be at the Ramsey home on Friday morning, Dec. 27, at 0900 hours.

Patsy told me ███████ has worked as her housekeeper for about the past 2 years. ███████ cleans the Ramsey home twice a week. Ms ███████ is paid $200 a week. Patsy told me that Ms ███████ husband ███████ ███████. Patsy provided me with Ms ███████ husband's name, ███████. Patsy also supplied me with Ms ███████ home phone number, ███████. Patsy further told me that Ms ███████ adult children have had problems in the past 2 months. Patsy believed that one of Ms ███████ adult daughters had been in contact with Safe House because of domestic violence problems. Patsy did not know the name of this daughter, nor where she lived. Patsy thought the daughter lived in ███████, ██. Patsy thought the adult daughter's domestic problems might have occurred prior to Thanksgiving of 1996.

After I had spoken briefly with Patsy I returned to the den area of the house. Each time the telephone rang I was present when John Ramsey answered the phone. There were at least 3 times when John Ramsey was not present in the den when the phone rang. I personally saw John Ramsey run to the den to answer the phone. For each incoming phone call received at the Ramsey home on the morning of Dec. 26, John Ramsey told me that the caller was not associated with the suspected ransom note.

While I was in the den the pastor from ███████ Church in ███████ relayed a message to me. Patsy had told this information to the pastor. I believe the pastor's first name was ██. The pastor told me about a telephone conversation Patsy had had with her mother. Patsy's mother had spoken with the housekeeper (███████) while Patsy's mother had been living in the Ramsey home. Ms ███████ had reportedly said that JonBenet was so cute that someone would kidnap her. I met with Patsy and asked her about her telephone conversation with her mother. Patsy told me that she had spoken to her mother after she had discovered JonBenet was missing. Patsy's mother is ███████. ███████ lives in Atlanta, GA. ███████ had told Patsy that Ms ███████ had said "many times" that JonBenet was such a beautiful girl, and wasn't ███████ afraid that someone was going to kidnap her. Patsy supplied me with ███████ home phone number. This home phone number is ███████.

Det. Patterson was going to follow-up on information regarding Ms ███████ and her family. Det. Patterson was going to attempt to have US West Communications place a trace on Ms ███████ home phone number.

Within about the first 20 minutes of arriving at the Ramsey residence I asked John Ramsey if he would consent to having his office telephones have a trap placed on them. John Ramsey did give

1 22

P96-21871 6

his verbal authorization. John Ramsey supplied me with the work number for himself, as well as his first assistant. These phone numbers were: [redacted] and [redacted], respectively. Arrangements were made through US West to have a trap placed on these two phone lines at Access Graphics.

There were 2 cellular phones at the Ramsey house when Det. Patterson and I arrived. These cellular phones were used to make phone calls from the Ramsey residence. The telephone at the Ramsey house was not used to make outgoing phone calls on the morning of Dec. 26. The cellular phones belonged to John Ramsey and [redacted]. The friends who had been contacted by the Ramsey's, and who were present with the Ramseys when I arrived, were: [redacted] and [redacted]; [redacted]; and Pastor [redacted] from [redacted]. [redacted] Church in Boulder. Burke, the Ramsey's 9 year old son, had already left the residence when I had arrived. Burke was staying at the [redacted] home located at [redacted]. in Boulder.

After I had connected the tape recorder to the telephone, and had briefly met with Patsy Ramsey, I talked with John Ramsey in the den. I talked with John Ramsey about things to say when the author(s) of the suspected ransom note called. I told John that he should demand to talk to JonBenet. If John Ramsey was going to be given instructions for meeting the purported kidnappers, I instructed John Ramsey to obtain very specific instructions from the caller. John Ramsey was told to say that he would not be able to obtain the money until at least 1700 hours this date. I supplied John Ramsey with a piece of note paper. I had John Ramsey write notes on this piece of paper regarding what to say when the author(s) of the suspected ransom note phoned. I retained this notebook paper and later placed it into evidence (item 4LKA). The third item written by John Ramsey was "must talk to JB." I had placed an asterisk by this sentence.

[redacted], a friend of John Ramsey's, told John Ramsey that he would be able to obtain the ransom amount from his bank. [redacted] left the Ramsey residence after I had arrived and met with his banker. [redacted] returned to the Ramsey residence prior to about 0930 hours. [redacted] told me that he had arranged with his banker to have $118,000 in cash be available. This amount was available when [redacted] returned to the Ramsey residence. The amount had been arranged in the denominations demanded in the suspected ransom note. [redacted] told me he was able to get this amount obtained within approx. one hour of notifying his banker. [redacted] told me that $118,000 is a relatively insignificant amount compared to John Ramsey's wealth. [redacted] told me that the persons who demanded the ransom could easily have asked for $10,000,000 and had obtained that amount.

Prior to 1000 hours I remained in, or near, the den area of the house. Patsy Ramsey remained in the front sitting room area. The

P96-21871 7

friends of the Ramsey's and the pastor divided their time between Patsy and John. John Ramsey paced between the area of the den and the formal dining room. John was usually by himself. I did not see John or Patsy interact with each other. No one in the house made any obvious comment to me that it was after 1000 hours and the suspected kidnappers had not called. From the time I arrived at the Ramsey house until approx. 1000 hours I had a few brief conversations with John. I had asked John if the doors to the house had been locked when the family went to bed last night. John told me that he personally checked all of the doors and all of the windows in the home this morning. All of the doors and windows were locked. John told me that although the house does have an alarm system, the family has not used the alarm system for months. I asked John who had keys to the residence. John told me his adult son has a key to the house. The son had been in Atlanta since Dec. 15, 1996. The adult son, John Andrew, had been attending college at the University of Colorado - Boulder. Another family member, Patsy's mother, also had a key to the residence. Patsy's mother is currently living in Atlanta, GA. I asked John if any keys had been hidden outside the house. John told me there were no hidden keys. I asked John of any keys had been lost or stolen. John told me there had been no stolen or lost house keys. John told me that the housekeeper, ████████, did have a key to the house. ████ ████ was the only person living in Colorado who had a key to the Ramsey house.

John Ramsey told me that he and his family had been at a dinner party held at the ████████ home on the afternoon and evening of Dec. 25, 1996. John, Patsy, Burke, and JonBenet had returned home at approx. 2200 hours. John told me that Patsy and Burke immediately went to bed. John had read a book to JonBenet, tucked her into bed, then John went to bed. John said he went to bed at approx. 2230 hours.

John told me that he is the President and CEO of Access Graphics. There was an article in the Boulder <u>Daily Camera</u> newspaper within this past month about Access Graphics. The news article had been written because Access Graphics had just grossed over $1,000,000,000. John told me that Access Graphics has over 300 employees. John told me that Access Graphics resulted from a merger of 3 businesses in the mid-1980s. John Ramsey had been the founder of one of these businesses. John's business had been in Atlanta, GA at the time. John informed me that Access Graphics has business offices located in Mexico City, Mexico and Amsterdam.

I asked John if he could think of any past, or current, employee of Access Graphics who might be responsible for the disappearance of JonBenet. John told me he was not directly responsible for hiring or firing. John talked about the employees at Access Graphics as being all part of a family. John did tell me that there was one employee that he was forced to "let go" approx. 5 months ago. The name of this employee is ████████. John said that ████ and his

1 24

P96-21871 8

wife, [redacted], are currently living in [redacted], CO. John told me he had not seen [redacted] since [redacted] left the company. John told me he could not think of anyone with whom he had disagreement with.

I asked John which interior lights, if any, were on when he went to bed on the night of Dec. 25. John told me no interior lights were on when he went to bed. I asked John which exterior lights were on when he went to bed. John told me that he didn't know if any exterior lights were on. John said the Christmas lights located in the front of the house may have been left on, and possibly an exterior light. There are small white Christmas lights lining the sides of the sidewalk extending toward the front of the house. These Christmas lights were on when I first arrived at the Ramsey residence.

After [redacted] had been named as a possible suspect, I asked John if he had any photos of [redacted] in the house. John Ramsey told me that he had a roll of film in his camera. Pictures had been taken of the Christmas party held at the Ramsey home on Dec. 23. John told me that [redacted] had attended that party. I asked John for the film from that camera. John personally provided me with the film from that camera. I gave the roll of 35 mm film to Ofc. Barry Weiss. I instructed Ofc. Weiss to have the file developed ASAP. I asked John if he had any paperwork in the house which might contain [redacted] handwriting. John checked the kitchen area for any note, but did not locate any. I asked John if he had cancelled checks which had been endorsed by [redacted]. John phoned his bank. John was told that the bank did have copies of checks which had been written to, and endorsed by, [redacted]. I asked John to have his bank fax those checks to me in care of the fax number located at the BPD Detective Bureau. This fax number is (303) [redacted].

I asked John and Patsy for current photos of JonBenet. I explained that the photos would be copied and distributed to local law enforcement agencies. I was given two 8x10 photographs of JonBenet as well as and 8x10 portfolio of JonBenet containing 2 pictures and her physical description. I gave these photos to Ofc. Barry Weiss and instructed him to have copies made and to relay the copies to Sgt. Larry Mason at the Boulder Police Dept. Ofc. Weiss and Ofc. Barcklow cleared the Ramsey residence at approx. 1015 hours.

At an unknown time between approx. 0900 hours and 0945 hours Det. Sgt. Robert Whitson arrived at the Ramsey residence. Sgt. Whitson talked with John Ramsey in the den area of the house. I was present during part of this conversation. Sgt. Whitson informed John Ramsey that the FBI had been notified and was assisting in this investigation. Sgt. Whitson told John Ramsey that we would need a sample of his handwriting. John verbally agreed to supply Sgt. Whitson with a handwriting sample. Shortly after Sgt. Whitson had requested this sample, John Ramsey wrote and line on a legal

1 25

P96-21871 9

pad in front of him and signed his name to this pad. I was sitting next to John Ramsey when he wrote this. John has written "Now is the time for all people," then signed his name. I removed this sheet of paper from the legal pad, secured it in my notebook, and later placed it into evidence (item 4LKA).

Before Ofc. Barry Weiss left, I asked him to show me what areas of the house he had processed for evidence. The first floor glass door located on the north side of the house, east of the spiral staircase, had been processed for latent fingerprints. John Ramsey had told me that this was the only door in the house that did not have a dead bolt to secure it. The spiral staircase located at the northwest corner of the house, extending from the first floor to the second floor, was processed for latent fingerprints. There was a green Christmas garland covering the handrail portion of this staircase. At the top of the spiral staircase was an open laundry area. JonBenet's bedroom door was located south of this laundry area. Ofc. Weiss walked to the patio door located at the south end of JonBenet's bedroom. Ofc. Weiss told me that there had been frost on the patio when officers had arrived. The frost had not been disturbed. Det. Patterson had entered JonBenet's bedroom. I walked into JonBenet's bedroom, only as far as the first bed. I did not touch anything. Ofc. Weiss pointed out a bedroom located west of JonBenet's bedroom. I entered into this bedroom a few steps, but did not touch anything. Ofc. Weiss then walked east along the second floor hallway into the children's playroom area. I noticed that there was a life size Barbie doll standing next to the north window. The doll was not clothed. Continuing east down this hallway there is a bathroom located on the north side of the hallway and a smaller bedroom located across from this bathroom. At the east end of the hallway is Burke's bedroom. Outside of Burke's bedroom is a stairway leading upstairs to the master bedroom. The stairway also leads downstairs to the front door. I walked upstairs into the master bedroom. I did not touch anything in the master bedroom area. I returned to the second floor using the west steps. The west steps enter the second floor area just east of JonBenet's bedroom, and just east of the open laundry area.

Sgt. Whitson requested that the door to JonBenet's room be sealed. Prior to his arrival, the door to JonBenet's room had been closed but not locked. I obtained a police crime scene tape and adhesive tape from Sgt. Whitson's vehicle. Det. Patterson and I sealed the entrance to JonBenet's room at approx. 1030 hours. At approx. 1035 hours all BPD officers, detectives, and victim advocates cleared the Ramsey residence. The only persons remaining in the residence were: John Ramsey, Patsy Ramsey, [redacted], [redacted], [redacted], [redacted], [redacted], and myself.

I talked with John briefly after all of the officers had left. John told me that he and Patsy had been married 16 to 17 years. Patsy had been diagnosed with ovarian cancer 3 years ago. Patsy recently discovered that she was free of cancer. John's adult

P96-21871 10

daughter had been killed in a car accident 4 years ago. I asked John if there had been any suspicious people at his residence within the last few weeks. John told me no. I asked John if he had received any suspicious phone calls or hang up phone calls within the last few weeks. John told me no.

John Ramsey, [redacted], [redacted], [redacted], and I were in the den area talking at an unknown time after 1040 hours. I had placed my copy of the suspected ransom note on the table in the den and had asked John to review the note. I had asked John Ramsey to tell me what unusual things he detected from reading the note. John Ramsey said very little. John Ramsey's friends asked me my opinion of the note. I told John Ramsey's friends that the note appeared to be directed towards John Ramsey. The note also appeared to be personal, as it referred to John Ramsey as "John" throughout the note. John Ramsey's friends made the following observations about the note: The author of the note directed the note to John Ramsey; the amount of $118,000 was an odd amount; the author of the note appeared to be somewhat educated, since the words "hence" and "attache" were used; the sentence "don't try to grow a brain John" seemed to be a slap in the face to John Ramsey; the closure "Victory! S.B.T.C." did not make sense; and the reference to John Ramsey being a southerner indicated to the friends the person did not really know John Ramsey because John was originally from Michigan. I asked John Ramsey if he had given a loan to anyone in the amount of $118,000. John said he had not. I asked John if he owed $118,000. John said he did not.

At an unknown time between approx. 1040 hours and 1200 hours John Ramsey left the house and picked up the family's mail. I was not present when John left. I did witness John Ramsey opening his mail in the kitchen. [redacted] also left the Ramsey home. [redacted] left sometime after 1015 hours. [redacted] told me he had also taken photos of the Christmas party held at the Ramsey's home on Dec. 23. [redacted] left to have his film developed at a one-hour photo lab. [redacted] returned within about 30 minutes to an hour. At approx. noon Patsy relocated to the den area. Patsy laid down on the couch in the den. [redacted] remained with Patsy. [redacted] also stayed with Patsy. [redacted], [redacted], [redacted], and John Ramsey were in the kitchen area and formal dining room area of the house. Patsy asked me what we (i.e. police) were doing. I told Patsy that we were attempting to locate [redacted]. I also told Patsy that the FBI was involved in this investigation. Patsy had asked me these questions when I initially spoke with her. Patsy talked with me about the suspected ransom note. Patsy told me that [redacted] did not use the language contained within the note. Patsy explained to me that [redacted] did not use the words "hence" or "attache" case. Patsy did not know why someone would ask for the amount of $118,000. Patsy said that amount had no significance to her. Patsy asked me why the author of the note had not asked for a larger sum of money, or at least a round sum of money. Patsy said the author of the note referred to John as being

1 27

P96-21871 11

a Southerner. Patsy told me that anyone who knows John Ramsey knows he's not from the South. I asked Patsy when ███ was next scheduled to be at their home. ███ was due to be at the Ramsey home at 0900 hours on Friday, Dec. 27. While I was talking to Patsy she would repeatedly start crying. Patsy would be unable to speak. Patsy repeatedly asked "why didn't I hear my baby?" Patsy looked physically exhausted. Patsy would close her eyes, but was not able to rest or sleep.

When I talked briefly with John Ramsey during the morning of Dec. 26 he was able to carry on a conversation and articulate his words. John Ramsey had smiled, joked, and seemed to focus during the conversation. Patsy seemed to be much less focused when I spoke with her. Patsy seemed to have a far-off look in her expression. Patsy's thoughts were scattered and it was difficult to get her to stay focused on one thought. Patsy would collapse in tears and repeatedly asked why had she not been able to hear her baby. There were 2 phone calls received by John Ramsey when I saw him act differently than he had all morning. When he received each of these phone calls, John stood in front of the north door located between the den and the kitchen. John looked outside during the phone call. John told the caller that JonBenet had been "kidnapped." John was sobbing and had difficulty speaking. At times, John was unable to speak. I was told by friends the identity of the 2 callers. One caller was John Ramsey's son, John Andrew Ramsey. The other caller was John Ramsey's daughter, Melinda Ramsey. John Ramsey told me that his Boulder family was planning on flying to Michigan this morning. John's adult children from another marriage, John Andrew and Melinda, had taken the family's private plane from Atlanta and had flown to Minneapolis, MN. John Ramsey, Patsy, JonBenet, and Burke were going to fly to Minneapolis, MN and meet with John Andrew and Melinda. The 6 Ramseys were then going to fly to their summer home located in Charlevoix, MI. They were going to return to Boulder on Sunday, Dec. 29.

At approx. noon I paged Det. Sgt. Mason and asked that he phone me at the cellular phone number for one of the phones at the Ramsey house. Patsy Ramsey had been repeatedly asking me for an update. At approx. 1230 hours I again paged Det. Sgt. Mason and asked him to phone me. I did not receive a call from either of these pages. At approx. 1230 hours I noticed that John Ramsey seemed to be by himself. John Ramsey was alone in the formal dining room area of the house. John Ramsey seemed to isolate himself from others. Earlier in the morning, I noticed that when John Ramsey was sitting down, he would look down and his leg would be bouncing. At an unknown time between 1230 hours and 1300 hours I talked with ███ ███. I told ███ that I needed his help to keep John Ramsey's mind occupied. I suggested to ███ that he and John Ramsey check the house "from top to bottom," excluding JonBenet's bedroom. I suggested to ███ that John Ramsey check to see if anything belonging to JonBenet had been taken or left behind. ███ told me

1 28

P96-21871 12

that he had reported his daughter missing to the Boulder Police Dept. this past year. ████ had checked the house and found his daughter inside the house. ████ said his daughter had been hiding. ████ told me it was hard for him at that time not to be able to do anything. I then spoke to John Ramsey. I suggested to John Ramsey that he and ████████ check the house "from top to bottom" to see if anything belonging to JonBenet had been taken or had been left behind. I talked with John Ramsey in the kitchen of the house. After I had spoken to John he immediately went to the basement door. I saw ████ following John Ramsey. I then returned to the den area. The time was approx. 1300 hours.

At approx. 1301 hours I received a page to phone BPD number ███-████. There was no answer. I had tried to make this call using one of the cellular phones at the house. I then returned to the den. At approx. 1305 hours I saw ████████ run from the area of the basement door to the den. I heard some type of shout or scream before I saw ████. I saw ████ grab the phone in the den, dial 2 to 3 numbers, then hang up the phone. ████ then ran back towards the basement door. ████ yelled for someone to call an ambulance. I followed ████ to the basement door. The door to the basement was wide open. I was standing in the hallway, facing the door to the basement, when I saw John Ramsey coming up the final three or four stairs. John was carrying a young girl in his arms. The young girl had long blonde hair. John Ramsey was carrying the young girl in front of him, using both of his arms to hold her around her waist area. The young girl's head was above John Ramsey's head while he was carrying her. From a distance of approx. 3 feet, as John was walking up the stairs, I was able to make the following observations to this young girl: both of her arms were raised above her head and were motionless; her lips appeared blue; her body appeared to have rigor mortis; there was a white string attached to her right wrist; there was a bright red mark, approx. the size of a quarter, at the front of her neck; the lower portion of her neck and the right side of her face appeared to have livor mortis. I told John to place the young girl's body on the rug just inside the front doorway. John did as he was instructed. The young girl was JonBenet. JonBenet appeared to have been dead for a period of time. I touched JonBenet's neck in an attempt to locate any sign that she was alive. JonBenet's skin was cool to the touch. There was dried mucus from one of JonBenet's nostrils. My face was within inches of JonBenet's face. I detected an odor of decay. John Ramsey asked me if JonBenet was alive. I don't remember the specific words John Ramsey used. I told John Ramsey that his daughter was dead. John Ramsey moaned. I told John Ramsey to go back to the den, where the other persons in the house were congregated. I told John Ramsey to phone 911 and have detectives and a coroner respond. I told John Ramsey to go to Patsy.

After John Ramsey left I picked up JonBenet and carried her into the living room. I laid JonBenet on the rug located inside the

1 29

P96-21871 13

living room. I noticed that JonBenet was wearing long white cotton pajama-like pants. JonBenet was also wearing a long sleeved white cotton or knit top. JonBenet's face was turned to her right side. There were no coverings on JonBenet's feet. JonBenet's feet appeared to be white (i.e. drained of color). I did not notice any marks to her feet. Shortly after I had moved JonBenet into the living room I heard a loud guttural moan and wail coming from the den area of the house. The noise sounded as though it was made by a woman.

John Ramsey came into the living room area approx. 1 to 2 minutes after I had sent him back to the den. As John entered the room he asked me if he could cover up JonBenet. John grabbed a throw blanket that was lying on a chair located immediately inside the living room. John placed this blanket over JonBenet's body before I had a chance to speak. I adjusted the blanket on JonBenet's body so that her clothing was covered from her neck down. I also covered the neck area of JonBenet. I had covered the wound on JonBenet's neck with her long sleeved shirt before John Ramsey arrived in the living room. I told John Ramsey that he could say good-bye to his daughter, but he could not move her body, touch her hands, or lower the blanket. John knelt on the floor next to JonBenet. John repeatedly referred to JonBenet as "my little angel." John stroked JonBenet's hair with one of his hands. John Ramsey laid down next to JonBenet, placed an arm around her body, and made sounds as though he was crying. I did not notice any tears. John Ramsey then rolled away from JonBenet's body and went into a kneeling position. When John rolled away from JonBenet's body he looked around, towards the hallway. John Ramsey then knelt by JonBenet's body, hugged her, and called her his little angel. After approx. 5 to 10 seconds John stopped hugging JonBenet and again looked toward the hallway. John remained kneeling near JonBenet when I looked into the hallway, towards the den. I was able to watch JonBenet, John Ramsey, and the people coming from the den toward the living room. I saw Patsy Ramsey. It seemed as though Patsy was unable to walk without the assistance of someone on each side of her, holding her up. [redacted], Patsy, [redacted], [redacted], [redacted], and [redacted] all came into the living room area. When Patsy saw JonBenet's body she immediately went to her and laid on top of her. As I faced JonBenet from the hallway, John Ramsey was to the right of her body, [redacted] was near JonBenet's head, Patsy Ramsey was next to [redacted], [redacted] was next to Patsy (near JonBenet's feet), and [redacted] and [redacted] were also near the lower portion of JonBenet's body. [redacted] left the living room and went into the kitchen area. [redacted] seemed to be very upset. When [redacted] entered the living room, she was shaking and her eyes were wide. [redacted] grabbed onto my arm and repeatedly told me not to leave. I asked [redacted] to pray for JonBenet and to lead everyone in a prayer. I then stood near the piano in the living room and was able to watch everyone in the living room, as well as [redacted], who was still in the kitchen area.

1 30

P96-21871 14

Patsy was crying and moaning while she was with JonBenet. Patsy raised herself onto her knees, lifted her arms straight into the air, and prayed. Patsy said "Jesus! You raised Lazarus from the dead, raise my baby from the dead!" At approx. 1312 hours there had been no officer response. There had also been no response from the coroner or an ambulance. The closest phone was a cellular phone in the kitchen. This phone was located approx. 12 feet away. I quickly walked into the kitchen, grabbed the cellular phone, and returned to the area in the hallway right outside the living room. I phoned 911. I reached Dispatcher Santiago. I told the dispatcher that I needed a detective response and a coroner at my location. I identified myself by my radio number, 156. Within approx. 3 to 5 minutes of this 911 phone call I made a second 911 phone call. I again reached a dispatcher whose voice I did not recognize. I was transferred to a supervisor. I informed the male supervisor that I needed detective response, the coroner, and an ambulance at my present location. I gave my location as 755 15th St. I told the dispatcher that I was at the scene of a homicide. Prior to making this second 911 phone call I had seen an ambulance drive slowly northbound on 15th St., past the Ramsey residence. At approx. 1320 or 1325 hours Ofc. Barry Weiss arrived at the Ramsey residence. Ofc. Weiss had responded to the first floor north door, located off the caterer's kitchen. Ofc. Weiss had been calling out my name. I briefly met with Ofc. Weiss and then returned to the hallway outside the living room area. I informed Ofc. Weiss of the current situation.

At an unknown time after JonBenet's body was found, and prior to Ofc. Weiss' arrival, I instructed ██████ to stand guard in front of the basement door. I told ███ that no one was to enter the basement area. After Ofc. Weiss arrived I met with the following BPD officers: Watch I Sgt. Dave Kicera, Ofc. Alaric Morgan, Ofc. Rick French, Det. Bill Palmer, and Sgt. Larry Mason. Agent Ron Walker with the FBI had accompanied Sgt. Mason. Paramedics from AMR Ambulance also arrived. After Ofc. Weiss arrived I had requested that an ambulance respond. Patsy Ramsey appeared to be swooning and I was concerned for her health. The paramedics did physically check Patsy Ramsey. The paramedics did not examine nor touch JonBenet. I was told that Patsy Ramsey was obviously very distraught, however she physically did not need to have medical attention. The two paramedics cleared the scene after Patsy was checked.

At 1315 hours I received a page from communications. The page stated that Sgt. Kicera was at the front door at 875 15th St. Sgt. Kicera was unable to find me. I also received a page on my pager at approx. 1329 hours. The page stated that my cellular 911 call had been received by Weld County. Weld County Communications did not understand me. I was instructed to call Boulder Communications Center if I needed assistance.

After BPD officers arrived everyone was cleared out of the living

P96-21871 15

room. JonBenet's body was left where I had placed her. At approx. 1340 hours Det. Bill Palmer told me that he overheard a phone conversation made by John Ramsey. John Ramsey was making arrangements to fly to Atlanta either that afternoon or that evening.

Arrangements were made for John and Patsy Ramsey, , , and to go to the residence. The live at in Boulder. At approx. 1400 hours I received a page to phone Det. Patterson. I phoned Det. Patterson using one of the cellular phones in the kitchen. Det. Patterson told me that he was going to attempt to contact and interview Burke Ramsey. Det. Patterson asked where Burke was staying. I informed Det. Patterson Burke was at the residence located at in Boulder. family members were watching Burke. One of the family members at the house was .

I cleared the Ramsey residence at approx. 1435 hours. The Ramsey residence was vacated after John and Patsy Ramsey and their friends had left the residence. Officers cleared the residence and awaited a search warrant before returning. John Ramsey had been wearing khaki pants and a blue and white long sleeved striped shirt when I had last seen him. Patsy Ramsey had been wearing black pants and a red turtleneck sweater when I had last seen her. There had been a paperbag containing children's clothing which was sitting in the doorway to the den throughout most of the morning. After approx. 11 a.m. I moved the bag to the cloak room area, which is located next to the door leading into the garage. told me the clothing contained outer clothing for JonBenet and Burke. Winter ski pants, two winter jackets, and boots had been contained within this bag. removed these items and placed them in the cloak room area.

When I had asked about doors being locked in the house, John Ramsey told me that the door leading from the garage into the house is always left unlocked. John further told me that the garage area is always secured from the outside. Before Ofc. Weiss left the residence on the morning of Dec. 26, I believe he opened the door leading from the house into the garage area. I briefly saw a utility vehicle and a car. Ofc. Weiss told me that the car was a Jaguar.

After I had cleared the Ramsey residence I returned to the Boulder Police Dept. I met with Det. James Byfield and assisted him in completing a search warrant for the Ramsey residence. I also attended a general detective briefing.

When John Ramsey met with me in the living room, after JonBenet's body had been found, I asked him where he had found JonBenet. John Ramsey told me JonBenet had been in the wine cellar. John Ramsey told me JonBenet had been lying underneath a blanket. John told me

I 32

P96-21871 16

that JonBenet's arms had been tied. JonBenet had a piece of tape covering her mouth. John told me he removed the tape from JonBenet's mouth. John said he then grabbed JonBenet and carried her upstairs. One of the first things John told me after he came into the living room and had covered JonBenet's body was, "It has to be an inside job." John told me I was right, it had to be someone who knew the family. John told me that no one knows about the wine cellar in the basement, and therefore it had to be an inside job.

Ofc. French briefly talked with me at the Ramsey residence after JonBenet's body had been found. Ofc. French asked where JonBenet's body had been discovered. I told Ofc. French that John Ramsey said JonBenet had been found in the wine cellar in the basement. Ofc. French asked me to describe this room. I had not been downstairs and could not describe it. Ofc. French told me that when he did check the house, he checked the basement area. Ofc. French had not checked behind one door in the basement. This door had a latch on the top frame of the door. The door was latched. I briefly talked with [redacted] after officers arrived at the Ramsey residence (after JonBenet's body had been found). I asked [redacted] where he was when JonBenet's body was found. [redacted] told me he was a few steps behind John Ramsey. John Ramsey had entered the wine cellar room located in the basement of the house. [redacted] was not able to see inside the room because his vision was blocked by the door. [redacted] heard John Ramsey cry out.

I obtained the following information from the general detective briefing held on the late afternoon of Dec. 26:

> Det. Patterson had conducted an interview with Burke Ramsey. Burke Ramsey said he and the three other members of his family had attended a party held at the [redacted] residence on Dec. 25, 1996. The Ramseys were at the dinner party from approx. 1630 hours until 2100 to 2130 hours. Crab was served at this dinner. John and Patsy Ramsey disciplined each of their children by talking to them. John and Patsy Ramsey do not use any corporal punishment on their children. Burke said there had been no family arguments prior to, nor on, Dec. 25.
> Det. Idler talked with the houseguests who were staying at [redacted] home. The houseguests told Det. Idler that John and Patsy Ramsey treat each of their children fairly. One of the houseguests did say that Patsy adored JonBenet. Det. Idler was told that an adult daughter of John Ramsey's, from a previous marriage, had been killed in a car accident approx. 5 years ago. Det. Idler had also been told that Patsy Ramsey had been diagnosed with ovarian cancer. Patsy had recovered from the cancer approx. 2 years ago. Det. Idler was told that John and Patsy Ramsey had held a Christmas party at their home on Dec. 23. Extra caterers had been hired to assist with this party.

1 33

P96-21871 17

John Ramsey had told me that he and Patsy had hosted a Christmas party at their home for their children's friends. I thought John Ramsey told me this open house had been held on Dec. 24. The children who attended the party had decorated gingerbread houses. The gingerbread houses decorated by JonBenet and by Burke had been sitting on the dining room table located just south of the kitchen in the Ramsey residence. John Ramsey told me this information after I had asked him about those two gingerbread houses. ████ had also talked with me about the gingerbread houses. ████ had told me that Patsy Ramsey was the only woman she know who would allow young children to decorate their own gingerbread houses. ████ children ████ and ████ had also attended this Christmas gathering.

Det. Idler had spoken with ████. ████ told Det. Idler that he had searched the Ramsey house after he had arrived at the Ramsey residence earlier this morning. ████ said he had opened the door to the wine cellar. ████ was unable to locate a light switch for the wine cellar. ████ did not enter the wine cellar. ████ had said the interior of the wine cellar was dark and he did not see anything inside. ████ said the latch to the wine cellar, located at the top of the door, was secured when he checked it. ████ re-secured the latch to the wine cellar after he closed the door.

The search warrant prepared by Det. Byfield was signed by Boulder County Judge Diane MacDonald on the early evening of Dec. 26, 1996. I was notified that the search warrant had been signed at approx. 2000 hours. I responded to the Ramsey residence. Det. Barry Hartkopp and I used crime scene tape and secured the exterior property of the Ramsey residence with this tape. The crime scene tape was placed along the south, east, and north borders of the Ramsey property. The crime scene tape was also attached to the two wooden fences located on either side of the driveway located at the rear (west) of the residence, and along side the alley. BPD officers had been positioned in the alley located in the rear of the residence, and also at the front of the residence, to ensure the security of the house.

The Boulder County Coroner, Dr. John Meyers, was the first person to enter the Ramsey residence after the search warrant had been obtained. Dr. Meyers entered the Ramsey residence at approx. 2023 hours. Dr. Meyers entered through the front door. Dr. Meyers placed protective booties on each of his feet before he entered the residence. Dr. Meyers also covered his hands with plastic gloves before entering the residence. Dr. Meyers was told the location of JonBenet's body. Dr. Meyers exited the residence through the front door. Dr. Meyers told me he had examined JonBenet's body. Dr. Meyers pronounced JonBenet dead. Dr. Meyers told me he had observed ligature marks on JonBenet's neck. Dr. Meyers had noted petechial hemorrhage to JonBenet's eyes. Based on my training and experience, it is my experience that petechial hemorrhage to the

1 - 34

The following is a BPD report from Detective Linda Arndt from Friday, December 27, 1996.

John Ramsey had asked if the BPD would send some officers by so he could talk with them. Arndt and another officer, Sergeant Larry Mason, responded.

P96-21871 8

given. Dr. Meyer invited Dr. Sirotnak to examine JonBenet, particularly the trauma to JonBenet's vaginal area. Dr. Sirotnak did conduct an examination on JonBenet after the conclusion of this meeting. Det. Trujillo was going to be present for this examination.

At approx. 2130 hours Det. Sgt. Larry Mason and I met with John Ramsey at the ████ residence. Sgt. Mason and I met with John Ramsey in an office area room located in the basement of the ████ residence. Other persons present in this room included: John Ramsey's brother, Jeff Ramsey; ████████████, who introduced himself as an attorney and a stockbroker with ████████ located in Atlanta, GA; Dr. ████, the physician for the Ramsey family; and Mike Bynum, who described himself as a friend of John Ramsey and also as an attorney who was providing John Ramsey with advice. Sgt. Mason and I met with John Ramsey for approx. 40 minutes. The following information was learned from this meeting:

I asked to speak with Patsy Ramsey. I was told by Dr. ████ that Patsy Ramsey was too medicated to talk to anyone. Dr. ████ had given Patsy valium.

John was told that there was a broken window located in the basement of his home. John told us that he had broken out a basement window approx. 4 to 5 months ago. This window was located in the room where the Christmas decorations were kept. The grate covering the window well to this window was not secured. John had been locked out of the house. John told us he removed the grate, kicked in the basement window, and gained entrance to the house from this window. John told us he had not re-secured the window nor had he fixed the window which he had broken.

Sgt. Mason had told John it would be helpful to our investigation if we could interview he and Patsy as soon as possible. Sgt. Mason requested that we interview John and Patsy on Saturday morning, Dec. 28. Dr. Beuff told Sgt. Mason he did not know if Patsy would be available for an interview at that time. Dr. Beuff said that Patsy was in a fragile emotional state and he did not want to subject her to anything which would further upset her. No definite answer was given regarding the request to interview John.

I again asked John if he could think of anyone who might be a possible suspect in this investigation. John told me that he could only think of two persons from Access Graphics who might be considered a suspect. John had previously given me the name of one of these individuals, ████████. The other person was a man who had been fired from Access Graphics approx. 3 years ago. John told me that he had talked to the person in charge of Human Resources at Access Graphics. John had asked if potential employees could be asked the question

1 121

P96-21871 9

of whether or not they smoked. John was told this question could be asked. The male employee was asked this question. The male employee stated that he was not a smoker. After the male employee was hired it was discovered that he was a smoker. John said the man was fired because he had lied on his application, not because he was a smoker. The man sued Access Graphics. The lawsuit was reported in the local newspaper. John told me that the lawsuit was settled. The former employee received a $15,000 settlement. John said he had not received any contact from this employee after the lawsuit had been settled.

John told us that this was a difficult time of year for him. John told me that his daughter, Beth, had been killed in a car accident on Jan. 8, 1992. John also told me that this was a difficult time for Patsy. Patsy had been diagnosed with ovarian cancer two years ago. Patsy had undergone treatment and the cancer had been removed.

John Ramsey told us that he was thinking about offering a reward. John did not ask any questions about the results of JonBenet's autopsy. John told us that there would be a private memorial service for JonBenet at St. John's Presbyterian Church in Boulder on Sunday afternoon. The memorial service would be held at 1400 hours. The memorial service was not open to the public. After the conclusion of the memorial service John and his family would be flying to Atlanta, GA. JonBenet's funeral was to be held on Tuesday, Dec. 31, in Atlanta, GA. JonBenet was going to be buried next to her half-sister, Beth Ramsey. When Sgt. Mason and I left John we told him we would phone him in the morning to arrange for interviews for he and Patsy.

End of Report.

cln

1 122

This is a report from the other detective who originally responded to the scene with Detective Arndt. Detective Fred Patterson left at approximately 9:45 to accompany Commander-Sergeant Bob Whitson back to the police department to debrief the FBI and other officers who were just arriving. This is the part of Patterson's report that deals with the morning of December 26, 1996.

Patterson

PCR P96-21871
Page 4

accompany Sgt. Whitson back to the police department for a briefing. Prior to leaving Sgt. Whitson asked that I attempt to obtain handwriting samples from John and Patsy Ramsey. I spoke with John Ramsey about the handwriting samples. He went out of the den to a counter near the bottom of the spiral staircase. He picked up two letter sized pads of white lined paper and handed them to me. He said that one was Patsy's and one was his that they used to write messages on. I identified each pad with the name of the person he identified as the writer and then gave the pads to Sgt. Whitson for later comparison with the ransom note. Sgt. Whitson maintained custody of the pads.

Sgt. Whitson and I then left the residence to return to the police department. We went to his vehicle and then drove around the neighbor. I used his video camera to tape vehicles that were in the area in a two-block radius of the residence. This had been suggested to Sgt. Whitson by the FBI. After completing the taping we returned to the police department.

At the police department, I contacted Det Chrisp and determined no further activity had occurred at the [redacted] residence. He said he would continue checking periodically.

I then attended a briefing at the police department. During the briefing I was supplied the name of [redacted] as the contact person at U.S. West for the trap/trace information. I also was advised that Legal Advisor Keatley was working on the affidavit for the court order based on the information I had provided. During the briefing we were advised that the body of JonBenet Ramsey was found in the house at 755 15th street in the basement.

After the briefing I met with Keatley and supplied him with the complete information he needed. He was working with U.S. West for the necessary information for the cover sheet. Keatley advised the affidavit would be ready to take to the judge later in the day.

Det. Idler and I were then assigned to go to [redacted] in Boulder and interview Burke Ramsey, the nine-year old son of Patsy and John Ramsey, about the kidnaping. We drove to that location and contacted several people at the residence. I conducted a taped interview with Burke Ramsey in an upstairs bedroom of the residence. [redacted] was present during the interview. She was the person watching Burke at the White's residence. Det. Idler conducted interviews with the other parties present at the residence. These were all relatives of the Whites. The tape was turned in of the interview with Burke and a transcript is available for review of the interview.

Det. Idler and I then transported Burke and the two Fernie children to [redacted] at the request of the Ramsey family. [redacted] is the address of the [redacted] residence. On arrival at the residence we were met by [redacted] who took custody of the children and escorted them inside the residence. Ofc. Morgan was also at the residence. We were told that Patsy and John Ramsey were inside the residence also.

1 40

The following is a report on the DNA testing for John, Patsy, Burke, Melinda and John Andrew Ramsey. The DNA samples were taken at the Boulder Sheriff's Department on Saturday, December 28, 1996 at separate times. The two officers who were in the room while the DNA was being taken wrote reports on the behavior and comments of each Ramsey family member.

This is that report.

**PCR P96-21871**
**page 2**

At approximately 3:50 pm, Detective Gosage and I met with **Melinda Bennett Ramsey**, dob/11-14-71 ( the half-sister of JonBonet ) in the BCSO Records Section fingerprint/photo room. Melinda Bennett Ramsey was friendly/cooperative/talkative, and samples were obtained. A photo was taken, and some basic personal information was obtained.

3:50 pm blood draw
3:55 pm hair samples
4:00 pm fingerprints

At approximately 4:09 pm, Detective Gosage and I met with **John Bennett Ramsey**, dob/~~11-14-71~~ ( the father of JonBonet ) in the BCSO Records Section fingerprint/photo room. John Bennett Ramsey was cooperative and reserved, and samples were obtained. A photo was taken, and some basic personal information was obtained. John Bennett Ramsey had present **David L. Williams** of David L. Williams, Inc., **Private Investigations**, 150 E. 10th Ave., Denver, Co 80203, 832-5113, who observed the proceedings.

4:09 pm blood draw
4:16 pm hair samples
4:24 pm fingerprints

At approximately 4:37 pm, Detective Gosage and I met with **Patricia "Patsy" Ramsey**, dob/12-29-56 ( the mother of JonBonet ) in the BCSO Records Section fingerprint/photo room. Patricia Ramsey was cooperative in our requests, but was crying/sobbing, withdrawn, and non-speaking, and unsteady on her feet. Samples were obtained without incident. A photo was taken, and some basic personal information was obtained. Patricia Ramsey had present **John F. Stavely, attorney**, 1900 15th Street, Boulder, Co 80302, 546-1363, who observed the proceedings.

4:37 pm blood draw
4:42 pm hair samples
4:50 pm fingerprints

During this processing, Patricia Ramsey sobbed/cried, and during fingerprinting asked Detective Gosage "Will this help find who killed my baby?", and made the statement "I did not murder my baby."

1 143

# ADDITIONAL RESOURCES

## DOCUMENTS

- BPD Officer Rick French's Report—Re: Thursday, December 26, 1996
- BPD Detective Linda Arndt's Report—Re: Thursday, December 26, 1996
- BPD Detective Linda Arndt's Report—Re: Friday, December 27, 1996
- BPD Detective Fred Patterson's Report—Re: Thursday, December 26, 1996
- Ramsey Family Times for DNA Testing and their Reported Behavior as written in a BPD Report—Re: Saturday, December 28, 1996

## ON THE WEBSITE WWW.WEHAVEYOURDAUGHTER.NET

- BPD Commander-Sergeant Robert Whitson's Report—Re: Thursday, December 26, 1996
- BPD Commander-Sergeant Robert Whitson's Supplemental Report—Written one year later upon request—Re: Thursday, December 26, 1996
- Full autopsy report on JonBenét Ramsey released in August 1997.
- Unsolicited letter from Donald Foster, PhD, to Patsy Ramsey claiming she's innocent based on his study of the language in the ransom note. He was later hired by the Boulder Police Department and claimed Patsy had written the ransom note.
- Patsy Ramsey's 911 call the morning of December 26, 1996—Audio and Transcript
- Federal Judge's 2003 Order dismissing a libel case against Patsy and John Ramsey. The judge lists her reasons for the dismissal of the case before trial in a 93-page document that was considered unusual for its detail and length by legal jurists.
- A video tour of the Ramsey home by two former homicide detectives. Unedited.

## QUOTATIONS

These were listed under "Quotations" from the JonBenét Ramsey Murder Book Index. They are from BPD reports on the Ramseys' behaviors after their daughter's body was found. This subtitle section is ten pages of single-spaced and double-spaced text. A few of the quotes as well as BPD report numbers are included here to give a sense of what the majority of the police reports contained about the Ramsey family.

- Mrs. Ramsey looked extremely distraught and was barely able to speak. BPD Report #1-134
- [Family Friend] I don't think he's mad at the Boulder Police, he just wants to find out whoever did this to his family . . . I've never seen 2 people grieve the way they have. BPD Report #5-4482
- [Patsy's Sister] When I was around him, oh . . . he was just crying and wailing and pacing the floor and breaking down with whomever he, you know, someone would hild [sic]him or whatever. He would just break down. BPD Report #5-4663
- [Patsy's Friend] I never even heard Patsy raise her voice at either of the children. BPD Report #5-5342
- [Victim Advocate] Re: (John Ramsey) But he would cry and then he would get it back again. BPD Report #5-2628
- [Housekeeper] said "I never saw a bad bond [sic] in Patsy's body. You know she was always just so good." BPD #5-982
- [Friend] . . . "but some sicko has gotten in there." BPD Report #5-2571
- [Friend] . . . "There's no possible way these two individuals could have possibly ever, ever, ever, ever have done this." BPD #5

# INDEX

NOTE: Page references in *italics* refer to photos and pictorial representations of documents.